Worldwide Space-A Travel Handbook

And RV, Camping Guide CONUS and Abroad

Sixteenth Edition

The most complete military travel handbook.

spaceatravel.com

P. O. Box 55
Hurst, TX 76053-0055
PH: 817.268.6000
FAX: 817.282.5900
E-mail:
publisher@spaceatravel.com

ISBN 1-881341-16-X

52500

9 781881 341161

0 374080 001517

Retail $25.00

WORLDWIDE
SPACE-A TRAVEL HANDBOOK
Sixteenth Edition

Additional Copies of Handbook

From Exchanges, Military Clothing, and Bookmarks:
If not stocked in your AAFES exchange, clothing store, or Bookmark, **tell store managers that our CRC# is 5440602**, & our AAFES Stock # is 469200742. Stores outside the U.S. are stocked by P.M.G. International. Within the U.S. ask store managers for names of their best *in store* vendor representatives. Send vendor name(s) and store location to us. If your effort connects us to a new vendor and our spinner rack is put in the store you'll earn $25 for your assistance. For Navy or Marine Exchanges within the U.S. the process may be slower but send potential vendor names and locations to us and we'll contact them with the same benefits.

Directly from spaceatravel.com:
Handbook, including Space-A Travel Update subscriptions, are $25 plus $5 S&H. Texas residents add $2.06 sales tax. Payment by check, money order, Visa, Master Card, American Express, or Discover. Ordering preference as given below.

1. **Whenever possible order by our secure Internet order page found at** http://www.spaceatravel.com.
2. **By mail:** Use order blank or send necessary information to address at bottom of this page.
3. **By Fax:** 817.282.5900
4. **By toll-free telephone: 888.277.2232** 0800-1700 M-F Central Time, *orders only* on this number.

For statistical purposes include birth year, pay grade, branch, and status. **Personal demographic information is not shared nor released.**

Others can obtain information about this publication by sending blank e-mail to our auto-responder at handbookinfo@spaceatravel.com.

For general suggestions and comments send e-mail to publisher@spaceatravel.com or if e-mail is unavailable call 817-268-6000 between 0800-1700 M-F Central Time. Trip reports, corrections, additions, or comments relating to material in the book should be in writing and can be sent by e-mail, mail,or Fax.

P. O. Box 55
Hurst, TX 76053-0055
PH: 817.268.6000
FAX: 817.282.5900
E-mail:
publisher@spaceatravel.com

Important Information

The *Worldwide Space-A Travel Handbook* is the premier reference book for travelers utilizing military aircraft and facilities. No three other titles provide what is within this publication. As the most inclusive military travel book ever published, it contains what travelers need and omits superfluous nonessential material. It is also supplemented by our helpful web site and *Space-A Travel Updates* which can be downloaded from the Internet while traveling.

Publication size and weight are important. Travel books covering only one segment of travel information are frequently available in larger formats. Aircraft photos, cartoons, and useless forms create filler and lack value. Our compressed format provides good information and includes over 450 facility maps. Experienced travelers know weight and compactness are essential; these benefits are accomplished with symbols and abbreviations. Entry symbols and abbreviations are explained in the front, with a sample facility lay out on the outside back cover.

Listed flight origination facilities frequently show where unposted flights may arrive from and provide transportation to. Travelers should thoroughly study the Appendices which provide a wealth of essential information.

Assuredly, information changes occur between verification and purchase dates. For over a decade, hundreds of travelers have assisted in maintaining content accuracy. This is where you, the traveler, join the space-a traveler fraternity. Input is essential. Most especially DSN numbers, area codes, base prefixes, and extensions. Whenever a new base directory can be obtained, receiving these provides essential help. No matter how minor changes may seem, submitting every change you learn about helps assure *Handbook* quality. When possible, providing reference sources and respective e-mail addresses supports future travel information accuracy. If Internet access is available, electronic conveyance helps, but is not essential. Postcards and letters are always welcome. Other travelers may benefit from reading your trip reports. If photos are included, your experiences may also be shared on our web site. If a map requires changes, please mark this on a map and mail it to the publisher. If it can be clearly explained by referencing points on the book's map, e-mail will be okay. Current construction, renovation, and demolition information which influences travelers is valuable input to *Space-A Travel Updates*.

Which is more important, the number of rooms or the likelihood of obtaining one; mission numbers and number of days out or likelihood of obtaining transportation? This publication provides seasonal likeliness of availability.

This compact publication provides nearly all necessary information for a successful space available trip. It is supplemented by our web site, where additional information is available and by *Space-A Travel Updates*. Updates can be downloaded from our web site from computers while you travel. Likewise, changes can be submitted on library and USO computers. Please encourage your friends to purchase a copy.

PREFACE

This edition, like the preceding, is dedicated to the late Major General Donal Turkal, AUS, Retired. August 14, 2000 General Turkal used his influence to schedule a meeting at Army Air Force Exchange Service (AAFES) Dallas, Texas Headquarters. The meeting resulted in AAFES providing a military travel publication market analysis. Product comparisons are warmly welcomed. Travelers purchasing Handbooks from AAFES save 33%. Our sincere gratitude also goes to AAFES Vice President of Consumables, Maggie Burgess, who proposed the test and to AAFES' Book Buyer, Yolanda Thursby, for her guidance and assistance.

In 1996 the original publisher asked me, the only traveler to ever ask, "What is the longevity of this book?" to write future *Space-A Travel Updates*. To assure publication of future *Handbooks*, I formed a corporation and purchased the company. Using credit cards to fund advertising, we released the 10th Edition. To assure sales, 52¢ on every dollar received went back into advertising. The following five years became an endurance test consisting of working very long hours without pay to hopefully assure publication continuance.

In December 1997, it became evident the only way AAFES would sell the Handbook was if their vendors provided it. Direct access was out of the question. They connected us with a vendor which, only by store invitation, had access to some clothing stores. They paid promptly and sales looked good.

Approximately 80 area codes have changed since 1996. Information rapidly became dated and cash flow remained low. During our first year over eighty percent of our customers ordered *Updates*. A difficult decision was made to package *Updates* with the *Handbook*. Even though the vast majority of our customers approved, AAFES' vendor panicked and dropped us. To sell books in AAFES Exchanges we were forced to use AAFES' contracted Exchange book vendors. Their largest (major!) vendor, who doesn't have access to clothing stores, stated, "If another supplier sells the book in the Clothing Store, we wouldn't supply that facility's Exchange." A year and a half after shipping approximately $35,000 worth of books to this vendor nearly all the books remained, unfunded, in their warehouses. This included warehouses supplying Travis, McChord, & Hickam AFBs. In September 1999, a very irritated AAFES customer called from the McChord Exchange to complain saying, "You are so tight fisted and money hungry that you won't give military people a break by making your book available in Exchanges," just as I was opening books returned by that vendor's warehouse!

General Turkal, in his retirement years, learned of our dilemma and pushed for a face to face meeting between AAFES personnel, himself, and me. Our success at having our own vendors stock AAFES stores is a direct result of General Turkal's concern and help.

On behalf of all those using this publication, "Thank you, General Turkal." I also wish to thank those who became our direct vendor representatives, without your help this edition wouldn't exist. Most important though are our many travelers who provide input to each edition and in turn support us with their book purchases.

Skip Shipe
spaceatravel.com

Foreward

As with many leading products, this publication was originated by necessity. The original compiler/author, found that only partial information was provided in other books and none provided everything needed by most travelers. Seventeen years later, many using this publication frequently call it, "My Travel Bible."

This book is helpful to tens of thousands of Active, Reserve, Guard, and retired military travelers using it to save money. It is also a very beneficial tool for career counselors, recruiters, and for lodging & terminal staff. Retired Affairs offices frequently use it to explain service benefits. Academy students use it during their break periods. Reservist and National Guard men & women also download travel authorization forms from our web site.

In early 1997, a corporation was established to assure availability of future Handbook editions. The 10th & 11th editions were compiled by the original author with Updates written by the new publisher. Following his ailing wife's departure and other events, the original author quit. Fortunately, the preceding years prepared us to continue. Beginning with the 12th edition, file updating is accomplished by the publisher.

Throughout the past decade travelers have supported information accuracy by submitting changes, trip reports, and helpful hints. To this day, travelers remain our best information source and sales promoters.

The Internet provides considerable benefit towards procuring and disseminating information. Since '911' access to many government web sites has become increasingly difficult and therefore information verification has again become more enduring.

With increased direct sales during the past few years the acquired name, "2-10-4 Publications," proved to be confusing, caused time loss, and created additional expense. When customers received credit card statements showing purchases from "2-10-4 Publications" not recognizing the name, they called their card company and stopped payment. Banks then removed their purchase and fined our account $15 for mail fraud. When customers were contacted they had received their publication and were happy with it. From receiving the chargeback from banks to clearing the matter we lost one hour of time, expense of faxing information to the card company, and $15 in nonrecoverable fines. Our new d.b.a. (Doing Business As) is our web address, spaceatravel.com. Since this change we have had few credit card chargebacks.

We hope you will, as others have, always remember to supply us with changes as you travel. Telephone number changes continue to proliferate and keeping an eye on these is of utmost importance.

A most sincere appreciation is extended to Priscilla McMullin, Judi Sheffler, Ray Thompson, Ralph Batchelor, Kat Batchelor, George Campbell, Debbie Stevenson, Cody Wilson, Debb Evans, Patti Schimpf & Kern Park, and many others around the world for their help in making this edition possible.

TIME

Standard time with respect to UTC (previously called GMT) is shown as Zulu ± hours, e.g., Zulu-5 is EST. When all installations in an area are in the same time zone, standard time difference is given at the beginning of area listing, otherwise on first line of details. Times are local standard time, make adjustment for daylight saving.

AVAILABILITY OF FLIGHTS OR QUARTERS

Probability of obtaining a seat on a selected flight by retirees (Category-VI) is shown by stars. One star represents 0-25% chance, additional stars 25% each, e.g., ★★★★ means 75-100% chance. Variations are given, e.g., ★★★★ x ★ Res weekends (75-100% chance except 0-25% on Reserve weekends), ★★★ x ★ Mildenhall (50-75% chance except 0-25% to Mildenhall). The same star system is used to express probability of walk-ins obtaining quarters, RV, or tent spaces (flight categories do not apply).

FLIGHTS

All installations and airports regularly served by Space-A flights are included: Air Force (AF), Air National Guard (ANG), Reserve (Res), Navy, Marine, Army, and Coast Guard. Destinations and days operated of scheduled flights are given, e.g., Dover SuW (Sun *and* Wed), if hyphenated (Su-W) means Sun *thru* Wed). Most-common destinations of unscheduled flights are also given. Frequently served destinations are marked√ (Pope√). Unusually high or low number of destinations or frequency of flights is noted (Flights rare). Access points for flights *to* selected destination are listed in Flight Destinations, page 235. This Section also serves as a comprehensive list of flights *from* an installation. Phone number is given for terminal (Base Operations (OPS) if no terminal). Hours answered are specified (7144 0700-1400 M-F). Fax number for remote sign up follows [Fax 1234], if also there is a special address for mail remote sign up, Fax number and address will be in [ ], e.g. [Fax 4241, APS/TRO 1245 Arnold Ave], then recording number (Recording 5432). Location of **Terminal** on maps is shown in **bold** (if no terminal **OPS** will be **bold**). Walking distance to BQ is noted, e.g., 1m BQ-Terminal (1 mile lodging office to terminal).

QUARTERS

Quarters are listed in the following order: BOQ, BEQ (BQ is combined **O** and **E**, some installations call them VOQ, VEQ), other on-installation quarters, e.g., Guest Houses (unless controlled by BQ office) and Navy Lodges. If there are separate BOQ and BEQ offices, both are listed with their phone numbers and hours answered and both shown on map. Rates per day of on-installation quarters are shown in the form $8per ($8 per person), $20unit ($20 per unit regardless of the number of persons), etc. Rates are rounded to nearest dollar. Following **Commercial:** nearby (or reachable by shuttle or bus) motels and hotels are listed.

RV and CAMPING

Available RV and tent spaces are listed under quarters. On maps symbol for installation with RV spaces is enclosed by a light circle ◐, if tent spaces also, by a heavy circle ● Rates follow RV and Tent, hookups by E (electricity), S (sewer), T (TV cable), W (water), e.g., RV $6, E $8, ESW $10. Tent $5. Rates rounded to nearest dollar.

TRANSPORT

Transport other than flights follows **Ground Transport:**. Installation shuttle listed first, next interinstallation shuttle, last hospital shuttle (✚ **Shuttle:**). Next special transport. Shuttles are free unless otherwise noted. Last in following order: Bus or tram, RR, limo, car rent, taxi. If both military and commercial transport exist, the latter follows **Commercial:**. On maps availability of transport other than on-base shuttle or taxi is indicated by solid-black triangles, circles, or squares:

QUICK REFERENCE INDEX

MAPS, SYMBOLS, and ABBREVIATIONS

Maps are north up. Key roads and traffic lights shown. Information of distances is expressed as short (most distances less than 0.5 miles), walkable (most distances less than 1.5 miles) and long (significant distances longer than 1.5 miles), as well as by key distances, e.g. 1m BQ-Terminal (1 mile BQ office to Passenger Terminal).

MAP SYMBOLS (Also used as text abbreviations)

§ Shown on maps only when usable by all space-A Travelers.

★	0-25% Availability	C	Commercial phone	NSY	Naval Shipyard
★★	26-50% Availability	CG	Coast Guard	O	Officer
★★★	51-75% Availability	coach	Intercity bus ¶	P	Parking, long-term
★★★★	76-100% Availability	CTV	Cable television	Pax	Passenger
§, ¶	Local reference	D, DSN	Defense Switched	POV	Private vehicle
√	Frequent flights		Network	Rec A	Recreation Area
A	Airevac (Medivac)	d	Day	Rec C	Center
Æ	Page reference	dump	RV sewage dump	Res	Reserve
AAF	Army Air Field	DV	Generally O6 up,	RON	Remain overnight
AB	Air Base		E9 at some locations	S	Sewer hookup
AD	Army Depot	E	Enlisted	Shuttle	Military transport,
AF	Air Force	E	Electric hookup		free unless stated.
AFB	Air Force Base	I	Internet access	T	Cable TV hookup
AFS	Air force Station	JRB	Joint Reserve Base	TLF	Temporary Living
AMC	Air Mobility Command	m	Mile or Month	W	Water hookup
ANG	Air National Guard	MB	Marine Base	w	Week
ANGB	ANG Base	MCAS	Marine Corps Air Sta	x	Except, Extension
ARB	Air Reserve Base	NAF	Naval Air Facility		
ARS	Air Reserve Station	NAS	Naval Air Station		
Bus	Commercial bus ¶	NS	Naval Station		

¶ In UK, Australia, New Zealand a city bus is called a bus, an intercity bus a coach.

DAYS of WEEK

Days are shown Su, M, Tu, W, Th, F, Sa. SaSu are SS, TuTh are TT. Two days connected by hyphen (M-F) are first thru second (M thru F). If no hyphen, a series of days is indicated (MF is M and F). When simpler to do so, except (x) is used, e.g., xSu is the same as MTWTFSa. This notation is used for days of scheduled flights, days meals served, days phones answered, and days facilities open.

GENERAL INFORMATION

MEAL DIAGRAM

Meal diagrams show days or hours meals are served. Clubs serving meals are always included. If all meals are covered, there may be other dining facilities on installation. McDonald's, Burger Kings, etc. are classed as snack bars but may be named.

	Break	Lunch	Dinner	Bruh
O Club	MF	xSu	7d	Su
NCO Club		M-F	xM	
Snack		0600-2200		

TELEPHONE

Military numbers (Defense Switched Network, DSN, D) numbers are first (left or above), commercial numbers last (right or below). When necessary for clarity DSN numbers are preceded by D, commercial numbers by C.
Operator-assist numbers are given directly below installation address. If a common operator serves all installations in an area, assist numbers are given in heading for that area. Prefix numbers for dialing extensions directly are in bold in the operator-assist number, e.g., **360**.0111. When extension prefix is different from operator prefix it is given as **Prefix**-xxxx or with the extension. Two or more extensions differing only in the last one or two digits are indicated by "/", e.g., 5001/2 is the same as 5001,5002. DSN access digits (to dial out via DSN from a CONUS or Alaska installation) are given in the top right corner of installation details, e.g., D-8. More complete telephone information is in Appendix G, Telephone Æ252.

GROUND TRANSPORT

Under **Ground Transport:** are on-installation or off-installation shuttles and hospital shuttles (✚ **Shuttle**). Shuttles are military and, unless specified, free. After shuttles, bus, RR, limo, car rent, and taxi follow in that order. If ground access is only by POV, rental car, or taxi, installation symbol on maps and some list will be ■, ◉, or ▲. If there is access by shuttle, bus, or RR, symbol will be ■, ●, or ▲. Some walking may be required.

QUARTERS

BOQ, BEQ, VQ, VOQ, VEQ, BQ, CBH, & **TLF** are all lodging offices, depending on the facility. Availability for walk-ins specified by stars, see Text Abbreviations facing page. Front-desk numbers and hours phones are answered follow stars. Should reservations be accepted, that will be stated. Any restrictions will be given, e.g., (no dependents). If there is a Space-A priority list, its starting time is given and the time quarters are assigned.
Rates per day are listed in following form: $20per ($20 per person), $16sgl ($16 single), $20dbl ($20 double), $20unit ($20 per unit regardless of number of persons) $15dbl=$5addper ($15 double+$5 additional person). BOQ and BEQ serve **O** and **E** respectively, exceptions are noted. VOQ, VEQ replace BOQ, BEQ as do BQ and CBH. Rates are rounded up to nearest dollar.
Other government quarters follow BQ and have the same information and form. Next are recreation areas having some form of accommodations ranging from cottages to tent spaces. When a Rec A is controlled by a single installation, it normally appears in details for controlling installation but is shown separately on maps if remote from controlling installation. On maps and lists ■ or ▨ indicates quarters usually available, ● or ◉ indicates quarters but difficult periods, ▲ or ▲ indicates no quarters. Should RV spaces be available, symbols above will be enclosed by a light circle, if both RV and Tent spaces, by a heavy circle.
If there are commercial quarters either nearby or on shuttle or bus routes, they are noted under **Commercial:**.

AIR FORCE CONUS CIRCUT MAP INDEX

CONUS, AIR FORCE CIRCUIT

AB, ARS, ANG, Airports within CONUS with Space-A flights.

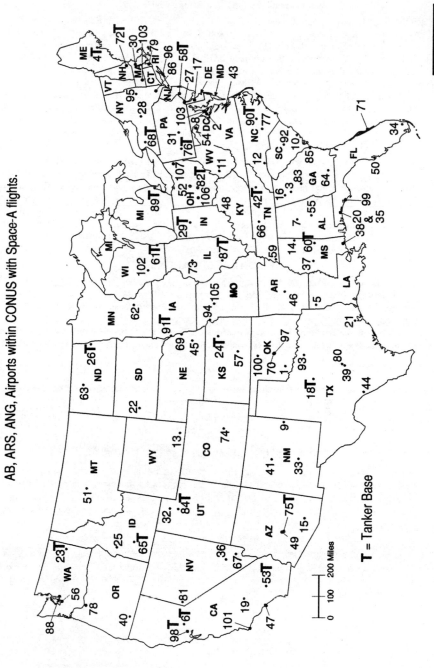

T = Tanker Base

0   100   200 Miles

CONUS, AIR FORCE CIRCUIT

International DSN Prefix for CONUS 312

CONUS Air Force (AF) Circuit consists of all Air Force Bases (AFB), Air Reserve Bases (ARB), Air National Guard Bases (ANGB), and airports having scheduled Space-A flights, also Naval Air Stations (NAS) regularly served by AF flights. Map on Æ10&11 shows locations with installation reference numbers which identify facilities in adjoining Map Index. Details of Navy & Marine facilities are given in Navy Circuit, Æ69-92. Chance of boarding a selected flight by Cat-VI is shown by stars (★★★★ 75-100%, ★★★ 50-75%, ★★ 25-50%, ★ 0-25%) in details. **Beginning 1 April 2003 a one year D.O.D. test allowed active and retiree dependents to accompany their sponsors on point to point CONUS trips. In February 2004 this program was extended indefinitely.** Until this program began, dependents could not fly between two CONUS points (see Æ243 for exceptions) but could transit intermediate CONUS points on a CONUS-outside CONUS flight in either direction.

Flights may be to CONUS Army or Coast Guard installations. Details of such installations are in the CONUS Ground Transport Section, Æ93-169. State maps in that Section show locations and page references to details of all installations and airports in each state including installations in AF and Navy Circuits. Airports often are intermediate stops but, unless there are special reasons, are omitted. Trips within CONUS are usually easier and faster by Navy than by AF if points of origin and destination are convenient. Navy flights often transit AF bases so it is simpler to start Navy and end AF than the reverse. In general, flights within CONUS are easy depending primarily on flights rather than on competition of other travelers.

FLIGHT DESTINATIONS

Under heading ✈✈✈ **Flights** ✈✈✈ destinations and days operated of scheduled flights are listed, e.g., Andrews WF (Wed *and* Fri, if hyphenated (W-F) means Wed *thru* Fri). Also listed are common destinations of unscheduled flights. Destinations with frequent flights are marked√, e.g. Andrews√. Unusually low or high number of destinations or frequency of flights is noted, e.g., Frequent flights to many destinations. Flight Destinations, Æ237-242 lists access points for flights *to* a given destination. That Section also serves as a comprehensive list of destinations *from* a selected installation.

TANKERS

On previous page installations with tankers (KC10, KC135) are marked **T**. Tanker flights are known in advance and availability is excellent. Common outside CONUS destinations are Hawaii (Hickam), Guam (Andersen), Alaska (Eielson and Elmendorf), Azores (Lajes), and England (Mildenhall). Dependents accepted. Changes in electronic systems of KC135 aircraft has minimized available seating.

EXPECTED AVAILABILITY OF QUARTERS

In details availability of quarters by walk-ins is expressed by the same system as used to show expected chance of obtaining a seat on a flight. Flight categories do not apply to quarters. On maps ■ ▨ indicate usually-available quarters, ● ◎ difficult periods, ▲ △ none. If RV spaces are available preceding symbols are enclosed by light circles, if both RV and Tent spaces, by heavy circles.

GROUND ACCESS

On maps access by shuttle, bus, or train (some walking may be required) is indicated by ■ ● ▲, no such access by ▨ ◎ △. When appropriate, shuttle or bus routes and stops are included on installation maps as well as RR stations. Installation maps show driving access routes from major highways or nearest towns.

LTS Zulu-6

AETC C5, C17,KC 135
C141 training,
Distances short.

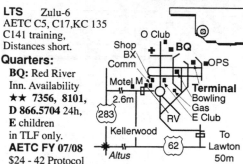

Quarters:

BQ: Red River
Inn. Availability
★★ **7356, 8101,**
D 866.5704 24h,
E children
in TLF only.
AETC FY 07/08
$24 - 42 Protocol
7044.

Commercial: Motel 0.8m from gate.
Fam Camp ★★★★ x ★★ holidays **6704** 24h,
reservations, check in at bowling, RV E, ESW $8.
Golf 481.7207 **Holes:** 18
Commercial: Motel 0.8m from gate.

Ground Transport:

Southwest Transit to Lawton (Ft Sill) 0830,1715
MWF, 482-5043, to Lawton $11. Limo to Lawton
Airport 800-522-2570. Taxi 482-0383,1427,3300.

Altus AFB D-94

Altus, OK 73523
866-1110 Operator **580-482**-8100
481-xxxx

➤➤➤➤➤➤➤ **Flights** ➤➤➤➤➤➤➤

Charleston	**During Thanksgiving**
Ft Worth	**& Christmas add**
McChord	Elmendorf:
Peterson	Selfridge
Scott	Seymour Johnson
Randolph	
Travis√	

Chance of seat ★★★★

Flight Information:

Terminal **6614, 5288** 0730-1630 M-F
[Fax 5573, 97 TRANS/LGTAP 516
S. 6th St] Recording 6350
OPS 6200,6415 M-F 24h. Tanker
scheduling 6311. Schedules out MF,
1427,3300.

	Break	Lunch	Dinner	Brun
O Club		M-F	xSa	Su
E Club	M-F	M-F	7d	Su
Bowling		24h		

ADW Zulu-5 Navy NSF

AMC & Navy, main base, Washington. 459th
AW Res, MD AF Res C12, C21, C22, C38,
C130, C141, VR-1, VR-48
Distances walkable x 3m AMC to Navy, 0.7m
BQ-AMC Terminal.

Quarters:

Availability ★. When full check again after
2100.
AF BQ: Gateway Inn **4614/0785/4624** 24h.
Reservations 9668/9547 **AMC $28 - 43** O7
up thru protocol 4525, E9 call 2316.
Navy BQ: ★ **301.817.2021** 24h (E no
dependents. Rates: **O** $10+2 add, assigned
1600. **E** $7per, DV O6 + up suite $20.
Fam Camp 4109 0800-1700 M-F, reserve.
Check in at Outdoor Rec in Services Area.
RV $10, ESW $16. Tent $6.
Golf 981.4404 **Holes:** 54
Commercial: Motels nearby 420-2800,
423-2323, 586-2800,5200, 899-7770,
hotlines in terminal.

NAF Washington DC

Andrews AFB D-88

Camp Springs, MD 20762
858-1110 Operator 301-981-1110

Hospital & Non-89th activities
D 857-XXXX **C 240-857-XXXX**
Toll Free: 888.360.8700

Calling on base:
To Navy, Hospital, or AFRES from
89th AW: **7-XXXX**. To 89th AW from Navy,
ANG, AFRES, or Hospital: **2-XXXX**. To ANG
6-XXXX.
Departures are from AMC, Navy & Marine
inbound flights often go to Navy Ops.

➤➤➤➤➤ **Flights**➤➤➤➤➤

Harrisburg	Maxwell 2-3/w	Ramstein 1-2/w
Jackson √ 3/w	McChord	Richmond VA
Jacksonville	McGhee Tyson	Robins
Jacksonville IAP	McGuire	Scott √
Johnstown PA	Miami	Shaw
Kansas City MO	Miramar	Stewart
Keesler	Nellis	Tampa
Keflavik A	New Orleans	Teterboro NY
Kelly	New River	Travis 2/w
Knoxville	Norfolk√	Tyndall
Lajes MF A	North Island	Whidbey Is
Langley 2-3/w	Orlando	Willington DE
Leavenworth	Otis	Willow Grove
Little Rock	Panama City	Wright-Pat√
Little Rock (Adams Fld)	Pensacola	
Las Vegas	Peterson 3-4/w	
MacDill 2/w	Quantico	
	Quonset	

Aberdeen PG	Burlington VT
Albany	Campbell
Atlanta NAS	Charleston 1/w
Atlanta (Brown Fld.)	Cherry Pt 2/w
Atlanta (Hartsfield)	Columbia SC
Barksdale	Dallas Love Fld
Beaufort	Davis-Monthan
Belvoir 2-3/w	Drum
Benning	Eglin 1/w
Bragg	Ft Worth
Brunswick	Hanscom

CONUS, AIR FORCE CIRCUIT
Andrews AFB continued

Ground Transport:

Shuttle: Base: 0600-1800 M-F, none on wkend or Hol. Lv AMC for BQ :44, for Navy: 32, from Navy: 07, 51.

Virginia Ave. & Main Gates are 24h, HQ & North 0800-1800.

Commercial: J12/3 Bus from North Gate to subway stations 0435-2145 M-F, 0800-1900 Sa, 0650-1950 Su, info 637-7000, to return use Addison station. Enterprise is Clinton, MD not Camp Springs, MD. Limo to Airport. Car rent at AMC 568-7900, 0730-1900 M-F, 0900-1300 SS, at Navy 899-8100. Taxis at AMC, expensive, 277-6000, 864-7700. Amtrak especially for destinations north 800-872-7245. Golden Touch Limo to Dover 301.599.1222.

Bus Stops off base are near Main Gate - Allentown Rd. & Suitland Rd.(also connects with Suitland & Branch Ave. Metro Station) (<.1 mi) - D13, D14, K11, K12 & from North Gate at 8431 Old Marlboro Pike (.33 mi) - J11, J12, J13.

	Break	Lunch	Dinner	Brun
O Club	xSu	xSu	Tu-Sa	Su
E Club	M-F	M-F	xM	Su
Terminal		Machines		

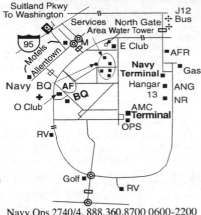

Navy Ops 2740/4, 888.360.8700 0600-2200 Food machines. Navy long-term parking, use Hanger 12 lot. **All space-a flights departing Andrews are manifested at and depart from AMC Terminal.**

Flight Information con't.:

AMC Terminal **1854, 3526, 3604** 0600-2200. [Fax 4241, 89APS/TROP, 1245 Arnold Ave]. AMC Recording 5851 tomorrow, 3527 today. OPS 3411. Terminal open 0600-2200. Food machines. Units with unposted flights: ANG C22 5004. AF Res 2800. VR48 9566/8/9.

BWI Zulu-5 DSN thru Ft Meade
Operator 923-1110.

Quarters:

Closest billets shown on map.
Motels near airport.

Baltimore-Washington Airport

D 243.6900   **410-918**-6900

Toll Free 877.429.4262

⤙⤙⤙⤙⤙⤙⤙⤙⤙ **Flights** ⤙⤙⤙⤙⤙⤙⤙⤙⤙

Some flights not every week

Adana	Lajes	Norfolk
Aviano	McGuire	Ramstein
		Thule Th

Flight Information:

0800-1600. **Rec** press 1, **Fax** 6932. $12 tax per person for overseas flights. AMC located on upper level of north wing of airport. customs on lower level under AMC,

Ground Transport:

From BWI USO, exit bldg and turn right. Go 200 feet to sign "regional buses". Find bus stop B30. **Fare is $3.00 pp - must have exact change!** Take bus to Greenbelt (DC) Metro for 40 min. underground ride to far end. With a credit card, from machine in terminal, before entering Metro, get a transfer ticket for a free bus ride from Branch Ave. Metro station to Andrews AFB. Total Metro cost is $3.95 per person & trip total is $6.95. Go left from Terminal to Buses. Turn left again and go down the side walk to the bus shelter at the end marked K12 (150 feet). Board bus and ride to Andrews entrance gate. This bus ride segment takes 15 min. Total time for trip from BWI to Andrews gate is 2 hours.
Taxi from BWI to Andrews is $70.00 for two people.
At Andrews, if you have large bag(s) ask gate guard for a "courtesy ride" to the Gateway Inn. No taxi or buses allowed on base. If all else fails then stick a thumb up and hitchhike inside the base to Gateway Inn. You will be glad you did. The walk from front gate to Inn is a challenging 15 - 20 minute walk when you are pulling bags or the weather is not cooperating. There is a McDonald's across the street from the gate (bus stop) if you need shelter. Many from the base eat here. Maybe you can barter for a ride to the Inn.

BGR Zulu-5 101ARW KC135, C12. Distances long, 2m ANG OPS-NG BQ.

Quarters:

BQ: Pine Tree Inn. Availability ★★★★ x ★ during NG training, **C 942-2081,** D thru operator, 24h. Rate: $13per.

Ground Transport:

The Bus from Airport, 947-0536.

ANG: Sign up in person, call 7d before flight, again 2d before.

Bangor Airport   D-85
Bangor, ME 04401
881.3450   698-7700
207.947.6593
                    207-990-7700
                ANG ↝↝ Flights ↝↝ NG

Nearby posts	Eglin	Mildenhall√ d
Andrews	Harrisburg	New Castle
Charleston	Kelly	Norfolk
Davison	Little Rock	Ramstein√ d
Drum	McGuire	Scott

               Chance of seat
★★★★   ★★
Flight Information:

7212 0730-1600 M-F, recording 7018.	7257 0700-1600

BAD Zulu-6
ACC
Distances walkable, 0.5m Terminal-BQ.

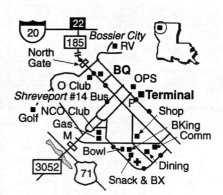

Barksdale AFB   D-8
Bossier City, LA 71110
781-1110   Operator   318-**456**-2252
↝↝↝↝↝↝↝↝↝ Flights ↝↝↝↝↝↝↝↝↝

Andrews	Maxwell
Dobbins	New Orleans NAS
Eglin	Offutt
Kelly	Scott
New Orleans Lakefront	Wright Pat
Langley	

No Pax Services
Chance of seat ★★★★
Flight Information:

OPS 3226 24h [Fax 4401] Without decal for parking contact Law Enforcement 2551.

	Break	Lunch	Dinner	Brun
O Club	M-F	M-F	Tu-Sa	Su
E Club	M-F	M-F	xSu	Su
Bowl	7d	7d	7d	
Dining	7d	7d	7d	

AF

Quarters:

BQ: Barksdale Inn. Availability ★★ x ★ Res weekends **3091** 24h. Fax 2267. **ACC FY 07/08 $30 - 43** O6 up thru protocol 4228. TLF $32.

Fam Camp ★★★★ check in at Fam Camp **2679** 0800-1700 xSu, other hrs pick site and check in morning or use envelope. RV $14/d, $90/w, $350/m, 20/30/50 Amp, Lodging $30/d **Commercial:** Motels outside both gates.   ESWD, WiFi

Golf: 456.2263 **Holes:** 18

Aero Club: C 8179

Ground Transport:

#14 Bus enters via North Gate, 0642-1753 M-F, 0730-1830 Sa, to Greyhound in Shreveport, 221-4205. Taxi 425-7000. Car rent in Shreveport.

BAB Zulu-8 940 R ARW KC135
ACC
Distances long, 3.7m BQ-
Terminal, 3.5m BQ-Club.

Beale AFB   D-8
Marysville, CA 95903 ←
368-1110 Operator **530.634**.3000
↣↣↣↣↣↣↣ **Flights** ↣↣↣↣↣↣↣
Miramar   Peterson

Few flights, no planes stationed.
Chance of seat ★★★★

Flight Information:

OPS **2002** 24h. Terminal in back of Bldg. 1086 No POV parking. PH: 2569, 0403, 0700-1600 M-F. Fax 2571 Recording 2567. 940 ARW EX: 1901

OPS & Snack, Marysville. P. 2m 3 3rd RV. Doolittle C St. A 'St. 10m. N Beale M. R. Linda. BX. Bowl 1.1m. Comm. Golf. Burger King. Warren Shingle. 70. Gas. BQ 3m. Club. To Sacramento 35m. Gavin Mandry. Gas &Shop. To Wheatland 8m.

Quarters:

BQ: Gold Country Inn. Availability ★★★★ **2953,3662** 24h. Reservation 3662/2953. Rates: ACC $30 - 43 O6 up thru protocol 2120.

Fam Camp 3382, reserve. Check in BQ, no restroom, shower. RV ESW $10.

Commercial: Motels on N. Beale.

Golf: 634.2124 **Holes:** 18

Aero Club: C 9011

Ground Transport:

Base Shuttle 0600-1700 M-F, 2543. ✚ Shuttle to Travis as required, 4001, if no answer 4831. Commercial: Limo to Marysville, Sacramento Airport, Travis 671-1199. Amtrak (north 0046, south 0416). Greyhound in Marysville. Super Shuttle 800.258.3826.

	Break	Lunch	Dinner
Club		Tu-F	WF
OPS Snack	0700-1500 M-F		
Golf	0700-1430		
Bowl	0600-2130 M-F		
	0900-2230 Sa		
	0900-2130 Su		
Burger King	0630-2100 M-F		
	0830-2100 Sa		
	0900-2130 Su		

BHM   Zulu-6   117ARW ANG (KC135)
Port of Entry by exception, there may be a problem manifesting from foreign origin but can accept Pax from outside US territory.

Ground Transport:

Usually transport available. Amtrak: North 1420, south 1225.

Birmingham Airport
5401 Eastlake Blvd
Birmingham, AL 35217
778-2201   **205-714**-2297

AF

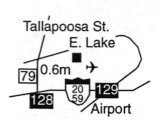

Tallapoosa St.
E. Lake

79 0.6m ✈

128 128 20 59 129

Airport

Andrews   Mildenhall
Bradley   Europe

Chance of seat ★★★★
Flight Information:
Pax 2208 0700-1730 Tu-F. Sign
up by phone 1w prior to flight. Fax
2610.

BKF   Zulu-7   On base prefix 7+XXXX
Distances walkable, 1.1m Terminal - Dining

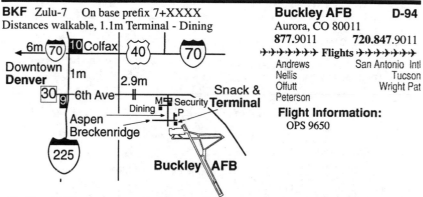

6m 70 10 Colfax 40 70

Downtown
Denver 1m   2.9m
30 g 6th Ave

Snack &
Dining M Security **Terminal**
P
Aspen
Breckenridge

225

Buckley AFB

Buckley AFB   **D-94**
Aurora, CO 80011
877.9011   **720.847**.9011
➤➤➤➤➤➤➤ **Flights** ➤➤➤➤➤➤➤➤
Andrews   San Antonio Intl
Nellis   Tucson
Offutt   Wright Pat
Peterson

Flight Information:
OPS 9650

Buckley ANGB was converted into Buckley AFB in 2001. Currently neither flights nor lodging exist. However, with the possibility of transient flights, basic information was placed in
this edition. The 6th Avenue Gate is open 24 hours. Air operations are still operated by the
Colorado ANG. Operations 9650, Lodging Referral Office 6117, Public Affairs 9431, Protocol 6370.

CVS   Zulu-7 On base prefix 4
ACC
Distances walkable,0.8m BQ-OPS.
Quarters:
BQ: Availability ★ **2918/9** 0500-2400, **ACC FY
07/08** $30 - 43
O6 up thru protocol 2729.
Golf: 784.2800 **Holes:** 18
Ground Transport:
Intercity buses in Clovis.

Cannon AFB   **D-94**
Clovis, NM 88103
681-1110   Operator   **505-784**-1111
➤➤➤➤➤➤➤➤ **Flights** ➤➤➤➤➤➤➤➤
Few flights Chance of seat
★★★★

Flight Information:
OPS **2801/2** 0545-2300 M-F
0700-2100 SS

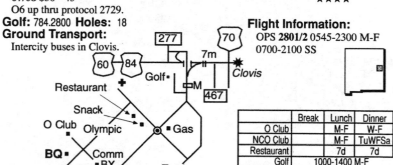

277 70
7m
60 84
Golf ▪ M *Clovis*
467
Restaurant
Snack
O Club Olympic ▪ Gas
BQ ▪ Comm
▪ BX
NCO Torch
Club
▪ P ▪ **OPS**
To US 70

	Break	Lunch	Dinner	Brun
O Club		M-F	W-F	Su
NCO Club		M-F	TuWFSa	Su
Restaurant		7d	7d	
Golf	1000-1400 M-F			
Snack	0630-2100 xSu			
	0730-2100 Su			

CHS   Zulu-5   On ase refix 3
AMC
437AW & 315AW Res (C17)
Distances walkable,
0.5m BQ-Terminal.

Quarters:
BQ: Inns of Charleston, Availability
★★★ x ★ summer, virtually impossible
Res weekends (1st 3) **D 3801/6,** C 552-
9900/8000 24h. **AMC FY 07/08** $28 - 43
LDVOQ: $44. **(E9** 5497 08-1600 Duty
Hours) Protocol 5644 O7+up. Space-A-
Limited Apr-Sept
Commercial: Motel hotlines in Terminal,
some with pick up.
Campground ★★★ check in at Outdoor
Rec **5271** 0900-1700 M-F, 1200-1700 Sa,
RV EW $10 Tent EW $7. Campers and
tents for rent.

Golf: 963.4177 Wrenwoods Golf **Holes:**
18 Course 0700-Dusk
Aero Club: C 5149 / 52

Ground Transport:
Greyhound on Dorchester
just east of I26. Amtrak in
Charleston, south 0805,2117,
north 0906,2035. Car Rent at
Airport. Taxi 552-5810, 554-
7575, 729-2910,6185.

Charleston AFB   D-94
Charleston, SC 29404
673.1100   Operator   **843-963-**1110
↣↣↣↣↣↣↣↣ **Flights** ↣↣↣↣↣↣↣↣↣

Andrews 2/w	Langley	Ramstein
Benning	Lajes	Rota 5/w
Cherry Pt	MacDill SuF ¶	Scott
Dobbins SuF ¶	McGuire	Shaw
Dover√	Mildenhall	Soto Cano WF
Gordon	New River	Travis 1/w Tu
Homestead FSu ¶	Norfolk	Willow Grove
Jacksonville SuF ¶	Pope SuF ¶	Wright Pat

¶ Reservist flight first 3 weekends
Chance of seat ★★★★ CONUS, ★ Europe
summer **Not advisable for retirees
to Europe June-Sept.**

Flight Information:
Terminal 3048,3083,3065 0500-2300. 3083
24h. [Fax 3060, 437 APS/TRO, 105 S. Bates
St, Bldg 178] Recording 3082. USO, ATM &
vending machines in Terminal. OPS 3024/26
24h.

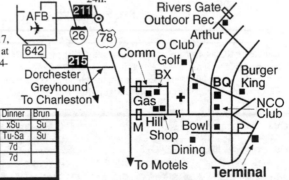

	Break	Lunch	Dinner	Brun
O Club		M-F	xSu	Su
NCO Club		M-F	Tu-Sa	Su
Bowl	M-F	7d	7d	
Dining	7d	7d	7d	
Burger King	0600-2230			

CRW   Zulu-5
130AW ANG (C130)

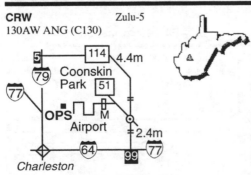

Charleston

Ground Transport:
Amtrak east 1035 SuWF, west 2005 SuWF.

Charleston Airport
(Yeager)
Charleston, WV 25311
366-9210   **304-341-**6000
↣↣↣↣↣ **Flights** ↣↣↣↣↣↣

Andrews	Nellis
Charleston AFB	Pope√
Charlotte	Richmond, VA
Davison	San Juan
Gill Rob Wilson Fld	St. Croix
Hickam	Travis√
Lajes	Wright-Pat
Morgantown	

Chance of seat ★★★
Flight Information:
OPS **6240** Scheduling 6109
0730-1600 M-F
For Parking contact Security

CLT   Zulu-5   145AW ANG (C130)

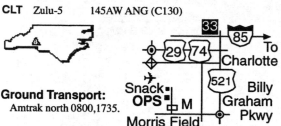

Ground Transport:
   Amtrak north 0800, 1735.

To Charlotte

Snack
OPS M
Morris Field

Billy Graham Pkwy

Charlotte Airport   D-8
(Douglas)
Charlotte, NC 28208
583-9210   **704-391-4**100
✈✈✈✈ **Flights** ✈✈✈✈
Andrews   Pope
Charleston WV   Chance of
      seat ★★★★
Flight Information:
   OPS **135** 0730-1600 M-F
   FAX: 704.391.4407

CYS   Zulu-7
153AW ANG (C130)

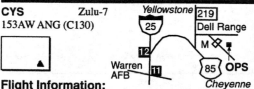

Yellowstone
25
Warren AFB
Dell Range
M
85 OPS
Cheyenne

Cheyenne Airport
Cheyenne, WY 82009
943-6110   **307-772**-6110
✈✈✈✈ **Flights** ✈✈✈✈
Gray AAF   Peterson
Offutt   Few flights
              Chance of seat ★★★★

Flight Information:
   OPS **6132,6354, 800-832-1959** 0730-1630 M-F. Call to list. Airevac handled by Warren AFB
   Air Freight (at airport) 3275 0730-1630 M-F. Info from Patient Affairs 3011 at Warren 1486.

CBM   Zulu-6
AETC
Distances walkable.
Quarters:
   BQ: Magnolia Inn.
   Availability ★★
   2548 or2372 24h. Fax
   2777. **AETC FY 07/08**
   $24 - 42 O6 up thru proto-
   col 7024. House $25
Golf: 434.7932
Ground Transport:
   Greyhound in Columbus,
   328-4732. SATO 2669.

1st
BQ
Club
Bowl
OPS
Simler
Independence
Golf
BX, Gas Comm
45
50
To Columbus, 5m

Columbus AFB   D-88
Columbus, MS 39710
742-1110   **662.434**.7322
✈✈✈✈ **Flights** ✈✈✈✈

                              Few flights
      Chance of seat ★★★★
Flight Information:
   OPS **2861** 0700-1900
   M-F, 0700-2100 F,
   1000-1500 Sa, 1200-1700 Su.

	Break	Lunch	Dinner	Brun
Club		Tu-F	WF	Su
Bowl	xSu	7d	7d	
Golf	7d	7d	7d	
Dining	7d	7d	7d	

DMA   Zulu-7   Prefix 8 on base.
ACC   Boneyard

Quarters: Inn at Davis-Monthan.
   BQ: Availability ★★ x ★ Res weekend
   228.3230 /748-1500 24h. **ACC FY 07/08** $30
   - 43 O6 up thru protocol 3153,228.3600, E9
   protocol 228.3559

Fam Camp ★★★★X★ winter C 747-9144
0800-1800, propane TTSa, check in at Fam Camp,
ESW $13. Known to be full Dec 20 - April 1st.
If full, max stay is 14 days. Map on door showing overflow area 1m away, arriving late check in
morning. Overflow is dry camping, no ESW. Very
nice facility with an 8 month long term special
rate.   **Continued on following page**

Davis-Monthan AFB   D-94
Tucson, AZ 85708
228-1110   Operator   **520-228**-3900
✈✈✈✈✈✈✈ **Flights** ✈✈✈✈✈✈✈
Andrews   Phoenix
Beale 1/m FSu§   Salt Lake City
Holloman   Scott
Miramar   Travis FSu 2/m §
Offutt   Wright Pat
Peterson
      § Reservist.   AF and Navy flights
                    Chance of seat ★★★
Flight Information:
   Terminal **2322** 0700-1600 M-F record-
   ing other hrs. Recording 3641. [Fax
   7229, 355 TRNS/LGTTI, 5275 E Gran-
   ite St. OPS 4315 0600-2230.

Continued on following page

Davis-Monthan AFB continued

AF

Commercial: Motels 0.9m outside main gate on Craycroft and #34 Bus, 747-1440, 790-5354,6021.

Golf: 228.3734 **Holes**: 18

Ground Transport:

Base Shuttle: 0700-1630 M-F

Commercial: #34 Bus from BX 0630-1758 M-F, 0824-1724 Sa, bus stop near BX, from 29th and Craycroft 0910-1710 Su, passes motels. Transfer to #8 Bus on Broadway to Greyhound, Amtrak east 0820 MWSa, west 2205 SuTT. Enterprise car rent 571-0886 0800-1700 M-F, 0900-1200 Sa. Taxi 623-1133,7979, 624-6611, 881-2227.

Broadway
Boneyard
Tucson   #8 Bus   #34 Bus
Motels Craycroft
Golf Links
Comm   M   1m   RV
Shop Gas
Gas   Burger King
Shop
BX   ■ BQ
Alvernon   ○ Club   To
Ironwood
E Club
Car Rent   Golf
Terminal   P   Kolb
OPS   #34 Bus
265
10
270

	Break	Lunch	Dinner	Brun
O Club		M-F	xSu	Su
E Club		M-F	Tu-Sa	
Golf	7d	7d		
Burger King		0630-2100 M-F 0800-2100 Sa 1100-1800 Su		

Sa, Su & holidays retirees can eat at dining.

Distances walkable, 0.9m BQ-Terminal.

D **MGE** Res, ANG 94AW (C130) AFRC
Δ **NCQ** Res VR46 (C9)
Zulu-5. Distances apprx. 3m to Navy.

BRAC 2005

280
Marietta
2.5m Lake Alatoona Rec A
Main BQ ■BOQ
Lockheed BX Club■■
Atlantic RV
Gas
NX Galley Rental P M 75
Club Center OPS 41
BQ■■ ITOPS ARB
3 M
NAS
To Atlanta 16m
3.2m NAS BQ to ARB OPS

Quarters:

Availability ★★★★ x ★ Res weekends.

AF: Main BQ **4745** 24h. Rates: $33 - 40 Protocol 4520.

Navy BQ: 6393 0600-2300. Rates: **O** $19per + 5 x DV suite $30-34, **E** 1-6 (no dependents) $14per, E6 up $19per. Protocol 678.655.6413

AF Fam Camp ★★★★ 4870 0800-1700 M-F, 0800-1600 Sa, 0800-1200 Su. Park on available site, report to Rental Center. RV W $5, EW $8.   **Continued on facing page**

Dobbins ARB
NAS Atlanta

D-94
Marietta, GA 30069

625-5000 Operator **678.655.**5000

Dobbins ⇥⇥⇥ Flights ⇥⇥⇥ Atlanta

Barstow-Daggett	Adams Fld AR
Bush Fld	Andrews 2/w
Cairns	Chicago O'Hare
Charleston FSu §	Davison AAF
Eglin	Gray AAF
Fulton Co.-Brown Fld.	Jacksonville 3/w
Godman	Key West
Greensboro FSu §	Langley
Keesler §	Lawson AAF
Langley	Mac Dill
Lawson	Maxwell
MacDill	Minneapolis St Paul
Norfolk	New Orleans 3/w
Peterson	Norfolk 3/w
Pope	North Island 2/m
Savannah §	Oceana 2/m
Seymour Johnson §	Pensacola
Simmons	Peterson
Washington NAF	Pope
Wright-Pat	Raleigh-Durham
	Savannah Intl GA
	Scott
§ Res flight 1st &	Washington NAF
2nd weekends	Whidbey Is
	Willow Grove
	Wright Pat

Dobbins ARB & NAS Atlanta continued

VR deploys to Italy and Japan several times a year, check with squadron for dates.

Lake Allatoona Rec A (Navy), ★★★★
Site C 770-974-6309, Rates: Cabin $34-55unit summer $29-50unit winter, houseboat $60unit. RV-tent April-Oct, go to lake. RV $8, tent $5. No pets. Discounts Golden Age, Access, Eagle. Army Rec A on same road 974-9420/3413, see Ft McPherson Æ128.

Ground Transport:
Greyhound in Marietta. Amtrak in Atlanta, north 1925, south 0912.

Navy has frequent flights to many destinations
Chance of seat ★★★

Flight Information:

Dobbins
4903 Fax 4915 0700-2300 94 LG/LGT
Traffic Management Office, 1538 Atlanta Ave, Bldg 812

Atlanta
6359 Fax 6155
0700-2300
VR46 6480

	Break	Lunch	Dinner	Brun
D Club		M-F		Su
A Club		Tu-F		
Galley	§	§	§	
§ May be permitted				

DOV Zulu-5
AMC 436 AW (C5) Reserve
512 AW (C5) Active Duty
Distances walkable, 1m BQ-Terminal.

Quarters:

BQ: Availability ★★★ x summer, Reservations: 5983 Res weekends, **2841/4 5983** 24h. AMC FY 07/08 $28 - 43
Commercial: Motels in Dover, nearest 1m, 735-4700.

Golf: 667.6039 **Holes:** 18
Aero Club: C 6365
Ground Transport:
Base bus schedule: Billeting 0638-1238, 1342-1742; Main gate 0645-1245, 1338-1738; Passenger Terminal 0651-1251, 1330-1730
FamCamp $15-18/d 50 Amp ESWD
Rental cars with key drop boxes include Avis, Hertz, & Enterprise.
Pay Shuttle M-F.
Commercial: Delaware Area Rapid Transit
#106 AFB to Dover Water St. Transfer Center M-F 0654-1643 800-652-3278, 30¢ including transfer. Transfer at TC to Wilmington Amtrack and Greyhound. SEPTA R2 to Philadelphia, north transfer to SEPTA R7 to Trenton then NJ Transit. From Philadelphia #317 NJT bus to McGuire, subway then #55 SEPTA bus to Willow Grove. From Wilmington south Amtrak or Greyhound to BWI or Washington, subway to Addison then J12/3 bus. Trailways/Greyhound from Dover 734-1417, North 1350,1920,2300, South 0050,1240,1605,2000. Taxi 734-5968. For the past three years limo service from AFB has been changeable.

Dover AFB D (CONUS) 94
Dover, DE 19902 D (OCONUS) 97
445-3000 Operator **302-677**-3000
➤➤➤➤➤➤➤➤➤ **Flights** ➤➤➤➤➤➤➤➤➤

Aberdeen PG	Norfolk 1/m
Andrews	Ramstein 7d
Aviano 2/m	Rota 2/m
Charleston 1-2/w	Scott
Kelly 1/w	Sigonella 1/m
McChord 1/w	Tinker 1-2/m
McGuire 1/m	Travis 2/w
Moron √	Willow Grove
New Castle DE	Wright Pat

Many flights ★★★★ CONUS,
★ Europe, especially tight summer
**Not advisable for retirees going
to Europe May-Sept.**

Flight Information:
Terminal 2854,4088 Dispatch 4089 24h. [Fax 2953, 436 APS/TROP Passenger Terminal]
Recording 2854. Terminal, cafeteria open 24h, lockers.

	Break	Lunch	Dinner	Brun
Club	Tu-F	M-F	Th-Sa	Su
Cafeteria		24h		
Bowling	M-Sa	M-Sa		

DYS Zulu-6 On base prefix 6
ACC 463AW (C130)
Distances long, 1.6m BQ-OPS.

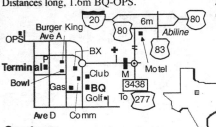

Quarters:
BQ: Dyess Inn. Availability
★★ **2681/1874** 24h, ACC FY 07/08 $30 - 43
O6 up thru protocol 5610.
Commercial: Motel on US80 3.7m from BQ.
Golf: 696.5067 **Holes:** 18
Ground Transport:
Greyhound 677-8127. Taxi 677-4334.

Dyess AFB   D-94
Abilene, TX 79607
461-1110/3113 Operator **325.696.**1110
➤➤➤➤➤➤➤➤➤ **Flights** ➤➤➤➤➤➤➤➤➤
Austin-Bergstrom   North Island
Kansas City   Scott

Flights to many destinations.
Chance of seat ★★★★
Flight Information:
OPS **2515/2258/5705** 24h [Fax 2700]
Terminal 4505. C130 planning 3078.
39th planning 3064, 40th planning 1113
Sign up at OPS. **Space-A 4045**

	Break	Lunch	Dinner	Brun
O Club		M-F	Tu-F	Su
NCO Club	M-F	M-F	Tu-F	
Dining	7d	7d	7d	
Bowl	1100-2300 M-F			
	1200-2300 Sa			
Snack	1200-2200 Su			
	0630-1330 M-F			

EDW Zulu-8
AFMC Flight test center
Distances long. 3.5m BQ-OPS

Quarters:
BQ: **High Desert Inn** (Bldg 5602) Availability
★★ x ★ **3394,3302,4101** 24h, list. Reservations
2 weeks in advance. **AFMC** $34 - 59
Protocol 277.3326.
Fam Camp: Check in at Outdoor Rec 2895 or
Host. RV ESW $10. Host is in 26.
Golf: 275.7888 **Holes:** 18
Aero Club: 275.2376 / 8341
Ground Transport:
Base Shuttle 0630-1400 M-F, 2620.
Commercial: Greyhound stops at Circle K in Rosamond, 800-231-2222 .Light rail Lancaster
to LA. Enterprise car rent at Gas, watch forcing insurance, 258-6006.

Edwards AFB   D-94
Rosamond, CA 93524
527-0111 Operator **661-277-**1110
Operator available 0600-1800
➤➤➤➤➤➤➤➤ **Flights** ➤➤➤➤➤➤➤➤
Andrews   Scott
Miramar   Willow Grove
North Island   Wright Pat
Pendleton   Few Flights
Chance of seat ★★★★
Flight Information:
OPS **2222** 0600-2200 M-F, 0800-
1600 SS. Sign up 0700 day of flight.
Tanker Ops 9797.

	Break	Lunch	Dinner	Brun
Club		M-F	M-F	Su
Cafeteria	0630-1300 M-F			
Burger King	0630-2130 M-F			
	0730-2100 SS			
Pizza	1100-2200			
BX Snack	1000-1700 xSu			
OPS Snack	0600-1400 M-F			
Bowl	1030-2100 Su-Th			
	1 100-2400 FSa			
Golf	0630-1900 xM			
	0730-1900 M			

VPS (Eglin) **EGI** (Duke)   Zulu-6
AFMC 919 OG (C130) at Duke
Distances long, 5m BOQ-Terminal.

Quarters:
AF BOQ (E with dependents). Eglin Inn
Availability ★★ x ★ March-Aug, 4534/5.
24h. **AFMC** $34 - 59
O7 up (& E9) through protocol 3011.
AF E: (O can use) Availability ★★★ x ★
March-August **5025** 24h. Rates: **E** $29
Navy BQ Availability ★★★ **5683** 24h, O
$14sgl, DV $20sgl, both + $4 additional per,
E (no dependents) $8per.
Duke Field:
AFSOC Duke Inn Availability ★★★★
x ★ Res weekends (1st) **(D 875, C 883)**
6203/2918 0715-1545 M-F, Res weekends
(1st). Rates: VAQ $23-26; VOQ $25-30; O7
& up $35; TLF $32
Fam Camp ★★★★ Recreation services
5058 0700-2100 summer, 0800-1800 winter,
report to Fam Camp, no provision for arrival
other hrs. RV EWS $20/d, $120/w, $400/m,
30/50 Amp Tent $5.

Eglin AFB   D-94
Valpariso, FL 32542
872-1110   Operator   **850-882**-1110
↣↣↣↣↣↣↣↣↣ **Flights** ↣↣↣↣↣↣↣↣↣
Andrews   Maxwell
Bangor   New Orleans
Barksdale   Peterson
Dobbins   Robins
Lakefront N.O.   Scott
Langley   Simmons AAF
                 Wright-Pat

Chance of seat ★★★
Flight Information:
Terminal **4757** 0700-1600 M-F.
[Fax 1461, 96 TRANS/LGTTP, 301
Biscane] Recording 3332. OPS 5313
24h.
Duke Field ★★★★ **(D 875, C883)**
6516 0800-2400 M-F. Command Post
6701. Transport provided for Duke
flights.

	Break	Lunch	Dinner	Brun
O Club	7d	M-F	xSu	Su
E Club	M-F	M-F	xSu	Su
Snack	7d	7d	7d	
Duke	SS	SS	Sa	
Club	Res weekends			

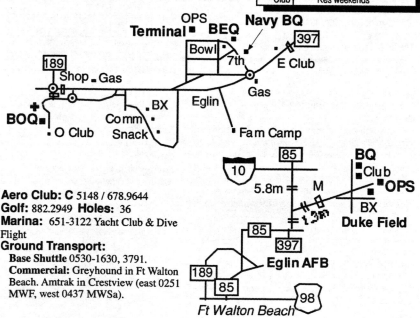

Aero Club: C 5148 / 678.9644
Golf: 882.2949 **Holes:** 36
Marina: 651-3122 Yacht Club & Dive
Flight
Ground Transport:
Base Shuttle 0530-1630, 3791.
Commercial: Greyhound in Ft Walton
Beach. Amtrak in Crestview (east 0251
MWF, west 0437 MWSa).

AF

EFD Zulu-6
No usable facilities nor formal source of flight information. Plane crews manifest.

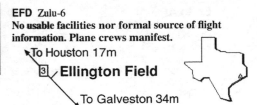

To Houston 17m

3 Ellington Field

To Galveston 34m

Ellington Field   D-8
Houston, TX 77209
954-2110   **281-929**-2110
No operator
➤➤➤➤➤ **Flights** ➤➤➤➤➤
Andrews   Wright Pat
Ft Worth FSu§
Few flights
Chance of seat ★★★★

§ Reservist flight originating and returning to NAS Ft Worth, usually the 4th weekend. Contact Ft Worth Æ75 for information. **May be parked at SouthWest Services 281.484.6551 who provides A/C fuel.**
Ground Transportation: Avis 281.488.4995

RCA Zulu-7 On base prefix 5

ACC Distances walkable, 0.8m BQ-OPS.
Quarters:
  VQ: Pine Tree Inn Availability
  ★★ **2844/1362**
  923-5861 24h.
  ACC FY 07/08
  $30 - 43 O6 up
  (& E9) thru protocol 1205.

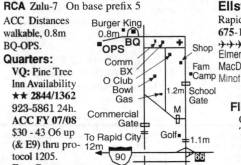

Fam Camp
15 May-15 Oct **2997** 0900-1700 M-F, check in at Fam Camp, RV 30/50 Amp, WiFi, ESWD $19/d, $120/w Tent $6. Outdoor Rec **2997**. No Reservations
Golf: 923.4999 **Holes:** 9
Ground Transport: Greyhound in Rapid City.

Ellsworth AFB   D-94
Rapid City, SD 57706
675-1110   Operator   **605-385**-1000
➤➤➤➤➤➤➤➤➤➤ **Flights** ➤➤➤➤➤➤➤➤➤➤
Elmendorf   Peterson
MacDill   Offutt
Minot
Few flights
Chance of seat ★★★★
Flight Information:
  OPS **1052,2861** 24h
  Terminal 1181-1630 M-F

	Break	Lunch	Dinner
O Club		M-F	Tu-F
Bowl	0600-2200 M-F		
	1200-2200 SS		
Golf	1100-1400 M-F		

SKA   Zulu-8
AMC
141ARW ANG (KC135), 116ARS (KC135)
Distances walkable, 1.6m BQ-OPS.
Quarters:
  BQ: Availability ★★★ **Res: C** 509.244.2290 Ex. 2120, **5519** 24h. **AMC FY 07/08** $28 - 43 O6 up (& E9) thru protocol 2127. Enquire about quarters at Survival School 3028/3751 (10-minute drive away).
  Fam Camp ★★★ **244.3247** 0800-1700 M-F, 0800-1300 SS. Check in with host. RV ESW $11.
  Clear Lake Rec A, cabins, campers, April-Oct ★★★ **5366** 0800-1700 M-F. Site C 299-5129 0700-1900 Th-M. Reservations. Rates: Cabin $15,20, camper $15unit. RV $5, EW $17. Tent W $3. Those in place may remain TuW.
Ground Transport:
  Commercial: #11 Bus thru base to Riverside and Howard 0705-2231, 328-7433. In Spokane, Greyhound, Amtrak (east 0115 MWFSa, Seattle 0240, Portland 0255 SuMWF). Car rent with pick up 838-1434. Taxi 2244.

Fairchild AFB   D-94
Spokane, WA 99011
657-1110 Operator **509-247**-1212
➤➤➤➤➤➤➤ **Flights** ➤➤➤➤➤➤➤
Hickam 1/w   Mildenhall 1/6m
Kadena 2/m   Scott
McChord 1/m
McConnell 1/ 1-2m
Reservist flight to McChord FSu, usually 1st weekend, sometimes 2/m.
Chance of seat
★★★★ x ★★ A
Flight Information:
  PAX **3406,** OPS 7115/7 5435/9 24h.
  Recording 4636x531. [Fax 4909, Base OPS 901 W. Boston]
  ANG scheduling 7116/8
  Parking near OPS

Fairchild AFB continued

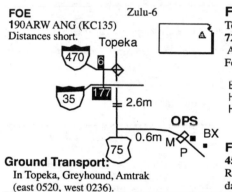

	Break	Lunch	Dinner
Club		M-F	Tu-Sa
Burger King	0630-2000 M-F		
	0800-2000 Sa		
	1030-1800 Su		

FOE   Zulu-6
190ARW ANG (KC135)
Distances short.

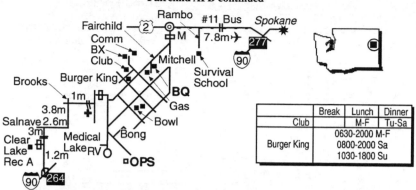

Ground Transport:
In Topeka, Greyhound, Amtrak
(east 0520, west 0236).

Forbes Field   D-83
Topeka, KS 66619
720-1234   No Op **785.861**.XXXX
ANG Command Post 4663
Forbes Base Locator 800.551.5276 **231**-xxxx

ANG ✈✈✈✈ **Flights** ✈✈✈✈ **Army**

Europe	Offutt	Riley
Henry Post AAF	Peterson	
Hickam		
	Norfolk Chance of seat	
	★★★★ x ★ Hickam	

Flight Information: **Air Refueling**
4557 0730-1600 M-F.   **Wing**
Recording 4558. Sign-up   **Scheduling 4695**
date given.   0700-1700

BOI   Zulu-7
Res training Distances short.

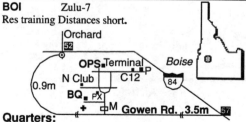

Quarters:
BQ: Availability
★★★★ x ★★ when schools operate, (no dependents x DV O5 & up) **4451**, 5011 0800-1630 M-F.
For arrival other hrs, call, make arrangement for key.
Rates: $21 single, Family Suites $24, DV $35. O6 & up must request through Protocol.
Fam Camp $10 full hookup, can make res. 48h in advance.
Ground Transport:
In Boise, Greyhound, Amtrak (east 2326 MWSa, west 0424 TTSa).

Gowen Field   D-88
(Boise Airport)
Boise, ID 83707
422-5011   **208-442**-5011

✈✈✈✈ **Flights** ✈✈✈✈

Coeur D'Alene Air ID	Nellis
Gray AAF	Pinal Airpark AZ
Helena Regional MT	Salt Lake City
Idaho Falls	Whidbey Island
March	

Few flights
Chance of seat ★★★★
Flight Information:
Terminal **(Army Ops) 5388**
0730-1600 M-F
OPS 5315,5303 0600-1800

	Break	Lunch
NCO Club	M-F	M-F

AF

RDR Zulu-6 On base prefix 7
AMC 905/6/11/12 ARS (KC135)
Distances walkable, 1m BQ-Terminal.

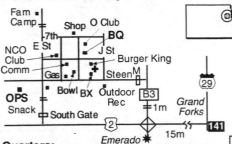

Quarters:

BQ: Warrior Inn. Availability ★★★★ x ★ summer **7200, Res: 7042** 24h. AMC FY 07/08 $28 - 43 O6 up thru protocol 5055, E9 4513.
Fam Camp May-Sept, check in Outdoor Rec, Outdoor Rec **3688** 0730-1800 MF, 1000-1800 TWTh, 0730-1400 Sa. RV ESWD Cable $12/d 50 Amp, Tent $5,10.
Golf: 4279 Holes: 9 Plainsview Golf Course
Ground Transport:
Base Shuttle 0700-1700 M-F. Greyhound 775-4781. Amtrak east 0058 STTS, west 0545 STTS. Taxi 746-7433, 772-3456.

Grand Forks AFB   D-94
Emerado, ND 58205
362-1110 Operator **701-747**-3000
↣↣↣↣↣↣↣ **Flights** ↣↣↣↣↣↣↣
Offutt

Few flights
Chance of seat ★★★★
Flight Information:
OPS **4409** 24h. [Fax 3169
OSS/OSA 695 Steen Ave]
Tanker scheduling 5858

	Break	Lunch	Dinner	Brun
O Club		M-F	TWT	Su
NCO Club		M-F	Tu-F	
Bowl		24h		
Burger King		0700-2030 M-F 0900-1900 Sa 1100-1800 Su		

ILG Zulu+5
166AW ANG (C130)
Distances short,
1m OPS-OPS.

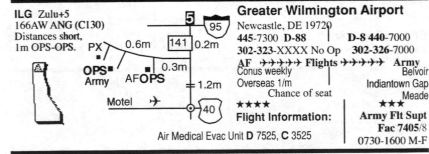

Greater Wilmington Airport
Newcastle, DE 19720
445-7300 **D-88** | **D-8 440**-7000
302-323-XXXX No Op   302-326-7000
AF ↣↣↣↣↣ **Flights** ↣↣↣↣↣ **Army**
Conus weekly   Belvoir
Overseas 1/m   Indiantown Gap
Chance of seat   Meade
★★★★   ★★★
Flight Information: Army Flt Supt
                                              Fac 7405/8
Air Medical Evac Unit **D** 7525, **C** 3525   0730-1600 M-F

RME Zulu-5
Supports Ft Drum

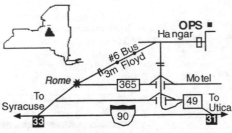

Griffiss Airfield   D-8
Rome, NY 13441
587-1110 No Operator   **315-330**-1110
↣↣↣↣↣↣↣ **Flights** ↣↣↣↣↣↣↣
Rare flights
Bangor
Chance of seat ★★★★
Flight Information:
OPS **7400** 24h. Recording 2089. ANG 330-2160.
Ground Transport:
Commercial: #6,10 Floyd Ave Bus to downtown enters base, 0645-1745 M-F, 0915-1745 Sa. Greyhound, Amtrak in Rome, east 1641, west 1201.

AF

GUS Zulu-5 (No daylight savings time.)

AFRC
434ARW
Res (KC135)
Distances
walkable,
0.9m BQ-
OPS.

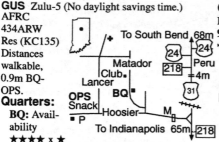

Quarters:
BQ: Avail-
ability
★★★★ x ★

summer, Res weekends **2844/2596** 0600-2200.
AFRC FY 07/08 $33-40 Space-A reservations - 24 ahead.
RV: No FamCamp, but have rental trailers
@ **$25 -55/d. State park 10 mile away.**

Ground Transport:

Indiana Bus on US 31, for stop at main gate call Peru, 472-1105, south.

Grissom ARB   D-8

Peru, IN 46971
928-1110   Operator   **765.6 88** .5211
➤➤➤➤➤➤➤➤➤➤ **Flights** ➤➤➤➤➤➤➤➤➤

Hickam 1/m	Nellis 1/w	Travis 1/m

8-10 flights/m, send SASE for schedule
Chance of seat ★★★★

Flight Information:

OPS **2254/5** 0700-2300 [Fax 3643, 434OSF/
ATB] Tanker scheduling 2958
No in-flight meals

	Break	Lunch	Dinner	Brun
Club	M-F	M-F	Tu-F	SS

BED   Zulu-5

AFMC No planes stationed
Distances walkable, 1m BQ-
Terminal.

Quarters:

BQ: Hanscom Inn. Availability ★★★ **6560/2044/2753**
377.2112 24h, reserve 0730-1630 M-F. AFMC FY
07/08 $34-59 Protocol 5151.
Fam Camp, ★★★ reservations, **4670** 0800-2100,
check in at Fam Camp, 2m from main gate. RV EW
$10, ESW $12. Tent $6.
Fourth Cliff Fam Camp, cabins ★ July,Aug, Outdoor
Rec **5316** 0900-1700, site C 837-6785, Info: 837.9269,
800-468-9547 0900-1630. Rates: Winter 3BD $75, 2BD
$60, TH $50 $45,70unit. RV ESW $15. Tent $10. No
pets in cabins.
Devens Inn at old Ft Devens **978-772**-4300, Fax 4903.
Meals at Conference Center.

Golf: 687.3114 Holes: 9

Commercial: Motel at I95.

Ground Transport:

Shuttle: From terminal & BQ to Boston subway, Airport
0530-1830 M-F, 1230,1530 Su if duty Pax, from Airport 1hr
later, reservations 2587/8, 800-522-8756. Free
bus airport-subway.
Commercial: #76 Bus to Alewife Red Line
subway station 0615-1915 M-F, 0815-1815 Sa,
from subway 0605-1830 M-F, 0730-1730 Sa.
222-3200, 800-392-6100. Car rent at Bedford
Airport, 274-7488. Taxi 275-6200.

Hanscom AFB   D-8

Bedford, MA 01731
478-5980 Operator **781-377**-4441
➤➤➤➤➤➤➤ **Flights** ➤➤➤➤➤➤➤

Albany	Scott
Andrews√	Simmons AAF
Barnes Muni MA	Washington NAF
Burlington VT	Wheeler Sack AAF
Langley	Willow Grove
Otis ANGB	Wright-Pat

Usually C12, C21, C21, & C26
Chance of seat ★★★★

Flight Information:

Terminal **2549** (Only open when
flights are scheduled) Transit 2549
0700-1600. [Sign-up by Fax **2383**,
66th MSG/LRDT 3 Robbins St
Hanscom AFB, MA 01731 Bldg
1721] Recording 3333

	Break	Lunch	Dinner
O Club		M-F	Tu-Sa
NCO Club		M-F	Tu-Sa
Bowl	M-F	7d	7d
Snack		1100-2300	
BX Snack		1000-1700	

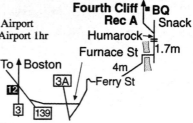

HA

AF

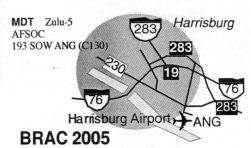

MDT Zulu-5
AFSOC
193 SOW ANG (C130)

Harrisburg

Harrisburg Airport ✈—ANG

BRAC 2005

Harrisburg Airport
Middletown, PA
423-2200 **717-948**-2312
↣↣↣↣↣ **Flights** ↣↣↣↣↣
Andrews   Davison   Norfolk
Burlington VT   Erie PA   Peterson
Capital City MI Langley
              Chance of seat ★
Flight Information:
    Numbers above 0700-1630
Ground Transport:
    Car rent at airport.

HIF   Zulu-7   On base prefix 7
AFMC
Distances short,
0.3m BQ-Terminal.

Quarters:
    BQ: Mountain View Inn.
    Availability ★★★ x ★★
    summer **1844 773**-0498
    24h. AFMC FY 07/08
    Rates: $34-59 Protocol
    7.5565.
    Rec Areas: 9666 0900-2100
    M-F, 1100-1800 SS.
    Fam Camp April-Oct, check in at camp after
    1300, **3250** 0800-2000. RV ESWD $10-14,
    15/30/50 **Amp power. Tents $5**
Golf: 777.3272 **Holes:** 18
    Carter Creek Rec A: June-Oct, cabins $35 unit
    Su-Th, $40 unit FSa, trailers $15unit. RV EW
    $10 Su-Th, $12 FSa. Tent $5, no dump. Reserve
    all x billets **at** Ticket & Tours, 3525 0800-1800
    M-F, 0800-1100 Sa.
Ground Transport:
    Shuttle: 0715-1515 M-F.
    Commercial: #70 Bus outside West Gate to
    Ogden, SLC. Also bus on Route 232, info 621-
    4636. Airport shuttle, make reservations 1843.
    Greyhound, Amtrak in Ogden west 2151, east
    0638. Taxi **9887.**

To West OPS
Gate 2nd
Terminal | BQ
Outdoor Rec | Cafe
Shop | OClub
Comm | Gas
BX | Bowl
E Club | 111th RV
193 | 232

Hill AFB   D-94
Ogden, UT 84056
777.1110   Operator   **801-777**-7221
↣↣↣↣↣↣↣↣ **Flights** ↣↣↣↣↣↣↣↣
Boise   McChord SuTu A FSu §
Helena   Scott

              Chance of seat ★★★
Flight Information:
    Terminal **2887** 0700-1700 M-Th, Sa
    0700-2200 F, 1700-2200 Su. Recording
    1854. Terminal may move to OPS build-
    ing. [Fax 3249, 649 ADG/LGTT PM]
    OPS 1861 24h

	Break	Lunch	Dinner
O Club		M-F	xSu
E Club	7d	7d	xM
Cafe	M-F	M-F	M-F
Bowl		7d	7d
Comuni		7d	7d

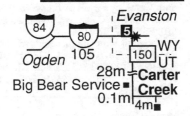

Evanston
84   80   **5**
                              WY
Ogden 105   – 150   ‾UT
              28m ═ **Carter**
Big Bear Service ■   **Creek**
              0.1m ┌ 4m ■

HMN   Zulu-7
ACC
Distances short, 0.5m BQ-AF
OPS x 2.5m between OPS.
Quarters:
    BQ: Availability
    ★★★★ x ★ summer,
    3311/7160 Res: 6131 24h. ACC FY 07/08 Rates: $30-43
    Protocol 572.5573.

Holloman AFB   D-88
Alamogordo, NM 88330
572.1110   505.572.1110
AF ↣↣ **Flights** ↣↣ **Army**
Rare flights | Rare flights
        Chance of seat
★★★★   ★★★★

Continued on facing page

Holloman AFB continued

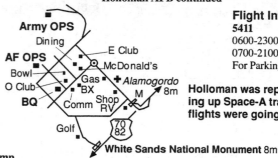

Flight Information:

5411	**1339/40**
0600-2300 M-F	0715-1600
0700-2100 SS	M-F

For Parking contact Security

Holloman was reported as not signing up Space-A travelers even when flights were going to Europe.

Fam Camp

★★★ **5369** 1100-1800 M-F, 1600-1900 SS, check in with host at Fam Camp. RV $3, ESW $10. No dump.

Golf: 572.3574 **Holes:** 9 Apache Mesa Golf Course

Aero Club: 572.3752 Holloman Aero Club

Ground Transport:

✈ **Shuttle:** To Ft Bliss 0600,1030,1330 M-F. Returns 0740,1300,1500, 3937.

Commercial:

Limo from BQ to Alamogordo, El Paso Airport 0645-1700, 800-872-2701.

	Break	Lunch	Dinner	Brun
O Club		M-F	Tu-F	Su
E Club	xSu	M-F	7d	
Bowl	xSu	7d	7d	
Golf	1100-1330			
McDonald's	0630-2230			

HST Zulu-5

AFRC Distances walkable.

Homestead ARB

Homestead, FL 33039

791-7000   Menu   **305-224**-7000

➤➤➤➤➤➤➤➤➤➤➤➤**Flights**➤➤➤➤➤➤➤➤➤➤

Charleston FSu§   Jacksonville F§

§ Reservist flight

Chance of seat ★★★★

Flight Information:

Terminal **7518/9** 1200-1930 FSu §

OPS 7516 0630-1930

Quarters:

Homestead Inn: Availability ★★★★ x ★ Res weekends, exercises **7168/7198** 0700-2300.

AFRC FY 07/08 Rates: $33-40, Fax: 7290

	Break	Lunch	Dinner
Club		M-F	M-F

HRT Zulu-6

Distances walkable 0.8m BQ-OPS

Quarters:

Commando Inn Availability ★ x ★★★ F **6245,7115** 24h. AFSOC FY 07/08 Rates: $23-46, O7 up thru protocol 2308.

RV: C 6653 ESW &10, tent $5.

Dive: Hurlburt Field Dive Club

Golf: 581.0007 **Holes:**18 Gator Lakes Golf Club

Marina: 6939

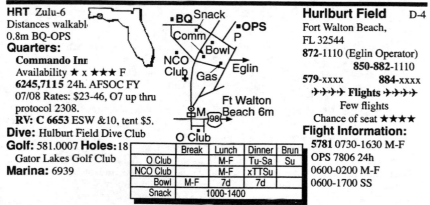

Hurlburt Field   D-4

Fort Walton Beach, FL 32544

872-1110 (Eglin Operator)

850-882-1110

579-xxxx   **884**-xxxx

➤➤➤➤ **Flights** ➤➤➤➤

Few flights

Chance of seat ★★★★

Flight Information:

5781 0730-1630 M-F

OPS 7806 24h

0600-0200 M-F

0600-1700 SS

	Break	Lunch	Dinner	Brun
O Club		M-F	Tu-Sa	Su
NCO Club		M-F	xTTSu	
Bowl	M-F	7d	7d	
Snack	1000-1400			

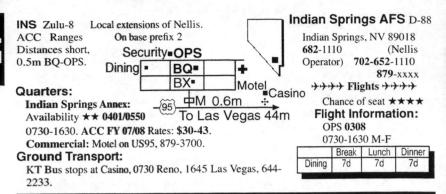

INS Zulu-8   Local extensions of Nellis.
ACC Ranges   On base prefix 2
Distances short,
0.5m BQ-OPS.

Indian Springs AFS D-88

Indian Springs, NV 89018
682-1110   (Nellis
Operator) **702-652**-1110
                              879-xxxx

++++ **Flights** ++++

Chance of seat ★★★★

Quarters:
Indian Springs Annex:
Availability ★★ **0401/0550**
0730-1630. **ACC FY 07/08** Rates: **$30-43**.
Commercial: Motel on US95, 879-3700.

Flight Information:
OPS **0308**
0730-1630 M-F

Dining	Break	Lunch	Dinner
	7d	7d	7d

Ground Transport:
KT Bus stops at Casino, 0730 Reno, 1645 Las Vegas, 644-2233.

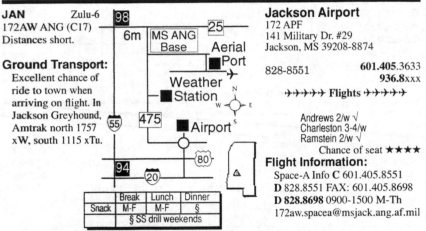

JAN   Zulu-6
172AW ANG (C17)
Distances short.

Jackson Airport
172 APF
141 Military Dr. #29
Jackson, MS 39208-8874

828-8551   **601.405**.3633
                        936.8xxx

++++++ **Flights** ++++++

Ground Transport:
Excellent chance of
ride to town when
arriving on flight. In
Jackson Greyhound,
Amtrak north 1757
xW, south 1115 xTu.

Andrews 2/w √
Charleston 3-4/w
Ramstein 2/w √
        Chance of seat ★★★★

Flight Information:
Space-A Info **C** 601.405.8551
D 828.8551 FAX: 601.405.8698
D 828.8698 0900-1500 M-Th
172aw.spacea@msjack.ang.af.mil

Snack	Break	Lunch	Dinner
	M-F	M-F	§
	§ SS drill weekends		

Amtrak May Save Both Money & Time

There are times continuing by rail is cheaper, faster, and more convenient than by commercial air or rental car as illustrated by an actual case observed at Andrews by a contributor. Another traveler was making call after call to airlines. The contributor asked where that traveler wanted to go - someplace south of New York City. The contributor suggested calling Amtrak [1.800.USA.RAIL (1.800.872.7245)]. It turned out the first train would get there before the first plane, at about half the cost, and much closer to where the traveler wanted to go than any airport.

There are many other places where Amtrak (or other rail transport) is appropriate, for example to many destinations around Travis or up the Coast from San Diego. Keep in mind that Amtrac delivers you to the city, not to some outlying airport. Also the train is more comfortable and has some spectacular routes such as up the Hudson from New York City. Amtrak schedules and station locations are found on the Internet at **http://www.amtrak.com.** Amtrak is considering major route reductions.

AF

BIX Zulu-6   On base prefix 7
AETC 403AW Res (C130)
Distances   ■Marina
short
x to Marina.

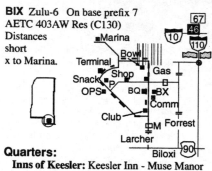

Quarters:
Inns of Keesler: Keesler Inn - Muse Manor 2420/4900 has Lodging desk, Tyler House 377.7867 provides officer & family quarters.
RES: 9986 Availability ★★★★ winter, ★★★ summer, x ★ Res weekends, Mardi Gras 2420 24h. **AETC FY 07/08** $24-42 Protocol 3359.
Fam Camp: At Marina **3160/86** 0600-1900 MThF, 0800-1800 TuW, 0530-2000 SS, check in with Host camper. RV $6, ESTW $12. BQ at NCB Gulfport Æ117 reachable by city bus. Firearms only in campers.
Commercial: Motels in Biloxi, $35 up.
Golf: 377.3832 **Holes:** 18
Marina: 3160/86
Ground Transport:
Base Shuttle: 0630-2000 M-F.
Commercial: Bus from Base to Biloxi afternoons M-F, all day SS, info 896-8080. Greyhound, Amtrak east 2131 SuTT, 1932, west 0924 MWSa, 0727. Car rent on base.

Keesler AFB   D-99
Biloxi, MS 39534
597-1110   Operator   228-377-1110
➤➤➤➤➤➤➤➤➤➤ **Flights** ➤➤➤➤➤➤➤➤➤➤
Andrews	New Orleans
Dobbins 1st Wend	Norfolk
Little Rock	Randolph
MacDill 1st Wend	Sheppard
Memphis 1st Wend	

Frequent flights, many destinations
Chance of seat ★★★
Flight Information:
OPS **2120** 0700-2300 [Fax 2459. 45 AS/ OSFAM 817 H St #11] Recording 4538 403AW 4181. Terminal open above hrs.

	Break	Lunch	Dinner	Brun
Club	M-F	M-F	xSu	Su
Bowl	xSu	7d	7d	
Snack	0630-1300 M-F			

SKF Zulu-6   On-base prefix 5, 3
AETC   to Lackland
433AW Res (C5) Distances short.

Quarters:
Inns of Lackland: Availability ★★7.
x ★ Res weekends **7201** 24h. Assigned at 1700. Rates $24-42
Ground Transport:
Commercial: Enterprise Rental Car has offices both at Lackland BX, 210.670.1104 & at Randolph, 210.566.4428, with vehicles available for one way transit at $37 a day. By calling either office prior to your arrival, a car can be awaiting your arrival at their respective terminal.
From former M gate #62 Bus to downtown, for airport transfer to #2, to Randolph only at 0515,0534,0554 M-F, transfer to #17 0607,0637, 227-2020. Greyhound 270-5824. Amtrak north 0700 SuTT, east 0400 SuTT, west 0535 SuTT.

Kelly USA Annex   D-88
NEW NAME *Lackland Passenger Terminal at Kelly Field.*
407 South Frank Luke Drive
San Antonio, TX 78241
473-1110   Operator   **210-925**-1110
924.XXXX
➤➤➤➤➤➤➤➤ **Flights**➤➤➤➤➤➤➤➤
Andersen 1/w	Norfolk
Andrews	Offutt
Dover 1/w	Osan√
Elmendorf	Peterson
Ft Worth	Ramstein√
Hickam √	Scott 2/wk C130
Kadena	Travis√
Langley	Yokota 1/w
Mildenhall	Wright Pat

Frequent flights to many dest.
Chance of seat ★★★ x ★★ Travis
Flight Information:
Terminal **925.0953**, 8714/5 0730-1630
Recording 925.8714/5,
OPS 6802 0630-2230. Fax2732.
Terminal open above hrs.
C5 schedules out 1st weekend.

Continued on following page

Kelly Annex continued from preceding page

AF

To downtown San Antonio
Comm NCO Hudnell
Mitchell Club
BQ & BX O Club
*Dining
Duncan
OPS
Lackland
Terminal Tinker
& *Cafeteria
Military Dr.
Berman
3
Gate 7

Frequent flights to many dest.
Chance of seat ★★★ x ★★ Travis

Flight Information:
Terminal 925.0953, 8714/5 0730-1630
Recording 925.8714/5,
OPS 6802 0630-2230. Fax2732.
Terminal open above hrs.
C5 schedules out 1st weekend.

* Security and Meal Notice: Kelly Annex is open to the public, lacks normal military security, and retiree meal availability at last report was quite questionable. Flight kitchen next to VQ is still provide sandwiches and drinks. **Before going to Kelly, plan ahead for meal arrangements.**

LMT Zulu-8
ANG Distances short.
Quarters:
BQ: Availability
★★★★ x ★ summer and when classes are in session **6365** 0800-1600 M-F, for arrival other hrs, keys at main gate 6653. Rate: $8,10per. In 1996 lodging taken over by state, not usable by Space-A except Guard. Retained as it may become available again.

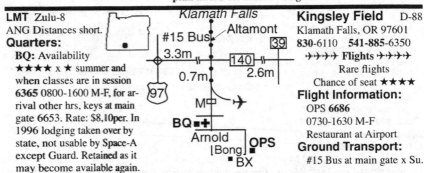

Klamath Falls
#15 Bus Altamont
3.3m
0.7m 140 39
97 2.6m
M
BQ
Arnold OPS
Bong BX

Kingsley Field D-88
Klamath Falls, OR 97601
830-6110 **541-885**-6350
✈✈✈✈ **Flights** ✈✈✈✈
Rare flights
Chance of seat ★★★★
Flight Information:
OPS **6686**
0730-1630 M-F
Restaurant at Airport
Ground Transport:
#15 Bus at main gate x Su.

ABQ Zulu-7 Two base prefixes 85**3** & 84**6**
AFMC 151AMC (C130)
Distances long, 5.2m BQ-OPS.

Quarters:
Kirtland Inn: Availability ★★ **6.9652/3**
2692.2141 24h. AFMC FY 07/08 $34-59 O6 up thru protocol 4119. 24h advance reservations.
Fam Camp 6.0337 [Outdoor Rec 6.1275,6.1499] 0900-2200 Su-Th, 0900-2400 FSa, check in Outdoor Rec. RV SW $5, ESW $10.
Commercial: Motels on Central.
Golf: 846.1169 **Holes:** 18
Aero Club: C 1072
Ground Transport:
Military taxi OPS-BQ 0500-2200 M-F, 2396.
Commercial: Bus on Carlisle, Gibson, Wyoming, change to **#50** for Airport (xSu). Greyhound, Amtrak in Albuquerque east 1324, west 1643. Car rent at Airport. Taxi 243-7777, 247-8888.

Kirtland AFB D-94
Albuquerque, NM 87117
246-0011 Operator **505-846**-0011
✈✈✈✈✈✈✈✈✈ **Flights** ✈✈✈✈✈✈✈✈✈
Andrews Offutt
Biggs § Peterson 2/w√

Chance of seat
★★★★ x ★★ Andrews

Flight Information:
Air Freight Office handles Space-A **6.6184, 6.7000** 0715-1600 M-F. Fax 6185 [377 TRNS/LGTT 3400 Clark Ave].
Recording 6184
OPS 8335/6 0700-2100 M-F
0800-1700 SS

	Break	Lunch	Dinner	Brun
O Club E	xSu	xSu	xSu	Su
O Club W		M-F		
NCO Club	M-F	xSu	7d	Sa
Snack		0600-2300		
OPS		0800-1700 M-F		
Snack		0800-1430 Sa		

Continued on facing page

AF

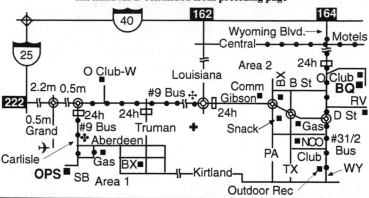

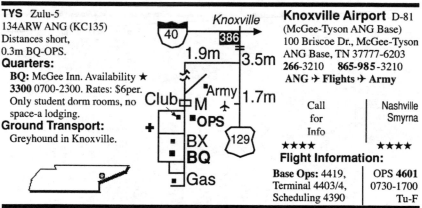

TYS Zulu-5
134ARW ANG (KC135)
Distances short,
0.3m BQ-OPS.
Quarters:
BQ: McGee Inn. Availability ★
3300 0700-2300. Rates: $6per.
Only student dorm rooms, no
space-a lodging.
Ground Transport:
Greyhound in Knoxville.

Knoxville

Knoxville Airport D-81
(McGee-Tyson ANG Base)
100 Briscoe Dr., McGee-Tyson
ANG Base, TN 37777-6203
266-3210 **865-985**-3210
ANG → Flights → Army

Call for Info	Nashville Smyrna
★★★★	★★★★

Flight Information:

Base Ops: 4419,	OPS **4601**
Terminal 4403/4,	0730-1700
Scheduling 4390	Tu-F

LFI Zulu-5
Prefixes: **C** 225 + **D** 575 use **5+XXXX**
C 985 + **D** 266 use **4+XXXX**
ACC 4500Sup (C130)
Distances walkable x to NCO Club, 1m BQ-
Terminal.
Quarters:
Langley Inns: Availability ★★ M-F, ★★★
SS, **4.4667** 766.1200 24h. ACC FY 07/08
Rates: **$30-43**, O6 up thru protocol 5041.
Rec A, April-Oct, Outdoor Rec **4.7170**
Commercial: Motel at King Gate
Golf: 764.4547 **Holes:** 36
Marina: 764-7220
Ground Transport:
Base Shuttle 0630-1730 M-F, 4.8347. ✚
Shuttle: M-F to Eustis, Portsmouth Naval ✚.
Commercial: #8 Bus thru base to Hampton
TC, 0645-2345 xSu, 723-3344. At Newport
News Amtrak north 0845 xSa. Limo to airports
(Patrick Henry & Norfolk). Car rent at Billet
1000-1800 M-F, 1000-1400 SS, 766-1163.

Langley AFB D-94
Hampton, VA 23665
574-1110   Operator **757-764**-9990
AF →→→→→ Flights →→→→ Army

Andrews √	Hanscom	Riley
Atlanta	Hurlburt	Pope √
Barksdale	Kelly	Randolph
Belvoir√	Knox	Scott √
Cherry Point √	Leavenworth	Tyndall √
Davison √	Maxwell	Wright-Pat
Dobbins	New River √	√ 2-3/w
Eglin	Norfolk √	
Godman AAF	Offutt	**Controls Monroe**

Frequent flights   ★★★★
Mostly C12,21   **C 878.2149**
Chance of seat ★★★
Flight Information:
Terminal **4.4311, 4.4563**
0700-1600 M-F. [Fax
5941]. Recording 4.5807. OPS 4.2504 24h

Continued on following page

Langley AFB continued from preceding page

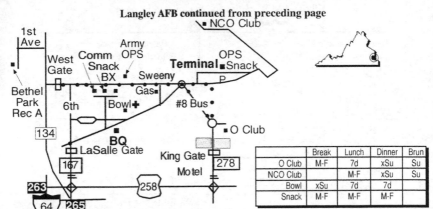

	Break	Lunch	Dinner	Brun
O Club	M-F	7d	xSu	Su
NCO Club		M-F	xSu	Su
Bowl	xSu	7d	7d	
Snack	M-F	M-F	M-F	

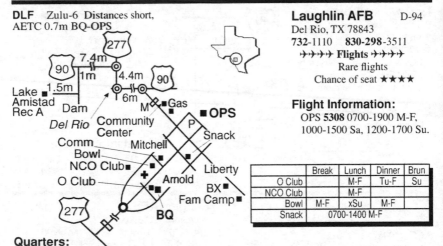

DLF Zulu-6 Distances short,
AETC 0.7m BQ-OPS

Laughlin AFB   D-94
Del Rio, TX 78843
732-1110   **830-298**-3511
✈✈✈✈ **Flights** ✈✈✈✈
Rare flights
Chance of seat ★★★★

Flight Information:
OPS **5308** 0700-1900 M-F,
1000-1500 Sa, 1200-1700 Su.

	Break	Lunch	Dinner	Brun
O Club		M-F	Tu-F	Su
NCO Club		M-F		
Bowl	M-F	xSu	M-F	
Snack	0700-1400 M-F			

Quarters:
Laughlin Manor: Availability ★★★ **5731/41** 24h. AETC FY 07/08 Rates: **$24-42** O6 up
thru protocol 5698.

Fam Camp ★★★ [Outdoor Rec **5830**] Camp Host 7593. 0800-2200 M-F, 1700-2400 SS,
reservations, check in at Community Center or Host. RV ESTW $12 no shower, dump. Regis-
ter firearms with security.

Lake Amistad Rec A: Trailers **C 775-5971,** D thru operator 0800-1800 Th-M. Rate: Trailer
$18unit. No blankets, linens. RV, Tent EW / ESTW D $12, W $80, M $250. Those already in
place need not leave TuW. **Marina** 775.7800

Commercial: Motels on US90 in Del Rio.

Golf: 298.5451 Holes: 9
Marina: 830-775-7800 South Winds Marina
Ground Transport:
Amtrak east 2259 MWSa, west 0830 SuTT. Car rent in Del Rio. Taxi 775-6344.

Send changes to
publisher@spaceatravel.com

LNK Zulu-6 155 ARW
KC135
Signups are recorded on Wednesday with local signup recorded prior to remote. **D** 279.1248/9 **C** 402.458.1248/9.

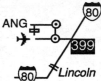

ANG

Lincoln

Lincoln Airport
ATTN: Space-A Travel
2945 NW 25th Street
Lincoln, NE 68524
279.7210 402-471-3241
OPS 1294

AF

LRF   Zulu-6   Prefix 7 on base
AETC/AMC, 189AW ANG (C130), 314AW (C130) Distances short x 1.5m BQ-OPS.

Quarters:
Razorback Inn: Availability ★ x ★★★
Dec **7769** 6752/3 988.1141 24h. Extensions if available. AETC FY 07/08 Rates: **$24-42**+7add per O6 up thru protocol 6828.
Fam Camp ★★★★ 5830 0730-1700, check in at Rec. RV EW $10. Dump by west gate. Deposit.
Commercial: Motels on US6/167.
Golf: C 6825 **Holes:** 18 Deer Run Golf Course

Ground Transport:
In Little Rock: Greyhound, Amtrak east 2302 SuTT, west 0808 MWSa.

Little Rock AFB   D-94
Jacksonville, AR 72099
731-1110   Operator   **501.987.**1110
➤➤➤➤➤➤➤➤➤ **Flights** ➤➤➤➤➤➤➤➤➤

Andrews	New Orleans
Dobbins	Patrick
Dyess	Pope
Eielson	Randolph
Elmendorf	Travis
McChord	Wright Pat
Langley	

2-3 flights per day, Chance of seat
★★★★
Flight Information:
Terminal 3342, **Rec 3684** 0730-1630 M-F, other hrs 3086. [Fax 6726, LG-TAP 314 TRNS] **Base OPS** 6123. **ANG Command Post** 6321

	Break	Lunch	Dinner	Brun
O Club	M-F	xSa	xSu	
NCO Club	xSu	xSa	xSu	Su
Bowl	M-F	7d	7d	
OPS Snack	0300-0200			
Snack	0730-1430 M-F			

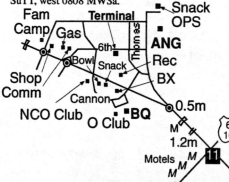

This compact travel book is provided for military travelers

We are open to including additional information in futher editions. If you would like something included in future editions, send us an e-mail.

Traveler input is requested.

AF

LAX   Zulu-8

To AFB planes: Mercury Aviation C 215-5745, get escort at American Airlines Post 1 end of World Way. Long-term parking **2190** at AFB, $30/m for large, $20/m for small space. Spaces can be rented 90/180/365d. Located by Gas. Shuttle to LAX until 1600

Quarters:
Fort MacArthur Inn (D 633) C
310.653.8296 Lodging facilities are located at Fort MacArthur 22 miles from Los Angeles AFB. From airport take 405S to 110S to San Pedro. L on Gaffey to L on 22nd St to R on Pacific Ave. to L on 24th St. **AFSPC**
FY 07/08 Rates: $25-44
   Fam Camp: ★★★★ 2190 0900-1500 M-F Equipment Rent **2081**. RV EW $8
Ground Transport:
   Shuttles: AFB-LAX. AFB to Ft MacArthur 1600 M-F.
   Commercial: From AFB: Bus: Los Angeles Airport #439 M-F, #225/6 xSu; Los

Los Angeles AFB, Airport
Los Angeles, CA 90009
833-1110   **310-363**-1110
Toll Free 800.756.2640
AMC ⤞⤞⤞⤞⤞ Flights ⤞⤞⤞⤞⤞ AFB
Peterson   Wright Pat

Flight Information:
AFB 1886, 2356 **Patriot Express flights no longer depart from or arrive at LA Airport.**

	Break	Lunch	Dinner	Brun
Club	M-F	M-F	W-F	Su

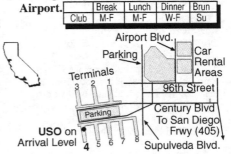

Angeles #439 **M-F**. MAX3 Bus to Ft MacArthur rush hrs. From Airport: Free C Bus on lower level at Airport to LAX Bus Terminal. From Bus Term: #225/6,439 to LA AFB; #232 to Long Beach for connection to Ft MacArthur and on to #50 for Los Alamitos; #42 to City Hall for connection to #496 to March. $15 shuttle to Greyhound.

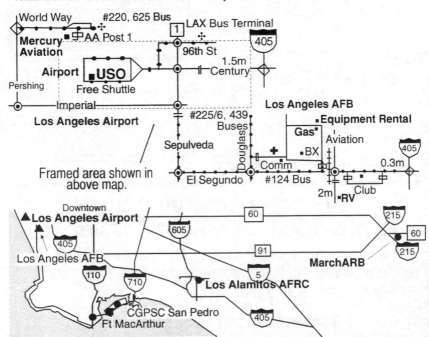

SDF   Zulu-5
123AW ANG (C130)

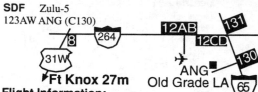

Ft Knox 27m   Old Grade LA

Flight Information:
OPS **460** 0630-1630 Tu-F. Fax 605. In-person signup,
0730-1600 M-F, Bldg 400. For Airevac, contact Ft
Knox, *ÆI29*, Patient Affairs, D 464-, C 502-624-9274
0800-1630 M-F. Contact Flight Managementat the
airport and staff will help with Airevac. Patient Affairs
office, reported as less than helpful.

Louisville Airport   D-94
(Standiford)
1019 Old Grade Ln
Louisville, KY 40213-2678
     Flight Management
741.4459   502-364-9459
➤➤➤➤➤ Flights ➤➤➤➤➤
        Belvoir
        Offutt
    Chance of seat ★★★★

Space-A 9473
USO 502.361.1888 in west wing of
airport. Open 0800 - last flight.

LUF   Zulu-7 (No Daylight Saving)
AETC Distances walkable, 0.6m BQ-OPS.
Prefix 6 on base.

Quarters:
Fighter Country Inn: Fighter Country Inn.
Availability ★ **3941** 24h. AETC FY 07/08
Rates: **$24-42** 22unit. Protocol 5604/5.
Ft Tuthill Rec A: A non-smoking facility.
Availability ★★★ x ★ summer, **623.856.3401**
24h, at site C 520-774-8893, **800-552-6268**,
reservations 6m ahead. Rates: A frames $80unit,
cabin $55unit, hotel $40-45,40unit, permanent
tents (communal facilities) $25unit. RV EW
$14. Tent $9. No pets in buildings. Firearms
must be unloaded and secured in vehicles.
Commercial: None close, BQ has list of motels
with discounts.

Golf: 535.8355 **Holes:** 18

Ground Transport:
Commercial: In Phoenix: Greyhound. Luke
Link Bus, $1.25, connections to city buses 0645-
1745 M-F 930-3521. Budget car rent at BX 267-
4000 x321 0900-1800 M-F, 1330-1600 Sa.

Luke AFB   D-94
Glendale, AZ 85309
896-1110   Operator   **623-856-**7411
➤➤➤➤➤➤➤➤➤➤ Flights ➤➤➤➤➤➤➤➤➤➤
      Few flights
    Chance of seat ★★★★

Flight Information:
OPS **7131/2** 0600-2230 M-F, 0800-1600
SS. Sign up day of flight starting 0730.
Does not accept remote sign up but will
Fax at no charge.

	Break	Lunch	Dinner
O Club		M-F	Tu-Sa
E Club		M-F	W-Sa
Burger King	0600-2200		
OPS Snack	Machines		

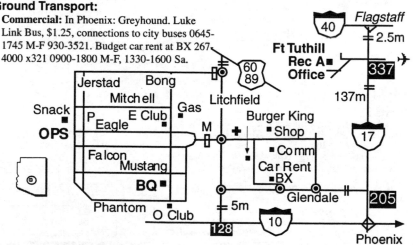

AF

MCF Zulu-5 AMC

KC-135 Distances walkable, 0.8m BQ-Terminal.

MacDill AFB
D-94

Tampa, FL 33621

968-1110 Operator **813-828**-1110

AF ⇥⇥⇥⇥⇥⇥ Flights ⇥⇥⇥⇥⇥⇥ Army

AF	Flights	Army
Andrews √	New Orleans	Andrews
Charleston FSu §	Norfolk	Belvoir
Dobbins	Peterson	Bragg
Eglin	Pope	
Hurlburt	Robins	
Jacksonville FSu §	Rucker	
Jacksonville NC	Scott	
Langley	Washington	
Maxwell	Wright Pat	

Numerous unscheduled flights.

Army Ops Aviation
2908
0700-1700
M-F

§ Reservist flight

Chance of seat ★★★

Flight Information:
Terminal **2485, 2440** 0800-1600 M-F. [Fax 3202, 6 TRNS/LGTA Hangar 4, Room 101] Recording 2310. OPS 2321/50 24h.

Old Tampa Bay
Tampa A/P
Orlando
Expressway
Dale Mabry
MacDill
Tampa
St. Petersburg
Tampa Bay
Gulf of Mexico

0 1 2 3 4
Scale in Miles

Tampa
#40 Bus Dale Mabry
#17 Bus Bayshore
Snack BX Comm
Gas
E Club
#17, 40 Buses
OPS
Terminal
Army
Shop
Florida Keys
Bowl
BQ
O Club

Fam Camp
Marina

Quarters:
MacDill Inn: Availability ★★★ x ★ summer, Res weekends **4259** 24h. **AMC FY 07/08** $28-43 Protocol O6 & up and E9 2056.

Fam Camp ★★★ **4982** 0700-2000 M-F, 0600-2000 SS, reservations, check in at Marina. RV $9, ESW $13. Tent $6.

Golf: 840.6904 **Holes:** 36 Bay Palms Golf Complex

Marina: 828.4983

Ground Transport:
Commercial: #17/40 Buses on base to downtown 0605-1835 M-F, 0817-1813, 254-4278. Greyhound, Amtrak north 2350, south 0703 in Tampa.

	Break	Lunch	Dinner	Brun
O Club		M-F	Tu-Sa	Su
E Club	M-F	M-F	M-F	
Snack	0800-2100			
Bowl	0900-2130 M-Th 0900-2330 FSa 1200-2130 Su			

GFA (Airport is GTF)   Zulu-7
Missile AFSPC Distances short,
0.5m OPS-BQ.

Malmstrom AFB   D-88
Great Falls, MT 59402
632-1110   Operator **406-731**-1110
➤➤➤➤➤➤➤➤ **Flights** ➤➤➤➤➤➤➤➤➤

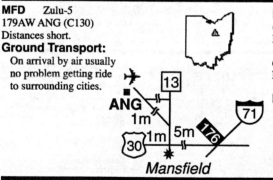

Fam Camp
Annex ■
Rec ⤴ Burger
NCO Club King
Comm ✦ P
O Club 4th
Ave B BX
4th ■Gas
BQ ■**OPS**
2nd N
Goddard
#3 M
Intercity 1st N Bus
& Bus
Great 87 Gateway FamCamp
Falls 89

**No flight line, few flights arrive
at airport.**

Chance of seat ★★★
ANG at Airport (C26), Flights rare
(279-2, 406-791-6) 202.

	Break	Lunch	Dinner	Brun
O Club		M-F	W-Sa	Su
NCO Club		M-F	M-F	
Burger King	0630-1900 M-F			
	0800-1800 Sa			
	1100-1700 Su			

Quarters:

Maimstrom Inns: Availability ★★★★ X ★ on Holiday weekends **3394** 24h. **AFSPC FY 07/08** $25-44 Protocol 3430.

Fam Camp ★★★★ **3263** 0730-1700 M-F, 0800-1300 SS, check in at Outdoor Rec 3263. **On Post** (Annex Fam Camp) open 1 April - 1 Oct RV $13/29 gravel pads 20A EW service, dump station, bathrooms. Shower & laundry off site. **Off post** (Gateway Fam Camp) open year round $17night $400/mo 25 concrete spaces w/ 50A service, shower, & laundry. Overflow $10. Tent $6. Military Camper Trailers @ Timber Wolf Resort [http://www.timberwolfresort.com]

Ground Transport:

#3 Bus at main gate to 4th and Central, take either direction, 0623-1743 M-F, 0943-1643 Sa, 727-0382. Amtrack at Shelby east 1117 MWFSa, west 1755 STTS. Bus connection 0800 from Bus terminal at Airport. Taxi 453-3241.

MFD   Zulu-5
179AW ANG (C130)
Distances short.
Ground Transport:
On arrival by air usually
no problem getting ride
to surrounding cities.

ANG
1m
30 1m 5m 176
Mansfield
13
71

Mansfield Airport   D-94
(Lahm)
Mansfield, OH 44901
   Operations Department
696.6124   **419.520**.6124
Flights Schedules out Th.
      Chance of seat ★★★★
Flight Information:
   Call recording at 6488.
   **Schedule is updated 15th day
   of each month.**
   OPS Numbers above.
   0745-1630 MF
   0745-2230 TWT

Telephone Area Codes

There was a time when area codes changes were infrequent. With the increasing presence of modems and cell phones, times have changed. Approximately 70 new area codes have been added since February 1997. To keep abreast of changes effecting this publication, considerable labor is necessitated. Calling individual facilities remains the only accurate way to verify numbers. These changes are detected with telephone calls. If you learn of any current or future changes, please share this information with us.

Free '411' Information by dialing 1.800.373.3411..

RIV Zulu-8 163ARW ANG (KC135)
AFRC
Distances short, 0.7m BQ-Terminal.

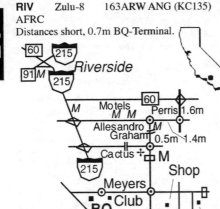

March ARB D-94

Riverside, CA 92518
447-1110 Operator **951-655**-1110
↣↣↣↣↣↣↣↣↣ **Flights** ↣↣↣↣↣↣↣↣↣

Eielson Th A	McChord
Elmendorf Th A	Nellis F §
Hickam Tu	Phoenix F §
Mather	Travis Tu Th A

§ Reservist flight
Frequent flights to many destinations
Chance of seat ★★★★

Flight Information:

Terminal **2397 3214** open for flights [Fax 3887, 722 TRNS/LGTA, 610 Myer Dr] Recording 2913. OPS 4404.
Order box lunches 24h in advance from the Hap Arnold Club at 653-2121.

	Break	Lunch	Dinner	Brun
Club	Tu-Sa	Tu-Sa	FSa	Su
Frank's		1100-1700		
Franks (BX)				

Quarters:

March Inn: Availability ★★★★ x ★ Res weekends **5241/3174/3347/3804/3812** 24h. Fax 3474. **AFRC FY 07/08** $33-40 Protocol 3060 O6 & up and E9.
FamCamp $15/night 20 sites w/full hookup
Aero Club: C 3875 March Aero Club

Fam Camp:

New restrooms & showers, no reservations, limited space.

Ground Transport:

Commercial: #16 Bus at main gate 0523-2104 M-F, 0635-2157 Sa, 0837-2002 Su to Riverside Transit. 800-636-7433. Ontario Airport transfer to #496. LAX #496, transfer to #42 at City Hall LA. Greyhound at Riverside Transit. Taxi 942-7172.

MRB Zulu-5
167AW ANG (C130)

Ground Transport:

On arrival no problem getting ride to some point with transport. Amtrak east 1151, west 1731.
Maryland Rail Commuter Service to Baltimore.

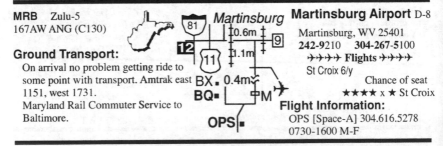

Martinsburg Airport D-8

Martinsburg, WV 25401
242-9210 **304-267-5100**
↣↣↣↣ **Flights** ↣↣↣↣
St Croix 6/y
Chance of seat
★★★★ x ★ St Croix

Flight Information:

OPS [Space-A] 304.616.5278
0730-1600 M-F

Air Force Quarters

Policy: Space-A may reserve three days ahead for quarters not on confirmed reservation status. On day of arrival rooms not held for confirmed reservations are supposed to be assigned to Space-A on request. This is assumed in this Handbook for all AF Inns. In practice it appears at least some billeting offices will at best allow 24 hour reservations while some still hold back empty rooms 'just in case'. Recommend that rooms be held with a credit card. AF-wide reservation number 888-235-6343.

CONUS, AIR FORCE CIRCUIT

MXF   Zulu-6   On base prefix 3
AETC 908AG Res (C130)
Distances walkable x Fam Camp,
0.7m BQ-Terminal.

Maxwell AFB   D-94
Montgomery, AL 36112
493-1110 Oper. **334-953**-1110
⤳⤳⤳⤳⤳⤳ **Flights** ⤳⤳⤳⤳⤳⤳
Atlanta   Hurlburt Fld
Beaufort   Langley
Bragg   New Orleans
Cherry Point   Offutt
Dobbins   Peterson
Eglin   Randolph
Knox   Rucker

Frequent flights to
many destinations.
Chance of seat ★★★★

Flight Information:
Terminal **7372** 0600-1800 M-F.
[Fax 6114, 220 W. Ash St]. Recording 6760, OPS 6961 0400-2300 C130 5924, lockers.

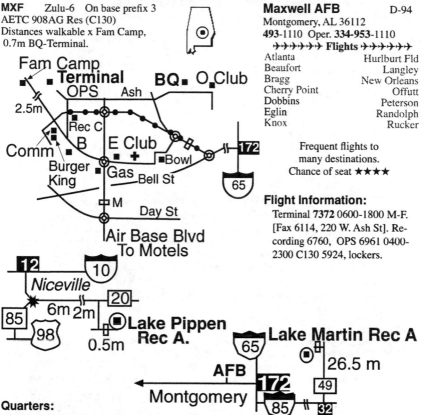

Quarters:
University Inn: Availability ★★★★ x ★ Res
weekends **2430/2055 334.240.5600**, 24h **AETC FY
07/08** Rates: $24-42 Protocol 2095.
Fam Camp ★★★★ 5161 0700-1600, check in
at Fam Camp. RV EDW $15/d, $85/w, $300/m.
20/30/50 Amp, Internet Tent $5.
Lake Martin Rec A, Lake Pippen Rec A (FL),
trailers ★★★★ winter, ★ summer **ITT 3509**
0900-1790 M-F, reserve at Maxwell Outdoor Rec.
Rates: Trailer $35unit summer, $20 winter, no linen,
towels. RV ESW $13. Tent $7. Site: Martin 256-
825-6251, Pippen 850-897-2411.
Commercial: Motels on Air Base Blvd.
Aero Club: 7342 Maxwell Aero Club
Golf: 953.2209 Holes: 36 Cypress Tree Golf Course
Marina: 256.825.6251
Ground Transport:
#7,10 Buses to Dexter Ave, Montgomery xSu 262-
7321. Taxi from Montgomery.

	Break	Lunch	Dinner	Brun
O Club	M-F	M-F	xSu	Su
E Club	xSu	xSa	MWFSu	
Bowl	1600-2200 xSu			
Burger	0630-2000 xSu			
King	0900-1800 Su			

41

AF

TCM   Zulu-8   On Base prefix 2
AMC, 4,7,8,72,97,313AS Res (C141)
Distances long, 2.1m BQ-
Terminal.

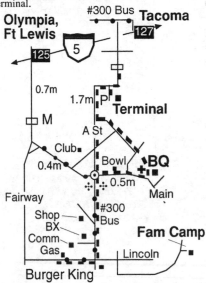

Olympia, Ft Lewis — 125 — 5 — #300 Bus — Tacoma — 127

0.7m — 1.7m P Terminal — M — A St — Club — Bowl — BQ — 0.4m — 0.5m — Main — Fairway — Shop — BX — Comm — Gas — #300 Bus — Fam Camp — Lincoln — Burger King

McChord AFB   D-94
Tacoma, WA 98438
382.1110   Operator   **253-982-**1110
✈✈✈✈✈✈✈✈ **Flights** ✈✈✈✈✈✈✈✈

Eielson F A	Osan
Elmendorf F A	Portland 1st FSu
Eugene	Tinker
Hickam	Travis√
Miramar A	Yokota

Chance of seat ★★★

Frequent flights to many destinations.
§ Reservist flight FSu McChord-Portland-
Eugene-Fairchild-McChord usually first
weekend, sometimes 2/m.

Flight Information:
Terminal 7259/60, 0555 24h, lockers.
[Fax 5659, 62 APS/TRO 1422 Union
Ave]. Recording 7268. OPS 5611. P 60d
limit.

Quarters:
Evergreen Inn: Availability ★★★ x ★ dependents summer 584.1471, **2505/3591/5613** 24h.
M-F 0730-1600 800.847.3899. AMC FY 07/08 Rates: $28-43 Protocol 2788. BQ at Ft Lewis
reachable by #300 Bus. To dial on base from billeting room dial 71+2+XXXX.
Fam Camp: Holiday Park ★★★★ 5488 24h, Reservations: **2206**, check in Fam Camp. RV
$5, ESW $11, Tent $3.
Commercial: Motels north on I5.
Golf: 982.4927 **Holes:** 18 Whispering Firs Golf Course
Ground Transport:
Base Shuttle 0530-0730,1100-1300,1430-1900,1900,
2300-0100 M-F, :00, :30 at terminal.

	Break	Lunch	Dinner	Brun
Club	xSa	M-F	xSu	Su
Bowl		24h		
Burger King		0630-2000 M-F		
		0800-1900 SS		

Commercial: Bus route to SeaTac IAP: Take #300 bus
which becomes #57 at Tacoma Mall, stay on bus (no new fare required) to downtown Tacoma
for transfer to #500 which goes to Federal Highway bus center. Then take #174 to SeaTac
IAP. Bus hours: #300 Bus to Ft Lewis 0509-2407 M-F, 0637-2400 Sa, 0715-2400 Su. 1h later starting time to Tacoma. #204 Bus 0625-1725 M-F, 0924-1725 SS connects with #300 and
#206, info 581-8000. Amtrak in Tacoma east 0826, south 0826, 0850, 1056, 1805. Greyhound
383-4612,800-231-2222. Limo to Sea-Tac Airport, Bangor, NSY 800-562-7948 0520-2320,
360-876-1737 24h. reservations required. Sea-Tac $10. Car rent hotline in Terminal, also BQ,
cheaper at Ft Lewis Æ162. Taxi 581-7190, 528-3000. 582-2800.

What Else Should Be Included?

Added in this and the prior edition are numerous CONUS origins and enroute facilities, Marinas,
Aero Clubs, USOs, and Foreign Holidays. As installations close room becomes available for more
or expanded information. Should there be something you would like to see added, please let us
know. Suggestions will be carefully considered.

AF

IAB   Zulu-6

Tankers. 184TFG ANG (C12)
Distances walkable, 1m BQ-OPS, 0.6m BQ-main gate.

Quarters:

Air Capital Inn: Availability ★★★★ **D & C 6999/6505** 24h. Fax 4190. AMC FY 07/08 Rates: $28-43 O6 up thru **3110**, E9 protocol **6999**.

RV: Report to BQ. Rate: EW $10.
Golf: 759.4036 **Holes:** 18
Ground Transport:

Greyhound 265-7711.

	Break	Lunch	Dinner	Brun
Club		Tu-F	W-Sa	Su
Burger King	0700-2000 M-F			
	1030-1800 SS			
Golf	1000-1400 X SuM 4038			

McConnell AFB   D-94

Wichita, KS 67221
743-1110   Operator   **316-759**-6100

⤳⤳⤳⤳⤳⤳⤳⤳⤳ **Flights** ⤳⤳⤳⤳⤳⤳⤳⤳⤳

Andersen   MacDill (few)
Bangor (few)   Mildenhall
Edwards   Ramstein (few)
Fairchild   Travis 2-4m
Grand Fork (few)
Hickam 1/45days
Lajes   Chance of seat
                        ★★★★ x ★★ Hickam

Flight Information:

Pax **5169**, 4810, OPS **3840** 24h [Fax 1032 22 RRS/LGRRT 53435 Kansas #101] Recording 5404, 3897. Mail sign-up (60d max) to: Passenger Terminal 5307 Hitchinson St., McConnell AFB, KS 67221.

Tanker scheduling 3116. Food machines in OPS

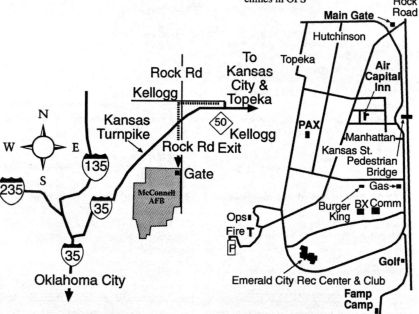

Lodging Reservations Telephone Numbers

AF

WRI   Zulu-5   On base prefix 4
AMC,108ARW ANG (KC135),
514AMW Res (C141B), 305 AMW (KC-10)
Distances walkable x to BX, 0.8m BQ-Terminal.

McGuire AFB   D-94
Wrightstown, NJ 08641
650-0111   Operator   **609-754**-1100
      800-569-8284 + 754-xxxx or 0

➤➤➤➤➤➤➤➤**Flights**➤➤➤➤➤➤➤➤➤

Albany NY	Norfolk 2-3/m
Andrews	Pope
BWI WSS	Ramstein F
Capital City MI	Rota
Charleston	Scott
Cherry Point	Tooele W
Dover M	Travis 0-10/m
Keflavik	Wheeler Sack
Lajes WSa	Willow Grove
McChord	Wright Pat
Mildenhall	

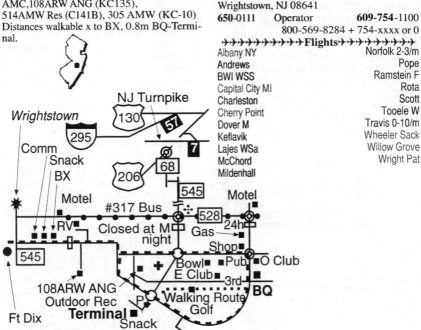

Quarters:

All American Inn: Availability ★★★ x ★
Res weekends **4856/3974/3336/3337/4667**
0700-0130 **AMC FY 07/08** Rates: $28-43
O6 up thru protocol 2405.
Commercial: Motel hotlines in Terminal.
Days Inns outside both gates, 723-6900.
Golf: 754.2169 **Holes:** 18 Falcon Creek
Golf Course

Ground Transport:
✚ **Shuttle**: Dix-McGuire-Monmouth 0715
Th.
Commercial: Buses from Terminal: #317
to Philadelphia 0541,0655, to Asbury
Park 0632,2119. #317 stops outside gates
0935-2100 for Philadelphia, 0923-1923 to
Asbury Park. To NYC or Newark #317 to
Lakewood, transfer to #139 for NYC, #67
for Newark RR or Airport. To Schedules in
Terminal or 800-772-2222. Limo to airports,
Philadelphia $20, 723-2001. Taxi hotline in
Terminal. Car Rental available at Exchange.

Frequent flights to many destinations Chance
of seat ★★★★ CONUS, ★ Europe summer,
Christmas

Flight Information:
Terminal 0500-2400 **2749,2864,5023,3655**
[Fax 4621, 305 APS/TROP 1706 Vandenberg Ave]. Recording **800-569-8284**
then enter 754.9950. OPS 2713, 170ARG
2756,2934, 108ARW 4212 0730-1600 M-F
Terminal closed 050-072400, opens for
flights, food machines.

	Break	Lunch	Dinner
O Club		Tu-F	
E Club		M-F	Th-Sa
BX Snack	Tu-Sa	7d	
Bowl		1600-2200 M-F	
		0800-2200 Sa	
		1200-1800 Su	
Golf		0730-1400	
Sidelines		0800-2400 MTh	
Sports		0800-2200 TuW	
Pub		1100-0200 Sa	
		1100-2200 Su	

CONUS, AIR FORCE CIRCUIT

MEM   Zulu-6
164AW ANG (C141)
Distances short.
Ground Transport:
City bus outside main gate. Amtrack north 2242 xTu, south 0635 xW.

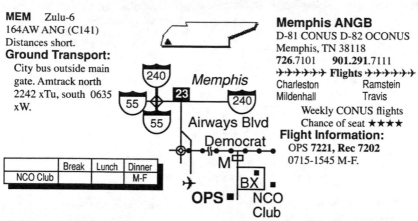

Memphis

Airways Blvd

Democrat

Memphis ANGB
D-81 CONUS D-82 OCONUS
Memphis, TN 38118
726.7101   **901.291.**7111
++++++++ **Flights** ++++++++
Charleston   Ramstein
Mildenhall   Travis

Weekly CONUS flights
Chance of seat ★★★★
Flight Information:
OPS **7221, Rec 7202**
0715-1545 M-F.

	Break	Lunch	Dinner
NCO Club			M-F

OPS ■ **BX** ■ **NCO Club**

MEI   Zulu-6   186ARW
(KC135)
Quarters:
At NAS Meridian, Æ79.

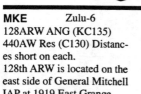

NAS Meridian

Meridian

Key Field, ANG

Entrance from US11

Meridian Airport (Key Field)   D-94
Meridian, MS 39309
778-9714   **601-484-**9714
++++++++ **Flights** ++++++++
Andrews 1-3/m   Europe 3-4/y

Chance of seat ★★★★
Flight Information:
OPS **9730,9413 recording** [Fax 9470]

MKE   Zulu-6
128ARW ANG (KC135)
440AW Res (C130) Distances short on each.
128th ARW is located on the east side of General Mitchell IAP at 1919 East Grange Avenue, Milwaukee, WI 53207-6143.
Ground Transport:
From Airport: #80 Bus to 6th and Wisconsin. Limo to town. Amtrack north 1651, south 0620-1912.

Milwaukee Airport (Mitchell)   D-94
Reserve address:
128 OSA, 1839 East Grange Avenue, Milwaukee, WI 53207-6143
580-8475   **Command Post   741.**5000
414.944.8476   **414.482.**5000
ANG ++++++ **Flights** ++++++**Res**
Europe   CONUS
Hickam

★★★★   Chance of seat   ★★★★
Flight Information:

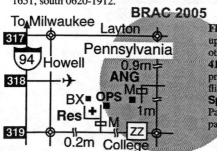

BRAC 2005

To Milwaukee   Layton
Pennsylvania
Howell
ANG   0.9m
BX ■ OPS
Res
0.2m   College

Flight Service 241, Sign up only 0830-0930, Tu, other hrs use recording at **414.944.**8732. Several days prior to flight call back for flight briefing information.
Space-A Parking:
Park at north end of south parking lot.

OPS 5918 0070-1500 M-F
Recording 5167

AF

MSP
Zulu-6

AFRC
133AW ANG (C130),
934AW Res (C130)

28th

Quarters:
North Country Lodge:
Availability ★★★ x
★ training weekends
1007/1983/4, 726-9440
0700-2200 Su-Th, 0700-
2400 F&Sa. Assigned
1800. AFRC FY 07/08
Rates: $33-40. After Hours
Arrivals: Utilize key boxes located off the lobby. Key
boxes are programmed with the last four of **SSN**. Security
713.1911

Ground Transport:
#7 Bus at Airport.
Amtrak south 0750, north 2355 MWFSa.

Minneapolis Airport
D-94

Minneapolis, MN 55450
783-1110 Switchboard **612-713**-1000

ANG→→ Flights →→Res

ANG	Res
Andrews	Muñiz
Atlanta	McChord
Cherry Point	McClellan
Chicago O'Hare	Norfolk
Kelly	North Island
Madison	Travis
Robins	Whidbey Island
	Willow Grove

Chance of seat ★★★★

Flight Information:

ANG 2461	1719, 2450
0600-1700 M-F	Recording 1741

	Break	Lunch	Dinner
O Club		Tu-Sa	Tu-Sa
NCO Club	M-F	7d	Tu-Sa

MIB
Zulu-6

ACC
Distances walkable.
0.9m BQ-OPS.

Minot AFB
D-94

Minot, ND 58705
453-1110   Operator   **701-723**-1110

→→→→→→→→→ **Flights** →→→→→→→→→

Few flights
Chance of seat ★★★★

Flight Information:
OPS **1854** 0545-2200 M-F, 0900-1700 SS.
[Fax 3637] Tanker scheduling 3495 Accepts
remote sign up.

Quarters:
Sakakiawea Inn: Availability ★★ **2184/6161/**
24h. **ACC** FY 07/08 Rates: $30-43 Protocol 3474.
Commercial: Motels in Minot.
RV FamCamp 3648
Golf: 723.3164 **Holes:** 9 Roughrider
Ground Transport:
Vehicle OPS 3121. Bus to Minot 1130, 1405 **Th**,
852-8008. Amtrak west 0935 STTS, east 2138
MWFSa, bus 852-2477 0800-1730 xSu, 1430-
1630 Su in Minot. Taxi 852-1391.

	Break	Lunch	Dinner	Brun
O Club		M-F	Tu-F	Su
NCO Club		xSu	ThFSa	
OPS Snack	24h Machines			
Burger King	0700-2200 M-F			
	0900-2000 SS			
Bowl	0630-2100 M-F			
	0800-2200 SS			

VAD
Zulu-5 On
base prefix 7+XXXX
ACC Distances
walkable, 0.6m
BQ-OPS.

Valdosta

Moody AFB
D-94

Valdosta, GA 31699
460-1110   **229.257**.1110

→→→→ **Flights** →→→→

Rare flights
Chance of seat ★★★★

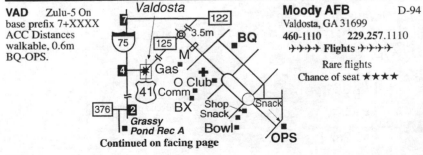

Continued on facing page

Quarters:
BQ:

Moody Inn: Availability ★★★ **3893/94** 24h, list starts 0730, assigned 1400. Rates: **$23-35** Protocol 4144.

Grassy Pond Rec A, cabins ★★★★ x ★ FSS summer **C 559-5840,** D thru Operator, 0700-1800 M-F, at site. Check in at Rec A. Reservations for cabins. Rates: Cabins (no linens) $25unit. RV EW $10. Tent $5. Outdoor Rec **2989.** Discount for Golden Age, Access, Eagle. **No pets in cabins.**

Golf: 257.3297 **Holes:** 9 Quiet Pines Golf Course

Ground Transportation:
Enterprise Car Rental 229-257-2989

Flight Information:
OPS **3305** Pax **4278** 0730-1630 M-F 0730-1630 SS [Fax 4664]

	Break	Lunch	Dinner
O Club		M-F	W-Sa
NCO Club			
Bowl	M-F	7d	7d
Snack		0700-1900 xSu	
OPS Snack		0630-1400 M-F	
E Dining	0630-0900	1100-1330	1630-1900

MUO	Zulu-7

ACC

Distances walkable, 0.8m BQ-OPS.

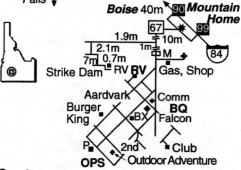

Mountain Home AFB
D-8

Mountain Home, ID 83648

728-1110   Operator   **208-828**-2111

⇢⇢⇢⇢⇢⇢⇢⇢ **Flights** ⇢⇢⇢⇢⇢⇢⇢⇢

Few flights

Chance of seat ★★★

Flight Information:
OPS **2222** 0630-2330 M-F, Fax: 4128 0800-1600 SS. [366 SS/OSAA] Tanker scheduling 2172

For Parking contact Security 2256

	Break	Lunch	Dinner
Club		M-F	ThF
Burger King	0630-2000 M-F		
	0900-1900 Sa		
	1100-1800 Su		

Quarters:
Sagebrush Inn: Availability ★★★ x ★ April-Nov

6451/5200 24h. **ACC FY 07/08** $30-43 E9 & O6 up Protocol 4536.

Fam Camp: ★★★ Check in, pay at camp. RV $6, ESW $10. Tent $5.

Strike Dam: ★★★★, information from Outdoor adventure **6333** 0900-1700 Tu-F, open camping mid May to early Sept, RV and Tent, free, no dump, showers. Same office handles trailers on right, $35unit, min 2 nights.

Commercial: Motels in Mt Home.

Golf: 208.828.6559 **Holes:** 18

Ground Transport:
Occasional transport to Boise 2339 24h.

Commercial: Greyhound in Mt Home. Car rent 587-3326,4321. Taxi to town $10.

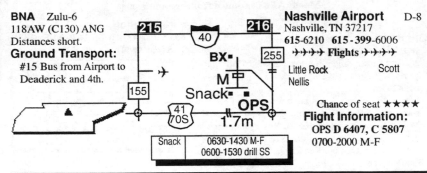

BNA Zulu-6
118AW (C130) ANG
Distances short.
Ground Transport:
#15 Bus from Airport to
Deaderick and 4th.

Nashville Airport D-8
Nashville, TN 37217
615-6210 **615 - 399**-6006
✈✈✈✈ **Flights** ✈✈✈✈

Little Rock   Scott
Nellis

Chance of seat ★★★★
Flight Information:
OPS **D 6407, C 5807**
0700-2000 M-F

Snack	0630-1430 M-F
	0600-1530 drill SS

LSV Zulu-8 On base prefix 2
ACC Distances walkable, 0.6m BQ-OPS.

Quarters:
Nellis Inn: Availability ★★★ **2711/9176**
24h. Fax 9172 **ACC FY 07/08** $30-43 **E9**
thru Command Chief O6 up thru protocol
2469.
Desert Eagle RV Park 4907 Fam Camp Dr.
★★★★ x ★★ winter 6017, C 643-
3060, reservations, check in at Fam
Camp. RV Full $17, ESW $13, Tent
$6. Discount Golden Age, Access.
Commercial: Motels with military
discounts on Craig.
Golf: 2602 **Holes**: 36 SUNRISE VISTA
GOLF COURSE
Ground Transport:
Base shuttle 8305. Occasional
transport to Indian Springs, 8305.
Commercial: #113/5 Bus outside
main gate 0555-2130. In Las
Vegas: Greyhound, Amtrak east
1750 SuTT, west 0820 MWSa.
Car rent, BX 644-5567 0900-
1800 xSu, 1000-1800 Su.

Nellis AFB D-94
Las Vegas, NV 89191
682-1110 Operator **702-652**-1110
✈✈✈✈✈✈ **Flights** ✈✈✈✈✈✈

Hill Su A   Mt Home Su A
March FSu 2nd & 4th   Phoenix F 2nd & 4th
weekends §   weekends §
McChord Su A   Travis Su A

§ Reservist flight
Chance of seat HHHH

OPS 4600, Pax 6099 Operation Red
Flag, about 4/year.

	Break	Lunch	Dinner
O Club		M-F	Tu-F
E Club	M-F	M-F	Tu-Sa
Burger	0600-2200 M-F		
King	0700-2100 SS		

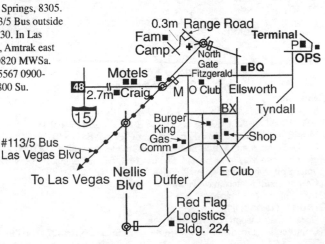

AF

IAG Zulu-5 914AW Res
AFRC (C130), 107ARW
(KC135)
Distances walkable, 1.2m BQ-
ANG OPS.

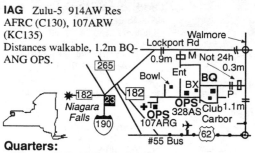

Niagara Falls ARB   D-94
Niagara Falls, NY 14304
238-3011   **716-236**-2000
914th ➤➤➤ **Flights** ➤➤➤ **107th**

Albany NY	McChord
Bragg	Travis
Johnstown PA	
Pope	
Stewart	
Westover	

Chance of seat ★★★★

Flight Information:
OPS **2174/5**
0730-1700
M-F

ANG
OPS **2534**
0900-1400 M-Th,
Recording 2475

	Break	Lunch	Dinner
Club		Tu-F	WFSa
Bowl	0800-1700 M-Th		
	0800-1300 F		

Quarters:
Niagara Falls ARB: Availability ★★★ x ★ 1 Apr - 15
Nov & Res weekends **2014/15** 0700-2300, reservations
accepted, confirmed 2d prior to arrival. AFRC FY 07/08
Rates: $33-40

Ground Transport:
#55 Bus at Carbor to Niagara Falls, 0630-1710 M-F,
285-9319. Amtrak north 1600, south 1300.

OFF Zulu-6
ACC 38th ReCon
Distances
walkable x ✚,
Fam Camp.
0.3m BQ-
Terminal.

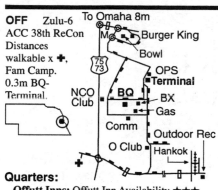

Offutt AFB ACC   D-94
Bellevue, NE 68113
271-1110   Operator   **402-294**-1110
➤➤➤➤➤➤➤➤➤➤ **Flights** ➤➤➤➤➤➤➤➤➤➤

Andrews	McCoy
Ankeny IA	Norfolk
Buckley	Peterson
Cheyenne WY	Rapid City SD
Forbes	Scott
Kansas City MO	Sill
Kelly	Tyndall
Langley	Travis
Louisville KY	Wright-Pat
Maxwell	

Frequent flights to many CONUS
destinations, mostly C21
Chance of seat ★★★

Flight Information:
Terminal **7111, Rec 6235** 0730-1630 M-F,
recording other hrs. [Fax 232-4070] OPS
3207, 3240 24h. 38th Recon Sqd 0694 OPS
3541

	Break	Lunch	Dinner	Brun
O Club	xSu	M-F	7d	Su
NCO Club		M-F	7d	SS
Bowl	1100-2200 M-Th			
	1100-2400 FSa			
	1500-2000 Su			
Burger King	0630-2100 M-F			
	0800-2100 Sa			
	1100-1800 Su			

Quarters:
Offutt Inns: Offutt Inn Availability ★★★
weekends, ★ weekdays & 1st weekend
3671 C 291.9000, 24h. **888.235.6343** ACC
FY 07/08 Rates: $30-43 O6 up thru protocol
4461.

Fam Camp, ★★★ **2108** 0800-2200 xSu,
1200-1800 Su, check in Outdoor Rec, other
hrs with host. RV E (Nov-April) $7, ESW
(May-Oct) $12-15. Tent $2. No dump.
Golf: 294.3530 **Holes:** 18
Aero Club: 3385 in Hanger 4
Ground Transport:
Shuttle: 0600-1830 M-F, 30min service.
Commercial: #60 Bus M-F, from BQ
0745,1708, from 17th & Dodge 0710,1620,
314-0800. Greyhound 341-1900, Amtrak
east 0644 SuMWF, west 0037 MWThSa in
Omaha. Limo to Omaha Airport. BX car
rent 292-9676 0900-1800 xSu, 1000-1700
Su.

AF

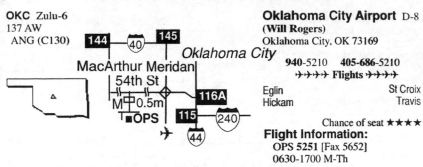

OKC Zulu-6
137 AW
ANG (C130)

MacArthur Meridan
54th St
M ☐ 0.5m
T ▪ OPS

Oklahoma City

144 — 40 — 145

116A

115 — 240

44

Oklahoma City Airport D-8
(Will Rogers)
Oklahoma City, OK 73169

940-5210   **405-686**-5210
✈✈✈✈✈ **Flights** ✈✈✈✈✈

Eglin   St Croix
Hickam   Travis

Chance of seat ★★★★
Flight Information:
OPS 5251 [Fax 5652]
0630-1700 M-Th

Oklahoma City A/P & Tinker AFB

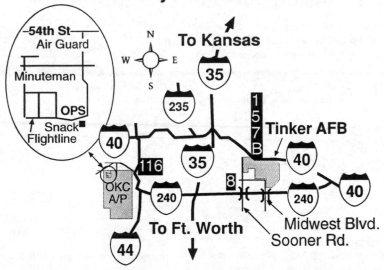

Using Amtrak May Save Both Money and Time

There are times utilizing rail is cheaper, faster, and more convenient than commercial air or rental car as illustrated by an actual case observed at Andrews by a contributor. Another traveler was making call after call to airlines. The contributor asked where that traveler wanted to go - someplace south of New York City. The contributor suggested calling Amtrak [1.800.USA.RAIL (1.800.872.7245)]. It turned out the first train would get there before the first plane, at about half the cost, and much closer to where the traveler wanted to go than any airport.

There are many other places where Amtrak (or other rail transport) is appropriate, for example to many destinations around Travis or up the Coast from San Diego. Keep in mind that Amtrac delivers you to the city, not to some outlying airport. Also the train is more comfortable and has some spectacular routes such as up the Hudson from New York City. Amtrak schedules and station locations are found on the Internet at **http://www.amtrak. com.**

When the 13th Edition was being prepared Amtrak was considering major reductions in routes.

COF Zulu 5 On base prefix 4+XXXX for listed extensions
AFSPC Missile support Distances walkable x to BX 1m BQ-Terminal.

Quarters:

Space Coast Inn: Availability ★★ x ★ during space shots **2075/5428/9/6590** 24h. AFSPC FY 07/08 Rates: **$25-44** O6 up thru protocol 4511, E9 4517. Reservations 24 h advance.

Fam Camp 1 Apr-1 Oct ★★★★, 1 Oct-1 Apr H **4787** 0900-1700 xSu (Fam Camp winter, Boat House summer). Boat House also 2042. Check in Fam Camp office when open, other hrs host. RV $7, EW $11. Tent $6. Ten person beach houses $150-175, $1,000 & 1,200 per week. All RVs must enter and exit south gate.

Commercial: Motels on A1A, ? north, 8m south.

Golf: 494.7856 **Holes:** 18
Ground Transport:

Base Shuttle M-F 0700-1600 every half hour x 0900,1000.

Commercial: C. Shuttle to Cocoa Beach, etc.m Sun Coast Shuttle to Orlando Airport 0645-1835, 676-4557. Greyhound in Melbourne, 723-4323. Car rent at BQ, 0930-1700 M-F, 0930-1330 SS. Taxi 784-2421.

	Break	Lunch	Dinner	Brun
O Club	M-F	xSu	7d	SS
NCO Club	7d	7d	7d	
Snack	0700-1430 M-F			
Bowl	1100-2200 M-F			
	1000-2200 Sa			
	1200-2200 Su			

Patrick AFB   D-94
Cocoa Beach, FL 32925
854-1110   Operator **321.494**.1110
✈✈✈✈✈✈✈✈✈✈ **Flights** ✈✈✈✈✈✈✈✈✈✈

Andrews Wkend
Antigua M *
Ascension M §*
Charleston 1st Wkend

Chance of seat ★★★
Flight Information:
Terminal **5631/2, 4623** 0730-1630 M-F closed SS & Holidays [Fax 7991]
OPS **2222** 0600-2300
§ Prior permission must be obtained from commander for visiting or transiting, write RANS/CCR, Patrick
* Check availability @ 1500 F, normal Space-A call 1100 M.

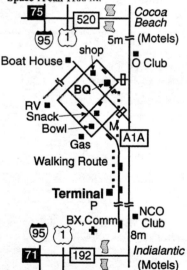

Getting Around by Navy

Destinations listed in the details of the Navy Circuit are the most-likely from each NAS but Navy is noted for unexpected flights to almost any other Navy installation in CONUS. As a general rule it is easier to move around CONUS by Navy than by AF. Going to any NAS with frequent flights (even if the destination you desire is not on their board) is a good way of playing the Space-A game. Obviously this does not apply to NAS listed as having rare or few flights such as NAS Whiting Field.

When at Navy and there is no flight to your destination, try calling that destination to determine their inbound flights. It may be possible to reach a point on such flights.

For the past several years C40, C9 & smaller aircraft mission assignments have been made at DOD level. It is common for Navy aircraft to transport personnel of another service and vice versa.

AF

PSM Zulu-5
157ARW (KC135) ANG
Distances short.
Sign in 1300-1600 W only, flight closed 1600 W before flight. No more Pax added or bumping after closing.

Ground Transport:
#4 Bus to downtown Portsmouth from Newington Mall. C&J limo hrly to Boston, Durham, Portsmouth.

Small BX
Motel 1.7m
Newington Mall
Limo
OPS
Newington
Newington
M
4 #4 Bus
2m
95
5 Motels
Portsmouth

Pease ANGB Newington, NH 03803
852-3323   **603-430**-3323
⤳⤳⤳⤳⤳ **Flights** ⤳⤳⤳⤳⤳
CONUS   Washington
Europe

Chance of seat ★★★★

Flight Information:
Nos. above 0800-1000
WTh, other hrs recording

DIA Zulu-6
186 AW (C130) ANG
Distances short.

Flight Information:
Logistics **5191** 0630-1600
Tu-F

474
ANG
✈
Airport Road
1.5m

Peoria Airport   D-94
2416 S. Falcon Blvd.
Peoria, IL 61607
724-4210   **309-633-5**210
⤳⤳⤳⤳⤳⤳**Flights**⤳⤳⤳⤳⤳⤳

Chance of seat ★★★★

COS   Zulu-7   On base prefix 6+XXXX
AFSPC
302AW Res (C130)
Distances walkable, 0.6m
BQ-OPS.

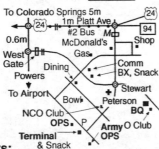

To Colorado Springs 5m
1m Platt Ave 24
24 #2 Bus M 94
0.6m McDonald's Shop
West Gas
Gate Dining Comm BX, Snack
Powers
To Airport Stewart
Bowl Peterson
NCO Club BQ
OPS P O Club
Terminal Army
& Snack OPS

Quarters:
Pikes Peak Lodging: Availability ★★★★
7851 24h. AFSPC FY 07/08 Rates: $25-44. Protocol 4225. Ft Carson BQ reached by #2 Bus.
Commercial: Motel hotlines in BQ. Motels outside main gate.
Golf: 556.4558 **Holes:** 18
Aero Club: 4310
Ground Transport:
Vehicle dispatch will transport on base if car available, 4307.
Commercial: #2 Bus to Colorado Springs, Ft Carson. 0650-1824 xSu. Greyhound 636-1505. Limo to Airport 578-5232. Car rent Budget 574-7401, Payless 576-1733, Enterprise on base (watch forcing insurance) 574-2800.

Peterson AFB   D-94
Colorado Springs, CO 80914
834-7011   Operator   **719-556**-7321
AF ⤳⤳⤳⤳⤳ **Flights** ⤳⤳⤳⤳⤳ **Army**

AF		Army
Andrews√	Long Beach	Hood
Bismark ND	March	Irwin
Bliss	Maxwell	Leavenworth
Buckley	Miramar	Riley
Cheyenne WY	Nellis	Ft Carson
Davis-Monthan	New Orleans	flights
Eglin	Norfolk	
Ellsworth W A	North Island	[Fax: 3556]
Fresno CA	Offutt	7542
Helena MT	Phoenix	0730-1700
Hill	Randolph	M-F
Holloman	Salt Lake City	Bldg 119
Hood	San Antonio	
Kelly	Scott	
Langley	Soto Cano	
Las Vegas	Travis	
LAX	Tucson	
Leavenworth	Warren MW A	
Lewis	Wright-Pat	

Frequent flights to many destinations
Chance of seat ★★★★

Flight Information:
Terminal **4521** 0600-2200 M-F [Fax 4979. 21 LSSI/CGITS, 621 W Stewart] Recording 4707. OPS 4778. In-flight meals available from Dining 4180, order 1.5h before, pick up. Can use crew lounge.

Continued on facing page

Peterson AFB Continued from facing page.

Ground Transport:
Vehicle dispatch will transport on base if car available, 4307.
Commercial: #2 Bus to Colorado Springs, Ft Carson. 0650-1824 xSu. Greyhound 636-1505. Limo to Airport 578-5232. Car rent Budget 574-7401, Payless 576-1733, Enterprise on base (watch forcing insurance) 574-2800.

	Break	Lunch	Dinner	Brun
O Club	M-F	M-F	xSu	Su
NCO Club	M-F	M-F	Tu-Sa	
Bowl	M-F	7d	7d	
Snack	0700-1600 xSu			
Terminal	0700-1430 M-F			
Snack	Machines other hrs			

PHX Zulu-7 (No daylight saving)
161ARW ANG (KC135)
Distances short x ANG-Commercial Terminals.

National Guard
853-2798 **602-267**-2798, 5636 E. McDowell, Phoenix AZ 85008. Controls C12 out of Sky Harbor, 5636 E McDowell. Flight information 0630-1630 Tu-F.
Reservist Flights
Crews manifest AF, P3 GTA Swift Aviation C 602.273.3770/7704 C9. Navy 800-828-9202, at North Island x2609.
Quarters:
Several motels nearby. Nearest base with billets Luke *Æ37*.
Ground Transport:
ANG #24 Bus on 24th St, 1.2m from OPS. Executive Terminal #13 Bus, NG #17 Bus, all xSu, 253-5000.

Phoenix Airport (Sky Harbor) D-4
Phoenix, AZ 85034
853-9210 ANG Operator **602-302**-9000
ANG ⇻⇻⇻⇻ Flights ⇻⇻⇻⇻ Reservist

Andrews	Navy C9
Los Alamitos	Davis-Monthan
Peterson	North Island
Out of CONUS 1/m	Navy P3
Chance of seat ★★★	Point Mugu
one way,	Nellis
★ round trip.	

Flight Information:
OPS **9162** 0600-1600
M-F. Recording 9058.
To sign up must call 10d prior.

Chance of seat ★★★★
Reservist flights, FSu 2/m

PIT Zulu-5
AFRC 171ARW ANG (KC135)
911AG Res (C130)
Distances short, 0.2m
BQ-OPS. Access to ANG only for sign up or flight.
Quarters:
Hospitality Inn: Availability ★★★★ x ★ Res, ANG weekends **AFRC FY 07/08 $33-44 8229/8805** 0700-2300, for arrival other hrs call, keys left at Club, 8227/8, then main gate.
Rates: $6per, DV $8per.
Ground Transport:
Amtrak west 2310, 2337, east 0625, 0825, 1300.

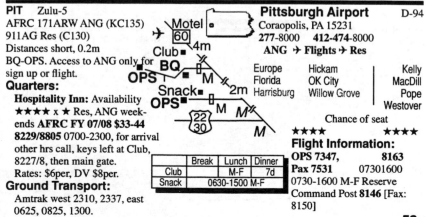

	Break	Lunch	Dinner
Club		M-F	7d
Snack	0630-1500 M-F		

Pittsburgh Airport D-94
Coraopolis, PA 15231
277-8000 **412-474**-8000
ANG ⇻ Flights ⇻ Res

Europe	Hickam	Kelly
Florida	OK City	MacDill
Harrisburg	Willow Grove	Pope
		Westover

Chance of seat
★★★★   ★★★★
Flight Information:
OPS **7347**,   **8163**
Pax 7531 07301600
0730-1600 M-F Reserve
Command Post **8146** [Fax: 8150]

POB Zulu-5
AMC Airlift for Ft Bragg
Distances walkable x 2m
BQ-Terminal.

Quarters:
Carlina Inn: Availability ★★★ x
★ Res weekends **4131**
24h. AMC FY 07/08
Rates: $28-43, O6 up thru protocol **4739**. Nearest Ft Bragg Guest House 2m from **BQ**.
Commercial: Motels in Spring Lake.
Golf: 394.1382 Holes: **18**

Labels in map: Terminal & OPS, Snack, Manchester, Bowl 24, BX, Gas, Comm, Spring Lake, Shop, O Club, BQ, M, To Ft Bragg Fayetteville

Ground Transport:
Base Shuttle 0630-1830, 2674.
Commercial: Car rental available on Fort Bragg. Greyhound 497-8746 on Ft Bragg Æ**145**. In Fayetteville Amtrak north 1226, 2348, south 0805, 2117. Taxi 43-5151.

Pope AFB D-8
Fayetteville, NC 28308
424-1110 Operator **910-394-0001**
↣↣↣↣↣↣↣↣ **Flights** ↣↣↣↣↣↣↣↣

Andrews	Norfolk
Belvoir	Raleigh-Durham
Charlotte√	Robins SuF §
Cherry Pt	Scott
Dobbins Su §	Shaw §
McGuire	Willow Grove
New River	

§ Reservist flight
Chance of seat ★★★★

Flight Information:
Terminal **5982,6527** 0715-1615 M-F. [Fax 6526] Recording 6525, OPS 4429, 6508/9
24h Terminal open 0700-2100

	Break	Lunch	Dinner
O Club		M-F	Tu-Sa
Snack	0530-1900 M-F		
Bowl	24h		

Quarters:
Howard Johnson motel nearby.
Ground Transport:
Amtrak.

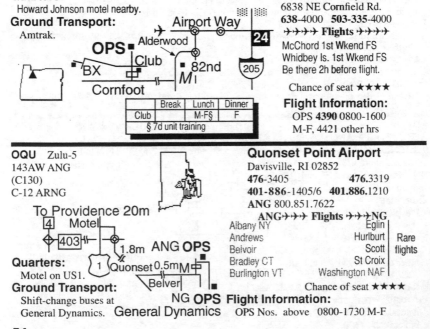

Labels in map: Airport Way, Alderwood, OPS, Club, BX, 82nd, Cornfoot, 24, 205, M

	Break	Lunch	Dinner
Club		M-F§	F

§ 7d unit training

Portland Airport
6838 NE Cornfield Rd.
638-4000 **503-335-4000**
↣↣↣↣ **Flights** ↣↣↣↣
McChord 1st Wkend FS
Whidbey Is. 1st Wkend FS
Be there 2h before flight.

Chance of seat ★★★★

Flight Information:
OPS **4390** 0800-1600
M-F, 4421 other hrs

OQU Zulu-5
143AW ANG
(C130)
C-12 ARNG

To Providence 20m
4 Motel
403 1.8m ANG OPS
1 Quonset 0.5m M
Belver
NG OPS General Dynamics

Quarters:
Motel on US1.
Ground Transport:
Shift-change buses at General Dynamics.

Quonset Point Airport
Davisville, RI 02852
476-3405 **476.3319**
401-886-1405/6 **401.886.1210**
ANG 800.851.7622
ANG↣↣↣ **Flights** ↣↣↣NG

Albany NY	Eglin	
Andrews	Hurlburt	Rare
Belvoir	Scott	flights
Bradley CT	St Croix	
Burlington VT	Washington NAF	

Chance of seat ★★★★

Flight Information:
OPS Nos. above 0800-1730 M-F

CONUS, AIR FORCE CIRCUIT

RND   Zulu-6 Distances walkab 0.5m BQ-Terminal.

To San Antonio

Ft Sam Rec A

Randolph AFB Rec A Jacob
0.5m Creek
Canyon 2.5m
Lake 306 14m

Quarters: 35
Randolph Inn: Availability ★★★ M-Th, ★ FSa **1844** 24h.
AETC FY 07/08 Rates: **$24-42.** Protocol 2061.
Canyon Lake Rec A: ★★★★ x ★ FSa summer, reservations for shelters **3702** 0900-1800 MF, 1100-1800 TWT, 0800-1200 Sa. Site 964-3804, shelter E $15, RV ESWD 50 Amp, $4 winter, $7 summer, tent $4 winter, $5 summer.
Commercial: Motels outside main gate.
Golf: 652.4570 Holes: 18
Ground Transport:
On base military taxi 652.8292. #17 Bus to Main & Travis 0658,0728,1645.1712, transfer to #62 to Kelly, #76 to Lackland. Return 0607,0637,1559,1615. info 277-2020. Amtrak north 0700 STT, east 0400 SuTT, west 0535. **See map & transportation information on Æ153**

Randolph AFB   D-94
Universal City, TX 78150
487-1110   Operator   **210-652**-1110
↣↣↣↣↣↣↣↣ **Flights** ↣↣↣↣↣↣↣↣
Andrews√	Keesler	Offutt
Fort Worth	Langley	Peterson
Eglin	Maxwell	Scott
Ft Hood	New Orleans	Wright-Pat

Frequent flights, mostly C21
Chance of seat ★★★
Flight Information:
Terminal **3725** 0730-1615 M-F [Fax **5718**, 555 E St]. Recording 1854. OPS **1861** 0600-2200 M-F, 0800-2000 SS

	Break	Lunch	Dinner	Brun
O Club	M-F	M-F	xSu	Su
E Club		M-F	FSa	
Cafeteria	0600-1330 M-F			
Deli	1100-2000 M-Th			
	1100-2200 F			
	1700-2200 Sa			

RNO Zulu-8
192AW ANG
Distances short.

Flight Information:
OPS **4709** 0730-1700 M-F, recording other hrs.

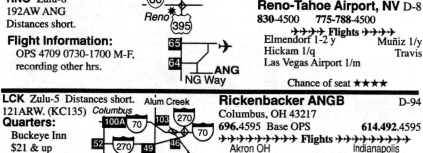

Reno-Tahoe Airport, NV D-8
830-4500   **775-788**-4500
↣↣↣↣ **Flights** ↣↣↣↣
Elmendorf 1-2 y	Muñiz 1/y
Hickam 1/q	Travis
Las Vegas Airport 1/m	

Chance of seat ★★★★

LCK Zulu-5 Distances short.
121ARW. (KC135)
Quarters:
Buckeye Inn $21 & up
614.409.2660
0700-1800 M-Th, 0800-2100 F, 1000-1800Sa, and 0800-1600 Su. Emergency quarters, contact security. Motel on route 317.
Ground Transport:
Taxi only public transport. Greyhound, car rent in Columbus.

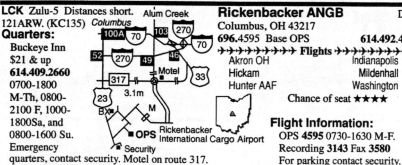

Rickenbacker ANGB   D-94
Columbus, OH 43217
696.4595 Base OPS   **614.492**.4595
↣↣↣↣↣↣↣↣↣ **Flights** ↣↣↣↣↣↣↣↣↣↣
Akron OH	Indianapolis
Hickam	Mildenhall
Hunter AAF	Washington

Chance of seat ★★★★
Flight Information:
OPS **4595** 0730-1630 M-F.
Recording **3143** Fax **3580**
For parking contact security.

WRB Zulu-5 On base prefix 6
AFMC 19ARW (KC135) Distances long,
1.5m BQ-Terminal.

Quarters:

Pine Oaks Lodge: Availability ★★ x ★ Res
weekends **2100/6503** 24h, AFMC FY 07/08
Rates: **$34=59** O6 up thru protocol 2761.
Fam Camp ★★★ **4500** 1330-1730 W-Sa.
Check in at camp. Drop box for payments if
office is closed. RV EW $6. Tent $4, dump on
main base.
Commercial: Motels in Warner Robins.
Golf: 926.4103 **Holes:** 18
Aero Club: 4867

Ground Transport:

Shuttle: Base 0700-1730 M-F. To motels 0630,0730,1630, 3493.
Commercial: Shuttle runs hourly to Atlanta IAP from main gate 0500-1800. City bus to
Macon M-F from town. Greyhound in Warner Robins. Taxi 923-6414.

Robins AFB D-88

Warner Robins, GA 31098
468-1001 Operator **478.92 6**.1110
⤙⤙⤙⤙⤙⤙⤙⤙ **Flights** ⤙⤙⤙⤙⤙⤙⤙⤙

Andrews	Maxwell
Belvoir	Mildenhall
Charleston FSu§	Pope F §
Cherry Point	Rucker
Dobbins F §	Scott§
Eglin	Willow Grove
Knox	Wright Pat

§ Reservist flight
Chance of seat ★★★★

Flight Information:

Terminal **3166** 0730-1600 M-F. [Fax
4355]. OPS 2114, Air Field OPS 2328.
Tanker scheduling 6221

	Break	Lunch	Dinner	Brun
O Club	M-F	M-F	7d	Su
NCO Club	M-F	M-F	7d	Su
Snack	xSu	xSu	M-F	
Restaurant	M-F	M-F	M-F	
Rec C		1030-2400		

SLC Zulu-7
151ARW ANG (KC135)
Distances short.

6th St
N 2200 W

Amtrak east 0430, west 0100.

Salt Lake City Airport

Salt Lake City, UT 84116
924-9**210** **801-245-2200**
⤙⤙⤙⤙⤙⤙ **Flights** ⤙⤙⤙⤙⤙⤙

AF Academy	Pease
Charleston	Stewart
Eielson	Tyndall
Hickam	Travis
Osan	Wright-Pat

Chance of seat ★★★★

Flight Information:

OPS **272/3/4** [Fax 559] 0700-1645
M-Th. Recording 415.

Installations Closing

Installations as they move toward closing often
phase down slowly so facilities shown in this
Handbook may be reduced or even eliminated
before next edition.

The other side of the coin is an installation
definitely closing, slated to close, even closed
may be assigned another mission or reopened
for the same task.

SA

AF

SAV Zulu-5
165AW ANG C130

To Savannah 7m

Quarters:
BQ: Barracks (no dependents)
912.963.3310 0730-1600 M-F. Difficult to reach.

Ground Transport:
In Savannah, Greyhound, Amtrak north 0715, 1255,1848, 2240, south 0514, 0951, 2303.

Savannah Airport D-90
(Travis Field)
Savannah GA 31402
Emergency Control Center
No Operator
860-8223 **912- 964**-1941
C thru operator
➤➤➤➤ **Flights** ➤➤➤➤

Andrews	Otis
Atlanta	Scott
Columbia	Spartanburg

Chance of seat ★★★★
Flight Information:
OPS **8230/5, 8433** 0730-1600 M-F.
Usually out F.

SCH Zulu-5
109AG Res (C130)
Distances short.
Quarters:
Ramada 2.6m from OPS.

Ground Transport:
Amtrak, Greyhound 3.2m from OPS.

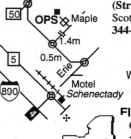

Schenectady County Airport D-94
(Stratton ANGB)
Scotia, NY 12302
344-9300 **518-344-** 2300
➤➤➤➤ **Flights** ➤➤➤➤

Winter Christchurch (no Space-A), April-June virtually none, several flights other months
Chance of seat ★★★★
Flight Information:
OPS **3326** 0800-1530 M-F. Not an airline airport.

BLV Zulu-6 Prefix 6 on base
AMC, Airevac HQ, 37AW (C130), 932AAG Res, 126 ARW ANG (KC135)
Distances short, 0.5m BQ-Terminal.

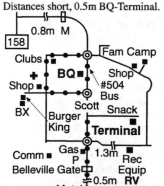

Scott AFB D-94
Belleville, IL 62225
576-1110 Operator **618- 256**-1110
800-851-7542
➤➤➤➤➤➤ **Flights** ➤➤➤➤➤➤

Andrews daily	McChord 1/w
Campbell	McGuire 2-3/m
Charleston	Minot
Cherry Pt 3-4/m	Norfolk 1/w
Davis-Monthan 1/w	Offutt 1/w
Fairchild 6/m	Peterson 2-3/w
Grand Forks 3-4/m	Pope 1-2/w
Kansas City	Tinker bi-weekly
Keesler 1/w	Travis 2-3/w
Kelly 1-2/w	Wood 1/w
Key West 2-3/y	Wright-Pat 2/w
Luke 3/y	
MacDill 1-2/m	Chance of seat

★★★★ x ★ Andrews, Travis

Continued on following page.

CONUS, AIR FORCE CIRCUIT
Scott AFB (Concluded)

AF

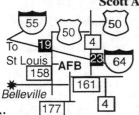

Quarters:

Flight Information:
Terminal **256.3017, 256.4042, 800-851-7542** 0500-1700. Recording 256.1854. [Fax 256.1946, Terminal, Bldg P8, Heritage Rd]. 256.1861, 256.3375. Small planes schedules **618.229.1701.** Terminal open 0500-1700. Lockers. Parking permits at terminal.

	Break	Lunch	Dinner	Brun
O Club		M-F	W-Sa	Su
E Club	xSu	xSu	M,Th-Sa	Su
Terminal	0530-1330 M-F			
Burger	0600- M-F, 0700- Sa			
King	0800- Su, all -2100			

Scott Inn: Availability ★★★★ x ★ Res weekends **256.1844/2045** 24h. AMC FY 07/08 Rates: **$28-43** Lobby closes 2200-0600 x for business. O6 up thru protocol: **AMC protocol D 779.2555, C 229.2555, Wing protocol D 576.3749, C 256.3749**

RV ★★★★ x ★★ summer **256.2067** 0730-1700 M-F, 0800-1500 Sa, 1200-1600 Su, other hrs pick site, reservations, check in Rec Equipment, RV EW $15. Tent $8. Dump 2m from site. Outdoor Rec **256.2304**

Commercial: Mid-American 0.5m outside Belleville gate, ≈$25, 744-1244. Super 8 234-9670, $42, picks up. Hotlines in terminal.

Golf: 256.2385 **Holes:** 18
Aero Club: 2170
Ground Transport:

Base taxi may take Terminal-BQ 256.1843, 256.4255.

Commercial: #504 Bus 0705-1905 M-F hrly, 0905-1705 Sa every 2h to 5th & **Missouri** E St Louis, transfer to MetroLink rail **to** St Louis downtown and Airport. $1.10 including transfer train to bus, 55¢ with Medicare card. MetroLink is a rapid-transit rail line starting St Louis Airport, crossing river and terminating at a bus-rail station in East St Louis. It has stops in St Louis near both Amtrak and Greyhound. Greyhound in Belleville 235-1220 (0645,1415,1955 south), also Car rent hotlines in terminal. Taxi 397-4334, 744-1300, 277-1515. Enterprise Car Rental in BX court area (618) 744-1000.

SEA   Zulu-8   AMC charters
Ground Transport:

Limo to Ft Lewis, McChord, Bangor, NSY, **Within WA only 800-562-7948** 0520-2320, **360-876-1737** 24h, One day advance reservation required when traveling TO Sea-Tac. Pickups are made at island #2 which in the parking garage on level three. NOTE: Drivers do not accept $100 bills.

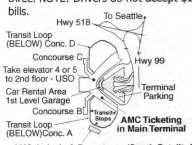

AMC Arrivals & Departures (South Satelite Terminal)

Sea-Tac Airport
Det. 1 62nd APS, Room 6411M , AMC, Sea-Tac IAP
17801 Pacific Hwy. South
Seattle, WA 98158
982-5555/6   **206-444**-9096/7
Toll Free: 877.863.1463
→→→→→→→→ Flights →→→→→→→→

Iwakuni Th	Misawa Tu
Los Angeles Su	Osan MW
Kadena MF	Yokota

Flight Information:
Numbers above. AMC counter next to America West. Fax 8358.
FAX: **D** 982.5557 **C** 253.512.5557 Open 0800-1600 & during all ops.

Sea-Tac USO:
Located on 2nd level of Main Terminal. 24h
206.433.5438

MTC   Zulu-5
927AG Res C130
Distances walkable x 3.4m AF OPS-Navy OPS.

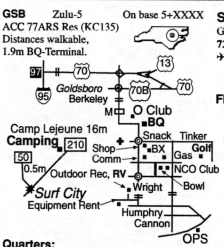

Mt Clemens ▼
To Detroit 25m

Quarters:
BQ: Lufberry ᴎᴀᴎ.
Availability ★★★★ x ★ Res weekends.
4435, 4062 24h. Rates: $15-40room, DV $50 room.
Commercial: Motel outside main gate 949-2750.

Ground Transport:
#560 Bus to Detroit on Route 3 (Gratiot Ave.).
One bus leaves Mt Clemens for Base 0700 M-F,
from OPS 1630 M-F.

Selfridge ANGB   D-94
Mt Clemens, MI 48045
273-0111   Operator   **586.307**.4011
✈✈✈✈✈✈✈ **Flights** ✈✈✈✈✈✈✈
Brunswick (P3) §
Various ANG locations
Ramstein
Willow Grove (P3) §
§ Navy drill weekend flights.
Chance of seat ★★★★

Flight Information:
OPS **5322**. Recording **5884**,
contact No. on recording. For
Parking contact Security **4673**.
Reserve Command Post **4634**.

	Break	Lunch	Dinner	Brun
O Club		Tu-Sa	W-Sa	Su
NCO Club		Tu-F	FSa	
Snack	xSu	7d	Th	
Golf	0700-2100			

GSB   Zulu-5   On base 5+XXXX
ACC 77ARS Res (KC135)
Distances walkable,
1.9m BQ-Terminal.

Goldsboro
Berkeley

Camp Lejeune 16m
Camping 210
50
0.5m Outdoor Rec, RV
✱ **Surf City**
Equipment Rent

Quarters:
Southern Pines Inn: Availability ★★★★ x ★ summer, exercises **722.0385** 24h. ACC FY
07/08 Rates: $30-43 Protocol **722.0013/14**.
Fam Camp ★★★ **5405** 1000-1700 M-F, 0800-1200 Sa, 1200-1800 Su, report to Outdoor
Rec, **1103/4** other hrs RV ESW $10, no dump, restroom, showers.
Golf: 772.0395 **Holes:** 18

Ground Transport:
Greyhound in Goldsboro, 734-3811, service to Fayetteville (Bragg,Pope). Car rent on Berkeley Blvd, Budget 778-3033, Sears 778-8787, Hi-Line 778-5677.

Seymour Johnson AFB   D-94
Goldsboro, NC 27531
722.1110   Operator   **919.7**22.1110
✈✈✈✈✈✈✈✈ **Flights** ✈✈✈✈✈✈✈✈
Few flights

Chance of seat ★★★★

Flight Information:
OPS **4097** 24h, Pax **722.4044**. 77ARW
coordinator 2026 handles their own flights,
0730-1630 M-F.

	Break	Lunch	Dinner
O Club			
NCO Club	M-F	M-F	xSu
Snack		7d	
Bowl	0800-2300 xSu		
	1300-2300 Su		
Golf	0700-1800 Summer		
	0700-1630 Winter		

CONUS, AIR FORCE CIRCUIT

SSC   Zulu-5   On base 5+XXXX
ACC Distances walkable,   **Comm Terminal**
1.1m BQ-Term.

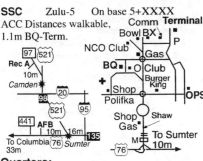

Quarters:
CAROLINA PINES INN: Availability ★★★ **3802/3/5**, 800-769-7429
24h. ACC FY 07/08 Rates: **$30-43**.

Protocol O6 + up 20FW **2007/8**, 9AF **3265/6**. Reserve, limit 3d. Limited space availability in TLF's during June-August due to high PCS.

Golf: 895.1399 Holes: 18

Wateree Rec A: ★★★ reservations BQ, site 803.895.0449, reserve 15d ahead. **Rates:** cabins $45,65unit, RV EW $9. Tent $5. No pets in cabins, firearms with permission during hunting season.

Ground Transport:
Shuttle: To Columbia Airport from BQ when needed for duty, **5017**.
Commercial: Greyhound in Sumter, 773-8113.

Shaw AFB   D-94
Sumter, SC 29152
965-1110   Operator   **803-895**-8110
↦↦↦↦↦↦↦↦↦↦ **Flights** ↦↦↦↦↦↦↦↦↦↦

Andrews   Pope
Burlington VT   Washington
Cherry Point

Chance of seat ★★★★

Flight Information:
Terminal **9517** 0800-1600 M-F
OPS **2357** 0530-2230

	Break	Lunch	Dinner	Brun
O Club	M-F	M-F	xSu,M	Su
NCO Club	xSu	M-F	xSu	
Bowl	M-F	7d	7d	

SPS   Zulu-6   On base 6+XXXX
AETC Distances walkable, 0.2m BQ-OPS.

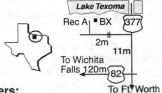

Quarters:
SHEPPARD INN: Availability ★★★★
1844/2707/2970/4538 24h, reserve day ahead.
AETC FY 07/08 Rates: **$24-42** Protocol **1102**.

Lake Texoma Rec A, cabins, ★★★ x
★ summer **4141** 0800-1700 M-F, site **C**
903-523-4612/3, reservations site only
0830-1630 xTuW, no towels. Rates: Su-Th
$20unit, FSa $25unit. RV EW $8, ESW
$10. Tent free. No pets in cabins. Hunting
firearms only, register at lodge. RV discounts Golden Age, Access, Eagle.
Commercial: Motels outside main gate.

Golf: 676.2381 Holes: 18

Ground Transport:
Base Shuttle 0500-1830 M-F.
Commercial: City Bus to downtown, Grey-
hound 7d. Bus to airport M-F.

Sheppard AFB   D-94
Wichita Falls, TX 76311
736-2511   Operator   **940-676**-2511
↦↦↦↦↦↦↦↦ **Flights** ↦↦↦↦↦↦↦↦

Randolph   Scott
Rare Flights
Chance of seat ★★★

Flight Information:
Terminal **9517** OPS **6474** 0730-1600 M-F

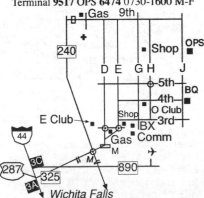

	Break	Lunch	Dinner	Brun
O Club	Tu-F	M-F	Tu-F	Su
E Club		xSa	7d	Su
Several Snack Bars				

MKC   Zulu-6
139AW ANG (C130
Distances short.

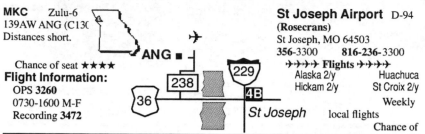

ANG ■

Chance of seat ★★★★
Flight Information:
OPS **3260**
0730-1600 M-F
Recording **3472**

229
238
36
4B

St Joseph Airport D-94
(Rosecrans)
St Joseph, MO 64503
356-3300   **816-236**-3300
✈✈✈✈ **Flights** ✈✈✈✈
Alaska 2/y   Huachuca
Hickam 2/y   St Croix 2/y
                          Weekly
St Joseph   local flights
                          Chance of

KSWF
Army, Marine aviation and AMC,
105MAW ANG (C5)
Distances walkable x to ANG OPS, 0.8m
PX-NY207.

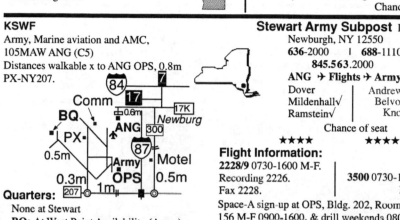

Comm
BQ
▪ PX ▪
0.5m
0.3m
1m
84
17
17K
0.6m
Newburg
ANG 300
87
Army ▪ Motel
OPS 0.5m
207

Quarters:
None at Stewart
BQ: At West Point Availability (Army)
★★★★ x ★ graduation, plebe week, summer, **D 220- 3311,3524, C 564-6309** 24h,
list starts 3d ahead. Rates: $29sgl shared
bath, $34sgl private bath, both+$5add per.
Commercial: Motel on NY300.
Ground Transport:
Taxi and limo available

Stewart Army Subpost D-8
Newburgh, NY 12550
636-2000   I   **688**-1110
845.563.2000
ANG ✈ Flights ✈ Army
Dover   Andrews
Mildenhall√   Belvoir
Ramstein√   Knox

Chance of seat
★★★★   ★★★★
Flight Information:
2228/9 0730-1600 M-F.
Recording 2226.   **3500** 0730-1630
Fax 2228.   M-F
Space-A sign-up at OPS, Bldg. 202, Room
156 M-F 0900-1600, & drill weekends 0800-
1500. **C** 845.563.2226 **D** 636.2226. Report to
✚, transport provided. Marine C130s 2904 do
not transport space-a.

	Break	Lunch	Dinner
O Club		Tu-F	Tu-Sa
E Club			Th-Sa

SUX   Zulu -6
ANG 185th ARW KC-135

Harbor
Drive

Sioux
Gateway
Halsey
970
Iowa
ANG
Sully Road
29 1st St
0.5mi

Sioux City Gateway Airport   D__
(Colonel Bud Day Field)
185th Air Refueling Wing
2920 Headquarters Avenue
Sioux City, Iowa 51111-1300
D 585.0200   Operator   **C 712.233.0**200
                       800.582.5718
✈✈✈✈✈✈ **Flights** ✈✈✈✈✈✈
McChord

Flight Information:
220 Toll Free 800.582.5718 ext. 0220
0730-1600 M-F.
Recording 2226.

**This is a new KC135 Air National Guard
unit. Likely, numerous destinations will be
available in the future.**

FOK Zulu-5
106ARRG ANG (HC-130)
Distances short.
Ground Transport:
Westhampton RR station
0.3m from
main gate.

To Riverhead

To
NYC 27
80m

31
63
2.2m
0.3m
M
OPS
Westhampton

Suffolk County Airport D-8
(**F. S. Gabreski**)
Westhampton Beach, NY 11978
456-7362   631-723-7362
↣↣↣↣ **Flights** ↣↣↣↣
Patrick   Lajes
Chance of seat ★★
Flight Information:
OPS **7362** [Fax 7420]
0730-1600 M-F

TIK   Zulu-6 Prefix 3 on base.
AFMC Distances walkable, 1m BQ-Terminal.
Quarters:
   INDIAN HILLS INN: Availability ★★★★
   x ★ Res weekends (**C 734**) **2822,5095** 24h,
   reserve day before. AFMC FY 07/08 Rates:
   $34-59 O6 up thru protocol (D 339,C 739)
   5511, **E9** 734.2175.
   Fam Camp ★★★ **D 2289, C 734-2289**
   0800-1700 M-Th, 0800-1800 SS other hrs
   caretaker. Check in Outdoor Rec. 734.3162
   RV $4, EW $10. Tent $4.
   Commercial: Motels on 29th.
Golf: C 734.2909 D 884.2909 **Holes:** 18
Ground Transport:
   Base Shuttle 0545-1830 M-F.
   Commercial: City bus Industrial Gate,
   0623,0745,1703,1813 M-F, 235-7433.

Tinker AFB   D-88
Oklahoma City, OK 73145
884-1110   Operator   405-732-7321
↣↣↣↣↣↣↣↣ **Flights** ↣↣↣↣↣↣↣↣
Andrews   Scott
Charleston 2-3/m   Travis 2/m
Hickam 2/m

Chance of seat ★★★★
Flight Information:
Terminal (**D 339, C 739**) **4339** 0715-1600
M-F. Recording 4360. [Fax 3826. Pass &
ID, 3165 5th St]
OPS (C 734) 2191 24h. Terminal open
0715-1600 M-F. Parking ½m from Termi-
nal through Security.

	Break	Lunch	Dinner	Brun
O Club	M-F	M-F	xSu	Su
NCO Club	xSu	xSu	xSu	
Bowl	M-F	7d	7d	

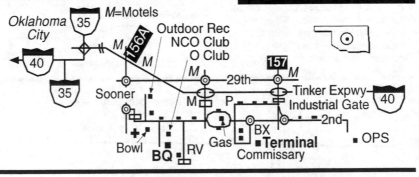

Oklahoma City 35   M=Motels
   40   Outdoor Rec
                     NCO Club
   35   Sooner   O Club
                     29th
                     Tinker Expwy
                     Industrial Gate 40
                     2nd
   Bowl BQ RV Gas BX Terminal   OPS
                     P   Commissary
156A 157

See Oklahoma City Map on Page 50

Air Force Quarters

Policy: Space-A may reserve three days ahead
for quarters not on confirmed reservation status.
On day of arrival rooms not held for confirmed
reservations are supposed to be assigned to
Space-A on request. This is assumed in this
Handbook for all AF BQ. In practice it appears

at least some billeting offices will at best allow
24 hour reservations while some still hold back
empty rooms 'just in case'. Recommend that
rooms be held with a credit card. AF-wide reservation number 888-235-6343.

CONUS, AIR FORCE CIRCUIT

SUU Zulu-8 Prefix 4 on base.
AMC 349MAW Res (C5,KC-10)
Distances walkable, 0.6m BQ-Term.

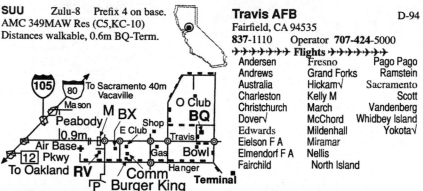

Travis AFB D-94
Fairfield, CA 94535
837-1110 Operator **707-424**-5000
➤➤➤➤➤➤➤ **Flights** ➤➤➤➤➤➤➤➤

Andersen	Fresno	Pago Pago
Andrews	Grand Forks	Ramstein
Australia	Hickam√	Sacramento
Charleston	Kelly M	Scott
Christchurch	March	Vandenberg
Dover√	McChord	Whidbey Island
Edwards	Mildenhall	Yokota√
Eielson F A	Miramar	
Elmendorf F A	Nellis	
Fairchild	North Island	

Quarters:

THE WESTWIND INN: Availability ★★ x ★ Res weekends & summer **2988/8000.** Dial 864 *only* when calling on base from a 424 prefix, 24h, additional nights reserved at 1000 if available. AMC FY 07/08 Rates: **$28-43** Protocol 3109/85/86.
Fam Camp ★★★★ 3583/2798 0830-1030, 1630-1700 xSu, other hrs follow instructions on window. RV $3, ETW $7, ESTW $12, Tent $5. Outdoor Rec 424.5659
Longterm vehicle parking $7/w, RV $10/w.
Commercial: Motel hotlines in Terminal, some with pick up.
Golf: 424.5797 or 448.7186 **Holes:** 18
Aero Club: C 437.3470
Marina C 415.332.2319 Travis Marina (north side of the Golden Gate Bridge)

Ground Transport:

Base Shuttle: 0600-0730, 1030-1300, 1530-1700, Red to BQ, Blue to P. 3404/5. ✚ **Shuttle:** Beale as required, contact Beale Æ10.

Frequent flights to many dest.
Chance of seat
★★★ CONUS, Europe, ★ Pacific
Flight Information:
Terminal or Recording (1) **1854**, recording. Agent 5703/4/6. [Fax 2048] 60 APS/TRP 90 Ragsdale Rd]. OPS 2836. Terminal Snack Bar machines, motel, car rent hot lines. Parking approx 2m from terminal, pay in advance in box at lot, cars $5 , RV $7w. Pay phone at lot. On Blue shuttle. USO 424.3316. Lockers at terminal.

	Break	Lunch	Dinner	Brun
Club	M-F	M-F	Th-Sa	Su
Bowl	xSu	7d	7d	
Cafeteria	0600-1400 M-F			
	0600-1230 SS			

Commercial: #2 Bus to Fairfield 0628-1828 M-F, 0935-1635 Sa, transfer at Solano Mall to #5 for Greyhound, Amtrak to McClellan, to #90 M-F to BART, to #85 xSu to BART, 800-640-2877, 422-2877. Amtrak at Fairfield for Sacramento, Oakland, San Jose. Supershuttle to Sacramento Metro (from local area) 800-258-3826. At BART's Cerrito Del Norte station take Colma train to last stop (Culma Station), then bus #3X to SFI airport. **Car rent with pick up:** Budget @ Terminal M-F 0830-1800, Sa 0900-1400, closed Su. Same Budget agency - located outside Travis 437-3366 or 800.952.5767 will provide p/u & drop off service, 0800-2100 xSu, 0800-1700 Su. Enterprise (Provides p/u & drop off service and is located outside M gate 425-5500 M-F 0730-1800, Sa 0900-1400, closed Su., Wreck 422-9853 0800-1900. Practical 437-7200 0800-1900. Taxi 422-5555, 449-8294, hotline in BQ. rate SF $80, Sacramento $70.

Travis-Yokota Via Elmendorf

Most of the time it is easier as well as faster for a Cat-VI to fly via Elmendorf than via Hickam. In winter many empty seats are the rule as well as available billets. M-F a tightly scheduled shuttle keeps travelers out of the cold. Terminal is open 24h and has a cafeteria if worst comes to worst.

AF

PAM Zulu-6
AETC Air defence weapons
Distances long, 1.6m BQ-OPS.
Quarters:
Sand Dollar Inn: Availability ★★★ 283.4210/1 24h. Fax 4800. Children in TLF only. AETC FY 07/08 Rates: **$24-42**, 22units. O6 up thru protocol 283.2800. Nearest other BQ Panama City.
Fam Camp ★★★ 283.2798 0800-1700. reserve cottages, check in at Fam Camp. Rates: Cottage $40, RV EW $9, ETW $10, ESTW $11. Tent $6. No pets in tages, no discharge of firearms.
Golf: 4389, 286.2565 **Holes:** 18
Aero Club: 4404
Marina C 283-3059 Beacon Beach Marina
Ground Transport:
Taxi on base 4872.

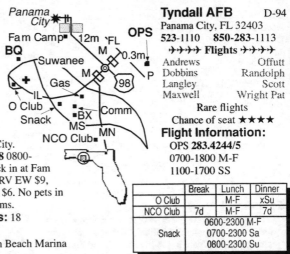

Tyndall AFB   D-94
Panama City, FL 32403
523-1110   **850-283**-1113
↦↦↦↦ **Flights** ↦↦↦↦
Andrews	Offutt
Dobbins	Randolph
Langley	Scott
Maxwell	Wright Pat

Rare flights
Chance of seat ★★★★
Flight Information:
OPS 283.4244/5
0700-1800 M-F
1100-1700 SS

	Break	Lunch	Dinner
O Club		M-F	xSu
NCO Club	7d	M-F	7d
Snack	0600-2300 M-F		
	0700-2300 Sa		
	0800-2300 Su		

END Zulu-6
AETC Pilot training
Distances short,
0.5m BQ-OPS.
Quarters:
Vance Cherokee Inn: Availability ★ **7358** FAX 6278, 24h, list 72h ahead. AETC FY 07/08 Rates: $24-42 Protocol 7253. Call in advance of arrival.
Commercial: Motels on US81.
Ground Transport:
Oklahoma Transit in Enid. Taxi 733-7433.

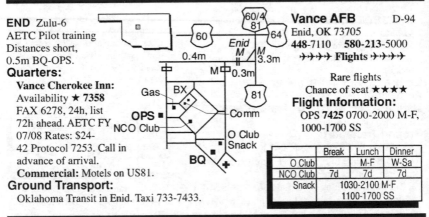

Vance AFB   D-94
Enid, OK 73705
448-7110   **580-213**-5000
↦↦↦↦ **Flights** ↦↦↦↦

Rare flights
Chance of seat ★★★★
Flight Information:
OPS 7425 0700-2000 M-F,
1000-1700 SS

	Break	Lunch	Dinner
O Club		M-F	W-Sa
NCO Club	7d	7d	7d
Snack	1030-2100 M-F		
	1100-1700 SS		

Remote Sign Up for Category VI

If starting point is near, certain, and accepts 60d sign ups, sign up in person so final destination will be reached before expiration of sign up. Otherwise send remotes by Fax, E-mail, or mail to all likely first points accepting remotes, and, for safety, to most-likely ocean-jumping points and possible intermediate outward stops. These may prove useful in the event there is a problem in carrying forward date-times. Always send remotes to every possible turnaround point. Remember there is a chance easy return will be by an unintended route, say Osan on a trip to Singapore.

On arrival at a base to which a remote sign up has been sent either as the originating base or as the base to which manifested, immediately obtain a print out of that sign up. Do not get such a print out if a thru Pax to maximize chance sign up will remain in the computer after you leave. If arrival with a carry-forward date-time is at a base with a remote, traveler can elect the one to use. Always keep all paperwork including boarding passes until final destination is reached. Make sure final destination appears on every boarding pass. Bases may add get-off point from flight as final destination.

CONUS, AIR FORCE CIRCUIT

TY

AF

VBG Zulu-8 Prefix 6 on base
AFSPC Missile
Distances long, 3m BQ-OPS.

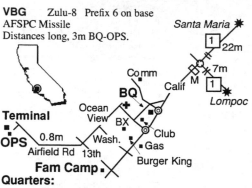

Terminal

OPS 0.8m

Airfield Rd 13th

Fam Camp

Quarters:

Vandenberg Lodge: Availability ★★★★ x ★ Th-Su May,Oct **D** thru operator. C 805.606.1844, 2245, 805.734.1111 24h, (children in TLF only). AFSPC FY07/08 Rates: **$25-44**. Protocol 3711 Reserve 3d in advance.

Fam Camp: ★★★★ **805.606.8579** 0730-1630 M-F, 0830-1600 SS, after hrs drop box. RV $5, EW $10, ESW $12.

Commercial: Motels in Lompoc.

Golf: 734.1333 **Holes: 18**

Ground Transport:

Base Shuttle 0630-1630.

Commercial: Greyhound at main gate for Oxnard, LA 0900, for San Luis Obispo, SF 1115. BX car rent 734-3644.

Vandenberg AFB   D-88

Lompoc, CA 93437
276-1110 Operator **805-606**-1110
✈✈✈✈✈✈✈ **Flights** ✈✈✈✈✈✈✈
Peterson   Travis

Few flights
Chance of seat ★★★★

Flight Information:

Terminal **1854**, MilCargo **7742/3**
0800-1630 M-F
OPS 6941 0800-1700 M-F
Sign up when flight is known

	Break	Lunch	Dinner	Brun
Club			M-F	
Burger King	0600-2100 M-F			
	0700-2000 SS			

VOK ANG
Distances short.

Quarters

BQ: Emergency only **244** 0730 1600 x Su winter.
Rate: Free.
RV, Tent: May-Oct, free.
Check in BQ.

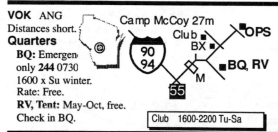

Club	1600-2200 Tu-Sa

Volk Field

WI 54618
946-3110   **608-427-1**236
✈✈✈✈✈✈✈ **Flights** ✈✈✈✈✈✈✈
Random flights to and from IL, MI, MN, WI locations.
Normally about 3 flights/w
No planes stationed

Flight Information

OPS 205 0800-1600 Tu-Sa

MTN Zulu-5
135TAS ANG (C130J)
Distances short.

Ground Transport:

#23 Bus (Wilson Point) outside main gate xSu.

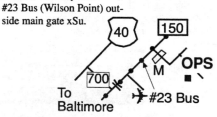

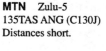

Warfield ANGB   D-77

(G L Martin Airport)
2701 Eastern Blvd.
Baltimore, MD 21220-2801
243-6210   **410-918-6**375
✈✈✈✈✈✈✈ **Flights** ✈✈✈✈✈✈✈
Aberdeen   Little Rock Adams Fld
Concord NH   Scott
CONUS   United Kingdom
Europe   Virgin Islands
Langley

Chance of seat ★★★★

Flight Information:

135th OPS **6308** 0630-1500 Tu-F
Recording **6551**, Base OPS 6229

65

AF

CEF   Zulu-5
439TAW Res (C5)
Distances walkable, 1m BQ-OPS.

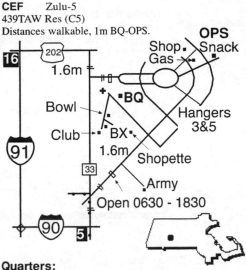

Westover ARB   D-8
Chicopee, MA 01022
589-1110 Operator **413-557**-1110
Toll Free 800.367.1110

⤙⤙⤙⤙⤙⤙⤙ **Flights** ⤙⤙⤙⤙⤙⤙⤙

Dover	North Island
Hickam	Ramstein
Italy	Spain
Kadena	Stuttgart
Langley	Travis
McChord	Yokota
Norfolk	All Shows

Chance of seat ★★★★

Flight Information:
Terminal [located in Hanger 3]
MWF 2622 & 2549 1000-1200,
1300-1500 WF. Recording 2549.
[Traffic Management Office 3009
LSS/TGTT AF Res]
OPS 2917/51 0700-2300 **As of Jan
04 taking Cat 3 but not Cat 6 pax.**
Terminal open above hrs
Sign up by phone.

	Break	Lunch	Dinner
Club	xM	xM	xM
Bowl		7d	7d
Snack	0700-2300 Machines		

Quarters:
BQ: Flyers Inn Availability ★★★★ x ★ Res weekends **2700 413.557.2700 413.593.5421** 24h FSa Res weekends, 0700-2300 other days. Rates: **O** $22+7add per, **E** $22+6add per, **DV E** $32+7, **O** $33

Ground Transport:
Base transport 3855.
Commercial: Bus to Springfield on Route 33.

SZL   Zulu-6
On base prefix 7
ACC Missile
Distances walkable,
1.4m BQ-OPS.

Quarters:
The Whiteman Inn:
Whiteman Inn. Availability ★★★★ x Summer ★ **1844/3753** 24h.
ACC FY 07/08 Rates:
$30-43 Protocol 7144.
Dining Hall reported
open to retirees.
Golf: 660.687.5572
Holes: 18

Ground Transport:
Greyhound in Knob
Noster, possibly discontinued.
Dining Hall reported
open to retirees.

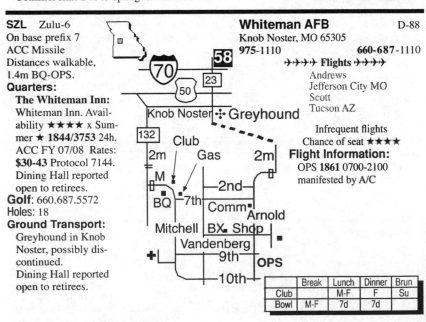

Whiteman AFB   D-88
Knob Noster, MO 65305
975-1110   **660-687**-1110

⤙⤙⤙⤙ **Flights** ⤙⤙⤙⤙

Andrews
Jefferson City MO
Scott
Tucson AZ

Infrequent flights
Chance of seat ★★★★

Flight Information:
OPS **1861** 0700-2100
manifested by A/C

	Break	Lunch	Dinner	Brun
Club		M-F	F	Su
Bowl	M-F	7d	7d	

AF

FFO   Zulu-5   Prefix 7 on base
AFMC 907TAG Res (C141)
Distances long, 1.5m BOQ-Terminal.
Quarters:

Wright-Patterson Inn: Availability ★★ x
★ M-Th **3451/3810** 24h, reserve day before.
AFMC FY 07/08 Rates: **$34-59** Protocol
4451.

Hope Hotel: ★★★★ **1285** 937.879.2696
Fax: 937.878.8731 24h. Rate: $68-110 (including tax)

Fam Camp 2579,9889 0900-2100. Report
to Fam Camp, select site, check with host.
RV E $3, EW $5. Tent $1. No water Nov-March. No shower.

Commercial: Motels on Route 444 starting
0.2m north of Gate 1C.
Golf: 879.5311 Holes: 27
Praire Trace 257.7961,Twin Base 257.4130
Aero Club: 7714, 937.253.2794
Ground Transport:

Shuttle: Areas ABC 0800-1600 M-F; BQ,
BX, Terminal 0630-1737 M-F; BOQ, O
Club, BX 1600-2400 M-F, 1000-1400,
1800-2200 SS. Vehicle Dispatch 3755.
Commercial: #11N Bus from Museum
and Visitors Center (Area B) to 1st & Main
1031-1523 M-F, 1015-1615 Sa, 1109-1709
Su. (Near Greyhound) Info 226-1144. Limo
to Vandalia Airport 0600-2000, 898-7171.
Car rent with pick up, 873-8303, 878-6651, Thrifty will pick up, 879-0023, Avis
873.9818.

	Break	Lunch	Dinner	Brun
O Club		M-F	7d	Su
NCO Club	Sa	Tu-F	Tu-Sa	
Snack		7d		
Hope	7d	7d	7d	
Hospital	7d	7d	7d	

**Reported that Dining Facility
serves retirees.**

Wright-Patterson AFB   D-88
Dayton, OH 45433
787-1110   Operator   **937-257**-1110
✈✈✈✈✈✈✈✈✈✈ **Flights** ✈✈✈✈✈✈✈✈✈✈

Andrews √	Kelly
Barksdale	Knox
Benning	Langley√
Buckley	Maxwell√
Campbell	McGuire
Charleston	Mildenhall
Cherry Point	Norfolk
Davis-Monthan	Offutt
Dover	Pensacola
Dulles Intl	Peterson
Eglin	Ramstein
Fulton Co. - Atlanta	Randolph
Hanscom	Robins
Hartsfield - Atlanta	Scott
Hickam	Travis
Hurlburt	Tyndall
Indianapolis	Washington
Keflavik	Willow Grove

Frequent flights to many destinations
Mostly C12, C21
Chance of seat ★★★
Flight Information:
Terminal **7741,7849** 0630-1630 M-F.
[Fax **D** 986.1580, **C** 937.656.1580 Rec
866.608.2976 88TRANS/CGTTM]. Passenger Terminal, will send Fax. Recording
6235. OPS 2131 0700-0130. Duty driver
will take OPS-BQ or Hope.

YNG Zulu-5
AFRC 910TAG Res (C130)
Distances short, 0.2m BQ-OPS.
Quarters:

Eagle's Nest Inn:
Availability ★★★ x ★
Res weekends, normally
1st, **1603,1268** 0700-1700
M-F, 0800-1200 SS. For
arrival other hrs, call,
keys at main gate or Club.
AFRC Rate: $33-40
Ground Transport:
Ride to airport generally
available. Taxis, possible
bus at airport.

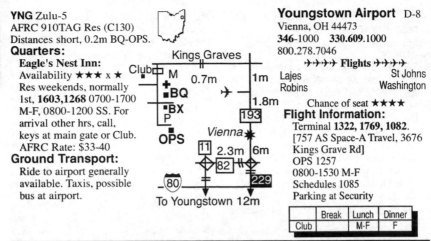

Kings Graves

Club M   0.7m   1m
BQ   1.8m
BX
P   Vienna   193
OPS
11 2.3m 6m
82
80   229
To Youngstown 12m

Youngstown Airport D-8
Vienna, OH 44473
346-1000   **330.609.**1000
800.278.7046
➵➵➵➵ **Flights** ➵➵➵➵
Lajes   St Johns
Robins   Washington
Chance of seat ★★★★
Flight Information:
Terminal **1322, 1769, 1082.**
[757 AS Space-A Travel, 3676
Kings Grave Rd]
OPS 1257
0800-1530 M-F
Schedules 1085
Parking at Security

	Break	Lunch	Dinner
Club		M-F	F

Cross References by Page Number

Following only accuracy and completeness among objectives for this Handbook are convenience and rapidity of use. It is far easier to find a cross-reference if its page is known rather than just its name. Every number in *italics* is a page number and all page numbers are in *italics*. *Italic numbers* have no other application. On tables the page locations are in a column marked page in most cases. On tables it is easy to locate page numbers for checking and for use. But when page numbers are distributed in text it is more difficult to locate them and, even more difficult to be sure all are found when checking accuracy of a new edition. Unfortunately PageMaker has no power to do this kind of checking nor does any other known application. To increase the accuracy and ease of manual checking as well as to make it clearer to readers that these are page numbers, not something else all page numbers in text follow the symbol Æ (pAgE). This symbol is used in no other way in this Handbook.

Date-Time Carry-Forward Warning

Frequently final destination of the plane is put in the lower right-hand corner of the boarding pass rather than the final destination of the traveler via continuing flights. The next base then assumes the traveler is terminating and requires a new date-time. Assure that the final destination as well as the original date time are entered on the boarding pass.

Keep all paperwork (including boarding passes) from the initial point until arriving at the final destination of the traveler. Get a new sign up

immediately at an intermediate stop from which you will continue on another flight. Make sure the original date-time and final destination appear on the new sign up. Always select as a final destination the most remote possibility. Often bases will permit a change in the final destination if that proves necessary as long as travel is in the same direction.

A strict interpretation of regulations requires that travel must be resumed on the first available flight but this is seldom if ever enforced.

About This Handbook

Unlike most publications, this book's complexity requires continual additions, alterations, re-indexing, and then page by page cross reference indexing. Blank areas exist to best enable future changes. Since we continually research to update information this book is never completed. Traveler input is an important element of this process. All of this is to insure that the most complete and best travel information is available to our travelers.

CONUS, NAVY CIRCUIT
International DSN prefix for CONUS: 312.

CONUS Navy Circuit consists of Naval Air Stations (NAS), Naval Air Facilities (NAF), and Marine Corps Air Stations (MCAS) and Marine Bases (MB) with flights, also Air Force Bases (AFB) and airports regularly served by Navy flights. Map on preceding page shows locations of such installations and page references for details in *italics*. Installations with frequent flights are in **bold**. Details of NAS in the Navy Circuit are in this Section (including NAS also in Air Force Circuit). Details of AFB included in the Navy Circuit are located in the AF Circuit Æ**10-68. Beginning 1 April 2003 a one year D.O.D. test allowed active and retiree dependents to accompany their sponsors on point to point CONUS trips. In February 2004 this program was extended indefinitely.**

Flights may be to CONUS installations or airports not included in either Circuit. Details of such are in CONUS Ground Transport Section, Æ**93-169.** State maps in that Section show locations of all installations and airports in each state and give page references to details in the form of *italic* numbers.

FLIGHT DESTINATIONS AND AVAILABILITY

Under heading **Flights** destinations and days operated of scheduled flights are listed, e.g. Andrews WF (Wed *and* Fri). If hyphenated (W-F) means Wed *thru* Fri. Also listed are common destinations of unscheduled flights. Destinations served more frequently than others listed are marked√, e.g. Yuma√. Unusually high or low number of destinations or frequency of flights is noted, e.g., Few flights. Details list most-common destinations *from* that installation or airport. Points having flights *to* a selected destinations are listed in Flight Destinations, pages Æ**235-240.** Particularly for installations having many flights, Flight Destinations also serves as a more comprehensive list of flights *from* a given installation.

Chance of obtaining a seat by Cat-VI on a selected flight is indicated by number of stars (★ 0-25%, ★★ 25-50%, ★★★ 50-75%, ★★★★ 75-100%). This same system is used to show expectation of obtaining quarters. Flight categories do not apply to quarters.

NAVY TRANSPORT FLIGHTS

Navy transport flights C9,C130, & C40 are by Reserve (Res) squadrons and tend to be round-trips from home stations. C40 squadrons have had numerous flights to non-military destinations around the world including to locations not normally served by American military aircraft. Many flights are scheduled in advance. Overseas C9 and C130 missions are normally scheduled well in advance. To learn about scheduled overseas flights contact squadrons. Prior to '911' we posted these schedules on our web site. Currently, schedules are constantly modified. When possible, we try to make information available.

When no direct flights exist, call destination to determine if a transport is expected. It may be possible to connect en route. If a transport is not shown as terminating at one of these stations, inquire, it may be continuing.

QUARTERS

The star system as described for availability of flights is used in details for availability of quarters on a walk-up basis (one ★ = 0-25%, each additional 25% more). See Appendix B, Space-A Quarters Æ**241.**

CONUS Navy Lodge reservations: **800-628-9466**, from Europe **D 565-2027**

Those Navy Lodges which cannot be reserved by this number are noted in details.

CONUS, NAVY CIRCUIT

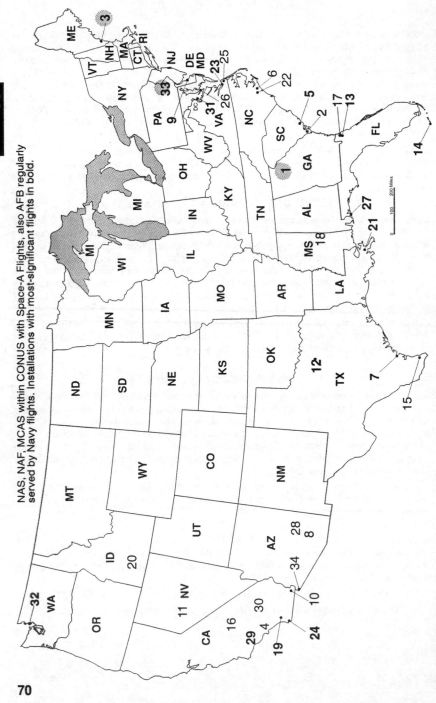

NAS, NAF, MCAS within CONUS with Space-A Flights, also AFB regularly served by Navy flights. Installations with most-significant flights in bold.

Navy

70

Most common CONUS facilities used by Navy & Marine Aircraft

Navy

NUMBER	FACILITY	SQUADRON	STATE	A/C	TAIL MARKING	QUARTERS	GROUND TRANS.	RV-TENT CAMPING
1	Atlanta, NAS	VR46	GA	C9/C12	JS/7B	W	Y	RT
2	Beaufort, MCAS		SC			S	Y	
3	Brunswick, NAS	VR62	ME	C130	JW	S	Y	
4	Camp Pendleton, MB		CA			U	Y	RT
5	Charleston AFB		SC			U	Y	RT
6	Cherry Point, MCAS		NC			U	Y	R
7	Corpus Christi, NAS		TX			S	Y	RT
8	Davis-Monthan AFB		AZ			S	Y	R
9	Dover AFB		DE			W	Y	R
10	El Centro, NAF		CA			U	Y	R
11	Fallon, NAS		NV	C12	7H	U	Y	
12	Fort Worth JRB, NAS	VR59	TX	C40/C12	RY/RNGR	W	Y	RT
13	Jacksonville, NAS	VR58	FL	C40/C12	JV/7E	U	Y	RT
14	Key West, NAS		FL	C12	MRLN	W	Y	RT
15	Kingsville, NAS		TX			U	Y	
16	Lemoore, NAS		CA	C12	75	U	Y	
17	Mayport, NS		FL			U	Y	
18	Meridan, NAS		MS			U	Y	
19	Miramar, MCAS		CA			W	Y	
20	Mt. Home AFB		ID			U	Y	
21	New Orleans JRB, NAS	VR54	LA	C130/C12	CW/GATR	W	Y	RT
22	New River, MCAS		NC			W	Y	R
23	Norfolk, NAS	VR56	VA	C9/C12	JU/7C	U	Y	RT
24	North Island, NAS	VR57	CA	C40/C12	RX/7M	U	Y	
25	Oceana, NAS		VA			U	Y	
26	Patuxent River, NAS		MD			U	Y	RT
27	Pensacola, NAS		FL			U	Y	RT
28	Phoenix (Sky Harbor) A/P		AZ					
29	Point Mugu, NAWC	VR55	CA	C9	RU	W	Y	
30	29 Palms, MB		CA			S	Y	
31	Washington, NAF (Andrews AFB)	VR53 / VR48	MD	C130/C12 / C20	WV/7G / JR	W	Y	RT
32	Whidbey Island, NAS	VR61	WA	C9/C12	RS/7G	W	Y	
33	Willow Grove JRB, NAS	VR52	PA	C9/C12	JT/7W	W	Y	RT
34	Yuma, MCAS	VR64	AZ	C130	BD	W	Y	RT

R Recreational Vehicle
S Summer
T Tent Camping
U Usually available
W Weekends difficult
Y Yes

Navy

See Dobbins AFB, *ÆE20*, Air Force Circuit

NAS Atlanta

NBC   Zulu-5
C12 2.4m BQ-Terminal.
OPS & Snack

To Savannah 10.4m
To Savannah

Car Rental
NCO Club
Guest House
Beaufort
Parris Island

Quarters:
BQ: Availability ★★★★ (no children)
843.228.6905/7618 24h. Rates: $18-40sgl+$3add per.
Guest House: ★★★★ x ★ Th, C 1663, D thru operator, 24h. Rates: $50-60sgl+$5. Reserve.
Marina: C 577.6733

Ground Transport:
Station taxi will take BQ-Terminal, 7550.
Commercial: Greyhound at main gate, call, 524-4646. Car rent 524-9140.

MCAS Beaufort   D-94
Beaufort, SC 29904
335.7100   Operator 843.228.7023/7100
↣↣↣↣↣↣↣↣↣↣ Flights ↣↣↣↣↣↣↣↣↣↣

Cherry Point√ 3/m	Norfolk
New River	Yuma

Frequent flights, few destinations
Chance of seat ★★★★

Flight Information:
Terminal 7143 0700-1630 M-F
OPS 7301 0700-2300 M-F, 1000-1800 Sa,
1200-2000 Su

	Break	Lunch	Dinner
O Club		M-F	W-F
NCO Club		M-F	M-F
E Club		M-F	7d
Cafeteria	xSu	xSu	
Bowl	MSa	7d	7d
Snack	1100-1300 M-F		

NHZ   Zulu-5
Distances short, 0.6m
BQ-OPS.

Quarters:
CBQ: Availability ★★★★ x ★ summer, Res weekends 2386 24h.
Rates: $8,12sgl, suite $15, all +$3add per, DV $24sgl+$12add per.
Protocol 2201.
BEQ Availability ★★★★ x ★ summer, Res weekends 2254 24h. (no dependents) $5per.
Navy Lodge:
★★★ x ★ summer D 2206, C 207.725.6268 0800-2000. Fax 721-9028. Rates: $40 unit.
Golf: 3250 **Holes:** 9 BRUNSWICK GOLF COURSE
Aero Club: C 729.4049
Commercial: Motels on US1.

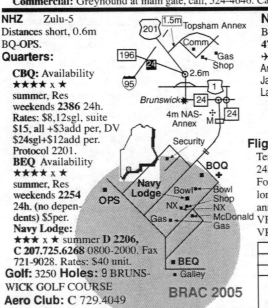

Topsham Annex
Comm
Gas Shop
Brunswick
4m NAS-Annex
Security
BOQ
Navy Lodge
Bowl
OPS
Bowl Shop
NX
NX
McDonald
Gas
Gas
BEQ
Galley

BRAC 2005

NAS Brunswick   D-800
Brunswick, ME 04011
476-1110   Menu 207-921-1110
↣↣↣↣↣↣↣↣ Flights ↣↣↣↣↣↣↣↣

Andrews	Norfolk√
Jacksonville	North Island
Lajes 2-3/mo	Whidbey Island
	Willow Grove

Frequent flights to many dest.
Chance of seat ★★★

Flight Information:
Terminal/OPS Duty Office 2682/92 24h, Recording 2689. Food machines.
For Parking contact Security 2775 for longterm storage. Sign up when flight announced. VPU1 2312, VP8 2108, VP10 2110, VP26 2126, VP92 2192, VR62 (C130) 1462.

	Break	Lunch	Dinner
Galley	7d	7d	7d
Bowl		M-F	7d
McDonald's	0600-1900 M-F 0700-1800 Sa 1000-1600 Su		

Ground Transport:
3/Town Connector, 443-8371: From Merry Meeting outside gate to Brunswick 0855, 1055, 1325, 1525; to Bath 1005, 1205, 1205, 1435, 1635; from Brunswick 0945. 1145, 1615; From Bath 0830, 1030, 1300, 1500. Sr, fare 60¢, 1414. Greyhound in Brunswick (Stow travel Agency), 725-5573. Limo 800-834-5000. Taxi 729-3688 0700-0100. Navy Lodge 207. 725. 6268 Bldg 31 - 1400 Burbank Ave.

NKT Zulu-5 Prefix 6 on station
Distances walkable x 4.4m BOQ-OPS.

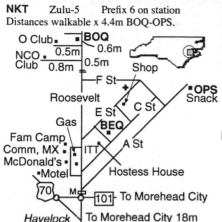

Havelock

To Morehead City

To Morehead City 18m

MCAS Cherry Point D-94
Havelock, NC 28533
582-1110 Operator **252.466**-2811
➤➤➤➤➤➤➤➤➤➤ **Flights** ➤➤➤➤➤➤➤➤➤➤

Andrews √	Langley	Pope
Beaufort√	McGhee-Tyson	Quantico
Belvoir	New River√	Scott
Charleston	Norfolk√	Washington√
Jacksonville	Patuxent River	Yuma

Chance of seat ★★★★

Flight Information:
Terminal **2379,3232** 24h
Recording 3225
OPS **2233,2671** 24h

	Break	Lunch	Dinner	Brun
O Club		M-F	W-Sa	Su
NCO Club		M-F	W-Su	
OPS Snack				
McDonald's		0530-2400		

Quarters:
BOQ: Availability ★★★★ O 5169 24h.
Rates: $16sgl, $19suite, $21 DV suite, all + $2 add per. O6 up thru protocol 2848.
BEQ: ★★★★ **3060** 24h. Rate: $16sgl, $19suite, $21 DV suite, all + $2 add per.
Fam Camp ★★★ ITT **2197** 0900-1800 M-F, 1000-1600 Sa, report to ITT, other hrs Rec
Director 4232. RV ESW $10, no restroom, shower.
Commercial: Motels in Havelock.
Golf: 3044 **Holes:** 18 Cherry Point Golf Course
Marina: C 466-3816 Hancock Boat Dock,C 466-5812 Slocum Recreation Area & Lodge;
C 466-2762/4874 Pelican Point Marina
Ground Transport
On-call shuttle to any point on station 2807.

NID
Distances walkable.

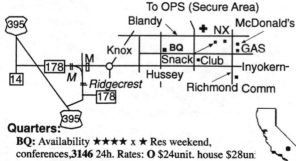

NAWS China Lake D-88
Ridgecrest, CA 93555
437-9011 **760-939**-9011
➤➤➤➤ **Flights** ➤➤➤➤
Miramar
Point Mugu√

Chance of seat ★★★★
Flight Information:
OPS **5267,5301** 0700-2230
M-F, 1500-2230 Su Flight
planning 5475. Restricted
field, call. MAC Air
939.5395

	Break	Lunch	Dinner
Club		M-F	7d
Galley	7d	7d	7d
Snack	0530-1500 M-F		
	0800-1300 Sa		

Quarters:
BQ: Availability ★★★★ x ★ Res weekend,
conferences,**3146** 24h. Rates: O $24unit. house $28uni.
DV $34unit. DV House $28unit. O6 up thru protocol
1365. E $4sgl, $15unit, house $42unit. No Space-A reser-
vations, first come first served after 1700.
Commercial: Motel outside main gate.
Golf: 2990 **Holes:** 18 China Lake Golf Course
Ground Transport:
Station Shuttle 0600-1630 M-F.
Commercial: Greyhound, car rent in Ridgecrest.

NGP Zulu-6 Prefix 1+XXXX on station 1.5m BOQ-OPS.

Quarters:
BQ: Availability ★★★★ 2380 24h. Rates: O $11+$3add per. $16sgl+$4add per. DV $24sgl+$6add per. Protocol 2331/2. **E** $10sgl, $8suite.
Navy Lodge: ★★★★ x ★ SS summer, **C** 937-6361/2 0800-1800. Rate: $32,40unit.
Commercial: Motels on Route 358 accessible by #4 Bus.
Rec A: 361.961.1293, (D 861). Check in at Marina, no shower. RV EW $7. Tent $3.

Golf: 3250 **Holes**: 18 GULF WIND GOLF COURSE

Marina: **C** 961-1293/1294/1295
Paradise Cove Marina

Ground Transport:
✈ **Shuttle:** From Kingsville about 0900, returns immediately. Check ✈ for shuttle to Kelly.
Commercial: #5 Bus via North Gate 0638-1808 M-F, #4 via main gate 0640-2015 M-F, 0715-2045 Sa, 882-1722. Intercity buses in Corpus Christi.

	Break	Lunch	Dinner	Brun
Club		M-F	W-Sa	Su
Snack	0500-2100 M-F			
	0600-2100 Sa			
	0900-2100 Su			

NAS Corpus Christi   D-8
Corpus Christi, TX 78419
861-1110   Operator   **361-961**-2811
➤➤➤➤➤➤➤➤➤➤ **Flights** ➤➤➤➤➤➤➤➤➤➤

Andrews   Norfolk
Ft Worth   Pensacola√
New Orleans

Frequent flights to many destinations
Chance of seat ★★★★

Flight Information:
OPS **2505/6/7** 24h. Recording 3385. Posts Kingsville flights. Will place on list by phone.
Army 2432 0630-1700 M-Th. Some Army flights posted at NAS OPS.

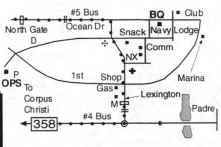

NJK Zulu-8
Distances short, 0.6m BQ-Terminal.

Quarters:
BQ: Availability ★★★ **C 2935, D** thru operator 24h. Rates: **O** $10sgl, **DV** $12,18sgl, both +$4add per, **E** $4per.
Navy Lodge: ★★★ Office at NX, **2342**, 1000-1700 M-F, at Gas 1700-2100 M-F. 0900-2100 SS, 339. Rate: $41unit. Not thru 800
Navy Inn. RV: ★★★★ 489 1000-2000 M-F, 1000-1800 SS. RV $3, ESW $9, check in Rec **C.** MWR **2481**
Commercial: Motels in El Centro.

NAF El Centro   D-8
El Centro, CA 92243
958-8524 [Base Info 2220] **760-339-2**555
➤➤➤➤➤➤➤➤ **Flights** ➤➤➤➤➤➤➤

Ft Worth   North Island
Kingsville   Oceana
Meridian   Whidbey Island

Chance of seat ★★★★

Flight Information:
T-Line **2425**, OPS 2411 0700 2300 M-F, 0700-1800 Sa.
Field closed **Su**

	Break	Lunch	Dinner
Club		M-F	M-F
Bowl	1100-2100 M-F		
	1400-2100 Su		

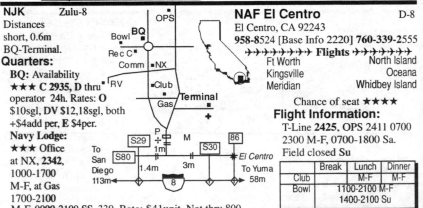

Ground Transport:
Shuttle: To El Centro from Club 1900,2030,2200,2330,0100-0100, return 1h later.
✈ **Shuttle:** San Diego 674/5.
Commercial: Greyhound in El Centro. Car rent in El Centro. Taxi 352-6141.

NFL   Zulu-8

Distances walkable x 3m BOQ-Terminal.

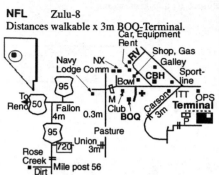

Quarters: All ★★★★ x ★ carrier planes in.

CBH Stillwater Inns C **428.3003/4**, 3199, 24h. Rate: $11+$7add per, DV $15 +$3add per. Reservations **2859**. Protocol 2700.

Navy Lodge: 426.2818, Fax 446-2944, office in NX 0930-1700 M-F, check in Shop 2583 0730-2200 xSu, 0730-2000 Su. Rate: $38unit. Not reservable via 800-NAVY INN.

Rec A: Currently closed for renovations. On base Pony Express Outfiggers **775.426.2598** 1000-1700 M-F, 0730-1600 SS, reservations up to 1m in advance, check in Equipment Rental. RV $5/5, $35/w, $150/m 50A EW Dump (on base) $3, no shower. Tent $3/d, 21/w, $90/m. Rose Creek cabin May-Oct $25unit, no towels, bedding. 70m south.

Commercial: Motels in Fallon.

Ground Transport:

Transport to Terminal. Free station taxi 2792 0700-1700. Pay shuttle to Fallon, 1700-2315 M-F, 423-3111.

Commercial: Greyhound in Fallon 322-4511. Taxi 423-9333. Hertz car rental near Terminal, 775-423-5998 M-F 0800-1800, SS 0900-1300

NAS Fallon   D-6

Fallon, NV 89406

890.2110   Operator   **775.426.5161**

➤➤➤➤➤➤➤➤➤➤ **Flights** ➤➤➤➤➤➤➤➤➤➤

Fort Worth	Nellis	Oceana
Key West	Norfolk	Whidbey Island
Lemoore	North Island √	Wright Pat
Miramar		Yuma

Frequent flights

Chance of seat ★★★★

Flight Information:

Terminal **3415** 0715-2245 M-F, 0745-1815 Sa, 1000-1800 Su.

OPS 2419/58, same hrs

Place on list by phone.

	Break	Lunch	Dinner
Club		M-F	7d
Galley	7d	7d	7d
Sportline	M-F	M-F	
Bowl		1000-2100	

NFW   Zulu-6

VR59 (C40), VMGR234 C130, 136 AW ANG (C130)

Distances walkable, BQ-OPS 0.5m.

Quarters:

BQ: ★★★★ x ★ Res weekend **5392/3** 24h. Fax 5391. Rates: **E7-O** $21sgl+$3add per, suite $26sgl+$5add per. E E1-6 $9sgl +$2add per. No space-a resevations, first come first served after 5 pm

Commercial: Motels on I30.

Ground Transport:

#92 Bus on route 183 0712-1850 M-F, 0810-1750 Sa, 0871-6200 Info 871-6200. Amtrak east 1425 SuTT, west 1658 MWSa.

Taxi charges as high as $75 are reported for travel from NAS Fort Worth to Dallas Love Field. Bus / Rail transportation is new to D/W region and routes shown are FW "T" and Dallas "Dart" systems which recently joined in the marked rail system. Amtrak may be discontinued and isn't shown here.

Continued on following page.

NAS Ft Worth, JRB   D-88
(Carswell Field)

Ft. Worth, TX 76127

739-1110   **817-782**-5000

➤➤➤➤➤➤➤ **Flights** ➤➤➤➤➤➤➤

Andrews	Kirtland FSu§
Atsugi	Kaneohe Bay
Barksdale FSu§	Miramar
El Paso FSu§	New Orleans √
Fallon	Norfolk
Hickam	North Island
Hood	Randolph
Jacksonville	Richards-G FSu§
Kelly	Rota
Key West	Sigonella
§ Reservist flight	Wake

Frequent flights, many destinations

Chance of seat ★★★★

Flight Information:

Terminal 6288 0700-2300. Sign up in person 45d ahead. Recording 6071/6289. VR 59 5380. C12 5755. Marine C130 5757/7525. 136 AW ANG C130 852.3202.

Navy

NAS Fort Worth, JRB continued from preceding page.

Navy

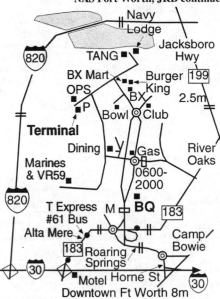

	Break	Lunch	Dinner
Dining	Su-Sa	Su-Sa	Su-Sa
Bowl	M-F	7d	xSu

Dallas - Fort Worth Metroplex

For bus and rail information call:
Fort Worth 'T' 817.215.8600
Dallas Area Rapid Transit 214-979-1111

Interstate Destinations from D/FW
I-20 west to Abilene
SH 287 north to Wichita Falls
I-35 north to Oklahoma City, OK
I-30 east to Little Rock, AR
I-20 east to Shreveport, LA
I-35 south to Waco, Austin, & San Antonio

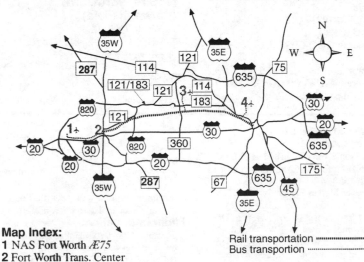

Rail transportation ······················
Bus transportion ······················

Map Index:
1 NAS Fort Worth Æ75
2 Fort Worth Trans. Center
3 D/FW Airport
4 Dallas Love Field Airport

Jacksonville, FL Area

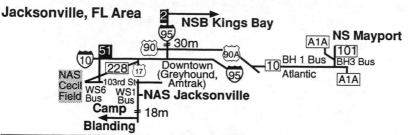

Navy

	Page	D	C	Quarters Summary	
Blanding	**122**	960	904-533	3381 0800-1630 xSu, RV3104 0800-1630 Tu-Sa	▧
Jacksonville	**77**	942	904-542	O 3138/9, E 3537 24h, Navy Lodge C 6000 24h	●
Kings Bay	**127**	573	912-673	O 2165 E 2163, Navy Lodge D 2132, C 882-6868	▧
Mayport	**80**	960	904-270	O 5423, E 5707 24h, Navy Lodge 5554	●

NIP Distances walkable, 2m BOQ-Terminal.

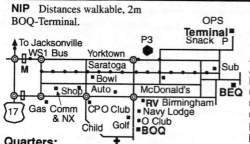

Quarters:

BOQ: ★★★★ **O 3138/9,3147** 24h, assigned 1800, extensions if available. Rates: $10sgl, DV $15,25sgl+$8add per. Protocol 2334.
BEQ (no dependents) **8195/6** 24h. Rate: $5
Naval Hospital $18-25 904.542.3138/9
Navy Lodge: ★★★★ **C 6000** 24h. Fax 77/-1/50. Rate: $42unit. No-shows assigned 1800.
Fam Camp ★★★★ **3227** 0830-2000 MThF, 0830-1600 TuW, 0900-1700 SS, reservations 0900-1600, 30d in advance, check in at Auto Hobby Shop on Birmingham, when closed go to RV, check in next day. RV $5, EW $10, ESW $13. Tent $5. Discounts Golden Age, Access.
Golf: 904.772.3249 / 542-3095 **Holes:** 27 Casa Linda Oaks Golf Course
Aero Club: C 786.9293
Marina: C 542-3260 Mulberry Cove Marina
Ground Transport:
Shuttle: Terminal to Cecil Field 0900, 1205, 1430 M-F.
✚ Shuttle M-F: Mayport 1100,1700, Kings Bay afternoon.

Commercial: WS1 Bus to downtown 0610-2325 M-F, 0640-2151 Sa, 0842-2050 Su, 630-1111. Amtrak north 0450, 1630, 2027, south 0200, 0800, 1135, MWF, 1237, west 2250 SuTuF. Car rent with pick up 264-785, 388-3553. Enterprise (watch forcing insurance) in terminal C 904.772.7007, 0700-1800 M-F, 0900-1200 Sa. On-station taxi $10sgl, 765-9999.

NAS Jacksonville   D-80
Jacksonville, FL 32212
942-2345 Operator **904-542**-2345
➤➤➤➤➤➤➤ **Flights** ➤➤➤➤➤➤➤

Andrews	Moody
Atlanta	Norfolk
Brunswick	Oceana
Charleston FSu §	Patrick
Cherry Point	Rota
Guantanomo Bay TuF	Scott
Homestead FSu §	Sigonella
Keesler WSa	Washington
Key West	Willow Grove
Lajes	Wright Pat
MacDill FSu §	

§ Reservist flight, 673-2458
Frequent flights to many dest.
Chance of seat ★★★

Flight Information:
Terminal **3825,3956** 24h. Sign up valid for 45d. {Fax 3257} OPS 2511/2/5 24h. Wing, all P3 flights 4080. VP5 3584, VP16 3560, VP30 3066, VP58 2302, VP62 2211, VR58 3302, 800-521-1317. Terminal closes at 2300, snack machines, car rent.

	Break	Lunch	Dinner
O Club		Tu-F	Tu-Sa
CPO Club		M-F	
Snack		Machines 24h	
McDonald's		0530-2300 M-F	
		0600-2300 SS	
Golf		0630-2000	

NQX Zulu-5

Distances short each location.

NAF Key West D-8
Key West, FL 33040
483-2178   Menu   **305-293**-3700
↳↳↳↳↳↳↳ **Flights** ↳↳↳↳↳↳↳
Andrews   Jacksonville√
Atlanta   Norfolk√
Bragg   Oceana
Cherry Point   Pensacola
Fort Worth   Willow Grove
      Chance of seat ★★★

Flight Information:
Terminal **2257,2769** 24h
OPS 2770 24h,
Field open 0700-2200

	Break	Lunch	Dinner	Brun
O Club			W-F	Su
McDonald	7d	7d	7d	
Galley	7d	7d	7d	
T Snack		0700-2200		

Quarters:
BOQ: 4110 Availability ★★★ x ★ winter.
Trumbo **293.4305** 24h, assigned 1600. Rates: $26 sgl+$6add per, Suite $33sgl+$6add per, Townhouse $50+$6add per. **Protocol** minimum 30 day advance, O6+up 2107/2866.

BEQ 2654 24h, handles BEQ at Truman Annex. Rates: $20+$2per **(no dependents)** common bath, $26/room shared bath.

Navy Lodge ★ C 292-7556 24h. Fax 296-4309. Rate $67unit winter , $48 summer.
Trailers ★ 4431 0800-1700 Tu-Sa $40unit.
Sigsbee Park RV Park ★★★★ Summer, ★ Winter **305.293.4432** 0700-1700, check in at Marina, overflow at Trumbo. RV $7 (Trumbo), 30/50A ESW, Dump, & Internet $16. Tent $9. Take US 1 to Sigsbee Park Annex, NAS Key West. Gravel & concrete pads, max stay 14d, no reservations, **E-Mail:** waited@naskw.navy.mil
Commercial: Motels on Roosevelt and downtown.

Ground Transport:
Duty driver 2268.
Commercial: City bus both directions on circular route around Key West and Stock 0640-2140. Greyhound 296-9072, to Miami Airport from Key West 0800,1245,1715, flag stop at Boca Chica. From Miami Airport 0750,1200,1850. Car rent 294-7550.

NQI Zulu-6 Local extensions of Corpus Christi.

Training
Distances walkable,
1.5m BQ-OPS.

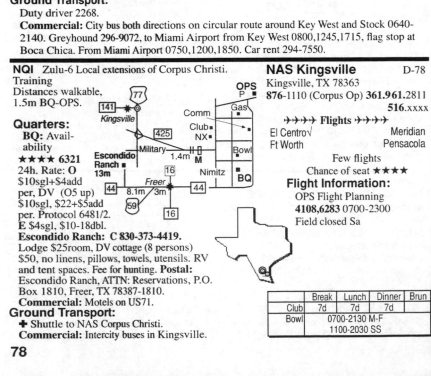

Quarters:
BQ: Availability ★★★★ **6321** 24h. Rate: O $10sgl+$4add per, DV (O5 up) $10sgl, $22+$5add per. Protocol 6481/2. E $4sgl, $10-18dbl.
Escondido Ranch: C 830-373-4419.
Lodge $25room, DV cottage (8 persons) $50, no linens, pillows, towels, utensils. RV and tent spaces. Fee for hunting. **Postal:** Escondido Ranch, ATTN: Reservations, P.O. Box 1810, Freer, TX 78387-1810.
Commercial: Motels on US71.

Ground Transport:
✚ Shuttle to NAS Corpus Christi.
Commercial: Intercity buses in Kingsville.

NAS Kingsville D-78
Kingsville, TX 78363
876-1110 (Corpus Op) 361.9**61.2811**
                        516.xxxx
↳↳↳↳↳ **Flights** ↳↳↳↳↳
El Centro√   Meridian
Ft Worth   Pensacola
      Few flights
   Chance of seat ★★★★

Flight Information:
OPS Flight Planning
4108,6283 0700-2300
Field closed Sa

	Break	Lunch	Dinner	Brun
Club	7d	7d	7d	
Bowl		0700-2130 M-F		
		1100-2030 SS		

CONUS, NAVY CIRCUIT

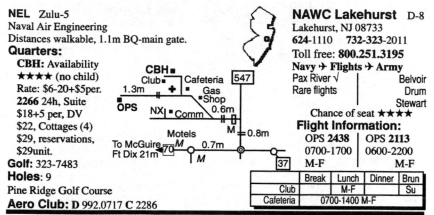

NEL Zulu-5
Naval Air Engineering
Distances walkable, 1.1m BQ-main gate.
Quarters:
CBH: Availability
★★★★ (no child)
Rate: $6-20+$5per.
2266 24h, Suite
$18+5 per, DV
$22, Cottages (4)
$29, reservations,
$29unit.
Golf: 323-7483
Holes: 9
Pine Ridge Golf Course
Aero Club: D 992.0717 C 2286

NAWC Lakehurst D-8
Lakehurst, NJ 08733
624-1110   **732-323**-2011
Toll free: **800.251.3195**
Navy ⇥ Flights ⇥ Army

Pax River √ | Belvoir
Rare flights | Drum
| Stewart

Chance of seat ★★★★
Flight Information:

OPS **2438**	OPS **2113**
0700-1700	0600-2200
M-F	M-F

	Break	Lunch	Dinner	Brun
Club		M-F		Su
Cafeteria	0700-1400 M-F			

NLC Zulu-8
Distances short x 5m to Terminal.

NAS Lemoore D-884
Lemoore, CA 93246
949-1110 Operator **559-998**-0100
⇥⇥⇥⇥⇥⇥⇥⇥⇥ **Flights** ⇥⇥⇥⇥⇥⇥⇥⇥⇥

El Centro | Norfolk
Fallon | North Island
Fort Worth | Whidbey Island
Miramar |

Frequent West Coast flights
Chance of seat ★★★★
Flight Information:
Terminal **1680** 0700-2400
OPS 1023 24h
Obtain Operation Area pass at main
gate for car or person, report to
Transit.

	Break	Lunch	Dinner
McDonald's	0600-2400		
Pizza	1100-2200		
Bowl	1100-2300		
Deli	0900-1730 xSu		
	1100-1500 Su		

Quarters:
BOQ: Availability ★★★★ E7 up & O **4609** 24h.
Rates: $13sgl+$2add per. Suite: $14sgl+$2add per,
Continental breakfast included DV $14+$3add per.
Protocol 3344.
BEQ ★★★★ **2670,4783** 24h. Rate: $5per.
Navy Lodge: ★ M-W, ★★★ Th-Su D **4861**, C **5791**
0700-2200. Fax 6149. Rate: $36unit.
Aero Club: 3526
Ground Transport:
Station Shuttle from Terminal 0615-2349. from Comm
0600-2342.
✚ **Shuttle** to Travis.
Commercial: Bus on NAS to Hanford Amtrak 0610-1810 M-F, 584-0101.
Amtrak south 1151,1507,1843,2218, north 0622,1044,1342,1713.

On-Installation Quarters Rates
The most-changeable data are those for quarters. For example rates for Navy Lodges almost-always have annual adjustments. Costs are often difficult to report as they vary room-to-room, rank-to-rank, active duty or retiree, and season-to-season. Fortunately exact rates are seldom of importance but a close approximation may serve as a means of selection when there is a choice of installations or to determine whether to go for quarters or to take commercial directly on the driving route. When the full list of rates is short it has been the practice to report all but should the list be involved only ranges have been given, e.g. $15-25sgl. This usually implies differences by rank but may depend on size of quarters. For simplicity rates are listed to the nearest whole dollar.

NRB Zulu-5
Distances walkable, 1.5m BOQ-Terminal.

NS Mayport D-80
Mayport, FL 32228
960-5011 Operator **904-270**-5011
↦↦↦↦↦↦ **Flights** ↦↦↦↦↦↦

Atlanta	Oceana
Key West	Pensacola
Norfolk√	

Frequent flights
to many destinations.
Chance of seat ★★★

Quarters:
TVQ Oceans Edge Transient Visitors Quarters (TVQ) Availability ★★★★ **5423/5707** 24h. Rates: $15+10, DV $17,25per. Protocol 5401 24h. Not available unless Navy Lodge is full or closed. Rate: E1-6 $5per (no dependents)
Navy Lodge: ★★★ **C 247-3964** 0800-1900, list starts 0800, call, assigned 1600. Fax 6153. Rate: $46,54unit, trailer $50unit.
Pelicans Roost RV ★★★★ X ★ mid-December - April $15 ESTW. **C** 904-270-7808 0700-1730M-F, **7808 SS** Fax 7810
Golf: 270.5380 **Holes**: 18 Windy Harbor Golf Club

Ground Transport:
✚ **Shuttle** to Jacksonville 0700,1200 M-F.
Commercial: BH3 Bus 0458-0253 M-F, 0533-0025 Sa, 0359-0053 Su, transfer to BH1 on Atlantic. 388-3553. Limo to NAS Jacksonville,Cecil 744-0804. In Jacksonville Amtrak north 0450, 1630, 2027, south 0200, 0800, 1135, MWF, 1237, west 2250 SuTuF. See Jacksonville Area map Æ77.

Flight Information:
Terminal **6023,6104,6604** 0600-2400. Recording 6104
Terminal open above hrs.
OPS 6130,6406 same hrs
Posts Jacksonville flights.

	Break	Lunch	Dinner	Brun
O Club		M-F	ThF	Su
CPO Club		M-F	Tu-Sa	
E Club		M-F	7d	
Bowl	Sa	7d	7d	
Snack		0530-2400		

NMM Zulu-6
Training Distances walkable x 2.5m to OPS.

NAS Meridian D-8
Meridian, MS 39309
637-2211 **601-679**-2211
↦↦↦↦ **Flights** ↦↦↦↦

| Corpus | North Island |
| Norfolk | Pensacola |

Infrequent flights
Field normally closed SS
Chance of seat ★★★★

Flight Information:
OPS **2470,2505**
0630-2300 M-F
C12 2468

Quarters:
BQ: Availability ★★★★ **2186** 24h. Rates: **All** $10sgl+$3add per, DV $18unit. Protocol 2181.
Commercial: Motels in Meridian.
Golf: 697.2526 **Holes**: 18
Ponta Creek Golf Course

Ground Transport:
Liberty buses to Meridian.
Commercial: Shuttle (pay), frequent service to Meridian. In Meridian intercity buses, Amtrak north 1125, south 1537.

	Break	Lunch	Dinner	Brun
O Club		M-F	M-F	
CPO Club		M-F	ThF	
E Club		M-F	xSu	Su
Snack	M-F	M-F	M-Th	
Galley	Su	Su	Su	

NKX Zulu-8 On station prefix 7
Distances walkable, 1m BOQ-Terminal.

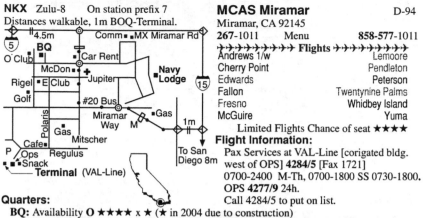

MCAS Miramar   D-94
Miramar, CA 92145
267-1011   Menu   **858-577-1011**
→→→→→→→→→→ **Flights** →→→→→→→→→→
Andrews 1/w   Lemoore
Cherry Point   Pendleton
Edwards   Peterson
Fallon   Twentynine Palms
Fresno   Whidbey Island
McGuire   Yuma
    Limited Flights Chance of seat ★★★★
Flight Information:
Pax Services at VAL-Line [corigated bldg. west of OPS] **4284/5** [Fax 1721]
0700-2400 M-Th, 0700-1800 SS 0730-1800.
OPS **4277/9** 24h.
Call 4284/5 to put on list.

Navy (sidebar)

Quarters:
BQ: Availability **O** ★★★★ x ★ (★ in 2004 due to construction)
Res weekends (2d,3d) **4233** 24h, assigned 1500. Reservations **4235** 0800-1600 M-F. Rates:
$14-21plus $5per,$26suite DV $31sgl. **E** ★★★★ $3, open bay, E1-6 $11sgl, E7-9 $10per,
E8-9 $18per, $15unit.
Navy Lodge: ★★★★ x ★ summer, Xmas,
FSa. **C 858.271.7111** 24h. Fax 695-7371. Rate: $45unit.
Big Bear Rec A, Chalets ★ weekends, reserve thru ITT 4126. Rates: FSa & Holidays
$60/n, Su-Th $55/n, 2+n Su-Th $45. **RV:** ★★★ x ★ summer Camp Res: **D 267.4126 C
858.577.4126** 0800-2200 EW $16, Tent $10 No pets.

Golf: 4155 **Holes**: 18 Miramar Memorial Golf Course

	Break	Lunch	Dinner
O Club		M-F	
E Club			
OPS Snack		0630-1430	
McDonald's		0600-2300	
Cafeteria		0630-1400 M-F	
Golf		0600-1800	

Ground Transport:
Commercial: #20 Bus from main gate through Station to Broadway, San Diego, 0533-2230
M-F, 0701-2031 SS. Transfer to #901 Bus to North Island, Coronado, #29 to Subase, trolley
for NS. NX car rent 695-7349 0830-1030 M-Th, 0830-1800 F, 0800-1500 Sa, 0900-1300 Sa
233-3004. Enterprise (watch forcing insurance) 574-249-9508 0800-1730 M-F, 0900-1200 SS.

NUQ Zulu-8 Prefix 3 on station
Distances long.
Quarters:
NASA Lodge Inn: ★★★ x
★ weekends $50
650.603.7100, Res 7101.
Navy Lodge: 962-1542
0700-2300. Fax 694-
7538. $60 Retirees can
reserve up to 30 days in
advance.
Golf: 650.254.2085
Holes: 18
Ground Transport
Buses on US 101. Train to San Francisco.

Moffett Federal Airport D-5
(Onizuka Air Station)
Santa Clara Naval Air Reserve, 500
Shenandoah Plaza
Mountain View, CA 94035
561-3000   **408.752.**3000
→→→→→→ **Flights**→→→→→→
Andrews   Pt. Mugu 1-2/m
Mather   Travis 1-2/m
North Island 1-2/m   Whidbey 1-2/m
      Res weekend flights
Flight Information:
OPS **9213** 0730-1530 M-F
Limited other space available
flights have been reported.

NBG Zulu-6 VR54
Res (C130)
Distances short,
0.3m BEQ-OPS.

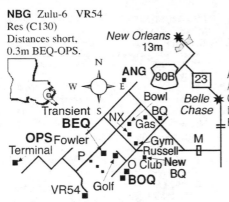

Quarters:
BOQ: Availability ★★★★ x ★ Res weekends, Mardi Gras, **O 3841** 24h. Rates: $8sgl+$5add per, DV $15sgl+$5add per. **BEQ (no dependents) 3419** 24h. Rate: $4per.
Golf: 678.3453
Ground Transport:
Liberty bus to New   Orleans Res weekend evenings. Amtrak east 1745, 1940 SuTT. **north** 1410 xW, west 515 MWSa. Car rent with pick up 366-**9400**, 0800-1800 M-F, 0900-1300 Sa. Taxi to Greyhound, Amtrak ≈$20.

NAS New Orleans, JRB
Belle Chase, LA 70143
678-3011   Menu   **504-678**-3011
(if necessary, use OOD at night 3253)
➻➻➻➻➻➻➻ **Flights** ➻➻➻➻➻➻➻

Andrews	Houston	Norfolk
Atlanta	Jacksonville	Pensacola
Corpus Christi	Lajes	Randolph
Dallas Love Fld	Mayport	Scott
Ft Worth 2-3/w	New River	Stafford VA
		Washington

Frequent flights to many destinations
Chance of seat ★★★

Flight Information:
Terminal **3213** 0700-2300. 800-222-7549. To speak with someone call T-Line at **3602**. [Fax 9575 (must include flight, front and back of ID), NAS Operations Bldg 1] Recording 3103, 800-222-7549. OPS 3100/1 24h. ANG OPS 391.8696. Terminal open 24h.

	Break	Lunch	Dinner
Club	SS§	Tu-Su	Sa§
Bowl		xM	7d
	§ Res weekends		

NCA Zulu-5
Distances: walkable,
1.3m BOQ-OPS.

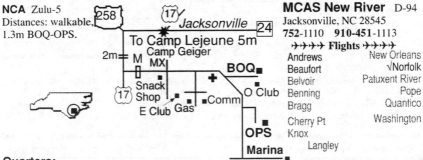

Quarters:
BQ: Availability ★★★★ New River Landing E6 up & **O** only **BOQ 449.6621** 24. Rates: $20sgl, Suites $25-27, both +$5 add per. **RV:** ★★★★ **449.6578** (also marina) 0730-1930, reservations, RV (small only) **W** $3. Tent $3, no dump. Popup rentals at Auto Hobby Shop **449.6709** 0800-1700.
Marina: C 449-6578 Air Station Marina
Ground Transport:
Shuttle: New River-Lejeune 0545-1700 M-F, 1100-1600 SS, 451.9480.
Commercial: At Lejeune bus station, Greyhound, taxi, 3632.

MCAS New River   D-94
Jacksonville, NC 28545
752-1110   **910-451**-1113
➻➻➻➻ **Flights** ➻➻➻➻

Andrews	New Orleans
Beaufort	√Norfolk
Belvoir	Patuxent River
Benning	Pope
Bragg	Quantico
Cherry Pt	Washington
Knox	
Langley	

Chance of seat ★★★★
Flight Information:
OPS **6316** 0700-2300 M-F,
0900-1500 Sa, 1500-1900 Su.

	Break	Lunch	Dinner
O Club		M-F	FSa
Snack	xSu	7d	
Bowl	Tu-Sa	7d	7d

Navy (side tab)

NGU Zulu-5 Prefix 4 on station.
Naval Base and NAS, AF flights, VR56 (C9)
Distances long, 3m NAS BOQ to Terminal.

Quarters:
Availability ★★★★ x ★ Res weekends,
all numbers 24h. BOQ assigned 1800. BEQ
rates $6-12sgl+$3add per by rank. Protocol
8595. **NS & NAS** Cental Res. 0700-2100
M-F, 08-1630 Sa **Toll Free 877.986.9258**
NAS: CBH 444.7466/4667/4983 $15sgl,
DV (O5&up $27sgl) Suite $18. O6+up Ely
Suite 444.2875 $40. BEQ -includes Officer
overflow **402.4553/445.4425** Central Billet-
ing Office) $8-15.
NS: BOQ 402.4444 & 3250 $15-27sg. DV
$27sgl+$4add per. **BEQ 445.0171.**
Navy Lodge: ★ C 489-2656 24h. Fax 489-
9621. $57unit.
Quarters at NAB Little Creek, Æ**163** reachable by #3 Bus, transfer to #1.
Commercial: Inexpensive motels on #3 Bus
route a few minutes outside gate.
Golf: 444.5572 Sewells Point Golf Course
Marina: C 462-7140 NS Norfolk Marina
Ground Transport:
Commercial: Hertz at AMC Terminal
757.489.1780, Fax 1783. Bus: See transit
map Æ159. #3 from NX, Gate 4 0654-2354
hrly xSu, from Gate 4 0554-0054 Su, to
low-cost motels Oceanview & Chesapeake,
downtown, Greyhound, waterfront, all
connections. Transfer to #1 to Little Creek,
transfer at Crossroads M-F to Eustis, Langley, Monroe, SS use Greyhound. Transfer
to #20 to Oceana, Dam Neck, Story. Bus
info 640-6300. Amtrak from Newport News
0845 xSa. Greyhound 627-5641. Limo to
airport $6.25, 857-1231. Taxi 622-3232,
489-7777, 855-3333,9009. Groome Transportation to airport 757.857.1231.

	Break	Lunch	Dinner	Brun
NAS O Club		M-F	M-F	Su
NS BOQ	xSu	M-F		
E Club		M-F	M-F	
Restaurant	M-F	7d	7d	
Cafeteria	0600-2200			
McDonald's	0515-2400			

NS Norfolk D-8
Norfolk, VA 23511
564-0111 Operator **757-444**-0000
D 564 for **C 444, D 565** for **C 445,
D 262** for **C 322, D 836** for **C 836,
D 464** for **C443; some prefixes require a
9 before 8 for DSN access.** Not all may
be needed for Space-A travel.
➤➤➤➤➤➤➤➤➤ **Flights** ➤➤➤➤➤➤➤➤➤

Andrews √	Lemoore
Atlanta	Mayport √§
Bahrain MF	McGuire Th
Beaufort √	Minneapolis St. Paul
Belvoir √	Miramar M A
Bragg	New London
Brunswick	New Orleans
BWI TuF	New River √
Cherry Point √	North Island √
Dobbins	Naples √
Dothan AL	Pensacola
Dover	Point Mugu
Fort Lauderdale √§	Pope F §
Fort Worth	Rota √
Gitmo	Scott
Gordon	Sigonella √
Jacksonville√	Souda Bay Su √
Jacksonville FL	St Croix Th
Jamaica Tu	Travis
Keflavik ThF	Washington √
Kelly M A	Willow Grove√
Key West	Wright Pat √
Lajes SuTh	
Langley √	

§ Flights from Navy Ops [at LP1]. OPS
has flights to most east coast Naval Air Stations, AMC has frequent flights many dest.
Chance of seat ★★★★

Flight Information:
Terminal **444.4148** press 0, 0400-
2400, Recording 4118. [Fax D 565, C
445.7501, **Toll Free 877.417.1695,** then
press '1' for Arrivals, '2' for Departures,
or '0' for assistance. AMC Air Terminal
Duty Officer **D 565 C** 445.6556/8659.
NAVAIRTERM/05]. OPS 2442 24h.
Parking permits at Terminal, VR56 7817.
C12, 21 and other smaller planes operate out of OPS. Contact OPS Terminal
444.0169 0500-1700 M-F. Terminal open
24h.

Continued on next page.

NS Norfolk continued

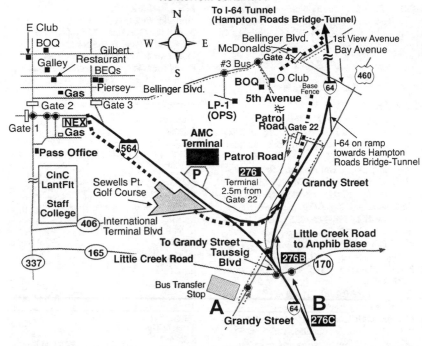

NZY   Zulu-8   On station prefix 5.
VR57 Res (C9)
Distances walkable x 2m Terminal,
Navy Lodge.

Quarters:

BOQ: Availability
★★★ x ★ Res week-
end **7545** 24h. Assigned 1800. Rates:
$10sgl, DV $16sgl, both+$5add per.
Protocol 8163.

BEQ ★★★★
9551/2 24h. Rate: E1-6 (No dep.)
$6per. E7up $10sgl+$3add per.

Navy Lodge: ★★★★ x ★ May-
Sept **435-0191 & 545.6940** 24h. Fax
522-7455. Rate: $66 unit.

**It is almost always possible to get
quarters somewhere in San Diego.**
See summary on Æ115. NAB Coronado closest.

Commercial: Motels on Orange,
nearest 0.5m from main gate.

Golf: 545.9658
Aero Club C 435.2525

NAS North Island   D-80

San Diego, CA 92135
(now part of NB Coronado)
735-1011   Menu   **619**-**545**-1011

⇢⇢⇢⇢⇢⇢⇢ **Flights** ⇢⇢⇢⇢⇢⇢⇢

Andrews 2/w	Miramar
Cherry Point 2/m	Moffett
Davis-Mon § FSu	Monterey 3/m
El Centro 1/w	Nellis FSu§
Fallon 3/m	New Orleans 2/m
Fresno	Norfolk 1/w
Fort Worth 1/w	Oceana 1-2/w√
GuantＤnamo Bay Tu	Pendleton
Hickam 1/w	Peterson √
Jacksonville 1/w	Point Mugu 1/w
Kaneohe Bay 1-2/w	
Lemoore 3-4/w√	San Clemente Is √
Los Alamitos	Travis
Los Vegas	29 Palms
Louisville	Whidbey Island √
Luke § FSu	Willow Grove
McChord	Yuma √

§ Reservist flight
Frequent flights to many dest.
Chance of seat ★★★

Continued on next page.

Navy

Ground Transport

Car Rental available on base; on weekends base taxi is available.

Station Shuttle: 0600-1700 M-F. Red route to terminal. On-call shuttle 1600-2300 895-1000.

Commercial: #901 Bus at main gate to motels, NAB Coronado, downtown 0533-0110 M-F, 0555-0118 SS. Change on Broadway to #20 Bus to Miramar. Change at Imperial to trolley for NS or Old Town and #28 Bus to Subase, info 233-3004.See transit map *Æ115.* Only taxi permitted to enter NAS 435-6211. Car rent Enterprise (watch forcing of insurance) 437-0145 0800-1800 M-F, 0900-1200 Sa. Adnural 435-14780900-1800 M-F, 0900-1700 Sa, 1000-1600 Su.

Ferry: North I 0550,0640,0730 to Antisub. 1520,1602,1644,1726 to Broadway pier,Antisub

Flight Information:

Terminal **9567** 24h. Recording 8273/8, [Fax 9532 60 days] OPS 8233, VR57 6921. Reservist flight 2609, 800-828-9202. P3 7591. Terminal open 24h. Get on register in person. Destination must be specific but can be changed by phone. Parking limited to 20d, for longer contact Security.

	Break	Lunch	Dinner	Brun
Club		M-F	F	Su
E Club		M-F	M-F	
Galley	7d	7d	7d	
Mexican		24h		
Bowling	7d	7d	7d	
Terminal	0530-1900 M-F1800SS		

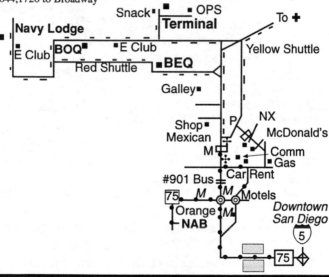

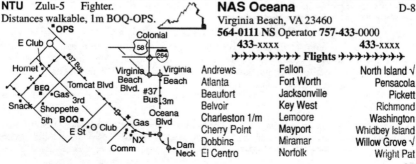

NTU Zulu-5 Fighter.
Distances walkable, 1m BOQ-OPS.

NAS Oceana D-8
Virginia Beach, VA 23460
564-0111 NS Operator 757-433-0000
433-xxxx   433-xxxx
✈✈✈✈✈✈✈✈ **Flights** ✈✈✈✈✈✈✈✈

Andrews	Fallon	North Island √
Atlanta	Fort Worth	Pensacola
Beaufort	Jacksonville	Pickett
Belvoir	Key West	Richmond
Charleston 1/m	Lemoore	Washington
Cherry Point	Mayport	Whidbey Island
Dobbins	Miramar	Willow Grove √
El Centro	Norfolk	Wright Pat

Navy

Quarters:
Chance of seat ★★★

BOQ: Availability ★★★★ **3293/2573** 24h. Rate: $12,15sgl+$3add per.
BEQ: ★★★★ **2574** 24h. Rates: $10sgl, E7 up suite $12sgl+$2add per.
See Dam Neck Æ161 for nearest other quarters.
Ocean Pines RV Park (757) 417-7140 **ESW 20/30/50 Amp**
Golf: 433.2866 / 2588 **Holes**: 36 Aeropines Golf Club

Ground Transport:
✚ **Shuttle** M-F: Naval Hospital 0700,1200; **Dam Neck** 0905,1135,1350,1540. Quarterdeck will transport O6 up to NAS Norfolk, 2366/7.
Commercial: #37 Bus to Dam Neck, Virginia Beach 1215-1705 FSu, 0945-0220 Sa, 1815-0015 M-Th, info 627-6300. for NAS Norfolk transfer to #20 then #15. To Little Creek #57, #20 then #1. 640-6300. Limo to Norfolk Airport. Taxi 486-4304. Car rent at NX 486-7700.

Flight Information:
Terminal **2902/3** 0730-1500 M-F
OPS **2162** 24h

	Break	Lunch	Dinner
O Club		M-F	Tu-Sa
E Club		M-F	FSa
Snack	0500-2300 xSu		
	0600-2300 Su		

NHK   Zulu-5
Air Test Center, On base dial 5 digits.
Distances long, 5m main gate-O Club.

Quarters: *Lexington Park*
BQ: Availability ★★★ **3601, 3291** 24h. Rates: **O** $15per, DV $25sgl+$8add per. Protocol 1104. **E** $6per (no dependents).
Navy Lodge: C 737-2400 0800-2000. Fax 862-7866. Rate $46unit.
Commercial: Motel outside main gate.
Golf: 342.3597 **Holes**: 18 Cedar Point Golf Course
Aero Club: 5087
Marina: C 342-3573 West Basin Marina
Rec A: Feb-Nov ★★★ **342.3519**, reservations, check in Gym. Trailers $15-40. RV $6, EW $10. Tent $6, no restroom, shower, pets.

Ground Transport:
Shuttle: To Pentagon 0700,1030 M-F, check with 4088, does not run if minimum duty not met, returns 1150,1530.
Commercial: Gold Line Bus Lexington Park to Washington 0620,1320,2000. Taxi 836-8147.

NAWC Patuxent River
D-8
Patuxent River, MD 20670
342-3000   Operator   **301-342-3000**
➜➜➜➜➜➜➜➜➜ **Flights** ➜➜➜➜➜➜➜➜➜
Andrews√   Jacksonville   Norfolk
Brunswick   New River   Willow Grove√
Cherry Point

Chance of seat ★★★★

Flight Information:
OPS **3340 3836/7** 0700-2300
Reported they do not manifest space-a.

	Break	Lunch	Dinner
O Club		TuF	xM
CPO Club		TuF	W-Sa
Cafeteria	0700-1430 xSu		
Snack	0700-1300 M-F		

Getting Around by Navy

Destinations listed in the details of the Navy Circuit are the most-likely from each NAS or JRB but Navy is noted for unexpected flights to almost any other installation within CONUS. As a general rule it is easier to move around CONUS by Navy than by AF. Going to any NAS with frequent flights (even if the destination you desire is not on their board) is a good way of playing the Space-A game. Obviously this does not apply to facility listed as having rare or few flights such as NAS Whiting Field.

When at a Navy installation and there is no flight to your destination, try calling that destination to determine their inbound flights. It may be possible to reach an intersecting point by using another flight destination. See Æ69 & Æ235-240.

NFG Zulu-8 1st
Marine Division
Distances long x on
Mainside, Del Mar.

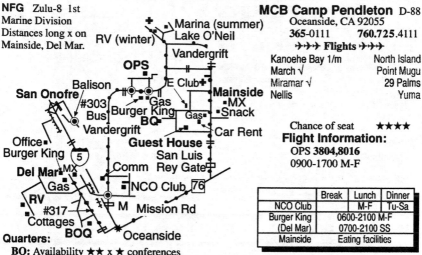

MCB Camp Pendleton D-88
Oceanside, CA 92055
365-0111 **760.725**.4111

➤➤➤ **Flights** ➤➤➤

Kanoehe Bay 1/m	North Island
March √	Point Mugu
Miramar √	29 Palms
Nellis	Yuma

Chance of seat ★★★★

Flight Information:
OPS **3804,8016**
0900-1700 M-F

	Break	Lunch	Dinner
NCO Club		M-F	Tu-Sa
Burger King	0600-2100 M-F		
(Del Mar)	0700-2100 SS		
Mainside	Eating facilities		

Quarters:

BQ: Availability ★★ x ★ conferences
732.3451 24h. Rates: **O** $22-25sgl+$5 add., DV $20-30sgl. O6 up thru protocol 5780. **E** $17sgl. All+$5add per.
Guest House Ward Lodge ★ **5194** 24h. Rates: $40-50 unit.
Del Mar: Harborside Inn BOQ ★★ summer **2305,732.2855**, 0600-2200. Rates: $22sgl, suites $24, DV $35sgl, all+$5add per. **Beach Cottages:** (trailers) ★★★★ x ★★ summer, **2134** 0800-1630, reservations, Rates: $30unit summer, $25unit winter. No linen, pillows, towels. RV EW $12, no restroom, shower.
San Onofre: ★★★★ x ★★ summer **7935** 0800-1630, reservations, trailers, cottages $30 summer, $25 winter, no linen, towels. RV $8, W $10, EW $12. Tent $8, W $10.
Lake O'Neil: ★★★★ x ★ summer holiday **4241** 0900-1600, reservations, check in RV summer, Rec A winter. RV $6,8, W $10, EW $12. Tent $6,8.
Golf: 760.725.4756/4704 **Holes:** 27 Marine Memorial Golf Course
Marina: C 760.725.2820/7245 Del Mar Marina
Ground Transport:
Buses: #303 via main, San Luis Rey gates lv Transit Center :00,:30 0700-2230; #317 to Del Mar :15, :45, start 0415 M-F, 1015 Sa, 0745 Su, end 0045. Intercity buses, Amtrak at Transit Center. Enterprise car rent (watch forcing insurance) C 6997, 0800-1700 M-F, 0900-1600 Sa.

NPA Zulu-6
Prefix 2 on station or to Whiting Field.
Distances long, 3m BOQ-Terminal.

Quarters:

BOQ: ★★★★ **2755** 24h. Rates:
$15sgl+$2add per. DV $25sgl+$2add per.
BEQ 452.7076 Reservations: **7782** 24h.
E1-4 $6sgl+$2add per, E5 up $10sgl+$2add per.
Navy Lodge ★★★★ C **456-8676** 24h.
Fax 457-7151. Rates: $37,46,57unit, trailer $50unit.
Golf: 452.2454 **Holes:** 54 A.C. READ
GOLF COURSE **Continued on following page.**

NAS Pensacola D-88
Pensacola, FL 32508
922-0111 Operator **850-452**-0111

➤➤➤➤➤➤➤➤ **Flights** ➤➤➤➤➤➤➤➤

Andrews √	Ft Worth	Norfolk
Atlanta, NAS	Jacksonville	Rucker
Beaufort √	Langley	Scott
Cherry Point	Meridian	Washington
Corpus Christi√	New Orleans	Wright Pat

Frequent flights to many destinations
Chance of seat ★★★★

Flight Information:
Terminal **3311** 0530-1830
Recording when not open
OPS 2431 24h

NAS Pensacola continued from previous page.

	Break	Lunch	Dinner	Brun
O Club		Tu-F	Tu-Sa	Su
O Club Annex		M-F		
Bowl	xMWTh	7d	7d	
Snack	0530-2300			

Marina: C 452.3369 Sherman Cove Marina, C 452-4152 Bayou
Grande' Sailing Marina
   Trailer Park: ★★★★ x ★ winter holiday 2535 0830-1700, reservations, check in office, other hrs host. Cabins $30unit, no pets. RV
EW $9. Tent $4.

Ground Transport:
   Duty driver to/from OPS 2431.
   Transportation dispatch 4563
   Commercial: #14 Bus to transfer
station 0630-1830 hrly M-F, 0730-
1730 2 hr, transfer to #2 to airport,
#10B to Greyhound, 436-9383. Greyhound 476-4800. Amtrak east 0140 SuTT, west 0556
MWSa. Car rent 453-2176 0800-1800 M-F. 0900-1500 Sa. Taxi 455-8506.

NTD   Zulu-8
VR55 (C9), VP65 (P3)
146TAW ANG (C130)
Distances short ANG, walkable NAWC x to
cottages, 1.4m Terminal-BQ.
Prefix 4 ANG-NAWC

NAWC Point Mugu   D-55
Point Mugu, CA 93042
351-1110   Operator   **D 893**-7000
805-989-1110 | **805-986**-7000

Navy ↣↣↣↣↣	Flights ↣↣↣↣↣↣	ANG
Andersen	Miramar	Pendleton
Brunswick	Nellis SuF §	Phoenix SuF §
Cherry Pt	Norfolk	Tinker
Hickam √	North Island	Washington
Jacksonville	Oceana	Whidbey Island

§ Reservist flight
                     Chance of seat ★★★★
Flight Information:

Terminal **7026,7305,** **7731** 0600-1800 M-F OPS 8521 0600-2200, VR55 Ops & Maintenance **D** 351.7129, **C** 986.7129. 5143, 5755, VP65 7295,8765 0800-1630. Retirees barred from flight line SS.	**Channel Island ANG OPS 7577** 0700-1530 Tu-F C130 Recording **D or C 893.7000** then "4". Call to sign up 5 working days ahead. P near OPS, contact OPS.

Frequent flights to many destinations
                     Chance of seat ★★★★
Flight Information:
   Terminal **6215/7** 0630-2300 Recording 6216. OPS
   6192/6,6202 VR52 6556, VP64 6414, VP66 6605,
   913TAG ANG (C130) 1073, Army 1585 0730-
   1630
   Terminal open 0700-2300. Field closed 2300-0700.

Quarters:

BQ: Availability ★★★★ x ★ Res weekends (dependents only in DV) BOQ **7510,8235/55** BEQ **8251** 24h. Rates: **O** \$10,12per, DV \$30unit. O6 up thru protocol 8672. **E** \$6,8,12,15per.

Motel, camping: ★★★ x ★ weekends **8407** 24h, reserve, AD 90d ahead, others 30d, check in motel.

Rates: Motel \$40sgl, suite \$57sgl with breakfast, all +\$4add per. RV \$8, E \$10, ESW \$15. Tent \$6.

Commercial: Motels in Oxnard.

Golf: 989-7109 **Holes:** 9 John E. Clark Golf Course

Ground Transport:

Shuttles: Station 0700-1630 M-F.

Commercial: Vista bus to Oxnard, connection on station. Greyhound stops at overpass, more buses (487-2706), Amtrak in Oxnard north 1106,1318.1657.1937. south 0818,1015,1500,1650,1905. Car rent with pick up 483-2326. Taxi 438-2444.

	Break	Lunch	Dinner
Restaurant		M-F	
Galley	7d	7d	7d
Pizza		M-F	7d
McDonald	0530-2130		

KPVD Zulu-5 *Providence*

Providence Airport
(T. F. Green)

555 Airport Rd., Warwick, RI 02886

Serves NSB New London and NTC Newport

Flights handled by Northstar Aviation

401-738-2600

⇥⇥⇥⇥⇥⇥⇥⇥⇥⇥ **Flights** ⇥⇥⇥⇥⇥⇥⇥⇥⇥

Concord   Peterson

Few flights

Warwick

NYG Zulu-5

Distances long, 2m BOQ-O Club.

Quarters:

BQ: Availability **O** ★★★★ **3148** 24h. Rates: \$22sgl, \$33suite. O6 up thru protocol 2756,4477.

Crossroads Inn: ★★★ x ★ summer, 800.965.9511 & 703.630.4444,

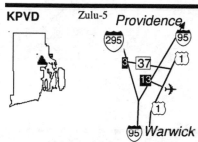

2983 0600-2200. Rate: \$49, \$57 Eff, \$66 Suite Toll Free 800.965.9511, 703.630.4444 Res. can be made 60d in advance.

RV: ★★★★ x ★★ weekends **5270** 1200-2000 Su,W-F, 0600-2000 Sa. RV \$6, EW \$12, ESW \$15. Tent \$6, no shower.

Golf: 2424 **Holes:** 18 Medal of Honor Golf Course

Marina: C 784-2359

Aero Club: 640.7200 / 6596

Ground Transport:

✚ **Shuttle** to Bethesda 0600 M-F.

Commercial: Amtrak south 1116, north 1654.

MB Quantico D-99

Quantico, VA 22134

278-2810   **703-784**-2121

⇥⇥⇥⇥ **Flights** ⇥⇥⇥⇥

Beaufort   New Orleans

Cherry Point   Washington

Flights rare

Flight Information:

OPS **2979** 0730-1700

	Break	Lunch	Dinner	Brun
O Club		Tu-F	Tu-Sa	Su
NCO Club		Tu-F	xSu	
E Club			7d	
Bowl			7d	
Cafeteria		7d		

TNP
Distances long, 8m BQ-OPS.
Quarters:
BQ #1565: Availability ★ 6642 24h. Rates:
$7,13,22per, DV $22unit. Protocol 6109. If possible
call one week in advance,re servations possible if
rooms are available.
TLF ★★★ x ★★ summer 6573/83 24h. Rate:
$30unit.
RV Twilight Dunes 6583 ESW must be self con-
tained. No public facilities. $15/d, weekly &
monthly rates available. Check in at TLF.
Commercial: Motels in 29 Palms.
Golf: 6132 **Holes:** 18 Desert Winds Golf Course
Ground Transport:
Desert Stage Line to Palm Springs, 1020 7d, 1730
F to Palm Springs, LA, schedules at bus station.

	Break	Lunch	Dinner
O Club		M-F	xSu
NCO Club		M-F	M-F
E Club	0600-2130 M-F		
	1000-2130 SS		
Cafeteria	0630-1800 M-F		
	1100-1800 SS		
Burger King	0600-2400		

NUW   Zulu-8 On base prefix 7+XXXX
VR61 Res (C9), VP69 (P3)
Distances walkable, 0.8m BOQ-
Terminal.
Quarters:
CBH: Availability ★★★★
x ★ Th-Sa Res weekends 2038 / 2529 / 3289 24h.
Fax 5962.Rates: O $10per, DV $17per. Protocol
2037.
E $6per.
Navy Lodge: 675-0633 0700-2300, Fax 675-1201.
Rate: $49unit.
RV Park: ★★★★ x ★ summer 2434 0830-1700
MF, 1100-1700 TWT, reservations, check in Out-
door Rec. Cliffside EW $6.50. Tent $3. Rocky Pt
RV $4.
Commercial: Motels in Oak Harbor.
Golf: 257-6585 / 2178 **Holes**: 18 GALLERY
GOLF COURSE
Marina: C 257.0853 Crescent Harbor Marina

	Break	Lunch	Dinner	Brun
O Club		M-F		
CPO Club		Tu-F	W-Sa	Su
E Club	M-F	M-F	M-F	
Galley	7d	7d	7d	
McDonald's	0600-2300			

MB 29 Palms
29 Palms, CA 92278
957-6000   **760-830**-6000
↦↦↦↦ **Flights** ↦↦↦↦

Beaufort	North Island
Cherry Point	Pendleton
El Toro	Washington
Miramar	Yuma

Chance of seat ★★★
Flight Information:
7815/6 0800-1600 M-F

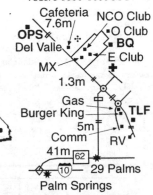

NAS Whidbey Island   D-8
Oak Harbor, WA 98278
820-0111 Operator **360-257**-2211
↦↦↦↦↦↦ **Flights** ↦↦↦↦↦↦

Andrews	Hickam √	Oceana
Atlanta	Jacksonville	Pensacola
Atsugi 2/y	Lemoore	Pt Mugu
Beaufort	Mayport	Sigonella 2/y
Brunswick	Miramar	Travis
El Centro	Misawa §	Wake
Fallon	Nellis	Washington
Fort Worth	Norfolk	
Lewis	North Island √	

§ No retirees into Misawa
or Atsugi. Retirees departing Japan via
Navy must first get stamped out with
Immigrations.
Frequent West Coast flights.
Chance of seat ★★★★
Flight Information:
Terminal 2604, 2328 0600-1900
OPS 2681 0700-2400
VR61 3701, VP69 2446

Continued on following page

Aero Club: C 679.4359

Ground Transport:

Station Shuttle 0600-0800, 1500-1800 M-F, 8962. ✚ **Shuttle** to Ft. Lewis 9500. Departs front of hospital MWF @ 0700.

Commercial: Free Island Transit bus: #2 to Oak Harbor then bus to ferry, schedule at BQ. #23 bus to Everett, #210 to Marysville then shuttle to NS. Bus to Seattle morning and afternoon, stop on Route 20 opposite McDonald's. Limo to Sea-Tac Airport 0740,1440 + 1110 M-F, 800-448-8443. Harbor Airline van to Oak Harbor Airport 1000 M-F, 1500 M-Th, 675-6666, schedule at BQ. Car rent with pick up Budget 675-590, Enterprise (watch forcing insurance) 675-6052. Taxi 675-1244, $5 to Oak Harbor. Ferry information 800-843-3779. Airporter Shuttle to Sea-Tac Marysville 0335-1550 800-235-5247.

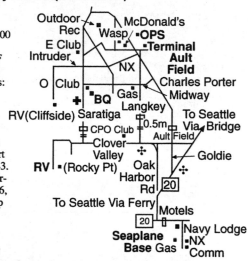

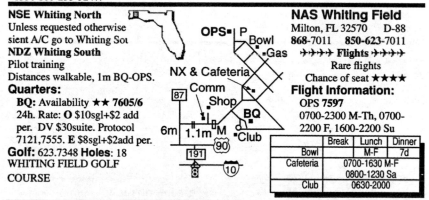

NSE Whiting North

Unless requested otherwise sient A/C go to Whiting Sou

NDZ Whiting South

Pilot training

Distances walkable, 1m BQ-OPS.

Quarters:

BQ: Availability ★★ 7605/6 24h. Rate: **O** $10sgl+$2 add per. DV $30suite. Protocol 7121,7555. **E** $8sgl+$2add per.

Golf: 623.7348 **Holes:** 18 WHITING FIELD GOLF COURSE

NAS Whiting Field

Milton, FL 32570   D-88

868-7011   **850-623**-7011

↣↣↣↣ **Flights** ↣↣↣↣↣

Rare flights

Chance of seat ★★★★

Flight Information:

OPS **7597**

0700-2300 M-Th, 0700-2200 F, 1600-2200 Su

	Break	Lunch	Dinner
Bowl		M-F	7d
Cafeteria	0700-1630 M-F		
	0800-1230 Sa		
Club	0630-2000		

NXX   Zulu-5

Res, 913AW Res (C130), VR52 Res (C9) VR64,66 Res (C130)

Distances short, 0.3m Terminal-M gate.

Quarters:

BQ: Availability ★★★★ x ★ Res weekends **(C 442) 5800/1**, 800-227-9472 24h, communal facilities. Fax 5817. Reserve 24h ahead. Rates: **O** $10per, suite $18sgl +$6add per, **E** $7per. Suite $15sgl +$3add per. Assigned 1500.

Continued on following page

NAS Willow Grove, JRB   D-81

Horsham, PA 19090

991-1000   Operator   **215-443**-1000

↣↣↣↣↣↣↣↣ **Flights** ↣↣↣↣↣↣↣↣↣

Alexandria LA √	Ft Worth	North Island
Andrews√	Harrisburg √	Oceana
Atsugi 2/y	Jacksonville	Pensacola
Belvoir √	Jacksonville FL	Rota
Bragg	Key West	Scott
Brunswick	Langley √	Sigonella 2/y
Beaufort √	McGuire	Washington
Cherry Point	Millington TN	Wright Pat
Corpus Christi	Norfolk√	

Frequent flights to many destinations

Chance of seat ★★★★

Willow Grove (Concluded)

Navy

Commercial: Motel south on US61.
Aero Club: 773..2165
Ground Transport:
  Shuttle: To Dix housing from Snack Bar 1600 M-F, from Dix 0600 parking lot behind playground, AMID 6490.
  Commercial: SEPTA #55 Bus outside main gate to Willow Grove RR and Olney Ave station N Broad subway.
Philadelphia, 0600-0150 M-F, 0640-0150 Sa, 0725-0033 Su. 589-7852/4. Taxi 572-6100, 654-1313.

Flight Information:
  Terminal **6215/7** 0630-2300 Recording 6216. **OPS** 6192/6,6202 VR52 6556, V**R**64 6414, **VP66** 6605, 913AW Res (C130) 1073, Army **1585** 0730-1630
  Terminal open 0700-2300. Field closed 2300-0700.

	Break	Lunch	Dinner
Club		W-Su	
Galley	7d	7d	7d
Subway	0630-1430 xM		

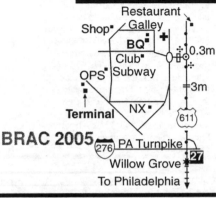

YUM (civilian) **NYL** (military)
Zulu-7 Distances walkable.

Quarters:
  BQ: Availability ★★★ x ★ Feb,**Mar**,Sept,Oct **3094** 24h. Rates: **O** $12sgl, $16dbl. DV $15sgl, $20dbl. Protocol 2226. **SNCO** $10per.
  TLF: ★★ x ★★★ weekends, **2262** 0800-2000 M-F, 0800-1630 SS. Reservations. Rate: $25unit. Building new TLF.
  Lake Martinez Rec A: Cabins ★★★★ x ★ weekend **2278**, 0730-1600 M-F, reservations, at site C 783-3422 0730-2200, 24h, no linens, utensils. **Rate:** Cabins $20unit, trailers $25unit. RV $4, EW $7. Tent $4. No dump. No pets in new cabins, trailers.

Ground Transport:
  In Yuma, Greyhound, Amtrak east **0258** MWSa, west **0013** MWF. Enterprise car rent (watch forcing insurance) 344-5444 0800-1800 M-F, 0900-1200 Sa but often not in office. Taxi 783-4444.

MCAS Yuma   D-94
Yuma, AZ 85369
269.2011   Operator   **928.269**.2011
➤➤➤➤➤➤➤ **Flights** ➤➤➤➤➤➤➤

Cherry Point	Nellis
El Toro	New Orleans
Fallon	North Island √
Grand Canyon NP √	Pendleton
Kaneohe Bay	29 Palms
Miramar √	

Chance of seat ★★★★

Flight Information:
  Terminal **2729** 0600-1630 M-F
  OPS **2326** 24h

	Break	Lunch	Dinner
O Club		M-F	
Burger King	0500-0100		

CONUS, GROUND TRANSPORT
ALL CONUS INSTALLATIONS OTHER THAN CIRCUITS
International DSN prefix for CONUS: 312.

Starting on page *ÆE103* are listings in alphabetical order of states with any installation or airport of use to Space-A travelers. All numbers in *italics* are references to pages for details. Each state listing is headed by a state map showing all installations and airports within that state with Space-A flights, quarters, or camping. Following maps are names in alphabetical order of all installations and included airports within each state. Should the details of an installation or airport be included in either Circuit, reference to that Circuit together with a page number is given. Details of other installations are given following their names. When several installations are in close proximity, an area billeting summary together with an area map showing locations and low-cost commercial transport is provided. Details, nevertheless, are listed in alphabetical order as if no area information were included.

Details of RV Camps, Rec A, or Rec C controlled by an installation are given in details of their controlling installation. If far enough from the controlling installations to so permit, they have their own map symbol with a page reference to the details of their controlling installations. Should such facilities be under their own control they are listed as separate installations.

FLIGHTS

Details for Air Force related installations with flights (AFB, AFS, ANGB, ARS) and airports regularly served by Space-A flights are in the Air Force Circuit tabbed section. Details for all Navy-related installations with flights (NAS, NAF, NS, MCAS) are in the Navy Circuit tabbed section. Details of all AF or Navy related installations with government quarters or camping but without flights are in this tabbed section as well as details of all Army and Coast Guard installations (with or without flights).

Under ((((**Flights** ((((destinations and days operated of scheduled flights are listed, e.g. Andrews WF *(*Wed *and* Fri). If hyphenated (W-F) means Wed *thru* Fri. Also listed are common destinations of unscheduled flights. Destinations served frequently are checked, e.g. Andrews√. Unusually high or low number of destinations or frequency of flights is noted. Chance of obtaining a seat by a Cat-VI on a selected flight is indicated by the number of stars under the list of destinations (★ 0-25%, ★★ 25-50%, ★★★ 50-75%, ★★★★ 75-100%). This same system is used to show expectation of obtaining quarters by walk-ins. Flight categories do not apply to lodging.

RECREATION AREAS

Recreation Areas (Rec A) or Centers (Rec C) with any form of lodging, camper or tent space are included. If linens, etc., are required that is specified. Rec Areas operating independently have their own separate listings. Those under the control of a major installation have their details with those installations. Independent Rec Areas or those remote from controlling installations are shown separately on state maps and on the CONUS maps. Trailer refers to an equipped, government-owned unit. They may be anything from mobile homes to pop-up units. Any deviation is given in details. The same applies to permanently located tents and similar shelters. Facilities for traveler-owned equipment follow **RV:** Unless otherwise indicated RV and tent spaces are available year round and have access to sewage dump, shower, and toilet. Hookup for campers or service to tent sites are as follows: E = Electricity, S = Sewer, T = Cable TV, W = Water. If more than one symbol applies, they are written in alphabetical order, e.g., ESW. Rec Areas use the same star system for showing availability as flights. Flight priorities do not apply.

EXPECTED AVAILABILITY OF QUARTERS OR RV SPACES

In details availability of lodging or RV spaces by walk-ins is expressed by the same system as used to show expected chance by a Cat-VI of obtaining a seat on a flight. Flight categories do not apply to lodging. On maps ■ ▨ indicate usually available, ● ◉ difficult periods, ▲ △ none. A light circle around such symbols indicate RV sites available, a heavy circle tent sites also.

Reservation numbers: For most Navy Lodges 800-NAVY-INN, most AF 888-235-6343, most

CONTINUED ON NEXT PAGE.

Army 800-GO-ARMY-1. The last is primarily for duty but may serve Space-A depending on the post.

GROUND ACCESS

On maps access by shuttle, bus, or train (some walking may be required) is indicated by ■▲, no such access by ▨◉△. When appropriate, shuttle and bus routes or stops are included on installation maps as well as RR stations. Map symbols are as follows: Shuttle stop ✛; Bus stop or station ✛; Combined bus and shuttle stop ✤; Rail station ◆. Shuttles are free unless otherwise indicated. Installation maps show driving access routes from major highways or nearest major town.

CONUS Maps

ID, MT, ND, MN, OR, WY, SD, NE

1	Cheyenne Airport	WY	Æ19
2	Ellsworth AFB	SD	Æ24
3	Gowen Field (Boise Airport)	ID	Æ25
4	Grafton, Camp Gilbert C	ND	Æ147
5	Grand Forks AFB	ND	Æ26
6	Kingsley Field	OR	Æ32
7	Lincoln Airport	NE	Æ35
8	Malmstrom AFB	MT	Æ39
9	Minneapolis Airport ARS	MN	Æ46
10	Minot AFB	ND	Æ46
11	Mountain Home AFB	ID	Æ47
12	Offutt AFB	NE	Æ49
13	Portland Airport	OR	Æ54
14	Rilea AFTC	OR	Æ148
15	Strike Dam (Mountain Home AFB)	ID	Æ47
16	Warren (Francis E.) AFB	WY	Æ169

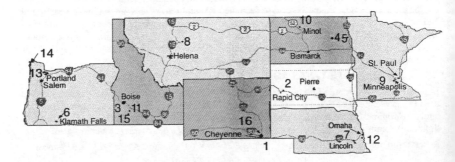

CONUS State Maps
NV, UT, CO, KS, AZ, NM, OK

1	Academy, USAF	CO	Æ118
2	Altus AFB	OK	Æ13
3	Cannon AFB	NM	Æ17
4	Carson, Fort	CO	Æ118
5	Davis-Monthan AFB	AZ	Æ19
6	Dugway PG (Michael AAF)	UT	Æ158
7	Fallon, NAS	NV	Æ75
8	Forbes Field	KS	Æ25
9	Fort Tuthill Rec Area	AZ	Æ37
10	Gila Bend AF Auxilary Field	AZ	Æ105
11	Hill AFB	UT	Æ28
12	Holloman AFB	NM	Æ28
13	Huachuca, Fort (Libby AAF)	AZ	Æ105
14	Indian Springs AFS	NV	Æ30
15	Kirtland AFB	NM	Æ32
16	Leavenworth, Fort (Sherman AAF)	KS	Æ130
17	Luke AFB	AZ	Æ37
18	McAlester AAP	OK	Æ147
19	McConnell AFB	KS	Æ43
20	Nellis AFB	NV	Æ48
21	Oklahoma City Airport (Will Rogers)	OK	Æ50
22	Peterson AFB	CO	Æ52
23	Riley, Fort (Marshall AAF)	KS	Æ131
24	Salt Lake City Airport	UT	Æ56
25	Sill, Fort (Henry Post AAF)	OK	Æ148
26	Sky Harbor (Phoenix) Airport	AZ	Æ53
27	Tinker AFB	OK	Æ62
28	Tooele Army Depot	UT	Æ159
29	Vance AFB	OK	Æ64
30	White Sands MR (Condron AAF)	NM	Æ142
31	Yuma, MCAS	AZ	Æ92
32	Yuma, PG (Laguna AAF)	AZ	Æ106

CONUS

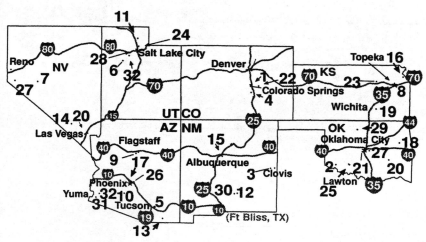

CONUS State Maps
IA, IL, IN, OH, MO, KY

1	Atterbury, Camp	**IN**	Æ130
2	Campbell, Fort	KY	Æ131
3	Columbus DCSC	OH	Æ147
4	Crane, NWSC	IN	Æ130
5	Great Lakes, NTC	IL	Æ129
6	Grissom ARS	IN	Æ27
7	Lake of the Ozarks	MO	Æ139
8	Leonard Wood, Fort	MO	Æ139
9	Louisville Airport	KY	Æ37
10	Mansfield Airport	OH	Æ39
11	Peoria Airport	IL	Æ52
12	Richard-Gebaur	MO	Æ139
13	Rickenbacker ANGB	OH	Æ55
14	Rock Island Arsenal	IL	Æ129
15	Saint Joseph Airport	MO	Æ61
16	Scott AFB	IL	Æ57
17	Sioux City ANGB	IA	Æ61
18	Whiteman AFB	MO	Æ66
19	Wright Patterson AFB	OH	Æ67

CONUS

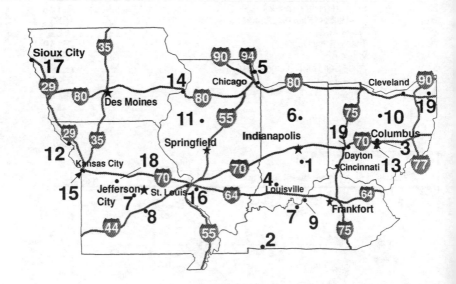

CONUS State Maps
WISCONSIN & MICHIGAN

1	Grayling, Camp	MI	Æ137
2	McCoy, Fort	WI	Æ168
3	Milwaukee Airport (Mitchell)	WI	Æ45
4	Point Betsie Recreation Cottages	MI	Æ137
5	Rawley Point Cottage, CG	WI	Æ169
6	Selfridge ANGB	MI	Æ59
7	Sherwood Point Cottage, CG	WI	Æ169
8	Volk Field	WI	Æ65

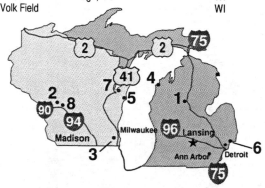

Washington

1	BANGOR, NSB	WA	Æ166
2	BREMERTON NSY	WA	Æ166
3	EVERETT, NS	WA	Æ166
4	FAIRCHILD AFB	WA	Æ24
5	GRAYS HARBOR, CGS	WA	Æ167
6	JIM CREEK, NRS	WA	Æ167
7	LEWIS, FORT	WA	Æ167
8	MCCHORD AFB	WA	Æ42
9	MURRAY, CAMP	WA	Æ167
10	PACIFIC BEACH CENTER	WA	Æ168
11	SEA-TAC AIRPORT	WA	Æ58
12	SNOMISH CO. (PAYNE FLD.) AIRPORT	WA	Æ166
13	WHIDBEY ISLAND, NAS	WA	Æ90

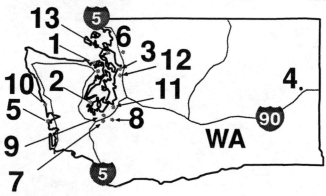

CONUS State Maps
WV, VA, & DC MAP

No.	Location	State	Code
1 C	A P Hill, Fort	VA	Æ162
2	Belvoir, Fort (Davidson AAF)	VA	Æ160
3	Bolling AFB (Anacostia, NS)	DC	Æ121
4	Charleston (Yaeger) Airport	WV	Æ18
5	Cheatham Annex, NSC	VA	Æ160
6	Dahlgren, NSWC	VA	Æ160
7	Dam Neck, FTC	VA	Æ161
8	Eustis, Fort (Felker AAF)	VA	Æ161
9	JAG School (Univ. of VA campus)	VA	Æ162
10	Langley AFB	VA	Æ33
11	Lee, Fort	VA	Æ162
12	Little Creek, NAB	VA	Æ163
13	Martinsburg Airport	WV	Æ40
14	McNair, Fort	DC	Æ121
15	Monroe, Fort	VA	Æ163
16	Myer, Fort	VA	Æ122
17	Norfolk, NAS, NS	VA	Æ83
18	Northwest, NSGA	VA	Æ163
19	Oceana, NAS	VA	Æ86
20	Pickett, Fort (Blackstone AAF)	VA	Æ164
21	Portsmouth, NSY	VA	Æ164
22	Quantico, MB	VA	Æ89
23	Richmond, DGSC	VA	Æ164
24	Story, Fort	VA	Æ165
25	Sugar Grove, NRS	WV	Æ168
26	Walter Reed Army Medical Center	DC	Æ122
27	Yorktown, CGTC	VA	Æ165
28	Yorktown, NWS	VA	Æ165

Map A

MAP B   National Capitol Area

Ft. Meade, MD

DC

Northern VA   Andrews AFB, MD

Washington D. C. (see Map B)

Charleston

Richmond

MAP C WV, VA & DC

VA

Norfolk (see Map A)

CONUS State Maps
NC, GA, SC, MAP

1	Albany, MCLB	GA	Æ125
2	Athens, NSCS	GA	Æ125
3	Beaufort, MCAS	SC	Æ72
4	Benning, Fort (Lawson AAF)	GA	Æ126
5	Bragg, Fort (Simmons AAF)	NC	Æ145
6	Cape Hatteras Rec Quarters, CG	NC	Æ145
7	Charleston AFB	SC	Æ18
8	Charlotte (Douglas) Airport	NC	Æ19
9	Cherry Point, MCAS	NC	Æ73
10	Dobbins ARB (NAS Atlanta)	GA	Æ20
11	Elizabeth City, CGSC	NC	Æ145
12	Fort Fisher Rec Area	NC	Æ146
13	Gillam, Fort	GA	Æ126
14	Gordon, Fort (Bush Field)	GA	Æ127
15	Hatteras Ferries	NC	Æ145
16	Jackson, Fort	SC	Æ151
17	Kings Bay, NSB	GA	Æ127
18	Lejeune, Camp	NC	Æ146
19	McPherson, Fort	GA	Æ128
20	Moody AFB	GA	Æ46
21	New River, MCAS	NC	Æ82
22	Parris Island, MCRD	SC	Æ151
23	Pope AFB	NC	Æ54
24	Robins AFB	GA	Æ56
25	Savannah (Travis Field) Airport	GA	Æ57
26	Seymour Johnson AFB	NC	Æ59
27	Shaw AFB	SC	Æ60
28	Stewart, Fort	GA	Æ128
29	Uchee Creek (Fort Benning)	GA	Æ126
30	Weston Lake Rec Area	SC	Æ151

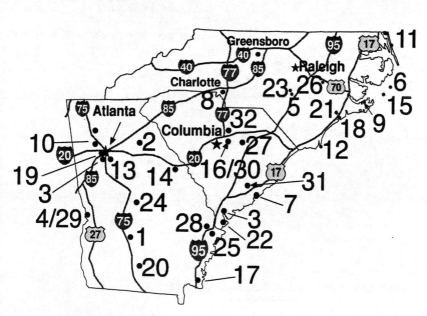

CONUS State Maps

1	Arnold EDC	TN	Æ152
2	Barksdale AFB	LA	Æ15
3	Birmingham Airport	AL	Æ16
4	Chaffee, Fort	AR	Æ106
5	Columbus AFB	MS	Æ19
6	Dauphine Island	AL	Æ103
7	Gulfport, NCB	MS	Æ138
8	Gunter AFB	AL	Æ103
9	Jackson Airport	MS	Æ30
10	Keesler AFB	MS	Æ31
11	Knoxville (McGee Tyson)	TN	Æ33
12	Lake Martin Rec Area	AL	Æ41
13	Little Rock AFB	AR	Æ35
14	Maxwell AFB	AL	Æ41
15	Memphis ANGB	TN	Æ45
16	Meridian Airport	MS	Æ45
17	Meridian, NAS	MS	Æ80
18	Mid-South, NSA	TN	Æ153
19	Mobile, CGATC	AL	Æ104
20	Nashville Airport	TN	Æ48
21	New Orleans, JRB	LA	Æ82
22	New Orleans, NSA	LA	Æ133
23	Pascagoula, NSF	MS	Æ138
24	Pine Bluff Arsenal	AR	Æ107
25	Polk, Fort	LA	Æ133
26	Redstone Arsenal	AL	Æ104
27	Rucker, Fort	AL	Æ104
28	Shelby, Camp	MS	Æ138

CONUS

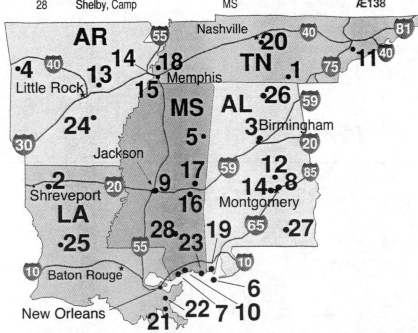

CONUS State Maps

1	Aberdeen PG (Phillips AAF)	MD	*Æ134*
2	Andrews AFB (Washington, NAF)	MD	*Æ13*
3	Baltimore-Washington Airport	MD	*Æ14*
4	Bethesda, Naval Medical Center	MD	*Æ121*
5	Carlisle Barracks (Army War College)	PA	*Æ149*
6	Curtis Bay, CGY	MD	*Æ135*
7	Detrick, Fort	MD	*Æ135*
8	Dix, Fort	NJ	*Æ140*
9	Dover AFB	DE	*Æ21*
10	Greater Wilmington Airport	DE	*Æ26*
11	Indian Head, NOS	MD	*Æ135*
12	Indiantown Gap, Fort (Muir AAF)	PA	*Æ149*
13	Lake Laurie Rec Area	PA	*Æ92*
14	Lakehurst, NAEC	NJ	*Æ79*
15	Martin, G. L. Airport (Warfield ANGB)	MD	*Æ65*
16	McGuire AFB	NJ	*Æ44*
17	Meade, Fort George G.	MD	*Æ135*
18	Monmouth, Fort	NJ	*Æ141*
19	New Cumberland AD	PA	*Æ149*
20	Patuxent River, NAS (NAWC)	MD	*Æ86*
21	Picatinny Arsenal	NJ	*Æ141*
22	Pittsburgh Airport	PA	*Æ53*
23	Solomons, Navy Rec Center	MD	*Æ136*
24	Tobyhanna AD	PA	*Æ150*
25	Willow Grove, JRB	PA	*Æ91*

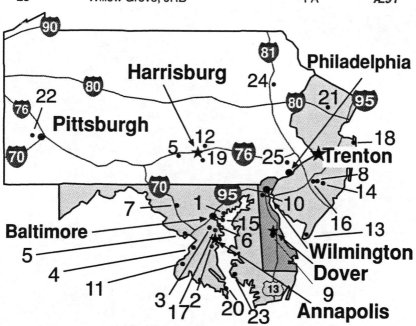

CONUS State Maps

CONUS

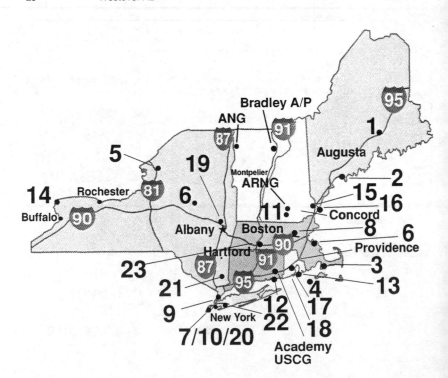

NOTES:

_____

_____

_____

_____

_____

_____

_____

_____

CONUS

Zulu-6

ALABAMA

On Æ16 Air Force Circuit **Birmingham Airport**

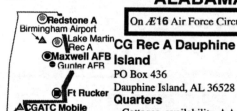

Redstone A
Birmingham Airport
Lake Martin Rec A
Maxwell AFB
Gunter AFB
Ft Rucker
CGATC Mobile
Dauphine Island CG Rec A

CG Rec A Dauphine Island
PO Box 436
Dauphine Island, AL 36528
Quarters
Cottages, availability ★★★★
x ★ summer **251.861.7113**
0800-2200. Reservations.
Rates: Summer $18-25unit,
winter $15-20unit, depending
on rank. RV $3, ESTW $8.
Tent $3.

Mobile
Grand Bay
Coden Bayou La Batre
Mississippi Sound
Intercoastal Waterway
Fort Gaines
Toll Ferry to 180
Dauphin Island Rec Area

Academy Distances
short, 0.4m BQ-
main gate. On base
prefix 6+XXXX.
AETC
Quarters:
University Inn:
Availability ★★
416.3360, 5501,
4611, 4656 24h.
AETC FY 07/08 Rates: **$24-42**
Ground Transport:
Bus xSu outside main gate, transfer to #7,10
for Maxwell.

Federal Dr 1.8m
M
1st
A D E Gas
2nd Comm
Club
BX
Bowl
BQ

231
3.2m
80
80
231
85

Gunter AFB D-94
Gunter Annex,
Maxwell AFB
Montgomery, AL 36114
596-1110 (Maxwell
Operator) **334-416**-1110

	Break	Lunch	Dinner	Brun
O Club		Tu	W-Sa	SS
NCO Club	M-F	M-F	xSu	Su
Bowl	M-F	7d	7d	

Retirees can eat in Dining Hall.

On Æ41, Air Force Circuit **Maxwell AFB**

ALABAMA (Concluded)

MOB

Distances short.
Ground Transport:

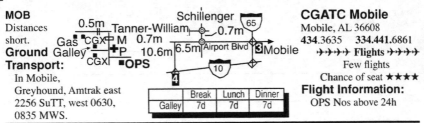

In Mobile, Greyhound, Amtrak east 2256 SuTT, west 0630, 0835 MWS.

	Break	Lunch	Dinner
Galley	7d	7d	7d

CGATC Mobile

Mobile, AL 36608
434.3635   **334**.441.6861
✈✈✈✈ **Flights** ✈✈✈✈
Few flights
Chance of seat ★★★★

Flight Information:

OPS Nos above 24h

HUA   On base prefix 6+XXXX

Distances walkable
x 4m BQ-OPS

Quarters:

BQ: Trailblazer Guest House
Availability ★ **838**.4130 **5713,8028** 24h. Rates: $25sgl+$5add per. Protocol 7135. Guest House: ★ M-F ★★★ SS. Rates: $22unit.

RV: ★★★ **4868,6854** 0930-1700, check in Outdoor Rec. RV, Tent EW $5 summer, $2.50 winter, no water winter.

Golf: 883-7977 **Holes**: 27 Redstone Golf Course Complex

Ground Transport:

Post Shuttle 0700-1500 M-F.
Commercial: Greyhound in Huntsville.

Redstone Arsenal D-8

Huntsville, AL 35898
746-0011   **256-876-2151**
✈✈✈✈ **Flights** ✈✈✈✈

Andrews	Hunter
Atlanta Airports	McCoy
Belvoir	Wright-Pat√
Benning√	

Chance of seat
★★★

Flight Information:

OPS **4299,4310** 0730-1630
M-Th 876.2186 0730-1530 F

	Break	Lunch	Dinner	Brun
O Club		M-F	Tu-Sa	Su
NCO Club		M-F	Tu-Sa	
Snack		0600-2400		

OZR

Distances long, 4.5m BQ-OPS.

Quarters:

BQ: Availability ★★★★ x ★ during conferences **D** 3780/2. Reserve 7d in advance. Rates: $15,17room, handles lake cottages $20sgl+$4add per. Protocol 255.1132/1025.

Guest House: 2888 0645-2200. Rate: $30unit.

Post Rec A: March-October **4305** 0730-1615 M-F, Sa 0800-1600, Su closed. Hunting season, check in Pro Shop. RV EW, dump $12, Tent $12, $50 /week. Golden Age, Access, or Eagle discount is 50%.

Commercial: Motels 1.3m from BQ.

Golf: 255-9539/2449 **Holes**: 27 Silver Wings Golf Complex

Ground Transport:

Post Shuttle 0800-1630 M-F, 4188.
Commercial: Bus: Tallahassee 0910,1950; Montgomery 0825,1815. PX car rent 598-2231, 0900-1700 M-F, 0900-1500 Sa. Taxi 598-3300,4464.

Ft Rucker   D-94

(Cairns AAF)
Ozark, AL 36362
558-1110   **334.255.1110**
SDO 334.255.3400
✈✈✈✈ **Flights** ✈✈✈✈

Atlanta	Knox
Hartsfield	Langley
Belvoir	Maxwell
Benning	Orlando
Bragg	Pensacola
Campbell	Pope
Gordon	Scott
Hood	Tampa

Chance of seat ★★★★

Flight Information:

OPS **2314** 24h.
Schedules 3800

	Break	Lunch	Dinner	Brun
O Club	W-F	M-F	Tu-Sa	Su
NCO Club		Tu-F	W-Sa	
Bowl	xSu§	7d	7d	
Snack		0630-2000 M-F		

ARIZONA

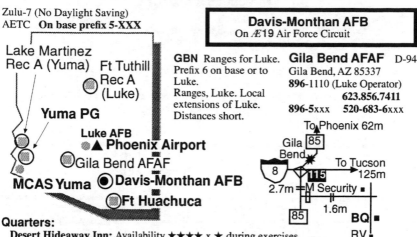

Zulu-7 (No Daylight Saving)
AETC **On base prefix 5-XXX**

Davis-Monthan AFB
On Æ19 Air Force Circuit

Lake Martinez
Rec A (Yuma)   Ft Tuthill
     Rec A
     (Luke)
Yuma PG

Luke AFB
  ▲ **Phoenix Airport**
  ○Gila Bend AFAF
MCAS Yuma ◉ **Davis-Monthan AFB**
  ○Ft Huachuca

GBN Ranges for Luke.
Prefix 6 on base or to
Luke.
Ranges, Luke. Local
extensions of Luke.
Distances short.

Gila Bend AFAF D-94
Gila Bend, AZ 85337
896-1110 (Luke Operator)
       623.856.7411
896-5xxx   **520-683-6**xxx

To Phoenix 62m
Gila 85
Bend
   8   115 To Tucson
              125m
2.7m = M Security ■
          1.6m
   85   BQ ■
              RV ■

Quarters:
Desert Hideaway Inn: Availability ★★★★ x ★ during exercises
290 0700-1600 M-F, other hrs keys at Security, 6220. AETC FY 07/08 Rates: **$24-42**
RV: ★★★★ x ★★ winter, check in at BQ when open, other hrs Security, 6200. RV $3,
ESTW $7.
Commercial: Motels in Gila Bend.

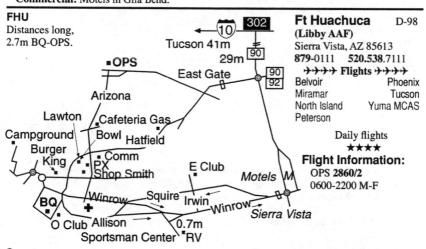

FHU
Distances long,
2.7m BQ-OPS.

Tucson 41m
       29m
 ■OPS
    East Gate
  Arizona
Lawton /Cafeteria Gas
Campground\ Bowl Hatfield
 Burger   ■Comm
  King ■PX   E Club
    Shop Smith   Motels M
 ■Winrow Squire Irwin
BQ   Winrow Sierra Vista
 O Club Allison 0.7m
  Sportsman Center ■RV

Ft Huachuca D-98
(Libby AAF)
Sierra Vista, AZ 85613
879-0111   **520.538.**7111
↣↣↣↣ **Flights** ↣↣↣↣
Belvoir   Phoenix
Miramar   Tucson
North Island Yuma MCAS
Peterson

Daily flights
★★★★
Flight Information:
OPS **2860/2**
0600-2200 M-F

Quarters:
BQ: Availability ★★★★ **(D 821, C 533)**
2222,5361,5950 24h. Rates: BOQ $49sgl+$2add per,
DV (O5 up) $44sgl+$2add per. Protocol (D 821, C
533) 1232. BEQ $44sgl+$2add per. Guest House $30-
25unit. BOQ, BEQ not available unless other lodging
is full. Barracks Manager 533.3083.

	Break	Lunch	Dinner	Brun
O Club		M-F	W-F	Su
E Club		M-F		Su
Cafeteria	M-F	M-F		
Bowl	xSu	7d	7d	
Burger	0600-2200 M-F			
King	0700-2300 Sa			
	0800-2200 Su			

Campground: ★★★★ Apache Flats RV Resort
520.533.**1335**. Check in at campground. RV EW $10, ESW $13. Two mountain cabins
$25unit 533-7085.
RV: ★★★★ **1335,7085** 1000-1700 M-F. Check in Sportsman Center **533.7085**. RV $3, EW

ARIZONA (Continued)
Ft Huachuca (Continued)

$7, ESW $10, Tent $3, no restroom, shower.
Golf: 533-7092/7088 **Holes**: 18 Mountain View Golf Course
Commercial: Motel outside main gate.
Ground Transport:
Shuttles 0645-1615 M-F, Yellow to main gate, Red to OPS, meet at ✚. Pay shuttle 459-1890,
also to Sierra Vista.
Commercial: Greyhound in Sierra Vista. Limo to Tucson Airport 458-3860. Car rent with
pick up, 458-3668. Taxi 458-3860. **PX** car rent 458-4800.

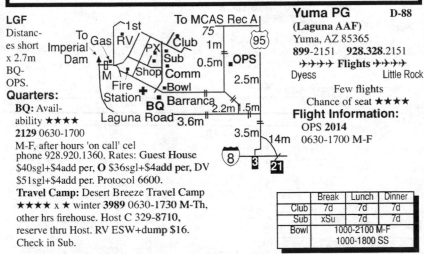

	On Æ37 Air Force Circuit	**Luke AFB**
On Æ53 Air Force Circuit	**Phoenix Airport**
On Æ93 Navy Circuit	**MCAS Yuma**

LGF
Distances short x 2.7m BQ-OPS.

To Imperial Dam

1st
To MCAS Rec A
75
Gas RV PX Club 1m 95
Sub 0.5m ▪OPS
M Shop Comm 2.5m
Fire ▪Bowl
Station ✚ BQ Barranca 2.2m 1.5m
Laguna Road 3.6m
3.5m 14m
8 3 21

Quarters:
BQ: Availability ★★★★
2129 0630-1700
M-F, after hours 'on call' cel
phone 928.920.1360. Rates: Guest House
$40sgl+$4add per, **O** $36sgl+$4add per, DV
$51sgl+$4add per. Protocol 6600.
Travel Camp: Desert Breeze Travel Camp
★★★★ x ★ winter **3989** 0630-1730 M-Th,
other hrs firehouse. Host C 329-8710,
reserve thru Host. RV ESW+dump $16.
Check in Sub.

Yuma PG   **D-88**
(Laguna AAF)
Yuma, AZ 85365
899-2151   **928.328.**2151
➤➤➤➤ **Flights** ➤➤➤➤
Dyess   Little Rock
Few flights
Chance of seat ★★★★
Flight Information:
OPS **2014**
0630-1700 M-F

	Break	Lunch	Dinner
Club	7d	7d	7d
Sub	xSu	7d	7d
Bowl	1000-2100 M-F		
	1000-1800 SS		

Ft Chaffee
Camp Robinson
Zulu-6
ARKANSAS

Little Rock AFB
540
Ft Smith 8
Pine Bluff Arsenal
Res & NG training
22
Ft Smith ▯M
4th Ave
RV▪ ▪BQ
PX
Snack ▪Club

Ft Chaffee   **D-8**
Ft Smith, AR 72905
962-3170 INFO **479.484.**3170

	Break	Lunch	Dinner
Club		7d	
Golf	0730-1500		

Quarters:
BQ: Availability ★★★★ x ★ summer,
Res weekends. 2252, **2917** 0730-1530
M-Sa, 0700-1530 Sa. List any time.
Rates: $19-33, cottage $25-33. **Reserve**
by fax 2259 with credit ,card.
RV Park: ★★★★ x ★ summer, check
in with billeting. RV ESW $8, dump available.

On Æ35, Air Force Circuit   **Little Rock AFB**

Distances walkable.

Ground Transport:

BQ: Availability ★★★★
3008, 2700 0630-1700
M-Th, Rate **O** $26 per
couple. For arrival other
hrs, keys left with Operation Center, Administration Bldg, 2700.

Golf: 540-3028 **Holes**: 9
Pine Bluff Golf Course

Pine Bluff Arsenal D-84
Pine Bluff, AR 71611
966-3000   **870-540**-3000

Operation Center

345   Gas

345   PX   BQ

65   256

270   Pine Bluff

	Break	Lunch	Dinner
Club	M-F	M-F	M-F

Quarters:

BQ: Availability ★★★★ x ★ summer &
drill periods. C 501.212.5274
Rates: $15-19
RV Park: 501.212.5274 (lodging office)
★★★★ x ★ summer & drill periods,
check in with billeting. RV ESW $9,
dump available.

Golf: 791-8592 **Holes:** 9
Duffers Club Golf Course

Exit I40 on Burns Park (Exit 150) to Military Drive. Follow signs approximately two miles to camp.

Camp Robinson NGB
North Little Rock, AR 72118
962.5100   501.212.5100

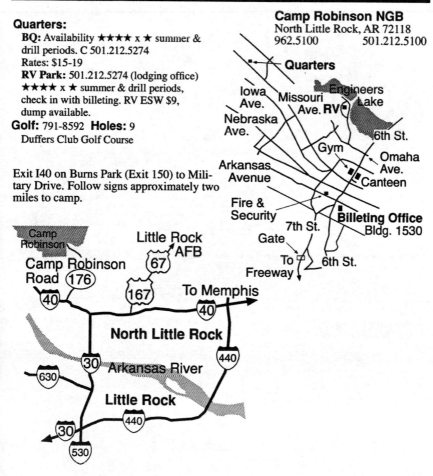

Quarters

Iowa Ave. Missouri Ave. **RV** Engineers Lake

Nebraska Ave.

6th St.

Gym   Omaha Ave.

Arkansas Avenue   Canteen

Fire & Security   7th St. **Billeting Office**
Gate   Bldg. 1530

To ⌂ 6th St.
Freeway

Camp Robinson

Little Rock AFB
67

Camp Robinson Road (176)
40   167

To Memphis
40

North Little Rock

30 Arkansas River 440

630

Little Rock
440

30
530

CONUS

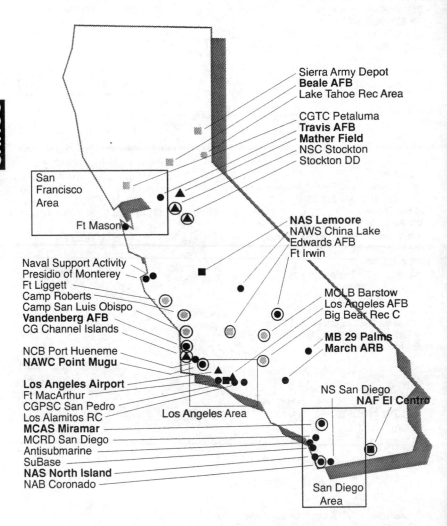

Sierra Army Depot
Beale AFB
Lake Tahoe Rec Area

CGTC Petaluma
Travis AFB
Mather Field
NSC Stockton
Stockton DD

San
Francisco
Area

Ft Mason

NAS Lemoore
NAWS China Lake
Edwards AFB
Ft Irwin

Naval Support Activity
Presidio of Monterey
Ft Liggett
Camp Roberts
Camp San Luis Obispo
Vandenberg AFB
CG Channel Islands

MCLB Barstow
Los Angeles AFB
Big Bear Rec C

MB 29 Palms
March ARB

NCB Port Hueneme
NAWC Point Mugu

Los Angeles Airport
Ft MacArthur
CGPSC San Pedro
Los Alamitos RC
MCAS Miramar
MCRD San Diego
Antisubmarine
SuBase
NAS North Island
NAB Coronado

Los Angeles Area

NS San Diego
NAF El Centro

San Diego
Area

DAG On base at Barstow 577.XXXX
Distances walkable,
1.8m Gate to Gate.

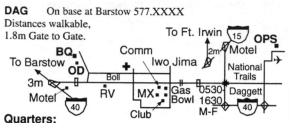

Quarters:

BQ: Availability ★★★★ x ★ June-July **6418** 0700-1530 M-F, reservations, for arrival other hrs, call keys with OD 6611. Rate: $25unit, DV 35unit. RV EW $10.

Golf: 6431 **Holes:** 9 Tees 'N Trees Golf Course
Commercial: Motel outside gate.

Ground Transport:

Dial-a-Ride 256-0311. Greyhound, Amtrak east 1221,1420 SuTT, west 0359,1140 MWSa.

MCLB Barstow D-94
Barstow, CA 92311
282-6211 **760-577**-6211

Daggett Airport
See Ft Irwin Æ110
No DSN 760.254.2542

↦↦↦ **Flights** ↦↦↦

Andrews	Irwin	Yuma
Belvoir	Las Vegas	
Dobbins	Riley	
Hood	Scott	

Chance of seat ★★★★

Flight Information:
Army OPS 760.380.0205
D 470.0205 (Irwin)

	Break	Lunch	Dinner
Club		M-F	W-F
Bowl	1200-1800 WTh		
	1600-2200 F		
	1200-2200 SS		

On Æ16, Air Force Circuit	**Beale AFB**
On Æ73, Navy Circuit	**NAWS China Lake**

C-130E

5 RV spaces suitable for largest units. **984.7705** Reservations numbers to right 0800-1630, ★★★★. Report to CG Station. EW $5. No restroom, showers on RV side but available in CG Station. RV spaces backed against busy road. Well suited for long-term occupancy.

CG Station Channel Islands
Oxnard, CA 93035-8399
Fax 805-984-1842 **805-985**-9822
Also ANGS **D** 893.7000
Hawaii 1/m

Adjacent to NCB Port Hueneme Æ114 with complete facilities. Closest gates not 24h.

Distances short. On base prefix 7. AT&T direct.

Quarters:

BOQ: Availability ★★★ x ★ M-Th, Res weekends **3860** Fax 3475 24h. Rates: $13sgl +$3add per, DV $29sgl+$7add per. Reserve 24h in advance.

BEQ: ★★★★ (no dependents) **3494/5/6** 24h. Fax 3475. Rates: $2.50 (open bay), $6per, E9 suite $12per.

RV Park: ★★★★ C **522.8680** 0800-1930, reservations. RV EW $17 14 nite limit.

Marina: C 522-8680/8681 Fiddlers Cove Marina & RV Park

Ground Transport:

#901 Bus 0533-0108 M-F, 0544-0108 SS, to North Island and downtown, transfer to trolley at Imperial for NS, on Broadway to #20 for Miramar. Trolley to Old Town, transfer to #28 Bus for Subase, Antisubmarine, to #8 Bus to MCRD xSu. Info 233-3004. See transit diagram Æ115.

NAB Coronado D-80
San Diego, CA 92155
577-2011 **619-437**-2011
North Island OOD 545.8123

To North Island & San Diego

Gas Shop

McDonald's ■ ■NX
✚ ■Bowl
BOQ ■ ■BEQ
■RV ■Club

#901 Bus 1.5m 0.3m

	Break	Lunch	Dinner	Brun
Club		M-F		Su
BOQ	7d	7d		
McDon	0600-2200			
Bowl	0700-2100 M-F			
	0900-2100 SS			

Distances short.
Quarters:
BQ: Availability ★★★★ x ★★ Res weekend (3d)
Army 5091 0600-1900 M-F, 0700-1600 SS, reserve. 888-719-8886. For arrival other hrs, SDO. Rates:
$25-45sgl+$2add per.
Navy Lodge 831.376.6133
Lake Tahoe: Condos,
motel rooms, call Outdoor
Rec at **5506,6133** 1030-
1400,
1500-1800 M-F. See Lake
Tahoe *Æ111*.
Golf: C 656-2167 Holes: 18
Monterey Pines Golf Course
[Naval Post Graduate School] 1250 Garden Road
Ground Transport:
Shuttle to Travis 0400, Ar 0700, Returns 1500, Ar 1800.
Buses on post and nearby.

#15 Bus Pine
Taylor BQ Lighthouse
Gas
Outdoor Rec
Club
PX Tunnel
Franklin Delmonte Naval Post
Pacific
To 'Language School'
Graduate School

Defense Language D-8 Institute
(Language School)
(formerly known as
Presidio of Monterey)
Monterey, CA 93940
878-5000   **831-242**-5000

	Break	Lunch	Dinner
Club		Tu-F	FSa
PX	1030-1900 M-F		
	1030-1700 SS		

On *Æ22*, Air Force Circuit	**Edwards AFB**
On *Æ74*, Navy Circuit	**NAF El Centro**

BYS,DAG Field training, isolated. Distances short x 4m
BQ-OPS, 1.2m BQ-RV.
Quarters:
BQ: Availability ★★★ x
★ summer, mid winter,
lodge, trailers **C**
386.4040 24h,
reservations ac-
cepted for same
day.
Rate: $36unit.
O6 up thru pro-
tocol 4223.
RV: C 3434 1200-1930 M-F, 0800-1200 Sa, RV, Tent
W $5.
Ground Transport:
Shuttle 0645-0800, 1430-1645 M-F, Transportation
motor pool 4156. Free taxi M-F 8294. Bus to Barstow
1800 7d, also 1400 SS, 2200 F-Su.

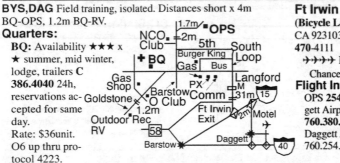
1.7m OPS
NCO 2m
Club 5th South
Burger King Loop
BQ Gas Bus
Gas Langford
Shop PX M
Goldstone Barstow Comm 31m 15
O Club Ft Irwin Motel
1.2m Exit
Outdoor Rec 58
RV Daggett
Barstow 40

Ft Irwin D-8
(Bicycle Lake AAF)
CA 923103
470-4111   **760-380**-4111
✈✈✈✈ **Flights** ✈✈✈✈
Chance of seat ★★★★
Flight Information:
OPS **254.3084/5** at Dag-
gett Airport *Æ109*,
760.380.4320 at Bicycle.
Daggett Airfield **C**
760.254.2542. See Barstow.

	Break	Lunch	Dinner
O Club		M-F	Tu-Sa
NCO Club		M-F	xSu
Burger King	0630-2300 xSu		
	0800-2200 Su		

Distances short.
Quarters:
BOQ: Admiral
Kidd Inn, ★★
5382 24h. Rate: $10-25, DV $30.
BEQ: ★ **1595** 24h. Rates: E1-4 (no dependents)
$10per. E5 up $14per, suite $21unit.
Ground Transport:
#28 Bus to Subase, Trolley. #22/3 Bus to Airport,
downtown, M-F. Ferry to North Island 0525-0755.
1520-1726 M-F. See transit diagram *Æ115*.

	Break	Lunch	Dinner
Cafe	M-F	M-F	SuTh
McDonald's	0600-2400		

Fleet Antisubmarine D-80
San Diego, CA 92147
524-1011   **619-524**-1011

To Old Town
209 Transit Center
#28 Bus To Airport, Downtown
Rosecrans Nimitz North Harbor Drive
M #22/3 Bus
To Subase BQ McDonald's
Ferry Cafe

CGS 2-Apartment A-Frame Cottages Lake Tahoe, Tahoe City, CA 96145 **530.583**.7438/4433, reserve, 12d limit. Availability H. Rates: By rank $15-30 1 bedroom, $30-45 2 bedroom. Check in at office.

CG Support Center Alemeda
510.437.3580 (formerly handled by Oakland AD) (BQ) 24h, reserve up to 6m in advance. Keys may be picked up not more than 3d in advance or mailed outside local area. No linen, bedding, towels, paper, cleaning supplies, firewood. **Rates:** $150 deposit. 1d stay $90unit Su-Th, $105unit FSa, 2-5d stay Su-Th $65unit. Weekly $600. Check in after 1300, check out before 1100. Both condos 3-bedroom with washer dryer, Tahoe Keys 2-bath, Lake Forest 2.5 baths. No pets in any of the above.

Defense Language Institute, CA 93940 **Outdoor Rec D 878-6133, C 831.242.5506,6133** 1030-1400, 1500-1800 M-F has condos $45-125/nt.unit (5-8 persons), motel $45-70unit (4 per) in south Lake Tahoe area. $50 Deposit.

Lake Tahoe Lodging
Coast Guard and Navy

On Æ79, Navy Circuit **NAS Lemoore**

HGT
Distances walkable x to RV.
Quarters:

BQ: Availability ★★★ during tests **3066, 2108, 2128** 0800-1630 M-F, other hrs call, keys left with police, 2613. Reserve then call 2d before arrival.
Rates: $17sgl+$5add per communal, $27,32sgl+$5add per private bath.
RV: ★★★★ x ★ hunting season **1205,2271,2928** variable hrs, register at Outdoor Rec. RV. Tent $3, W $5. Pet $1. No dump, shower, discharge of firearms.

Ft Hunter Liggett
Jolon, CA 93928
359-xxxx   481-386-xxxx

	Break	Lunch	Dinner
Club	M-F	M-F	F
Bowl		1400-2200 Tu-F	

SLI
Res Center
Distances short,
0.3m BQ-OPS.
Quarters:

BQ: Availability ★★ x ★ summer, drill weekends **2124/6/60** 0800-1630 Su-W, 0600-1800 Th, 0600-200 F&Sa Rate: $19-26sgl by rank, DV $29sgl, all +1/2 add per.

Ground Transport:
#50 Bus east to Anaheim (Amtrak), west transfer to Long Beach transit center, then train to downtown or #232 Bus to LAX airport.

Los Alamitos AFRC
Los Alamitos, CA 90720
972-2000 562.795.2000
↦↦↦↦ **Flights** ↦↦↦↦
Fresno   Mather
Miramar   Phoenix
North Island
Infrequent flights
Chance of seat ★★★★
Flight Information:
OPS **2571**
0600-2200 Tu-F
0730-1600 SMS

Snack	0700-1400	xM

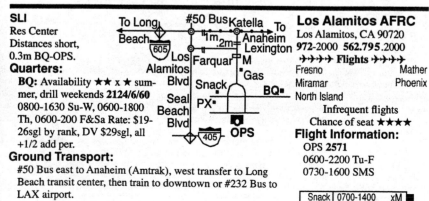

CONUS

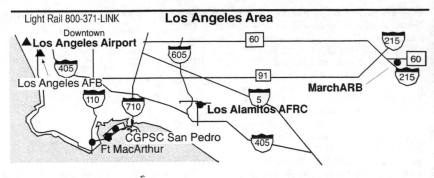

Light Rail 800-371-LINK **Los Angeles Area**

	Page	D	C	Quarters Summary	
Los Alamitos AFRC	111	972	310-795	2125 0800-1630 xF, 0800-2000 F	■
Ft MacArthur	112	833	310-363	8296 0500-2400 M-F, 0600-2100 SS	■
March ARB	40	947	909-655	5241 24h	■
CGPSC San Pedro	117		310-514	6450 0730-1530 M-F	▨

Quarters:

BQ: Fort MacArthur Inn Availability ★★★★ x ★ April-Sept **8296** 0600-2000. Rates: $29per, family $33, Reservations 24h, DV $39per. O6 up thru protocol 8119.

Ground Transport:

Shuttle: LA AFB 0600 M-F.
Commercial: #446 Bus to Union Station, change at City Hall to #496 for March. MAX3 Bus to LA AFB rush hrs.

Ft MacArthur   D-94

San Pedro, CA 90731
833-1110   (LA AFB
Operator) **310-363**-1110

Gaffey #446 Bus
Coast BQ■
Defense
Museum   M
12-1600 SaSu
36 26 Pacific
Korean Bell

On Æ40, Air Force Circuit   **March ARB**

Hints to increase financial travel security

1. Only print your initials instead of first and last name on checks.
2. Put your work phone # on your checks instead of your home phone.
3. If you have a PO Box use that instead of your home address.
4. Never have your SS# printed on your checks.
5. Place the contents of your wallet on a photocopy machine, do both sides of each license, credit card, etc. and all of the account numbers and phone numbers to call and cancel. You will know what you had in your wallet. Keep the photocopy in a safe place. Carry a photocopy of your passport when traveling either here or abroad.
6. To limit the damage in case of theft cancel credit cards immediately. The key is having the toll free numbers and your card numbers handy so you know whom to call. Keep those where you can find them easily.
7. File a police report immediately in the jurisdiction where it was stolen, this proves to credit providers you were diligent, and is a first step toward an investigation (if there ever is one).
8. Call the three national credit reporting organizations immediately to place a fraud alert on your name and Social Security number. Equifax: 1-800-525-6285; Experian (formerly TRW): 1-888-397-3742; Trans Union: 1-800-680-7289 Social Security Administration (fraud line): 1-800-269-0271

Zulu-8

To Sacramento
Watt Ave 4m

50

#72 Bus

In ANG hangar
east of OPS

OPS■

Mather Field

NG C12 Flight Coordinator
(Fixed wing scheduling)   916-854-3814

➤➤➤➤➤➤➤➤➤ **Flights** ➤➤➤➤➤➤➤➤➤

Fresno   Paseo Robles
Gulfport   San Diego
Los Alamitos   San Luis Obispo
Monterey

| On Æ81 Navy Circuit | **MCAS Miramar** |

Quarters:

BOQ: Availability ★ **2060/9** 24h. List
30d in advance. Assigned 1500. Rates: **O**
$15sgl+$3add per, DV $33sg+$6add per,
$25sgl+$6add per. **E** in BOQ.

Golf: 656-2167 **Holes:** 18 Monterey
   Pines Golf Course
   Commercial: Motels nearby,

Aero Club: 831-372-7033 Monterey Navy
   Flying Club 1600 Airport Road Monterey Airport

Marina: C 656-7953/2597/2159 Blue Water
   Cove Marina

Naval Post Graduate School D-8

Monterey, CA 93943
756.2441   No operator **831.656**.2441/2

During break periods limited services.

	Break	Lunch	Dinner	Brun
_O Club	xSu	M-F	7d	Su
E Club	M-F	M-F		
Snack	0900-1630 xSu			

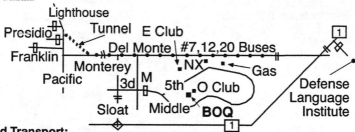

Ground Transport:

Base shuttle around base and main housing area. Presidio of Monterey/Defense Language
Institute (POM/DLI) shuttle picks of at NPS. Buses on Delmonte.

RV:Oct-Apr ★★★-★★★★,other ★ W,S,E,30&50A,I laundry & shower

Rates: $22 full, $18 partial, max. two pets allowed. Reservations: Made by phone or mail for
14 d plus 7 if available 4029.

Attention Travelers with RV and Tents

Hopefully all essential information has been included such as phone numbers, hours answered,
rates, and maps showing access from nearby major highways. Availability of obtaining a site
when arriving without a reservation is given when known. But there may be other matters those
traveling in this manner feel should be added. If so, please let us know. You can help other RV and
tent travelers by sending in changes or additions. Information of special interest to RV travelers
is always welcome.

| On Æ84, Navy Circuit | **NAS North Island** |
| On Æ87, Navy Circuit | **MB Camp Pendleton** |

CGTC Petaluma
Petaluma, CA 94952
707-765-7215

Coast Guard Training
Distances short,
0.6m BQ-main gate.

Quarters:
BQ: Availability
★★★★ **7248** 0900-
1900 M-F, no provision
for arrival other hrs. Rates: E4 up and **O**
$30 room, DV (O5 up) $35room, E1-3 $25 room.
Campsite: Reservations (Gym) 7348, check in BQ RV $16 EW&Cable. Tent $3.
Ground Transport:
Car rent 7340 0730-1630.

	Break	Lunch	Dinner
Club			Pizza
Deli	0700-2000 M-F		
	1100-2000 SS		

On Æ88, Navy Circuit **NAWC Point Mugu**

NCB Port Hueneme D-88
Naval Construction Bn
Distances walkable,
0.7m E Club-O Club.
(Naval Base Ventura County, Port
Hueneme)
Port Hueneme, CA 93043
551-4711 **805-982**-4711

Quarters:
BOQ: Gold Coast Inn. Availability
★★★ x ★ Res
weekends, **5785/6025**
24h. Assigned 1800. Rates: $14sgl
+$3add per, DV $29sgl +$3add per. O6 up thru proto-
col 2058.
BEQ ★ (no dependents) 24h. Rate: $4per.
Golf: 2620 **Holes**: 18 SEEBEE GOLF COURSE
Navy Lodge ★★★★ **C 985**-2624 0800-2100. Fax
985-7364. Rates: $48,54unit.
RV: CG Channel Islands, Æ109.
Commercial: Motels in Oxnard.

Ground Transport:
#3 Bus on Ventura to Tran-
sit Center 0643-1856, info
487-4222, Vista Bus to Pt
Mugu. Greyhound 487-2706,
Amtrak in Oxnard north
1106,1318.1657.1937, south
0818,1015,1500, 1650,1905.
Taxi 483-2444.

	Break	Lunch	Dinner
O Club		M-F	W-Sa
E Club		M-F	7d
McDonald's	0530-2100 M-F		
	0600-2100 Sa		
	0700-2000 Su		

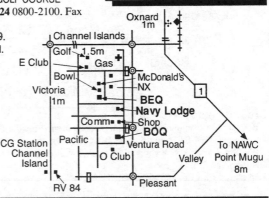

Presidio of Monterey is now named Defense Language Institute (Language School) and is
listed under **Defense Language Institute**.

Camp Roberts Army NG
CA 93451
949-8210 **805-238**-3100

National Guard 5+XXXX on post.
Distances short x 2.8m to RV.

Quarters:
BQ: Availability ★★★★ x ★ sum-
mer **8312** 0800-1630 M-F, reserva-
tions. Rate: $15per.
RV: Reserve, check in at BQ. RV.
Tent ESW $10.
No commercial close.

Snack	0730-1300

CALIFORNIA (Continued)

San Diego Area

Buses and trolley interconnect all bases. Vans between MCRD, North Island and downtown Broadway. Almost always billets are available somewhere.

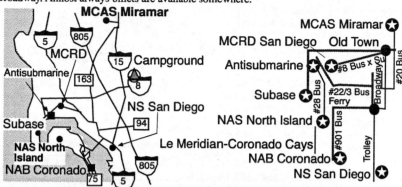

very highFor on station or interstate dialing, prefix last digit of DSN prefix. Bus 233-3004.

	Page	D	C	Quarters Summary` NL = Navy Lodge
MCRD	116	524	619-524	4401 24h
NAB Coronado	109	577	619-437	O 3860 24h, E (no dependents) 3496 24h
Fleet Antisubmarine	110	524	619-524	O 5382 24h, E 1595 24h
MCAS Miramar	81	577	619-537	1172,4233 24h, Navy Lodge 4855 24h NL
NAS North Island	84	735	619-545	O 7545 24h, E 9552 24h, Navy Lodge 6940
NS San Diego	115	526	619-556	O 8156, E 8672. NL C 234-6142 all 24h NL
Subase	116	553	619-553	O 9381 24h, E (no depen.) 7533 24h

Naval Station   On station prefix 6

Distances walkable.

Quarters:

BQ: O: Availability ★★★ x ★ summer **8156/9,8762** 24h, assigned 1800 Rates: $10per, DV $19per. Protocol 2400.

E: ★★★★ (dependents only E7 up) **556.8672/3** 24h. Rates: $10sgl+$2add per.

Navy Lodge ★★★★ C **234-6142** 24h, list starts 0700, assigned 1800.. Fax 238-2704. Rate: $45sgl room, $51unit.

Admiral Baker Campground reservations **5525** 0900-1630, check in office. RV $8,10, EW $10,12.

Golf: 556.7502/5162 **Holes:** 36 ADMIRAL BAKER GOLF COURSE **Holes:** 9 NAVAL STATION GOLF COURSE

Commercial: Motel on Main St.

Ground Transport:

Shuttle: To ships 0545-1730 M-F.

Commercial: Trolley to downtown, for North Island, Coronado transfer to #901 Bus at Imperial, for Miramar transfer to #20 Bus. For Subase, Antisubmarine, trolley to Old Town then #28 Bus. #8 to MCRD x Su. Vans Pacific Fleet Station to downtown.

NS San Diego   D-80

San Diego, CA 92136

526.0400 619-556-1011

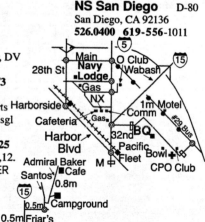

	Break	Lunch	Dinner
O Club		M-F	Su
CPO Club		Tu-F	Tu-Sa
Bowl	7d	7d	7d
Cafeteria	0700-2100 M-F		
	0700-1900 SS		

very high**115**

Marine Corps Recruit Depot On base prefix 4.
Distances walkable.

Quarters:

BQ 524.4401 Availability ★★★ x
★★ weekends **0117/6451** 24h. Rates:
O $15sgl+$5add per, $20+5 suite, DV
$30sgl+$7add per. Protocol 8710/2. **E**
$15sgl+$5add per.

Ground Transport:

#28 Bus to Subase or Old Town Transit
Center. #8 Bus xSu to Old Town. Transfer
at Old Town to trolley for downtown and
all installations except Miramar. For
Miramar transfer to a bus to Fashion Valley
then to #20.

**Dining hall allows retirees to each for $1.60
(Breakfast); $3.25 (Lunch and Dinner)**

MCRD San Diego D-80
San Diego 92140
524-1011   **619-524**-1011

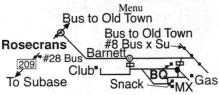

See transit map for San Diego Æ115.

	Break	Lunch	Dinner	Brun
Club		M-F	Tu-F	Su
Snack	0600-2200			

Distances short. On base prefix 3.

Quarters: AT&T direct

Availability ★★★★ x ★ Res weekend, **BOQ 9381** 24h, assigned 1800. Rates: $15sgl+$5add per, suites $25+5, DV $30.
BEQ 9381 24h. Rate:$15+5add per.

Ground Transport:

#28 Bus to Antisubmarine, MCRD Su,
Old Town Transit Center, change there for all other
installations,NS,MCRD xSu and downtown, 0519-0022 M-F,
0515-1240 SS. Info 233-3004.

Subase San Diego D-80
San Diego, CA 92106-3521
553-1011   **619-553**-1011

To Old Town
Transit Center

	Break	Lunch	Dinner
O Club		Tu-F	
Galley	7d	7d	7d
E Club	1100-2100 M-F		
McDon	0600-2100 M-F		
	0700-2100 SS		

San Francisco Area

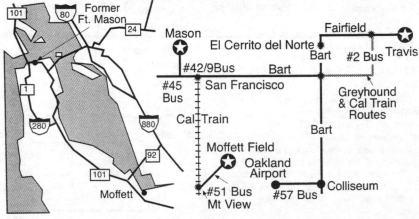

NG training, distances long. Dial 6+XXXX on base

Quarters:

BQ: Availability ★★★★ x ★
April-Sept **6500** 0800-1630
M-F summer, 7d summer.
Rate: $17 per.
RV Park: Check in BQ, res-
ervations. RV $10-12, EW
$10, ESW $12. Tent free. No pets.

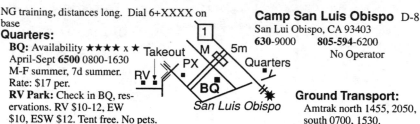

Camp San Luis Obispo D-8

San Lui Obispo, CA 93403
630-9000   **805-594**-6200
No Operator

Ground Transport:
Amtrak north 1455, 2050,
south 0700, 1530.

Distances short.

Quarters:

BQ: Availability ★★★★ x ★★
spring, summer, No. to right 0730-
1530 M-F. Check in at PRU. 2-bed-
room house on ocean front, max 7d
stay. Launder linens, make beds before leaving. $10-
25unit by rank.

Ground Transport:
#143 Bus to Long Beach 0644-1121 M-F, # 446 to
downtown.

CGPSC San Pedro

San Pedro, CA 90731
310-514-6450

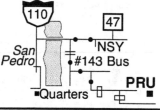

AHC

Distances walkable,   0.9m BQ-Club.

Quarters:

BQ: Availability ★★★★ **4544** 0630-1500 M-F, 0900-1400
SS. Rate: $42-53room.

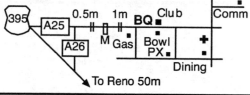

Sierra Army Depot D-8

(Amadee AAF)
Herlong, CA 96113
855-4910   **530.827**.2111
Restricted field

	Break	Lunch	Dinner
Club		M-Th§	TWT§
Dining	7d	7d	7d
Bowl		0800-2100	

Best to contact on site person, Wanda Thompson at
209.639.1016.

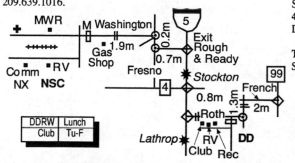

DDRW	Lunch
Club	Tu-F

Stockton DDRW

Stockton, CA 95296
462-2000   **209.839**.4000
Distances short.

Trailer Camp: ★★★★ On
Site 24/7 PH: **209.639.1016**
1000-1630 M-F, check in
Rec office. RV ESW $12,
no dump. Discount Golden
Age, Access, Eagle. Trailer
Camp is located in Lathrop,
CA.

On Æ63, Air Force Circuit	**Travis AFB**
On Æ90, Navy Circuit	**MB 29 Palms**
On Æ65, Air Force Circuit	**Vandenberg AFB**

Zulu-7 On base dial 3+XXXX

AFF Distances long.

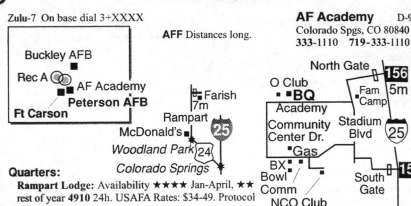

Buckley AFB
Rec A
AF Academy
Peterson AFB
Ft Carson
Farish 7m
Rampart
McDonald's
Woodland Park 24
Colorado Springs

North Gate 156 5m
O Club
BQ
Fam Camp
Academy
Community Center Dr.
Stadium Blvd 25
Gas
BX
Bowl
Comm
NCO Club
South Gate 150
To Colorado Springs 8m

Quarters:

Rampart Lodge: Availability ★★★★ Jan-April, ★★ rest of year **4910** 24h. USAFA Rates: $34-49. Protocol O8 up **3540**

Rec Areas ★★★★ x ★ weekends, reserve up to 89 days ahead, **4356,4753** Outdoor Rec 0900-1630.

Farish Rec Area: ★★ Site C 687-9098 0800-1630 M-F. Rates $20-65unit. RV $8, E $9, 15,Yurt $15. Tent $7.50. Altitude over 9,000'. No pets lodge or cottage.

Fam Camp, check in with host (no host winter) **4980**. RV $5, ESW $12. Tent $5, EW $12.

Golf: 4735 **Holes**: 36 Eisenhower Golf Course

Commercial: BQ has list of motels with military discounts.

Ground Transport:

Taxi to airport 2230.

	Break	Lunch	Dinner	Brun
O Club	Tu-F	Tu-Sa	Tu-Sa	Su
NCO Club		M-F	Tu-Sa	Su
Bowl	xSu	7d	7d	

FCS
4th Inf Div
Distances long,
6.5m BQ-OPS.

Quarters:

BQ: Colorada Inn Availability ★★ x ★ families, **4832** 24h. Rates: $23sgl +$10add per DV $28sgl+$13add per. O6 up thru protocol 4601.

Golf: 4122 **Holes**: 9>18 Cheyenne Shadows Golf Club

Ground Transport:

#2 Bus on post to Colorado Springs and Peterson, 0600-1855 M-F, 0650-1850 Sa. PX car rent 576-8811 . Limo to airport 578-5232.

	Break	Lunch	Dinner
O Club	M-F	M-F	M-F
NCO Club	7d	M-F	xSa
Snack	0530-2300 M-F		
	0700-2300 SS		

Ft Carson   D-8
(Butts AAF)
Colorado Springs, CO 80913
691-5811 Menu 719-526-5811
↦↦↦↦ **Flights** ↦↦↦↦
See Peterson AFB Æ52.

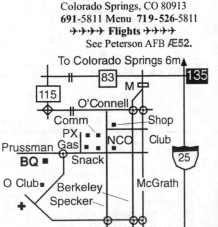

To Colorado Springs 6m
135
83 M
115
O'Connell
Comm
PX
Prussman Gas NCO
BQ Snack
O Club Berkeley
Specker
Shop
Club
25
McGrath
132
OPS

On Æ52, Air Force Circuit   **Peterson AFB**

Zulu-5

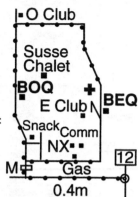

Distances walkable,
1m main gate-O Club.

NSB New London D-8
Groton, CT 06349
694-4500   860-694-3011

NSB New London

Car ferry to
Orient Point, Long Island,
New York

Quarters:

BOQ: Availability ★★★★ x ★ June-Sept **O** 3416 24h. Rate:
$8per, DV $25sgl+$8add per. All space-a can use BOQ.
Susse Chalet (govt. contract housing): **C** 445-6699 24h,
D thru operator. Rates: $58,68sgl +$5add per.
BEQ: ★★★★ (E1-6 no dependents) 3117 24h.
Rates: $8,10per, Chief $15per.
Navy Lodge ★★★★ x ★ summer, **C** 446-1160 24h,
D thru operator. Rate: $42unit.
Golf: 3763 **Holes**: 9 Goose Run Golf Course
Marina: C 694-3164 Thames View Marina
Ground Transport:
Shuttle: 0750-1520 M-F.
Commercial: #10 Bus to RR station, car ferry xSu.

	Break	Lunch	Dinner	Brun
O Club		M-F	W-Sa	Su
BOQ	7d	xSa	xSa	
E Club		7d	7d	
Snack	7d	7d	7d	

Zulu-5 # DELAWARE

▲Greater Wilmington Airport

●Dover AFB

In Air Force Circuit

Dover AFB Æ21

Greater Wilmington Airport Æ26

Facilities Shown on Maps

To avoid clutter normally only facilities important to Space-A travelers are included. Of prime interest are terminals, BQ, other quarters, and RV/tent offices. Where meals can be obtained is significant. Should locations shown cover all meals, there may be other eating facilities. Because medical emergencies may require prompt action, locations of hospitals/clinics are indicated. Useful shuttles and commercial transit are shown if possible without confusion. Principal roads, gates, and landmarks such as traffic lights appear. Exchanges, commissaries, shoppettes and gas stations are shown if they can be used by all Space-A.

Shuttles interconnect most installations but, except those so indicated, cannot be used by retirees.

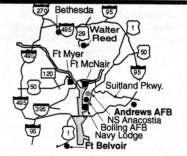

CONUS

DISTRICT OF COLUMBIA
District of Columbia Area Operator assistance for
DC, Northern VA, & MD suburbs
D 227-0101, C 703-545-6700

Special Coding	
A	Air Force
E	Enlisted
N	Navy
O	Officer

Lodging Availability Index	
UA	Usually Available
UN	Usually Not Available
DP	Difficult Periods
ND	Not Difficult

BQ in or near Washington, DC

Facility	Page	DSN	Comm	Exten	Spec.	Availability
Aberdeen PG	ÆE134	298	410-278	5148		DP
NS Anacostia	ÆE121	288	202-433	2006		ND
Andrews AFB	ÆE13	858	301-981	2750	N	DP
				4614	A	DP
Ft Belvoir	ÆE160	655	703-805	2333		DP
NMC Bethesda	ÆE121	295	301-295	5855		DP
Bolling AFB	ÆE121	297	202-767	5741		DP
Ft Detrick	ÆE135	343	301-619	2154		ND
NOS Indian Head	ÆE135	354	301-743	5543	O	UN
			301-743	4845	E	UN
Ft McNair	ÆE121	355	703-696	3491		UA
Ft Meade	ÆE135	923	301-677	5884		UA
Ft Myer	ÆE122	226	703-696	3491		UA
Naval Academy	ÆE136	281	410-267	3906		DP
Navy Lodge	ÆE121		202-563	6950		UN
NAS Patuxent	ÆE86	326	301-826	3610		DP
MC Quantico	ÆE89	278	703-640	3148		UA
NRC Solomons	ÆE136	326	301-863	3566		DP
Walter Reed MC	ÆE122	291	202-576	2076		DP

Greater DC Metropolitan Bus Information

Bus routes that begin with FFX (e.g. FFX107) are Fairfax Connector routes. Information can be found at www.fairfaxconnector.com
Routes starting with RO (e.g. RO42) are Ride-On buses.
You can learn more at www.rideonbus.com

All other routes are Metrobus routes. You can find maps and timetables here: http://www.wmata.com/timetables/default.cfm
Also, the Metro System Route Map can be found here: http://www.wmata.com/metrobus/maps/metrobus_service_maps.cfm
Andrews AFB (Main Gate) - Allentown Rd. & Suitland Rd. (<.1 mi) - D13, D14, K11, K12
Andrews AFB (North Gate) - 8431 Old Marlboro Pike (.33 mi) - J11, J12, J13
Fort Belvoir (Defense Logistics Agency HQ) - 9A, FFX107, FFX304
Fort Belvoir (Building 1000) - Belvoir Rd. & Harris Rd. (<.1 mi) - 9A
Fort Belvoir (Pence Gate) - Richmond Hwy. & Belvoir Rd. (.17 mi) - FFX107
Fort Belvoir (Walker Gate) - Mt. Vernon Memorial Hwy. & Mt. Vernon Rd. (.16 mi) - FFX114, FFX102
Bethesda Naval Medical Center - Wisconsin Ave. & South Dr. (.21 mi) - 14B, J1, J2, J3, RO42
WRAMC (Main Hospital) - 16th St. NW & Main Dr. (.16 mi) - S4
WRAMC (Building 2) - Georgia Ave. & Fern St. (.18 mi) - 70, 71, K2
Bolling AFB - Malcolm X Ave. SE & S. Capitol St. (<.1 mi) - W4, W9
Anacostia Naval Annex - Malcolm X Ave. SE & S. Capitol St. (<.1 mi) W4, W9
US Naval Station - 8th St. & M St. SE - A42, A46, A48, P1, P2
Fort Myer (Hatfield Gate) - S. Courthouse Rd. & S. 2nd St. (<.1 mi) - 16Y, 24M, 24P
Fort Myer (Henry Gate) - Arlington Blvd. & Pershing Dr. - 4A, 4H, 4S
Fort McNair - 4th St. & P St. SW - 70, 71

DISTRICT OF COLUMBIA (Concluded)

DC

Navy Medical Center
Distances short.

Quarters:

BQ: Availability ★ (no dependents)
5855 24h. Rate: $24per. Space-A at 1600,
check out at 1100.
Navy Lodge ★ 301-654-1795, 0800-
2200. Rate: $52,62unit.

Ground Transport:

#34 Bus front of ✚.

	Break	Lunch	Dinner	Brun
O Club	M-F	xSu	Tu-Sa	Su
CPO Club		Tu-F	F	
Snack	M-F	7d	7d	
Bowl		0900-2300		

NMC Bethesda   D-94

Bethesda, MD 20814
295-xxxx   **301-295**-xxxx

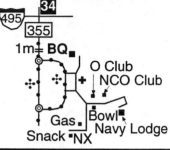

Distances walkable.

Quarters:

Bolling Inn: ★ 5771 24h. AFDW FY 07/08 Rates:
$26-70. Protocol 5584.
NS Anacostia: E7 to O6 only (no dependents) ★★ x
★ summer **(D 288,**
C 433) BOQ 2235 0630-2100 M-F, 0900-
2100 SS. Rate: $8sgl.
Navy Lodge ★★★ C 202-563-6950 0700-
2300, assigned 1830. Rate: $52unit.
Marina: C 202.563.7025 Capital Cove
Marina

Ground Transport:

W4 Bus to downtown.

	Break	Lunch	Dinner	Brun
NS O Club		M-F	M-F	
AF O Club				
NCO Club			M-F	W-Sa	Su
Snack	xSu	7d		
Restaurant		SS	7d	
Bowl				

Bolling AFB   D-94

Washington, DC 20332
297-xxxx   **202-767**-xxxx
DOD Operator 703.545.6700

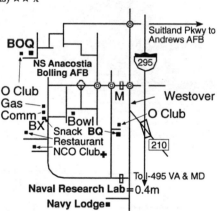

Naval Research Lab ⊨ 0.4m
Navy Lodge ■

Distances short.

Quarters:

BQ: Availability ★★ **O**
only, report to Ft Myer
(next entry) for assign-
ment and keys. Key drop
at Ft McNair. Rates:
$45sgl+$5add per, Suites
$50. **McNair Protocol
685.2975 serves McNair,
Belvoir, &Myer.**

Golf: (202)685-3138 **Holes**: 9 Ft. McNair Golf Course

Ground Transport:

City bus outside main gate and METRO subway..

Ft McNair   D-94

Washington, DC 20319
335-xxxx   **202-457**-xxxx

	Break	Lunch	Dinner
O Club		Tu-F	FSa
NCO Club	M-F	M-F	
Bowl		xSu	xSu

CONUS

DC   DISTRICT OF COLUMBIA (Concluded)

HQ   Distances walkable, 0.8m BQ-NCO Club.

Quarters:

BQ: Availability HHH **3576/7** 0600-2200 xSa,
0800-1600 **Sa**, list starts 0600, call back. DV
assigned at 1400. Controls **O** BQ at Ft McNair
(202.685.2975). Rate: $50+$5add per. Protocol O7
up (Pentagon) 703.697.7051 Wainwright reservations, Emergency Protocol 697.0692. DV Suite
Su-F $70+8; F&Sa, & holidays $62+5. BOQ $50.

Ground Transport

City bus on US50. Bus on Columbia Pike 24h to
Pentagon transfer point.

Ft Myer   D-8 or 94
Arlington, VA 22211
426-xxxx   **703-696**-xxxx

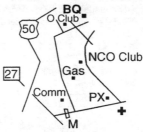

	Break	Lunch	Dinner	Brun
O Club	xSu§	xSu	xM	Su
NCO Club		M-F	xSu	Su

Army Medical Center
Distances short on each area.

Quarters:

BQ: Availability ★★
7096 24h. Rate: $76unit.
Guest House ★ 3044, 24h, Call after
0630. Rates: $30-38unit.
Mologne House: 782-4600, Fax 2297.
Rates: $88room to $125suite

Ground Transport:

Shuttle to Annex, 7d, frequent service.
✚ Shuttle: Ft Meade: 1100,1430 M-F;
Ft Lee 1500 TuW.
Commercial: Buses on Georgia and on
16th, also at Annex.

BRAC 2005

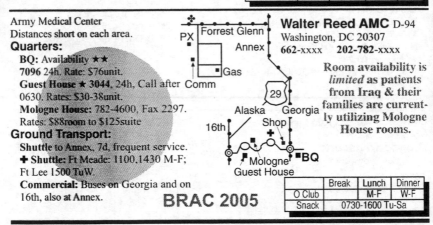

Walter Reed AMC D-94
Washington, DC 20307
662-xxxx **202-782**-xxxx

Room availability is
limited as patients
from Iraq & their
families are current-
ly utilizing Mologne
House rooms.

	Break	Lunch	Dinner
O Club		M-F	W-F
Snack		0730-1600 Tu-Sa	

FLORIDA

NG training
Distances walkable.

Quarters:

BQ: ★★★★ x ★ training & summer
3381 0800-1630 x Su.
Reservations. Lodge,
trailers, huts, various
rates. Dry camp $4per tent.
RV $13, report to MWR.

Recreation 3104

Camp Blanding   D-8
Rt. 1 Box 465, Starke, FL 32091
960-3100 (Police) **904.682**.3100

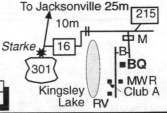

	Break	Lunch	Dinner
Club	7d	7d	7d

Dining - Galley Meals for Space-A Travelers

Only some dining facilities are usable by all Space-A travelers. These are shown on page entries.
Most commonly these are Navy and Coast Guard. Whenever you learn of a dining facility serving
retirees please forward this information.

FLORIDA (Continued)

FL

Camping & Recreation Key

C	Cottage / Cabins
H	Hotel
RV	Rec Vehicle Facilities
S	Summer Difficult Times
T	Tent Camping
W	Winter Difficult Times

No.	Facility	Rec & Camping
1	Blanding, Camp	RV, T
2	Blue Angel Rec Park	W, RV, T
3	Clearwater, CGAS	RV, C
4	Destin Rec Area	RV, T
5	Eglin AFB	RV, T
6	Homestead ARS	
7	Hurlburt Field	
8	Jacksonville, NAS	RV, T
9	Key West, NAS	RV, T
10	Lake Pippen Rec Area	S, RV, T
11	MacDill AFB	RV, T
12	Marathon, CG	RV
13	Mayport, NS	RV
14	Panama City, NCS	S, RV
15	Patrick AFB	RV, T
16	Pensacola, NAS	W, C, RV, T
17	Shade of Green AFRC	H
18	Tyndall AFB	C, RV, T
19	Whiting Field	

CONUS

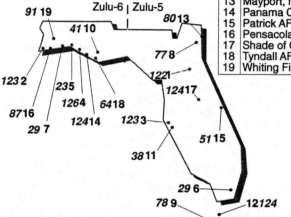

Quarters:
Availability ★★★★ x ★ winter, holidays, reservations C **850.453.9435**, D thru operator.
Campers: Rate Primitive cabins $25 unit, mobile homes $50.
RV: EW $8. Tent $4, dump, 30A E Boat House 453.4530.

Blue Angel Rec Park   D-88
2100 Bronson Field Rd
Pensacola, FL 32506-5000
922-0111 NAS Pensacola **850.452**.0111

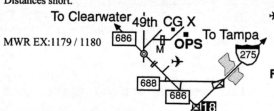

PIE
Coast Guard C130
Distances short.

MWR EX:1179 / 1180

CGAS Clearwater
Clearwater, FL 33502
                    727.535.1437
✈✈✈✈✈✈ Flights ✈✈✈✈✈✈

No Flights

Flight Information:
OPS Numbers above
0715-1530 M-F

See Ft Benning, Æ126	**Destin Rec Area**
On Æ23, Air Force Circuit	**Eglin AFB**
On Æ29, Air Force Circuit	**Homestead ARB**
On Æ29, Air Force Circuit	**Hurlburt AFB**
On Æ77 Navy Circuit	**NAS Jacksonville**
On Æ78, Navy Circuit	**NAS Key West**
See Maxwell AFB, Æ41	**Lake Pippen Rec Area**
On Æ38, Air Force Circuit	**MacDill AFB**
On Æ80, Navy Circuit	**NS Mayport**

CG Marathon Rec Cottages

Distances short. 1-bedroom cottages, All reservations are made thru Miami at 305.535.4565. Check in with OOD, CGS, 1800 US1, $33-47unit. Marathon's cell phone 305.481.4934. **Their form must be used** and reservations can be made 6m in advance. Minimum 2 nights. **C 743-3549** provides recorded reservation instructions. EW $5. No dump, shower, restroom, pets.

CGS Marathon, FL 33040
305.743.3549

To Miami 111m
Mile Post 48
Marathon 6m — Rec Cottages
Key Vaca
Key Marathon

AFRC Orlando Hotel
Shades of Green

Availability ★. Reservations numbers to right, 0800-2100 M-F, 0800-1700. Standard Rates: $72-119 room depending on grade. Reduced-price admissions to Disney attractions. Free shuttles. All meals served in hotel.

Lake Buena Vista, FL 32830
407-824-3600 Fax 3665
Reservations 1-888-593-2242
Internet Reservations:
http://www.armymwr.com/shades/index.html

NCS Panama City D-8

Naval Coastal Systems
Distances short.
Quarters:
BQ: Availability ★★★★ x ★ April-Sept **Res: 4217** 24h. **BEQ** 236.2920, **BOQ** 236.2921 Rate: **O** $8,12sgl+$4add per, DV $20sgl+$5add per. Protocol 5486. **E** 236.2920 $8sgl+$3add per.

98 M Panama City
Club Marina
CBH BOQ
Galley
(Easiest Gate)

Panama City, FL 32402
436-4011   850-234-4011
Amtrak in Orlando, north 1251, 1700, south 1116, 1554.

Rec A, ★★★★ x ★ summer, Outdoor Rec 4374, 0900-1700 summer, xTuW winter, check in Marina 1200-2400 xTuW. Rates: Campers (without linens) $25unit, park models (with linens) $35unit. RV ESW $10. No dump.

Marina: 4402 Hidden Cove Marina

	Break	Lunch	Dinner
Club		M-F	
Galley	7d	7d	7d

On Æ51, Air Force Circuit	**Patrick AFB**
On Æ87 Navy Circuit	**NAS Pensacola**
On Æ64, Air Force Circuit	**Tyndall AFB**
On Æ91, Navy Circuit	**NAS Whiting Field**

	Page	D	C	Quarters Summary	
Blue Angel Rec	123	972	850-453	**D 0111** 9435	🔵
Destin Rec A	126		850-837	2725, **RES:** 800-642-0466	🔵
Duke Field	23	875	850-883	6203, 0715-1545 M-F	🔵
Eglin AFB	23	872	850-882	**O** 8761, **E** 5025 24h	🔵
Hurlburt Field	29	579	850-884	6245 24h	🔵
Lake Pippen Rec A	41	493	850-953	5496 0730-1700 M-F	🔵
NAS Pensacola	87	922	850-452	**O** 2755, **E** 3438, Navy Lge. 456-8676	⬛
NAS Whiting Field	91	868	850-623	7605 24h	🔲

Florida Panhandle

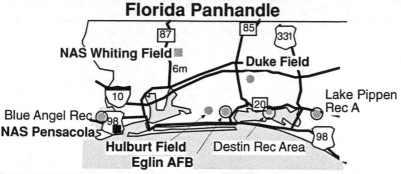

NAS Whiting Field

Duke Field

Lake Pippen Rec A

Blue Angel Rec
NAS Pensacola

Hulburt Field / Destin Rec Area
Eglin AFB

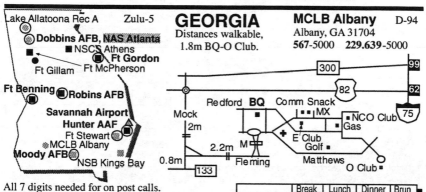

Lake Allatoona Rec A   Zulu-5

Dobbins AFB, NAS Atlanta
NSCS Athens
Ft Gordon
Ft Gillam   Ft McPherson

Ft Benning   Robins AFB

Savannah Airport
Hunter AAF
Ft Stewart
MCLB Albany
Moody AFB
NSB Kings Bay

All 7 digits needed for on post calls.

GEORGIA
Distances walkable, 1.8m BQ-O Club.

MCLB Albany   D-94
Albany, GA 31704
567-5000   **229.639**-5000

Quarters:
BQ: Availability ★ **5614** 0800-1600 M-F, accepts reservations 1d in advance. Rates: **O** $12-24per, E6 up $9per. TLF $20unit. Protocol O7 up 5759.
Golf: Driving Range Only
Marina: C 912-439-5267/8

	Break	Lunch	Dinner	Brun
O Club		M-F	F	Su
NCO Club		M-F		
E Club		M-F	M-F	
Golf	xM	xM		
Snack	1000-1900 xSu			

Navy school
Distances short.
Quarters:
BQ: Availability ★★★★ **7360** 0730-0100, other hrs quarter deck 7305. Rates: **E** $15, **O** $15-28sgl+$4add per, DV $32unit, TLF $28. Protocol 7200.
Ground Transport:
#5 Bus to downtown, 0700-1800, M-F, 0902-1755 Sa.

NSCS Athens   D-8
Athens, GA 30606
354.7305   706-354-1500

	Break	Lunch	Dinner
O Club		M-Th	
Galley	M-F	M-F	M-F

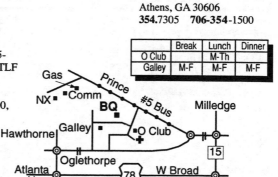

On Æ20, Air Force Circuit — **NAS Atlanta**

XLE All 7 digits needed for on post calls.
Infantry school.
Distances long, 2.5m BQ-OPS.

Columbus
5m — 185
Benning Blvd
Motel — 27/280
2.5m
2.3m
Marne
Gas
Gillespie
Vibbert
Wold
Shop
Indianhead
Gas Snack
O Club
Lumpkin
PX
Comm
BQ
BQ
PX
E Club
Eckel — Bowl
OPS.
Ft Mitchell
Sightseeing
Sunshine
RV
Uchee Creek
Benning
Water Tower — 1.4m
To *Destin*
Ft Walton Beach
98

Ft Benning D-8
(Lawson AAF)
Columbus, GA 31905
835-2011   706-545-2011

↣↣↣↣ **Flights** ↣↣↣↣

Andrews	McGuire
Beaufort	Milwaukee § ThF
Belvoir	Minneapolis § ThF
Bragg √	Peoria § ThF
Campbell √	Pope § ThF
Charleston § ThF	Rucker
Dyess	Savana § ThF
Little Rock § ThF	Wright Pat √
Knox √	
McChord § ThF	

§ Res C17/130 for airborne training arrive Su, return to home Th or F.

Chance of seat ★★★
Flight Information:
OPS 3524 24h

	Break	Lunch	Dinner	Brun
O Club		M-F	Tu-Sa	Su
E Club		M-F	7d	
Bowl	xSu	7d	7d	
Snack	0600-0200			

Quarters:
BQ: Olson Hall, Availability ★★★★ D 3146, **C 689-0067** 24h. Rates: Range from $41 motel to 3 bed $73 cabins.
Guest House: $16unit. O6 up thru protocol **4662**.
Destin Rec A, FL, cabins, motel ★★★★ x ★ summer, **5600**, site (info number) 850-837-6423 0800-2000. Reservations only @ 800-642-0466 0800-1400 M-F. Rates: $37-58unit winter, $26-36unit summer. RV ESW PH&Cable 1 Nov-15 Mar $19/d, $114/w, $375/m; 16 Mar - 31 Oct $16/n, $98/w, $280/m. Tent E $6. No pets. See also on Florida & Pensacola Area maps Æ120, 122.
Uchee Creek: Cabins ★★ x ★ winter, RV ★★★★ 7238 0900-1800 M-F, 0700-1900 SS, reservations. Rates: Cabins $17-40 by rank and size, no towels, sheets. RV EW $8,9, ESW $10,11. Tent $5.
Golf: 682.1937 **Holes**: 36 Follow Me Golf Complex
Marina: C (706) 685-3060 Uchee Creek Marina; C 850.837-6423 Destin
Ground Transport:
Post Shuttle 0600-0100.
Commercial: Bus to Columbus xSu. PX car rent 689.0896 0900-1700 xSu.

On Æ20, Air Force Circuit — **Dobbins AFB**

Subpost of Ft McPherson
Distances long.
Quarters:
BQ: 469.5410 Book thru McPherson.
Availability ★
0730-1600 M-F.
Protocol **C**
464.5388.
For arrival after 1600 F thru weekend, call, keys left at Security 5981. Reservations taken F. Rates: **O** $25sgl, DV $30sgl, **E** $23sgl, all +$2add per.
Ground Transport:
MARTA Bus morning and afternoon.

To Atlanta
54 — 285
54
2.5m
Jonesboro — 160
NCO Club
Bowl
Hood
0.7m
Commissary
PX, Snack
O Club
1.7m Security
BQ
58
23

Ft Gillam D-88
Forest Park, GA 30050
McPherson Operator
367.1110 404.464.3113
Fort Gillam
797-xxxx   469-xxxx

	Break	Lunch	Dinner
O Club		MF	F
NCO Club			FSa
Snack	xSu	7d	
Bowl			7d

AGS
Quarters:
BQ:
Availability
★★★★
780.2277
24h. Rates:
$25sgl+$2add
per,
DV $26per. Proto-
col 2017,6552.
Guest House: ★24h.
Rates: $27-31unit.
Rec A: Cabins, trailers ★★★★
x ★ weekends, reduced Nov-March
706.541.1057 0730-1600 M-F. Site C 541-
1057 0730-2300. Rate: Trailers $45unit, cottages $65unit.
M-Th +$5 F-Su. RV E $5, ESW $14. Tent $3. No pets in
cabins, trailers.
Golf: 791-2433 **Holes**: 27 Gordon Lakes Golf Course

Ground Transport:
Post Shuttle 7d. ✚
Shuttle for A flights.
Commercial: Post
bus station: To
Augusta 0640-2300;
Greyhound.

Distances long, 1.8m BQ-Snack Bar,
12.5m BQ-Airport. Dial all 7 digits
on post.

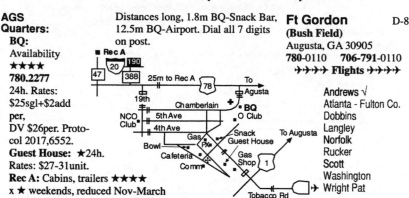

	Break	Lunch	Dinner	Brun
O Club		M-F	Tu-Sa	Su
NCO Club		M-F		
Cafeteria	7d	7d		
Snack				
Bowl	1000-2300			

Ft Gordon D-8
(Bush Field)
Augusta, GA 30905
780-0110   **706-791**-0110
✈✈✈✈✈ **Flights** ✈✈✈✈✈

Andrews √
Atlanta - Fulton Co.
Dobbins
Langley
Norfolk
Rucker
Scott
Washington
Wright Pat ✈

Chance of seat ★★★
Flight Information:
Airevac 2644, Hospital Info
706.787.5811 0730-1600
M-F, 0900-flight time Su,
call after 0900 day of flight.
Transport provided from ✚.

SVN Distances walkable, 1.1m BQ-OPS.
Quarters:
BQ: Availability ★★★★
5834, 5910 0600-2100,
other times call. Keys at
Garrison HQ security
office. Rate: $38-48 room,
DV $53unit. O6 up thru
protocol 8610 (Stewart).
Landmark Inn-Hunter
(civilian co-op) **C** 692.0139 $69- 79.
Travel Camp: ★★★
352.5722/7744/7824/7833 1130-1900 Th-M, reservations,
check in Outdoor Rec. Rates: Trailer $25 (pop up). RV. Tent
W $3. No shower. Dump at equipment Rental.
Golf: 315.9115 **Holes**: 18 Hunter Golf Course
Ground Transport:
City bus outside main gate and on Route 204.
Amtrak north 0715, 1255,1848, 2240, south 0514, 0951, 2303.

Hunter AAF D-95
Savannah, GA 31409
729-1110 (Stewart
Operator) **912-767**-1110
729-xxxx   **352**-xxxx
✈✈✈✈ **Flights** ✈✈✈✈
Andrews   Campbell
Belvoir   Rickenbacker
Bragg   Rucker
Chance of seat ★★★★
Flight Information:
OPS **5110, 5210, 5531**
0000 M to 2300 F

	Break	Lunch	Dinner	Brun
O Club		Tu-F	Tu-F	Su
NCO Club		Tu-F		
Bowl	xSu	7d	7d	

Submarine base
Distances walkable.
Quarters:
TVQ: **Availability** ★★★★ x4871/4971/8258
Fax 2752. **24h. Rates:** $15-20 DV $25sgl+$7add per.
Navy Lodge: ★★★★ x✚ F-Su, **C** 882.6092, 0700-2000. Fax 6800. Rate: $37unit.
Golf: 573.8475/6 **Holes**: 18 KINGS BAY GOLF COURSE

NSB Kings Bay D-80
Kings Bay, GA 31547
573-2111   912.573.2000

Continued on following page

NSB Kings Bay continued from preceding page

NSB Kings Bay continued from preceding page

CONUS

Ground Transport:
Base Shuttle 0600-2300, 8294, Taxi 8632. ✦ **Shuttle:** To
NAS Jacksonville 0820 M-F.
Commercial Greyhound at Gulf station on I95.

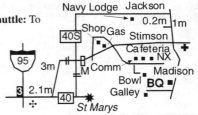

	Break	Lunch	Dinner
Galley	7d	7d	7d
Bowl		7d	7d
Cafeteria	xSu	xSu	

Distances short,
1.1m BQ-main gate.
Quarters:
BQ: Availability ★★ **2253/3833**
0630-2330. Rates: $25sgl +$2add
per. DV $35sgl +$2add per. Protocol
(D 367, C 669) 5388.

Rec A cabins, trailers, Active Duty
assigned to McPherson have priority ★★★★ winter, ★ summer **C**
770-974-3413,9420, D thru operator,
0800-1700 Su-Th, 0800-2000 FSa. Rates: $30-66unit
summer, $32-50unit winter. RV ESW $15. Tent EW
$10. No pets. Navy Rec A also, see NAS Atlanta Æ20.
Golf: 2178 **Holes:** 18 Fort McPherson Golf Course
Ground Transport:
MARTA RR and Bus outside main gate. Bus on Cam-
bellton. Amtrak north 1925, south 0912.

Ft McPherson   D-88
Atlanta, GA 30330
367-1110   **404-464**-3113

	Break	Lunch	Dinner
NCO Club		M-F	F-Su
Bowl	xSu	7d	7d
Cafeteria	xSu	7d	

On Æ**46**, Air Force Circuit   **Moody AFB**
On Æ**56**, Air Force Circuit   **Robins AFB**
On Æ**57**, Air Force Circuit **Savannah Airport**

Dial all 7 digits on post.
24th Inf Division Distances walkable.
Quarters:
BQ: Availability ★★★★ **8384 Guest House** 0730-
2345. Rate: $22unit. Protocol 8610/7744.
RV: ★★★★ **2717/2771** 0800-1900 xW, check in
Outdoor Rec, map on building. RV EW $5. Tent $3.
Discount Golden Age, Access.
Golf: 912.767.2370 **Holes:** 18 Taylor's Creek Golf
Course
Ground Transport:
Greyhound in Hinesville. PX car rent 368-9191
0900-1700 M-F. Taxi 368-4172.

Ft Stewart   D-95
Hinesville, GA 31314
870-1110   **912-767**-1110
Also Hunter AAF.

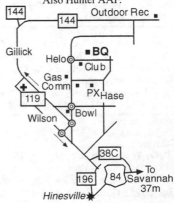

	Break	Lunch	Dinner	Brun
Club			Tu-Sa	Su
Bowl	7d	7d	7d	

IDAHO

Gowen Field
Macks Inn
Henry's Lake
Yellowstone
Mt Home AFB

On Æ25, Air Force Circuit **Gowen Field**
On Æ47, Air Force Circuit **Mountain Home AFB**

Recreation trailers controlled by Outdoor
Adventure, Mt. Home AFB Æ47.

ILLINOIS

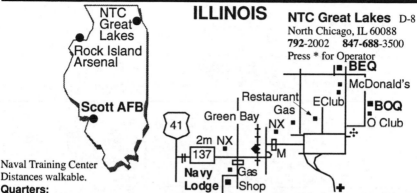

NTC
Great
Lakes
Rock Island
Arsenal

Scott AFB

Naval Training Center
Distances walkable.

NTC Great Lakes D-8
North Chicago, IL 60088
792-2002   **847-688**-3500
Press * for Operator

Quarters:
CBO: Availability ★★★★ x ★ School needs &Res weekends
847.688.2170 24h, Rates: **E** $18sgl+$3add per, **O** $23sgl+$6add per. DV
O6 up thru protocol **6996** $29+7.
BEQ ★★★★ (no children) **2170,2241** 24h. Rate: $4per.
Navy Lodge: C 847.689.1485 24h. Fax 689-1488. Rate
$48,51unit.
RV ★★★★$13 CESW 20 Hard surface spaces, contact
Marina, 5417
Golf: 847.668.4593 Holes: 18
Marina: C 688-5417 NS Great Lakes Marina

	Break	Lunch	Dinner
O Club		Tu-Sa	Tu-Sa
E Club		M-F	7d
McDon		0600-0200	

Ground Transport:
Shuttle 0730-1600 M-F.
Commercial: City bus on center. Limo to O'Hare Airport. RR Chicago,
Kenosha.

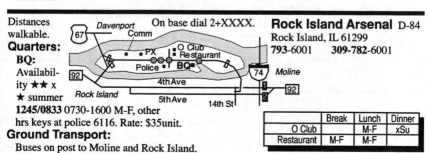

Distances
walkable.
Quarters:
BQ:
Availabil-
ity ★★ x
★ summer
1245/0833 0730-1600 M-F, other
hrs keys at police 6116. Rate: $35unit.
Ground Transport:
Buses on post to Moline and Rock Island.

Rock Island Arsenal D-84
Rock Island, IL 61299
793-6001   **309-782**-6001

On base dial 2+XXXX.

	Break	Lunch	Dinner
O Club		M-F	xSu
Restaurant	M-F	M-F	

On Æ57, Air Force Circuit   **Scott AFB**

129

IOWA

Camp Dodge Billeting
7700 Northwest Beaver Drive
Johnston, Iowa 50131

BQ
M-F 0700-1930, SS 0700-1630 $17-30
515-252-4238 (Duty Hours)
Toll Free **1-800-294-6607 X4010** (After Hours Reservations)
DSN 431-4238 / 4010
E-Mail: cdtngsite@ia.ngb.army.mil

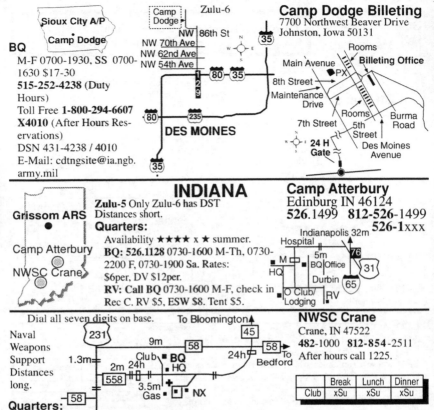

INDIANA

Zulu-5 Only Zulu-6 has DST
Distances short.

Camp Atterbury
Edinburg IN 46124
526.1499 **812-526**-1499
526-1xxx

Quarters:
Availability ★★★★ x ★ summer.
BQ: 526.1128 0730-1600 M-Th, 0730-2200 F, 0730-1900 Sa. Rates: $6per, DV $12per.
RV: Call BQ 0730-1600 M-F, check in Rec C. RV $5, ESW $8. Tent $5.

Dial all seven digits on base.

Naval Weapons Support Distances long.

NWSC Crane
Crane, IN 47522
482-1000 **812-854**-2511
After hours call 1225.

	Break	Lunch	Dinner
Club	xSu	xSu	xSu

Quarters:
BQ: Availability ★ **1176** 0730-1500 M-F, other hrs quarterdeck has keys, 1222/5. Rates: **O** $9unit, DV $18unit. Protocol 1411. **E** $4per.
RV: ★★★★ **6255/3947/1368**, check in Marina. RV ESW $5,10. Tent $3.5. Max stay in one site 30d. Cabins $20-40.

Marina: C 854-**1368** Lake Greenwood Marina

On Æ**27**, Air Force Circuit   **Grissom ARS**

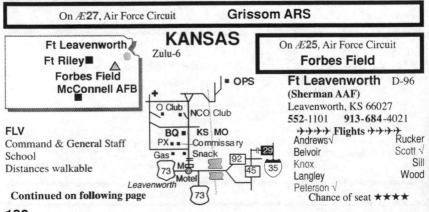

KANSAS

Zulu-6

On Æ**25**, Air Force Circuit
Forbes Field

Ft Leavenworth D-96
(Sherman AAF)
Leavenworth, KS 66027
552-1101   **913-684**-4021
✈✈✈✈ **Flights** ✈✈✈✈

Andrews√	Rucker
Belvoir	Scott √
Knox	Sill
Langley	Wood
Peterson √	

Chance of seat ★★★★

FLV
Command & General Staff School
Distances walkable

Continued on following page

CONUS

Ft. Leavenworth continued from preceding page

Quarters:

BQ: Availability ★★★ x ★ May-July & with children **684.4091** 24h. Reserve 0730-1600 M-F. Rates: $46-55sgl+$5add per. DV $58 Protocol 684.5042. Guest House $58 unit. DVQ 684.5051

Commercial: Motels on US73.

Golf:

Flight Information:
OPS **684.1782,7717** 0730-1630 M-F.

	Break	Lunch	Dinner	Brun
O Club		M-F	Tu-Sa	Su
NCO Club		M-F	W-Su	
Cafeteria	M-F	M-F		

On Æ43, Air Force Circuit   **McConnell AFB**

CONUS

FRI
1st Inf Division Distances long, 2.2m BQ-OPS.

Quarters:

BQ: Availability ★★★★ **239.3525** 24h.
Reserve. Rates: $20-40 unit. Protocol 239.8843.

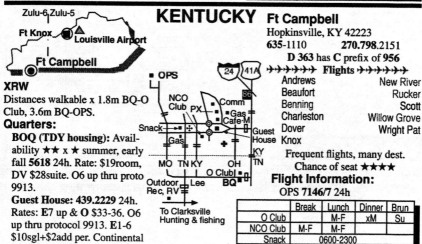

Golf:
Ground Transport:

Post Shuttle: Main post-Custer Hill-Junction City 0700-2000 M-F, 1300-2000 SS.
Commercial: Frequent pay service to Junction City, Greyhound.

Ft Riley (Marshall AAF)   D-8
Junction City, KS 66442
856-1110   **785.239**.3911

↣↣↣↣↣↣ **Flights** ↣↣↣↣↣↣

Carson	Kelly M A
Hood	McConnell MA
Irwin	Scott W A
Kansas City W A	Wood W A

Rare flights other than A
Chance of seat ★★★★

Flight Information:
OPS **2530/75** 0745-1700.
Airevac at Manhattan Airport, 3810 24h. Report to ✚, transport provided.
Hospital info: 239.7000

	Break	Lunch	Dinner	Brun
O Club		M-F	W-Sa	S
NCO Club		M-F	W-Su	
Cafeteria	M-F	M-F		

KENTUCKY

Zulu-6, Zulu-5

Ft Knox   Louisville Airport

Ft Campbell

XRW
Distances walkable x 1.8m BQ-O Club, 3.6m BQ-OPS.

Quarters:

BOQ (TDY housing): Availability ★★ x ★ summer, early fall **5618** 24h. Rate: $19room, DV $28suite. O6 up thru proto 9913.

Guest House: 439.2229 24h. Rates: E7 up & O $33-36. O6 up thru protocol 9913. E1-6 $10sgl+$2add per. Continental breakfast.
Golf: 798.1822

Ft Campbell
Hopkinsville, KY 42223
635-1110   **270.798**.2151
D 363 has **C** prefix of **956**

↣↣↣↣↣↣ **Flights** ↣↣↣↣↣↣

Andrews	New River
Beaufort	Rucker
Benning	Scott
Charleston	Willow Grove
Dover	Wright Pat
Knox	

Frequent flights, many dest.
Chance of seat ★★★★

Flight Information:
OPS **7146/7** 24h

	Break	Lunch	Dinner	Brun
O Club		M-F	xM	Su
NCO Club	M-F	M-F		
Snack	0600-2300			
Cafeteria	0600-1600 xSu			

Continued on facing page

KENTUCKY (Concluded)

Ft Campbell continued from facing page

Travel Camp: ★★★ 3126,5590 0730-1700
M-F, 0900-1700 SS, reserve cabins, no bedding, $20unit. RV EW $9. Firearms permitted for hunting. Discount Golden Age.
Commercial: Roadway Inn, Clarksville picks up, 615-645-2100.

Ground Transport:
Post Shuttle 0700-1530 M-F to near OPS.
Commercial: Greyhound on post. Limo Clarksville, Nashville Airport 0435-2030.

CONUS

FTK
Armor
Distances long,
1.5m BQ-OPS.

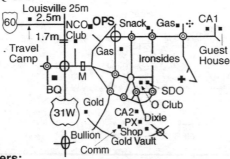

Quarters:
BQ: Availability ★★★★ D 3491, C 943-1000 24h.
Rates: $16sgl
+$5add per. DV $46sgl+$5add per. O4 up thru protocol 6615. Space-A only when Guest House is full.
Guest House: ★★★★ x ★★ WFSa C 943.1000,
D thru operator, 24h, assigned 1800, reserve 90d in advance. Rates: $28-31sgl+$5add per. Continental breakfast.
Camp Carlson Travel Camp ★★★★ 4836 0800-1700, reservations. Check in Travel Camp. Rates: Cottages $22, Youth cottage $3per. RV $7, EW $10. Tent $7. Discount Golden Access,Age,Eagle.
Golf: 0984 Lindsey Golf Course

Ground Transport:
Post Shuttle 0700-1800 M-F.
Commercial: Greyhound on post.
Taxi C 942-0042.

Ft Knox
D-8
(Godman AAF)
Tip Top, KY 40121
464-1000   **502-624**-1000
D 464/536-XXXX

C (502) 624/626-XXXX
➜➜➜➜➜ **Flights** ➜➜➜➜➜

Adams Fld AR	McCoy √
Andrews √	New Orleans
Belvoir	New River
Benning √	Norfolk
Bragg	Ohio State Univ
Capital City KY √	Peterson
Dobbins	Scott √
Indianapolis IN	Sill √
Jefferson City MO	Wright Pat √
Langley √	
Leavenworth	

Chance of seat ★★★

Flight Information:
OPS **6047**, 1727 24h, Res. C-12 6359 0800-1700 M-F. For Airevac contact Patient Affairs 9494 0800-1630 M-F, report to ✚, transport provided to Louisville Airport.

	Break	Lunch	Dinner	Brun
O Club		M-F	Tu-Sa	Su
NCO Club		Tu-F	xM	
Snack	7d	7d	7d	
Cafeteria 1	7d	7d	7d	
Cafeteria 2	7d			

On Æ37, Air Force Circuit   **Louisville Airport**

Zulu-6

LOUISIANA

●**Barksdale AFB**
Rec A   Camp
    Beauregard
Ft Polk
NSA New Orleans●
JRB New Orleans●

Camp Beauregard
Pineville, LA (Alexandria, LA) 71360
318.640.2080   (Switchboard)

Rooms $18 - 28, RV trailer $13
Lake trailers $18 **Place billeting request 72 hours in advance.**

Zulu-6   Distances short.

NSA New Orleans D-8
Algiers, LA 70146
678-5011   **504-678**-5011
Ground Transport:
Shuttle boat across
Mississippi.
Commercial: Algiers bus
to New Orleans, local bus
to free ferry to New Or-
leans. Amtrak east 1745,
1940 SuTT. north 1410 xW,
west 0315 MWSa.

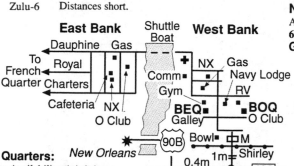

CONUS

Quarters:
Availability ★★★★ x
★ Res weekends, Mardi
Gras
CBH: 2220/52 24h Rates: $10sgl+$3add per, suites
$15sgl +$3add per. DV $31sgl+$4add per. O6 up thru
protocol **9422**.
Navy Lodge ★★★★ D 2700, C 366-3266 0700-2000.
Rate: $43unit.

	Break	Lunch	Dinner
E-O Club		M-F	
W-O Club		M-F	F
CPO Club		M-F	
Bowl			

POE
Distances long,
2.2m BQ-OPS.

Ft Polk   D-94 + PIN
Leesville, LA 71459
863-1110   **337.531**-2911
↣↣↣↣ **Flights** ↣↣↣↣

Bragg
Hood

Chance of seat ★★★★
Flight Information:
OPS **7328** 0700-2200 M-F

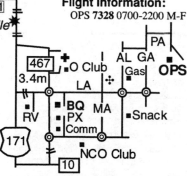

Quarters:
BQ: Availability ★★★★ **2941** 24h. Rates:
$33+5per, cottages $41, DV $33, O6 up thru
protocol 1720.
Golf: 337.531.4661
RV: 1948 Handled by BQ. RV ESW $8, 30d
limit.
Toledo Bend Rec Area 888.718.9088
★★★★ x ★ summer weekends, **1974** 1000-
1600, reservations, site **318**.565.4235, no
linens. Rate: Trailers $25unit, RV ESW $8.
Tent $2. Discount Golden Age for RV.
Commercial: Motels in Leesville.
Ground Transport:
Military taxi 531.4982 0600-2300.
Commercial: Greyhound on post. Taxi 239-
6000,224.13 05, 239.3680.

	Break	Lunch	Dinner	Brun
O Club		M-F	Tu-Sa	Su
NCO Club		M-F		
Snack	0600-2300 M-F			
	0700- Sa, 0900- Su			

On Æ15, Air Force Circuit	**Bangor Airport**
On Æ72, Navy Circuit	**NAS Brunswick**

Naval Shipyard Distances short.

Quarters:

CBH:
Helmsman Inn Availability
★★★★ x ★ when ship
is in **1513,2015** 24h. Rates:
$15+4 & $26+7, DV $31unit.

Ground Transport:
Yard Shuttle 0800-1600 M-F.
Marina: C 207-438-1583/1280
Back Channel Marina & Sound
Basin Marina

Both Maine and New Hampshire laid claim to the naval base until the U.S. Supreme Court ruled in favor of Maine.

NSY Portsmouth D-81
Kittery, ME 03904
684-1000 **207-438**-1000

Bangor Airport
NAS Brunswick
NSY Portsmouth

	Break	Lunch	Dinner
O Club		M-F	F
CPO Club		M-F	
E Club		M-F	
Bowl		7d	7d
Cafeteria	0500-20000 M-F		

On base 3-xxxx   Zulu-5   **MARYLAND**

Ft Detrick
Aberdeen Warfield ANGB
Ft Meade
CGY Curtis Bay
NMC Bethesda   Naval Academy
Andrews AFB
NSWC Indian Head
NRC Solomons
NAS Patuxent

APG   Distances long.

Quarters:

BQ: Availability ★★★ **5148**
24h. Rates: $31sgl+$5add per, DV
$45sgl +$5add per. O6 up thru protocol
1038/9.
Guest House: 3570/8,3856 0800-1600
M-F, other hrs BQ. $20-32unit.
Skipper's Point: ★★★★ **436.2733**

Outdoor Rec 4124 0800-1630 M-F, reservations,
Outdoor Rec. Site 617-4732. Report to RV 0700-
1900 F-M Memorial-Labor, otherwise Outdoor
Rec. RV $5. Tent $2.
Commercial: Motels in Aberdeen.

Ground Transport:
Shuttle to Aberdeen 1700-2255, more SS.
Commercial: Greyhound, Amtrak in
Aberdeen. Taxi 272-0880.

Aberdeen PG   D-8
(Phillips AAF)
Aberdeen, MD 21005
298-1110   **410-278**-5201
↣↣↣↣ **Flights** ↣↣↣↣
Andrews   Bragg
Belvoir   Warfield
Chance of seat ★★★★
Flight Information:
OPS **3483,4902**
0600-2000 M-F

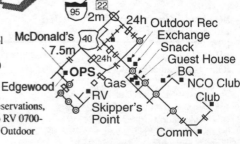

	Break	Lunch	Dinner	Brun
O Club		M-F	Tu-F	Su
NCO Club		M-F	xSu	
Snack	0630-2200 xSu			
	0800-2200 Su			

CONUS

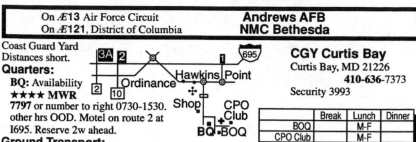

On Æ13 Air Force Circuit — **Andrews AFB**
On Æ121, District of Columbia — **NMC Bethesda**

CGY Curtis Bay
Curtis Bay, MD 21226
410-636-7373
Security 3993

Coast Guard Yard
Distances short.

Quarters:
BQ: Availability
★★★★ MWR
7797 or number to right 0730-1530.
other hrs OOD. Motel on route 2 at
I695. Reserve 2w ahead.

Ground Transport:
City bus at main gate.

	Break	Lunch	Dinner
BOQ		M-F	
CPO Club		M-F	
Galley	7d	7d	7d

Ft Detrick D-84
Frederick, MD 21701
343-1110 **301-619**-8000

Medical
Distances walkable.

Quarters:
BQ: Availability Guest House & BOQ
★★★ **2154** 0745-1630, M-F, for
arrival other hrs, call, keys left with
Security 7114. Rates: **O** $13unit, DV
$18unit, Guest House $24unit.

Ground Transport:
Greyhound in Frederick.

	Break	Lunch	Dinner
Club		M-F	TuF
Bowl		7d	7d
Dining	7d	7d	7d

NSWC Indian Head
Indian Head, MD 20640
354-4000 **301-744**-4000

Naval Surface Warfare Center
Distances walkable.

Quarters:
BQ: Availability ★★★★ **2091**
4845 24h. Rates: **O** $9per, DV
$20 M-F **E** 1-4 $5, 5 up $9per
M-F, all free SS.
Golf: 301.743.4662 **Holes**; 9
INDIAN HEAD GOLF COURSE
Marina: C 744-6314/3573/6591 Dashiell Marina
Ground Transport: Bus to Baltimore xSu. Taxi
647-6660.

	Break	Lunch	Dinner
O Club		M-F	W
CPO Club		M-F	

Ft George G. Meade D-94
(Tipton AAF)
Ft Meade, MD 20755
622-1311 **301-677**-6261

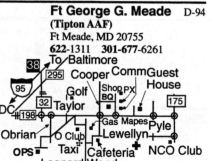

FME
Distances long, 1.6m BQ-OPS

Quarters:
BQ: Availability ★★★★ (no depen-
dents)
5884 24h. Rate: $32-52 room.
DV $52 unit. O6 up thru protocol
4130/3420.
Guest House ★★★ **5660** 24h. Rates:
$39+5
Golf: 4308 **Holes**: 36 Ft. Meade Golf
Courses

Ground Transport:
✚ **Shuttle:** Walter Reed 0820,1230 M-F, returns
1100,1430, 8392.
Commercial: #16 Bus to Baltimore xSu. Ask O
Club manger for directions to obtain long term
parking.

	Break	Lunch	Dinner	Brun
O Club		Tu-F	Tu-Sa	Su
NCO Club		Tu-F	Tu-Sa	
Golf	xM	xM	xM	
Cafeteria	0630-1500 M-F			

Distances short each area.

Quarters:

BOQ: Availability ★ **3906** 0800-1600, accepts standby reservations, keys left at Gate 3. Rates: $31+8per, DV $45+11. O6 up thru protocol 1512.

Fam Camp: ★★ **9200** 0700-2200, check in Rec C. RV EW $15. Tent $2. Discount Golden Access, Eagle.

Golf: 410.757.2022

Marina: 410.293.37313732/2058 Mill Creek Marina & Carr Creek Marina & Sailing School

Ground Transport:

Greyhound in Annapolis.

Naval Academy D-8
(Annapolis)
Annapolis, MD 21402
281- 1000 **410-293**-1000
0700-1530

450   658   Gas   M

Comm■
NX■ ■
Snack■   E Club
BOQ   Galley
O Club
Gate 3   RV■ ■
Rec C

	Break	Lunch	Dinner	Brun
O Club		xSu	xM	Su
E Club				
Galley	7d	7d	7d	
Snack	Tu-F	xSu		

On Æ86, Navy Circuit   **NAS Patuxent**

Navy Rec Center
Distances walkable.

Quarters:

Availability ★★★★ x ★ summer, weekends. Admin office **3566** 0730-2000, reservations C 9024 0900-1800 xF, 0900-2000 F. Cottages, trailers, no linens, blankets, rent at Office. Rates depend on rank and size of unit, and time of year. On season prices $44-125/d, $264-750/w.

RV: $20-35/d, $88-175/w, $150-315/m; $20 basic, E $27, EW $32, ESW $35 No pets in lodging facilities.

Commercial: Motels, restaurants in town of **Solomons**.

Marina: C 410-326-4009/5408/5104/7165 Point Patience Marina

To DC 55m   Shop ■Office
3.8m   Gas■ M
235   4   2,4
4.5m✗   Solomon ✳
NAS Patuxent

NRC Solomons D-8
Solomons, MD 20688
342-0111   (Patuxent Operator) **301-342**-3000/2
Admin   410.326.5003
Marina   410.326.5204
Security 5410
Toll Free From VA, DC, VA
800.628.9230

On Æ65, Air Force Circuit   **Warfield ANGB**

Zulu-5

MASSACHUSETTS

Hanscom AFB■
Westover AFB■
Fourth Cliff Fam Camp
CG Cuttyhunk Island   Otis ANGB,
Rec Cottage   Camp Edwards,
CGAS

Telephone Area Codes

There was a time when changes in area codes were infrequent. Today it is different. Approximately 80 area codes changed in CONUS since February 1997. In normal practice all numbers are checked once between editions. As preparation of the next edition changes are put into that edition. Traveler input is essential, not even the Pentagon Operator has a commercial telephone listing as accurate as provided here. If you discover any change, please help other readers by submitting this information.

Distances short on island, 0.2m ferry to apartments. Availability ★★★★ x ★ summer.
Advance Reservations &payment required from address to right. Summer Sa-Sa only, other seasons may be shorter but preference given to week. Rates $285/w up depending on rank. other times, Cuttyhunk Boat Lines, 508-992-1432. Departs from State Pier, New Bedford. Caretaker meets ferry. Priority 1 AD CG, P-2 other AD, P-3 all others.

CG Cuttyhunk Island Rec
CO (fm) USCG ICS Boston
427 Commercial Street
Boston, MA 02109-1027
617-223-3181/3338
Ferry daily 25 May - 4 Oct,2002 twice weekly

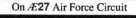

★New Bedford
Ferry 16m
Cuttyhunk Island

On Æ27 Air Force Circuit	**Hanscom AFB**

FMH
C26, ANG &
ARNG,
Coast Guard,
National Guard
Distances long.
Quarters:
All ★ summer (1
June - Sep 30).
Coast Guard:
6461 0800-1600 M-F.
For arrival other hrs, call
with credit card, key left
at OOD (at CG OPS) 6330.Rates: By pay
grade, Summer $50 Suite, $40 Room, Off season $40 Suite, $35 Room. CG OPS 6352.
National Guard: (no dependents) **5916** 0730-
1600 xF, 0730-2000 F. Rate: $11per.

495
3
25
195
Cape Cod Canal
6   6
CG AS
4m
1.5m M
0.4m
0.6m
OPS
0.9m
Comm
28
Gas
BQ   Lee **OPS**
NG   **ANG**
PX **Snack**
Turpentine
BQ
CG   Club

Otis ANGB   D-94
Camp Edwards, NG
MA 02542
557-4401   **508-968**-1000
CG ⇥⇥ Flights ⇥ ANG
Rare flights
Andrews   Hanscom
Barnes Muni MA   Hunter √
Dobbins   Washington
Harrisburg
          Chance of seat
★★★★   ★★★★
Flight Information:
4832

	0730-1600 M-F, **6360** 24h xSu.	0730-1600 ARNG 5291 Scheduler

	Break	Lunch	Dinner	Brun
Club		7d	WTh	Su
Snack	0600-1400 M-Th 0600-1500 F			

On Æ66, Air Force Circuit	**Westover ARB**

Zulu-5

MICHIGAN
NG Training Distances short.

Grayling
72
256
Lake Michigan
93   254
Point Betsie Rec A
RV   75
Camp Grayling
Selfridge AFB ●
PX
Snack
(Summer)
BQ

Camp Grayling   D-8
Grayling, MI 49739-7621
623-3100   **989.344**.6154
Quarters:
BQ: Availability ★★ x ★ summer (no
dependents) **6208.** 0745-1630 M-F,
Bldg 560. Rate: Free.
RV: ★★★★ **6604** reservations, check
in Trailer Park. Season 15 May-15
Sept. RV ESW $9. Tent $9.

Coast Guard
Quarters:
BQ: 2 bedroom cottage ★★★★ x ★
summer, reservations a must, up to
30d ahead (active CG 60), number to
right. Check in at CG Station, Frankfort
616.352.4242/9151 after 1000, Frankfort,
MI. Rate: $20-30unit by rank. No pets.

Point Betsie Rec Cottage
CG Group Grand Haven
650 Harbor Ave, Grand Haven MI 49417
Cottage   **616-850**-2509
Lighthouse   22   M-F 0800-1600
Point Betsie Rd
6m ─ Traverse City
2nd   115   40m
CG Station   Frankfort

On Æ59 Air Force Circuit	**Selfridge ANGB**

CONUS

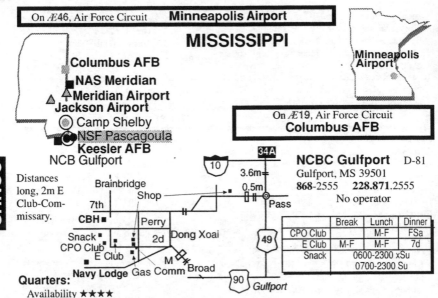

On Æ46, Air Force Circuit **Minneapolis Airport**

MISSISSIPPI

Minneapolis Airport

Columbus AFB
NAS Meridian
Meridian Airport
Jackson Airport
Camp Shelby
NSF Pascagoula
Keesler AFB
NCB Gulfport

On Æ19, Air Force Circuit
Columbus AFB

Distances long, 2m E Club-Commissary.

Brainbridge
Shop
7th
CBH
Perry
Snack
CPO Club
2d
Dong Xoai
E Club
Navy Lodge Gas Comm Broad
M

34A
10
3.6m
0.5m
Pass
49
90 Gulfport

NCBC Gulfport D-81
Gulfport, MS 39501
868-2555 **228.871**.2555
No operator

	Break	Lunch	Dinner
CPO Club		M-F	FSa
E Club	M-F	M-F	7d
Snack	0600-2300 xSu		
	0700-2300 Su		

Quarters:
Availability ★★★★
CBH: 2505/6, 2226 0800-2300. Rates: $25per (dependents only E7 up). No Space-A guest.
Navy Lodge: ★★★ x ★ May-Aug, **C 864-3101** 0830-1800. FAX 868-7392. Rate: $42unit.
Golf: 871.2124 **Holes**: 18 PINE BAYOU GOLF COURSE
Ground Transport:
City bus to Keesler. In Gulfport Greyhound, Amtrak east 2114 SuTT, 916, west 0914 MWSa, 0743.

On Æ30, Air Force Circuit   **Jackson Airport**
On Æ31, Air Force Circuit   **Keesler AFB**
On Æ45, Air Force Circuit   **Meridian Airport**
On Æ80, Navy Circuit   **NAS Meridian**

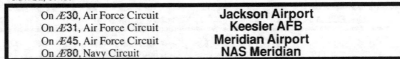

Housing for ship crews, in one building

Quarters:
BQ: Availability ★★★★ x ★ when ship in port 761.2444 24h. Rates: $9per, (shared bath), DV $25unit, families $25.
Ground Transport:
Greyhound on US90. Amtrak east 2154 SuTT, 1954, west 0902 MWSa, 0706.

10
69
63
90
1.2m
Chicot
0.6m BQ

NS Pascagoula
Pascagoula, MS 39567
457-4999 **228-769**-6160

BRAC 2005

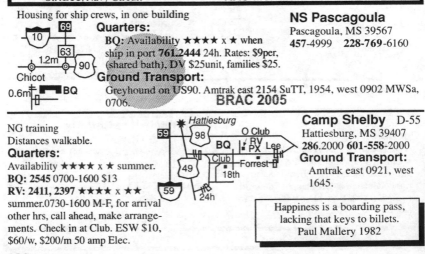

NG training
Distances walkable.
Quarters:
Availability ★★★★ x ★ summer.
BQ: 2545 0700-1600 $13
RV: 2411, 2397 ★★★★ x ★★ summer.0730-1600 M-F, for arrival other hrs, call ahead, make arrangements. Check in at Club. ESW $10, $60/w, $200/m 50 amp Elec.

Hattiesburg
59
98
O Club
BQ
RV
PX Lee
Club
Forrest
49
18th
59
24h

Camp Shelby D-55
Hattiesburg, MS 39407
286.2000 **601-558**-2000
Ground Transport:
Amtrak east 0921, west 1645.

Happiness is a boarding pass, lacking that keys to billets.
Paul Mallery 1982

CONUS

GVW Zulu-6
Quarters:
BQ D 894.3850, C 843.3850
ALL $15-40

On Æ61, Air Force Circuit
St Joseph Airport
On Æ66, Air Force Circuit **Whiteman AFB**

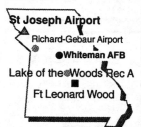

St Joseph Airport
Richard-Gebaur Airport
●Whiteman AFB
Lake of the Woods Rec A
Ft Leonard Wood

Richards-Gebaur Airport
Marine Corps Support Activity
465-7106 816-322-7106
Flights handled by Millionaire.
Reservist flight FSu, contact JRB Ft
Worth.
Quarters:
BQ: Availability
★★★★ $15-20 + $5, DV
$30+$10 add. 816.843.3850.

OPS
155th St 1m
Kensington 0.8m M Motels
Club ■■PX
■Billet
435 470
=5.5m
150
M
71

TBN
Distances long,
3m BQ-OPS.
Quarters:
BQ: Avail-
ability
★★★★ **0999**,
800-677-8356
24h. Rates: $20sgl , DV
$22sgl both+$4add per.
Protocol 6157/83. Guest
House $36sgl+$1add per.
Golf: 5730329.4770 **Holes:** 18
Piney Valley Golf Course
Marina: C 573.346.5640
Lake of the Ozarks Rec A:
Trailers, duplex ★★★★ x ★
weekends **573.346.5640/5673**
0730-1630 M-F, site Fax
573.346.3578, reserve May-Sept
0900-1800 M-F. Check in after
1400. Rates: $31-73 depending on rank and
accommodations. No bedding, towels.
RV $4-7, EW $7,8. Tent $4-7.
Commercial: Motels outside main gate.
Ground Transport:
Shuttle 0700-1700 M-F. **Commercial:**
Greyhound on post. Fort Taxi.

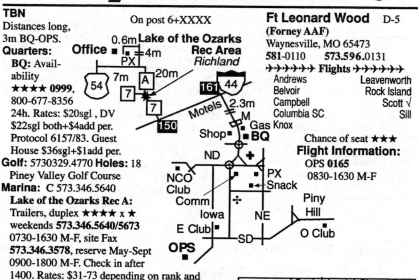

On post 6+XXXX

Office ■ 0.6m **Lake of the Ozarks**
Rec Area
Richland
PX ≑4m
7m 20m
54 A
7
7
150 Motels 2.3m
Shop■ M Gas Knox
■ **BQ**
ND ✚
NCO PX
Club ■◄ Snack
Comm ÷
Iowa NE
E Club■ Piny
SD Hill
OPS O Club
■

Ft Leonard Wood D-5
(Forney AAF)
Waynesville, MO 65473
581-0110 **573.596**.0131
↔↔↔↔↔↔ **Flights** ↔↔↔↔↔↔
Andrews   Leavenworth
Belvoir   Rock Island
Campbell   Scott √
Columbia SC   Sill
Knox

Chance of seat ★★★
Flight Information:
OPS **0165**
0830-1630 M-F

	Break	Lunch	Dinner	Brun
O Club	M-F	Tu-F	Tu-Sa	Su
NCO Club		W-F	FSa	Su
E Club	M-F		W-Su	
Snack		0600-2200		

●Duval's
Malmstrom AFB
Lionshead Resort

Zulu-7

MONTANA

On Æ39, Air Force Circuit
Malmstrom AFB

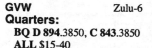

Offutt AFB
Lincoln Airport △

Zulu-6

NEBRASKA

On Æ35 Air Force Circuit **Lincoln Airport**
On Æ49, Air Force Circuit **Offutt AFB**

NEVADA

Zulu-8

Reno Airport
NAS Fallon

Indian Springs AFS

Nellis AFB

On Æ75, Navy Circuit	**NAS Fallon**
On Æ30, Air Force Circuit	**Indian Springs AFS**
On Æ48 Air Force Circuit	**Nellis AFB**
On Æ55 Air Force Circuit	**Reno Airport**

NEW HAMPSHIRE

Zulu-5 **Rec A:** Availability ★★★ **2452**
0730-1600 M-F, reserve, site
2234, season Memorial-Colum-
bus. Rates: Trailer $15,30unit. RV
$3, EW $10. Tent $4.

**Pease
ANGB**

New Boston
AFS

New Boston AFS
Amherst, NH 03031
489-2000 **603-471**-2000

114 Manchester

7m
M
101 101 293
3
293

On Æ52, Air Force Circuit	**Pease ANGB**

NEW JERSEY

Zulu-5
Distances walkable.
Quarters:
BQ: Availability **O** ★, **E** ★★★★
3188, 4849, 24h. O6 up thru proto-
col 3061. Rates: $22sgl +$5add per.
Guest House ★★★ x ★ summer,
6663 24h, reservations 0800-1800
M-F. Rates: $35dbl+$5add per,
$45max
Golf: 609.562.5443 **Holes**: 18
Fountain Green
Travel Camp ★★★★ **6667** 1100-
1700 M-F, 0900-1200 SS, check in
Outdoor Rec, with reservation go to
site. RV $8, no dump, shower.
Commercial: Motels in area.
Ground Transport:
Shuttles: To Willow Grove Æ91
0600 M-F from parking lot behind
playground.
✚ **Shuttle** to McGuire, Monmouth
0700 Th, 3004.
Commercial: #307 Bus to
McGuire, NYC, Newark Airport.
#317 Bus to Philadelphia, Asbury
Park. Transfer at Lakewood to #139
for NYC, to #67 for Newark Airport
or RR. Purchase ticket on first bus.
800-582-5946. Taxi 723-2000.

Picatinny Arsenal

Ft Monmouth

NAEC Lakehurst
Ft Dix
McGuire AFB

Campground

Ft Dix
Wrightstown, NJ 08640
944-1110   **609-562**-1011
✈✈✈✈ **Flights** ✈✈✈✈

Belvoir

Chance of seat ★★★
Flight Information:
OPS **5287,5659**
0800-1700 M-F

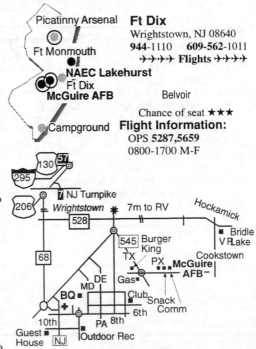

	Break	Lunch	Dinner	Brun
Club		Tu-F	W-Sa	Su
Burger K	0700-2000			

On Æ79, Navy Circuit
On Æ44, Air Force Circuit

**NAEC Lakehurst
McGuire AFB**

Distances walkable, 1.7m East-West Gates.

Ft Monmouth   D-88
Oceanport, NJ 07703
992-9110   **732.532**.9000

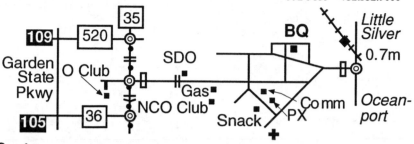

Quarters:

BQ: Availability ★★★★ x ★★ summer **1092** 0730-2400. For arrival other hrs, call, keys left with SDO, 1100. Retirees reserve 7d prior 1300-2400 M-F. Rates: $21sgl, $27family, DV $32sgl, $37dbl. Protocol 4015.

Golf: 732.532.4653/4307 Holes: 18 **Suneagles Golf Course**

Commercial: Motel outside West Gate.

	Break	Lunch	Dinner	Brun
O Club		M-F	Tu-Sa	Su
NCO Club		M-F		
Snack	0700-2000 M-F			
	0800-2000 Sa			
	1030-1830 Su			

Ground Transport:

Post Shuttle 0730-1600 M-F. ✚ **Shuttle** to Dix, McGuire 1300 Th, Dix 3004.

Commercial: Buses at West Gate: M21 to Red Bank, Long Branch; M22 to Asbury Park xSu. RR in Little Silver to Newark.

Armament R&D
Distances long.

Picatinny Arsenal
Dover, NJ 07801
880-4021   **973.724**.4021
Info only.

Quarters:

BQ: Picatinny Guest House Availability ★★★X May-Oct Reservations 973.724.8855 **3506** 0830-1500 M-F, for arrival other hrs, call, keys left with Security 6666. Rates: $38-54 O6 up thru protocol 7024.

Golf: 973.989.2466 **Holes**: 18 Picatinny Golf Club

	Break	Lunch	Dinner
O Club		Tu-F	
NCO Club		M-F	M-F
Cafeteria	0630-1300 M-F		

Trailers: ★ **4014,4186** 0730-1530 M-F, reservations, check in Trailer Office. Rates: $33-40unit. No pets.

Lake Denmark: **973.724.3853** ★★★★ x ★ with hook up 1000-1300, for arrival other hrs, call ahead. Water late spring to early fall. RV $5, ESW $10. Tent $5.

Ground Transport:

Morris County Metro, 285-6145.

NEW MEXICO

Zulu-7

On Æ17, Air Force Circuit	**Cannon AFB**
On Æ28 Air Force Circuit	**Holloman AFB**
On Æ32, Air Force Circuit	**Kirtland AFB**

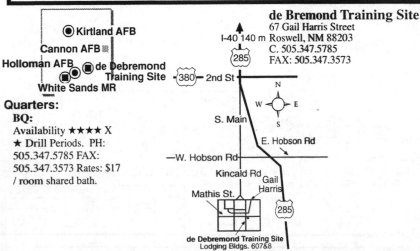

⊙ Kirtland AFB

Cannon AFB ▓

Holloman AFB
▣ de Debremond
Training Site
White Sands MR

de Bremond Training Site
67 Gail Harris Street
I-40 140 m Roswell, NM 88203
C. 505.347.5785
FAX: 505.347.3573

Quarters:
BQ:
Availability ★★★★ X
★ Drill Periods. PH:
505.347.5785 FAX:
505.347.3573 Rates: $17
/ room shared bath.

de Debremond Training Site
Lodging Bldgs. 607&8

WSD
Missile Range
Distances short x 6.2m BQ-OPS.
Quarters:
BQ: Availability ★★★★ **2966,4559**
0745-1600 M-F, other hrs SDO has keys, 2031. Rate:
$18,25unit. O6 up thru protocol 1028.
Travel Camp: ★★★★ **1713** 0900-1700
M-F, reserve, check in Equipment Issue. RV ESW $8.
Maximum 21d in 60 d period.
Golf: 678.1759 **Holes**: 9 WSMR Golf Course
Ground Transport:
✚ **Shuttle** Ft Bliss 0730, 1300 M-F. Post taxi will take
OPS-BQ, 2340.
Commercial: Intercity buses in Las Cruces. Car rent C
437-7922.

White Sands MR
(**Condron AAF**)
White Sands, NM 88002
258-2211   505-678-2121
✈✈✈✈ **Flights** ✈✈✈✈
Army posts in Southwest
Holloman

Infrequent flights
Chance of seat
★★★★

Flight Information:
OPS **5111** 0800-1600 M-F. See
Holloman Æ28.

To Las Cruces 25m
Picatinny

To
Alamogordo
3.8m 47m

Gas · PX · Bowl
· Rock I
Comm
· HQ Avenue
· SDO
BQ ▪
Aberdeen/ Shop
RV NCO Club
O Club Equipment Lease
Cafeteria ✕ ▪ **OPS**
To El Paso, Ft Bliss 60m

	Break	Lunch	Dinner	Brun
O Club		M-F	Tu-F	Su
NCO Club		M-F	WFSa	
Bowl		1100-2300 xSu		
		1300-1900 Su		
Cafeteria		0700-1400 M-F		

GTB
Zulu-5 On post dial 2+XXXX
Distances long, 2m BQ-OPS.

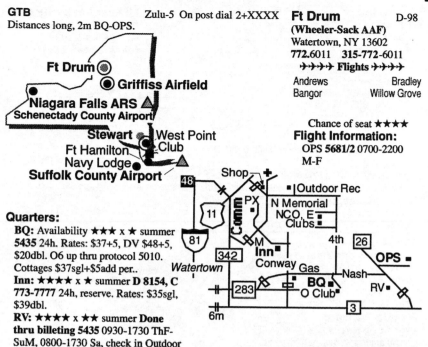

Ft Drum ◉

◉ **Griffiss Airfield**

Niagara Falls ARS △
Schenectady County Airport

Stewart ⬡ **West Point**
Ft Hamilton ⬡ **Club**
Navy Lodge ●
Suffolk County Airport ↙ △

Quarters:
BQ: Availability ★★★ x ★ summer
5435 24h. Rates: $37+5, DV $48+5,
$20dbl. O6 up thru protocol 5010.
Cottages $37sgl+$5add per..
Inn: ★★★★ x ★ summer **D 8154, C**
773-7777 24h, reserve. Rates: $35sgl,
$39dbl.
RV: ★★★★ x ★★ summer **Done**
thru billeting 5435 0930-1730 ThF-
SuM, 0800-1730 Sa, check in Outdoor
Rec. RV $20. No dump. Discounts
Golden Age, Access, Eagle.
Ground Transport:
Post Shuttle 0600-2300 M-F, 0900-
2300 SS.
Commercial: Buses in Watertown.

Ft Drum
D-98
(Wheeler-Sack AAF)
Watertown, NY 13602
772.6011   315-772-6011
✈✈✈✈ **Flights** ✈✈✈✈

| Andrews | Bradley |
| Bangor | Willow Grove |

Chance of seat ★★★★
Flight Information:
OPS **5681/2** 0700-2200
M-F

	Break	Lunch	Dinner	Brun
O Club	M-F	Tu-F	Tu-Sa	Su
NCO Club		M-F	W-Sa	
Snack	7d	7d	7d	

On Æ26, Air Force Circuit   **Griffiss Airfield**

Distances short.
Quarters:
BOQ Availability ★★★★
x ★★ summer **4892, 4348**
24h. Rates: $45-60+$5add
per.
Guest House 4052,4892
24h. Rates: $60sgl+$5add
per. **DV $62**
Ground Transport:
Subway, buses on 4th Ave.
#53 Bus at 95th and 4th to
Navy Lodge New York.

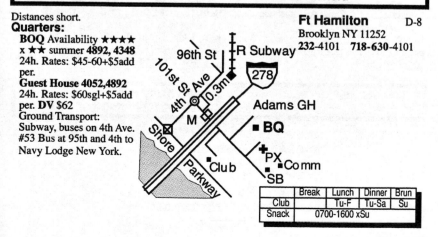

Ft Hamilton
D-8
Brooklyn NY 11252
232-4101   718-630-4101

	Break	Lunch	Dinner	Brun
Club		Tu-F	Tu-Sa	Su
Snack		0700-1600 xSu		

Distances long.

Quarters:
Thayer Hotel: Availability ★★★★ x ★ graduation **C 446-4731**, 800.247.5047 D thru operator, 24h. Rates: $60sgl to $175dbl. **Five Star Inn** 845.446.1028/1034/5943 Rates: $47-67 + $5 per. **RV:** Round Pond **4455, 3860,** season 15 April-15 Nov ★★★★ x ★★ mid season **2503** 0700-1800, shorter ends of season, reserve. RV EW $14. Tent $8.

Military Academy D-98
(West Point)
West Point, NY 10996
688-4011 **845-938**-4011

	Break	Lunch	Dinner	Brun
O Club		M-F	Tu-Sa	Su
NCO Club		M-F	TTFSa	
Hotel	7d	7d	7d	

Golf: 845.938.2435 **Holes**: 18 West Point Golf Course
Commercial: Motels on Route 218, 1.1m south. See Stewart Army Subpost Æ61.

Ground Transport:
Post Shuttle 0630-1700 M-F, pay shuttle to Stewart 0500,1635,2018, active duty only.
Commercial: Bus to NYC. Limo to Airport.

Quarters:
Navy Lodge: ★★★★ **C 718-442-0413** 0800-2300. Fax 816-0830. Rate: $56unit. Carriage House 876.6489

Ground Transport
#51 Bus to ferry to Manhattan. #53 Bus to Brooklyn and Ft. Hamilton. Nearest other quarters Ft. Hamilton across bridge, see preceding page.

Navy Lodge NY
Bldg 408
North Pass
Ft Wadsworth
Staten Island. NY 10305
718-442-0413

On Æ49, Air Force Circuit	**Niagara Falls ARS**
On Æ57, Air Force Circuit	**Schenectady County Airport**

Converted 5-story residence, no elevator, communal facilities.
Rates: Active Duty **E**, 2-bed room $25-30 per, **O** $40 and retirees $40per.
Reservists, former service $45. 3 or 4-bed room $25per. All +$5 FSa, holidays. Smoking permitted & permeates Club.

Soldiers', Sailors', and Airmen's Club
283 Lexington Ave. (between 36th and 37th)
New York City, NY 10016, 212-683-4354
800-678-8443, Fax 683-7374

On Æ61, Air Force Circuit	**Stewart Army Subpost**
On Æ62, Air Force Circuit	**Suffolk County Airport**

Zulu-5

NORTH CAROLINA

CGAS Elizabeth City
Seymour Johnson AFB
Pope AFB
Charlotte Airport
Ft Bragg
MCAS New River
MCAS Cherry Point
Camp Lejeune
Ft Fisher Rec A

FBG

82d Airborne Division Distances long, 4.3m BQ-OPS.

Quarters:
   BQ: Availability ★★ x ★ summer **5575** 24h. Rates: $11per, $19sgl, DV (O5 up). $25sgl+$5add per. Protocol 2804.
   Guest Houses: E5 up & **O** ★★ Rate: $30unit. Nearest other quarters at Pope AFB 3m north, *Æ54.*

Golf: 910.396.3980 **Holes**: 18 Stryker Golf Course; **Golf:** 910.907.4653 **Holes**: 18 Ryder Golf Course

RV: ★★★★ **5979** 0900-1900, check in RV. EW $7, ESW $8. Discount Golden Age, Access.

Rec A: KOA, 5th south of Myrtle Beach SC. Trailers ★★★★ x ★ summer, **2713**, site C 803-436-1065, reserve 0800-1700 M-F $30unit.

Ground Transport:
   Check motor pool for transport 7283.
   Commercial: Greyhound on post, 497-8746.
   Amtrak north 2333, south 0221. Car rent 436-2202, 0800-1800 xSu, 1200-1800 Su.

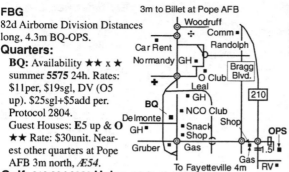

Ft Bragg

(Simmons AAF)
Fayetteville, NC 28307
236-0011   910.396.0011
✈✈✈✈ **Flights** ✈✈✈✈

Aberdeen	Langley
Atlanta	Maxwell
Atlanta Hartsfield	New River
Belvoir	Norfolk √
Benning	Richmond VA
Dobbins	Rucker
Jacksonville √	Washington
Johnstown	Willow Grove √
Knox	

Chance of seat ★★★★
Flight Information:
   OPS **7804,9387** 24h
   Scheduling 3303,3766

	Break	Lunch	Dinner	Brun
O Club	M-F	M-F	xM	Su
NCO Club	7d	7d	xSuW	
Snack	0530-2300 M-F			
	0700-1400 Sa			
	0800-2300 Su			

CONUS

Hatteras Ferries

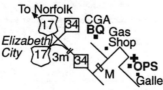

When driving along the East Coast consider ferries. The two most-important are to the left. Schedule information 800-293-3779. Hatteras-Okracoke free 0500-2500 essentially 30min service, 40min crossing. Cedar Island-Oracoke $10 0700-2030 x 0700-1600 Nov-May, make reservations, From Cesar Island 800-956-0343, from Okracoke 800-345-1665, 2.25h crossing.

On *Æ*19 Air Force Circuit	**Charlotte Airport**
On *Æ*73, Navy Circuit	**MCAS Cherry Point**

ECG

Coast Guard Support and Air Station Distances walkable, 0.6m BQ-OPS.

Quarters:
   BQ: Availability ★★★★ x ★ summer **C 6727** 0800-1630 M-F, other hrs OOD, C 6130. Trailers $25-37 unit, RV ESW $4-7. No pets.
   MWR 6482
   Commercial: Motels in Elizabeth City.

Ground Transport:
   Liberty bus to Elizabeth City evenings 7d.
   Commercial: Taxi 335-7180.

CGSC Elizabeth City

Elizabeth City, NC 27909
723-1540   **252.335.**6085
✈✈✈✈ **Flights** ✈✈✈✈
Gander,Groton Feb-July
St. Johns 2/m Spring & Summer

Chance of seat ★★★
Flight Information:
   OPS **6333**
   0800-1600

	Break	Lunch	Dinner
CPO Club		M-F	
Galley	7d	7d	7d

Distances short.
Quarters:
Availability ★★★★, cottages, lodge
C 6546, D thru operator. Reserve.
Reservations only **800.645.9725.** Fax
458-6298. **Rates:** Various depending
on season and accommodations $15-
135unit. RV ESW $18. Tent $10-15.
No pets in lodge, fee in cottages.

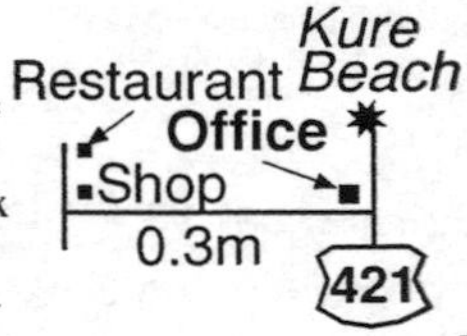

Kure Beach
Restaurant
↙ **Office** ✳
▪**Shop**▪▪
0.3m
(421)

Ft Fisher Rec A D-98
Air Force Rec. Area
118 Riverfront Road
Kure Beach, NC 28449
488-8011 (Sunny Point
Operator) **910-457**-8000
Res 458-6549, **Admin** 6723

	Break	Lunch	Dinner
Dining	7d	7d	7d

Distances long, 4m BOQ-
snack.
Quarters:
BOQ: ★★★ I ★ summer
1385, 2146 24h. Rates:
$16sgl+$5add per. O Club
O6 up thru protocol 2523.
DV $20+5
SNCO (E6 up) **5262** 24h.
Rate: $20sgl +$5add per.
Hospitality Inn: ★★★ x ★ summer **3041** 24h.
Rate: $26unit.
Golf: 910.451-5445 **Holes:** 36 Paradise Point
Golf Course
Marinas: C 910.450.7386/7119
Courthouse Bay; C 910.451.8307/8345 Gottschalk
Marina
Onslow Beach: ★★★ 450.7572, 7473,7502
0730-2000, reservations, trailers, apartments,

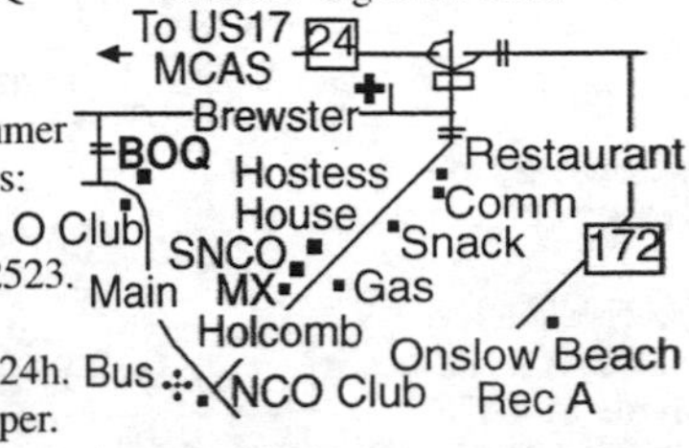

Dial all 7 digits on base.
To US17 [24]
← MCAS
Brewster
┌BOQ Hostess
│ SNCO▪ House
Main MX▪ ▪Snack
\ Holcomb ▪Gas
Bus ⋮ NCO Club
Restaurant
Comm
[172]
Onslow Beach
Rec A

Camp Lejeune D-94
Jacksonville, NC 28542
751.1110 910-451-1113

Ground Transport:
Shuttle: Lejeune-New
River 0545-1700 M-F,
1100-1600 SS, 3585.
Commercial: Bus station,
Greyhound, taxi, 3632.

	Break	Lunch	Dinner	Brun
O Club	xSa	M-F		Su
NCO Club		M-F		
Snack	7d	7d	7d	
Restaurant	M-F	M-F	7d	

On Æ82, Navy Circuit — **MCAS New River**
On Æ54, Air Force Circuit — **Pope AFB**
On Æ59, Air Force Circuit — **Seymour Johnson AFB**

Zulu-6
NORTH DAKOTA

On Æ26, Air Force Circuit — **Grand Forks AFB**
On Æ46, Air Force Circuit — **Minot AFB**

Minot AFB Camp Grafton NGTS
Grand Forks AFB

NORTH DAKOTA (Concluded)

Quarters:
Availability ★★★★ X ★ Drill periods. Rates $9.
PH: 701.662.0239

Billeting Office
Camp Gilbert C Grafton, ND
4417 Highway 20
Devils Lake, ND 58301
701.662.0200

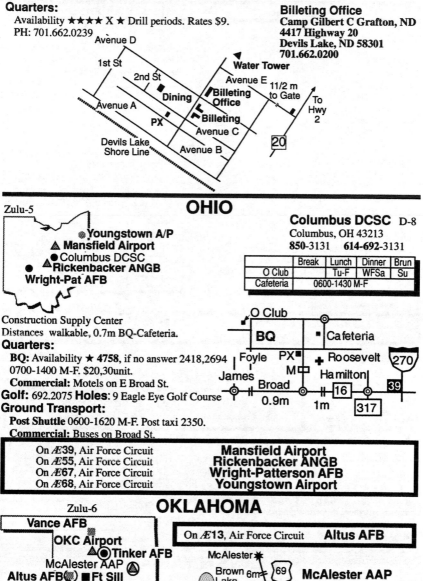

OHIO

Zulu-5

- ●Youngstown A/P
- ▲ Mansfield Airport
- ●Columbus DCSC
- ●▲Rickenbacker ANGB
- ● Wright-Pat AFB

Columbus DCSC D-8
Columbus, OH 43213
850-3131   614-692-3131

	Break	Lunch	Dinner	Brun
O Club		Tu-F	WFSa	Su
Cafeteria	0600-1430 M-F			

Construction Supply Center
Distances walkable, 0.7m BQ-Cafeteria.

Quarters:
BQ: Availability ★ **4758**, if no answer 2418,2694
0700-1400 M-F. $20,30unit.
Commercial: Motels on E Broad St.
Golf: 692.2075 **Holes**: 9 Eagle Eye Golf Course

Ground Transport:
Post Shuttle 0600-1620 M-F. Post taxi 2350.
Commercial: Buses on Broad St.

On Æ39, Air Force Circuit	**Mansfield Airport**
On Æ55, Air Force Circuit	**Rickenbacker ANGB**
On Æ67, Air Force Circuit	**Wright-Patterson AFB**
On Æ68, Air Force Circuit	**Youngstown Airport**

OKLAHOMA

Zulu-6

- ■Vance AFB
- ●OKC Airport
- ▲●Tinker AFB
- McAlester AAP ●
- Altus AFB●) ■Ft Sill ●

| On Æ13, Air Force Circuit | **Altus AFB** |

McAlester AAP
McAlester, OK 74501
956-6642   **918-420**-6642
No operator, Security
D thru Security

Distances short.
RV: Availability ★★★★ x
Oct-Nov for hook ups **C 7484**
0630-1700 M-W, 1150-1730
Th-Sa, closed Su. Reservations, park, they will collect, check in at Equipment Rental, or use box. Cabins $65, Deuplex $30-50. Rental campers, tents available, RV $10 ESW $7. Tent $5.
Discount Golden Age, Access.

On Æ50, Air Force Circuit — Oklahoma City Airport

FSI
Distances long,
1m BQ-OPS.
Quarters:
BQ: Availability
★★★★ **5000**
24h (no children under 18). Rate: $33-50
+$7add per. O6 up
thru protocol 3902.
Guest House: ★★★★
580.355.4475 24h.
Rates: **O** $22-36room, **E** $22-32room.
Commercial: Motels on US62, I44.
Golf: 3875 Holes: 18 Cedar Lakes Golf Course;
580.353.0411 **Holes:** 36 Fort Sill Golf Courses
Ground Transport:
Post Shuttle 0600-1730 M-F, connects at ✚ with shuttle to Lawton. On Sa shuttle has Lawton stop. Southwest Transit from Lawton to Altus MWF. On-post taxi 248-1234, 355-5555.

Quinette
Comm
Gas
PX ■ ■
Macomb
Sheridan
Shop ■ Snack
Gas ■
Sheridan
Ft Sill
Condon Rogers
O Club 44
62
Burril M
Guest House
■ NCO Club
Motel
Lawton
39A
39
38
62
44

Ft Sill (Henry Post AAF)   D-94
Lawton, OK 73503
639-7090   **580-442**-8111
✈✈✈✈✈✈✈✈✈✈ **Flights** ✈✈✈✈✈✈✈✈✈✈
Carson   Peterson
Hood   U of OK Westheim
Leavenworth

Chance of seat ★★★★
Flight Information:
OPS **5643, 5808** 0600-2000 M-F.
Schedules 5012 M-F. A at Lawton
Airport, 0752 0730-1600 M-F, **D866**
C458-2752, 353.5012

	Break	Lunch	Dinner	Brun
O Club		Tu-Sa	Tu-Sa	Su
NCO Club		Tu-F	Tu-Sa	
Snack	0600-2300 M-F			
	0700-2400 Sa			
	0900-2200 Su			

On Æ62, Air Force Circuit — Tinker AFB
On Æ64, Air Force Circuit — Vance AFB

Zulu-8

OREGON

Rilea AFTC
Portland Airport
Kingsley Field

On Æ32, Air Force Circuit — Kingsley Field
On Æ54, Air Force Circuit — Portland Airport

Quarters:
BQ: ★★★★ | ★ 1st weekend & summer **C**
4052, D thru operator 0800-1630 7d, reserve
90d in advance, no bedding $7per, bath,
$10,15-30 shared bath, Koshi Hall Hotel
suite $25-40.

Astoria ✳
101
PX
Restaurant
8m
■ **BQ**

Rilea AFTC   D-9100
91390 Rilea Pacific Road
Warrenton, OR 97146-9711
355-3972   **503-861**-4004

Restaurant Lunch, Dinner xSu

PENNSYLVANIA

Zulu-5

Pittsburgh Airport
Tobyhanna AD
Harrisburg
Airport   Ft Indiantown Gap
Carlisle Barracks ● ■
New Cumberland AD **NAS Willow Grove**

Army War College
Distances short.
Quarters:
BQ: Availability ★★ x ★ summer **4245** 0700-1800 M-F, 0800-1600 SS. Other hrs Security has keys, 4115. Reservations accepted, confirmed 60d ahead, x 3d June-Aug. Rates: $20sgl communal, $25sgl, $35sgl private bath. DV $40sgl all+$5add per.
Commercial: Motels in Carlisle.
Golf: 717.243.3262 **Holes**: 18 Carlisle Barracks
Ground Transport: Capital Area Transit, Greyhound in Carlisle.

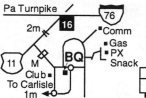

Carlisle Barracks
(War College)
Carlisle, PA 17013
242-4141   **717-245**-3131

	Break	Lunch	Dinner
Snack		7d	

MUI
Summer training
Distances walkable,
0.7m BQ-PX.
Quarters:
BQ: Availability ★★★★ x ★ March-Sept, **2540/12,** Fax 2821 0730-1630 Sa-Th, 0700-2000 F, for arrival other hrs, call, keys left with Security.
Rates: $7sgl suites $20sgl, cottages $30-40 all+$6add per. **Space-A should call 24 in advance.**

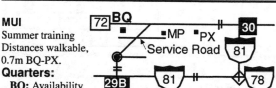

Ft Indiantown Gap D-8
(Muir AAF) PANG
Annville, PA 17003
491-1110   **717-861**-2000
✈✈✈✈ Flights ✈✈✈✈
Rare flights

Flight Information:
OPS D 2123,2813,
C x2123

	Break	Lunch	Dinner
Club	M-F	M-F	Tu-Sa§
	§ xSu summer		

Distances walkable.
Quarters:
BQ: Availability ★★★ x ★ summer **7251/7035** 0800-1630 M-F, other hrs Security has keys, 6270. Rates: $30sgl+$5add per, DV $30unit.
Golf: 717.770.5199 Holes: 9 Riverview Golf Course
Ground Transport:
Capital Area Transit in New Cumberland, on post rush hr. Greyhound, Amtrak in Harrisburg.

New Cumberland AD
(Defense Distribution Region-East)
17070
New Cumberland, PA
977-1110   **717-770**-6011

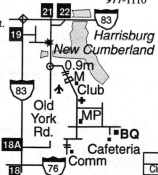

	Break	Lunch	Dinner
Club		M-F	Tu-F
Cafe	M-F	M-F	

On Æ53, Air Force Circuit   **Pittsburgh Airport**

Signal depot
Distances walkable,
1m BQ-Club.

Quarters:

BQ: Availability ★★★ x ★ ski and foliage seasons **7501** 0730-1600 M-F, for arrival other hrs, call, keys left at Security, 7550. Reservations accepted 30d in advance, confirm 2d ahead. Rates: $15sgl+$5add per. Protocol 6223.

Cottages: 8529 Rate: $41, add $5 per. No confirmation by mail, call to confirm. Keys picked up at BQ (Community Services) or Security.

Ground Transport:
Monroe County Transit outside PA423 gate, to Stroudsburg.

Tobyhanna AD
Tobyhanna, PA 18466
795-7110   570.895.7000

Security
To Scranton 25m
Club
Gas
BQ
Comm
PX 1.2m
423
611
380

	Break	Lunch	Dinner
Club		M-F	F
NCO Club	Sa		

On Æ91, Navy Circuit **NAS Willow Grove JRB**

RHODE ISLAND
Zulu-5

Providence Airport

Quonset Point Airport

NETC Newport

NETC Newport   D-5
Newport, RI 02841
948-3456   401-841-3456
Quarterdeck

Naval Education and Training Center
Distances walkable,
1m CPO Club-O Club.

Quarters:

Availability ★★★ x ★★ summer **CBH 2200, 7900** 24h. Rate $15. DV $26. O6 up thru protocol 3715,6464. Check in at **CBH. 3845 O & E** Check in at **CBH.** Rates: E1-4 $5per, E5 up $15per.

Susse Chalet: ★★ C 0800, D thru Quarterdeck, 24h. Rate: $63-106room, reserve 6d ahead.

Navy Lodge: C 849-4500 24h. Fax 1807. Rates: $41-66.

Ground Transport:
Center shuttle. City bus through center to Newport.

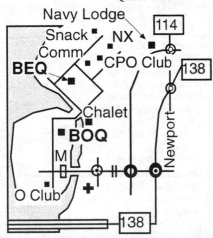

Navy Lodge
Snack   NX   114
Comm
CPO Club   138
BEQ
Chalet
BOQ
M
Newport
O Club
138

	Break	Lunch	Dinner	Brun
O Club	M-F	M-F	Tu-Sa	Su
CPO Club	M-F	M-F	W-Sa	
Snack	0600-2200			

On Æ54, Air Force Circuit **Quonset Point Airport**
On Æ89, Navy Circuit **Providence Airport**

Zulu-5

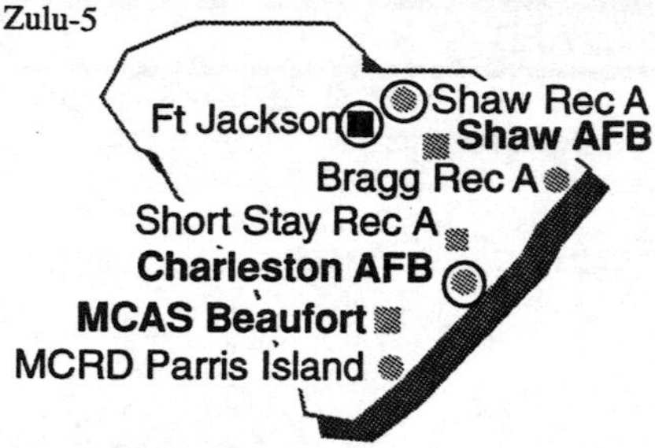

On Æ72, Navy Circuit
MCAS Beaufort
On Æ145
Ft Bragg Rec A
On Æ18, Air Force Circuit
Charleston AFB

CONUS

Distances walkable,
1.5m BQ-Snack.
Quarters:
   BQ: Availability ★★★ **7576** 24h
   (no child).
   Rates: $42sgl+$5
   add per. Protocol
   5218,6618.
   Guest House: ★★★ 24h. Rate:
   $40unit.
   Weston Lake Rec A ★★★★ x
   ★ **803.751.5253** summer, weekends, cabins, **5253,6013** 0900-
   1700 summer, 0900-1700 winter,
   reservations. No linens (can rent).
   Rates: $30-50unit depending on
   size, no pets. RV EW $9 ESW
   $11. Tent EW $5.
Golf: 803.787.4344 **Holes:** 36
Fort Jackson Golf Club
Ground Transport:
   #14,15 Buses 0620-2320 M-F,
   0715-2220 SS, Greyhound,
   Amtrak 0326 north, 0053 south.

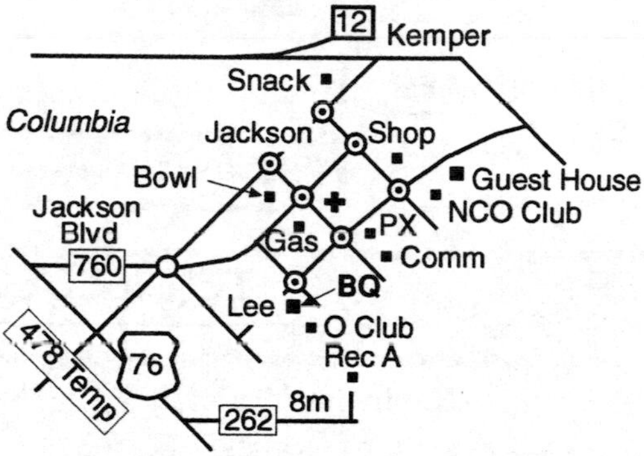

Ft Jackson D-88
Columbia, SC 29207
734-1110   803-751-7511

	Break	Lunch	Dinner	Brun
O Club		Tu-F	Tu-Sa	Su
NCO Club	xSa	xSa	Tu-Sa	
Snack	7d	7d	7d	
Bowl	xSu	7d	7d	

Distances walkable x to O Club.
Quarters:
   BQ: Availability ★ **3962, 2744** 24h. **O** $32+8per, DV
   $20sgl, Protocol O6 + up
   228.4442. **E** (no child)
   $26+8per. All+$4 add per.
   TLF: ★★★★ x ★★ WTh **2976**
   24h. Rates: $50-60, Res 30d
   advance, 35unit. Nearest
   other quarters, MCAS Beaufort,
   12m. Reservations up to 30 days
   prior.
Golf: 843.228.2240 Holes: 18
Legends at Parris Island
Ground Transport:
   Greyhound Bldg 646, 3717.

MCRD Parris Island D-94
Parris Island, SC 29905
335-1110   843.525.2111

	Break	Lunch	Dinner	Brun
O Club		M-F	ThF	Su
NCO Club		M-F	M-F	
E Club	Su	xSu	xSa	
Snack	0600-2000 xSu			
	0800-2000 Su			

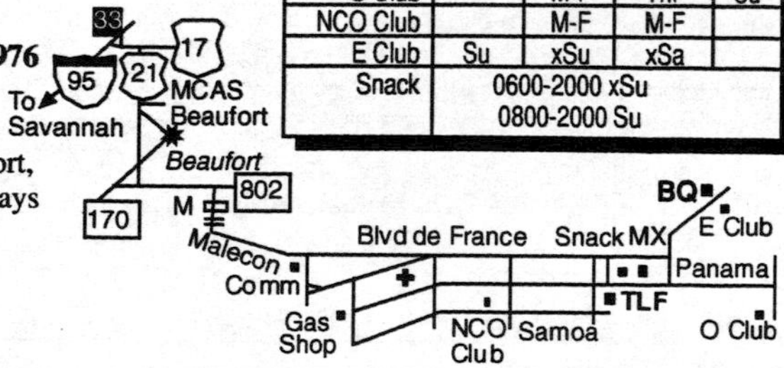

151

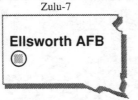

On Æ60 Air Force Circuit — **Shaw AFB**

Short Stay USN Outdoor Rec A Lake Moultrie
211 Short Stay Road
Moncks Corner, SC 29467
Toll Free 800.447.2178
Charleston #**743.2366**
Local (Moncks Corner) Area
PH: 843.761.8353 FAX: 843.761.4792
0730-1700 7d Office open 0730-1700 7d.
Low Season Nov - Feb, $45-73, **High Season** $57-73, **Cabins** $73. AD Reserve up to 1y in advance, retirees 6 m. Check in 1500 until closing, checkout 1100.

SOUTH DAKOTA

Zulu-7

Ellsworth AFB

On Æ24 Air Force Circuit **Ellsworth AFB**

TENNESSEE

Zulu-6 | Zulu-5

Nashville Airport △
Arnold EDC ◎
● NSA Mid-South
▲ **Memphis ANGB**

Knoxville Airport

TUH Zulu-6
AFMC
Distances long.
Secure station, access only to facilities on map.
Quarters:

Wingo Inn: Availability ★★★ x ★ winter **3098/9** 0600-2200 M-F, 0600-2200 SS, 1100-1900 Su. AFMC FY 07/08 Rates: $34-59. Protocol 5202.
Fam Camp March-Oct, reservations.
Rec C **6084** 1300-1900 Tu-F, 1000-1800 Sa, 1200-1800 Su, 24h in season. Site 4520 0800-1700, 24h in season. RV EW $8. Tent $5. Firearms permitted.
Golf: 7076 or (931) 455-5870 **Holes**: 9 Arnold Golf Course
Ground Transport:
Greyhound in Manchester and Tullahoma.

Arnold EDC D-88
Tullahoma, TN 37389
340-5011 931.454.3000

To *Manchester* 4m

Comm 117 24
BX ■
Cafeteria ■ M 0.6m

Rec C

To 2.8m
Tullahoma BQ
RV ■■ ■■ Club

	Break	Lunch	Dinner
Club		xM	Tu-Sa
Cafeteria	M-F	M-F	

On Æ33, Air Force Circuit	**Knoxville Airport**
On Æ45 Air Force Circuit	**Memphis ANGB**

NQA Zulu-6
Distances walkable, 0.8m BOQ-BEQ.

RV
Navy Lodge
Millington 2m
Attu
Gas
M
Golf
0.8m Motel
Navy Road
51
G St
205
40
Inn
Lodge
To Memphis 18m
NX
Club
To Memphis
Exit 25
McDonald's
Bowl
Comm
5th
7th

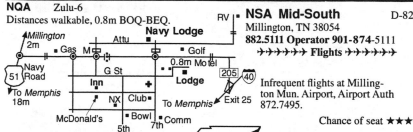

NSA Mid-South

D-82

Millington, TN 38054
882.5111 Operator 901-874-5111

Flights

Infrequent flights at Millington Mun. Airport, Airport Auth 872.7495.

Chance of seat ★★★

Quarters:

BQ taken over by the Navy Exchange, E1-O6 **Inn** (former BEQ) **C 873.2901** E1-O6 $28; **Lodge C 872.0121** mostly O6 up $32reg - $45 suite.

Rec A: Navy Lake RV Park RV & T **C 872.3660.**

Commercial: Econo Inn motel 0.8m from gate, 873-444, others on US51.

	Break	Lunch	Dinner
CPO Club		xSu	7d
Bowl	7d	7d	7d
Golf	7d	7d	
McDonald's	0430-2400 M-F 0600-2400 SS		

Golf: 901.874.5168 Holes: 18 GLEN EAGLES GOLF COURSE

Ground Transport:

Limo to airport 7d 527-0100, 1030-1630. Greyhound in Millington, Amtrak north 2242 xTu, south 0635 xW. Car rent with pick up 872-8181. Taxi 872-3321.

On Æ48, Air Force Circuit	**Nashville Airport**

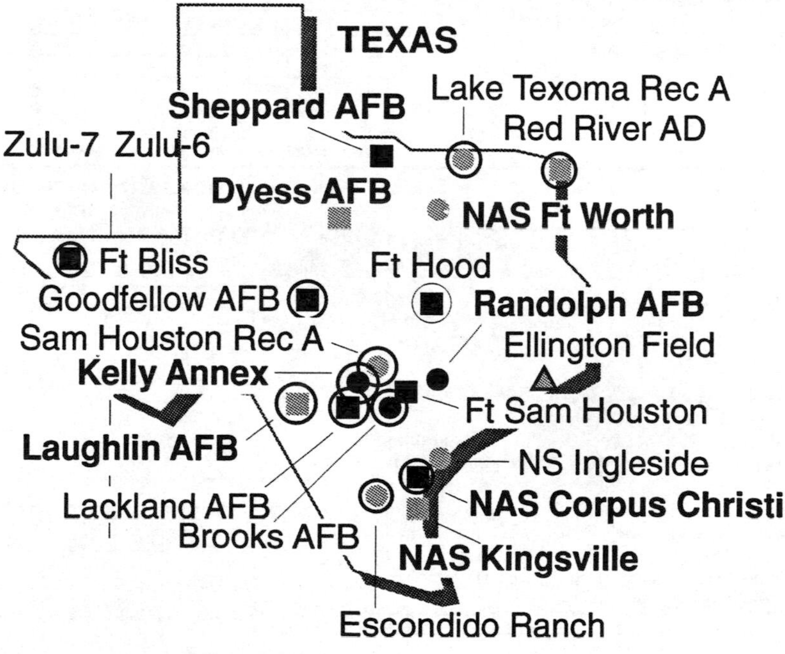

TEXAS
Sheppard AFB
Lake Texoma Rec A
Red River AD
Zulu-7 Zulu-6
Dyess AFB
NAS Ft Worth
Ft Bliss
Ft Hood
Goodfellow AFB
Randolph AFB
Sam Houston Rec A
Ellington Field
Kelly Annex
Ft Sam Houston
Laughlin AFB
NS Ingleside
NAS Corpus Christi
Lackland AFB
Brooks AFB
NAS Kingsville
Escondido Ranch

BIF Prefix 3 on post, 4 to Med Distances long, 4.7m BQ-OPS.
Quarters:
BQ: Availability ★★★ O6 up thru protocol 5323.
Army Hotel ★★★★
915.565.7777, 6078 24h. Rates: $40-43+$5add per.
Fisher House ★★★★ (D 979) **2381**, 0800-1600 M-F, other hrs BQ. Rates: $5unit.
Golf:
915.562.2066/1273 **Holes**: 18 General George V. Underwood, Jr. Golf Complex
Campground:
★★★ 4693 0800-1600 M-F, check in RV office or host. RV EW $8. Tent $3. Discount Golden Access,Age
Commercial: YMCA near Med Center. Rate: $25.
Ground Transport:
Shuttles: BQ-✚–Biggs PX, 0700-1700 M-F, 4028. ✚ **Shuttle:** Holloman 0740,1300,1530 M-F.
Commercial: #30,31 Buses (#32,40/1 Med Cen) to El Paso. PX car rent (C 562) 4895 0900-1800 xSu, 1100-1700 Su. Amtrak east 1440 MWSa, west 1620. Taxi 562-0022.

Ft Bliss   D-8
(Biggs AAF)
El Paso, TX 79916
978-0831   **915-568**-2121
✈✈✈✈✈ **Flights** ✈✈✈✈✈
Army posts 2/w   Langley
Fort Worth   Peterson √
Hood   Scott
            Chance of seat ★★★
Flight Information:
OPS **8048/88** 0600-2200, M-F 0800-1600 Sa

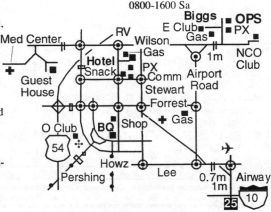

	Break	Lunch	Dinner	Brun
O Club	M-F	M-F	FSa	Su
E Club		M-F		
NCO Club	M-F	M-F		
Snack	0600-2200			
OPS Snack	0630-1400 M-F			

Distances short, 0.6m BQ-Bowl.   On base dial 4+XXXX
Quarters:
Brooks Inn: Availability ★ x ★★★★ FSa **1844** 24h. AFMC FY 07/08 Rates: $34-59. O6 up thru protocol 3238.
RV: ★★★ handled by Outdoor Rec in Bldg 1154 PH: 536.2881. RV $3, EW $8, ESW $10. Tent $3.2881
Golf: C 536-2636 Holes: 9 Brooks Golf Course
Ground Transport:
Shuttles: M-F Base 0630-1630. Transportation **1843.** Wilford Hospital, Lackland 0600-1900.
Commercial: #34 Bus on base to downtown 0536-2153 M-F, 0620-2120 Sa, 0733-2120 Su. #550 clockwise 0617-2210, #551 counterclockwise 0623-2106 loop around city. Amtrak north 0700 SuTT, east 0400 SuTT, west 0535 SuTT. Greyhound downtown.

Brooks City Base D-94
San Antonio, TX 78235
240-1110   **210-536**-1110

	Break	Lunch	Dinner
Club	M-F	M-F	M-F
Bowl	1000-2200 M-F		
	0900-2200 Sa		
	1300-2200 Su		

BRAC 2005

TEXAS (Continued)

On Æ74, Navy Circuit	**NAS Corpus Christi**	
On Æ22, Air Force Circuit	**Dyess AFB**	
On Æ24, Air Force Circuit	**Ellington Field**	
On Æ75, Navy Circuit	**NAS Ft Worth, JRB**	

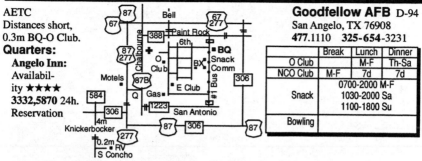

AETC
Distances short,
0.3m BQ-O Club.
Quarters:
  Angelo Inn:
  Availabil-
  ity ★★★★
  3332,5870 24h.
  Reservation

Goodfellow AFB D-94
San Angelo, TX 76908
477.1110   **325-654**-3231

	Break	Lunch	Dinner
O Club		M-F	Th-Sa
NCO Club	M-F	7d	7d
Snack		0700-2000 M-F	
		1030-2000 Sa	
		1100-1800 Su	
Bowling			

3686. AETC Rates: **$24-42**. O6 up thru protocol **5401**.
RV: On Lake Nasworthy. ★★★★ C **325.944-1012**, D thru operator, Th-M. Those in place need not leave. RV EW **$8**. Tent **$3**.
Commercial: BQ has list of motels with military discounts.
Ground Transport:
#1 Bus thru base to downtown 0650-1840 xSu. Kerrville Bus in San Angelo.

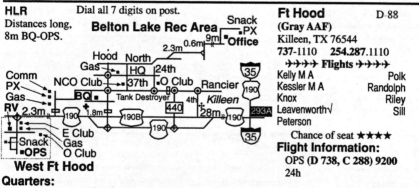

HLR
Distances long,
8m BQ-OPS.

Ft Hood   D-88
(Gray AAF)
Killeen, TX 76544
737-1110   **254.287**.1110
✈✈✈✈ **Flights** ✈✈✈✈

Kelly M A	Polk
Kessler M A	Randolph
Knox	Riley
Leavenworth√	Sill
Peterson	

Chance of seat ★★★★
Flight Information:
OPS (**D 738, C 288**) **9200**
24h

Quarters:
BQ: Availability ★★ **532.8233** 24h. **Guest House** ★ **287.3067** 24h (same bldg as BQ).
Rates: **$20,25**unit. DV **$34**suite. O5up thru protocol **5001**.
Belton Lake Rec A, cabins ★★★★ x ★ May-Aug, weekends **4907** 24h. Rates: E1-4 **$25**unit, E5 up & O **$30**unit, **$5** less winter, no towels, pets. RV EW,ESW **$8**. Tent **$3**, EW **$6**. Discount Golden Age, Access, Eagle, **$2** entry fee per car.
West Ft Hood: ★★★★ (**D 738, C 288**) **9926** 0700-1745 M-F, 1000-1745 Sa, check in office.
RV ESW **$9**. Tent **$2**. Discount Golden Age,
Access.
Commercial: Motels in Killeen.
Golf: 254.287.4130 Holes: 27 The Courses of Clear
Creek

	Break	Lunch	Dinner	Brun
O Club		M-F	Tu-Sa	Su
NCO Club		M-F		
	Many Snack & Cafeteria			

Ground Transport:
Post Shuttle 0700-1700 M-F. Pay shuttle to Killeen, Greyhound 0900-1900.

Distances long, 1.3m Snack-✚.

Prefix 1 on post.

Ft Sam Houston D-88
San Antonio, TX 78234
471-1110   210-221-1211

Quarters:
BQ: Availability
★★★★ x ★ week-
ends 24h.Rate:
$24sgl+$15 add per.
Protocol 6803.
Guest House:
★★★★ x ★
July,Nov,Dec
210.357.2705 then
EX: 2000 24h. Rate:
$40dbl, $45suite.
O Club, 10 rooms, C 224.4211, D thru operator
1000-1400 MTu, 1000-1800 WTh, 1000-1900 F,
1200-1800 Sa. Rate $45unit/break.
Golf: 5675 **Holes:** 36 Fort Sam Houston Golf
Courses: La Loma & Salado Del Rio
Canyon Lake Rec A: ★★★★ x ★, summer,
weekends, trailers **888.882.9878** 0800-1700
M-F, 0900-1400 Sa. Site 210-964-3318 0800-
2000, reserve 21d ahead. Rates: **O** $30unit,
E1-6 $20unit, E7-9 $25unit. RV EW $8. Tent
$5. Discounts Golden Age, Access, Eagle.
Ground Transport:
Bus lines on post. Amtrak north 0700 SuTT, east
0400 SuTT, west 0535 SuTT.

Ft Sam Rec A
Jacob Creek
Randolph 0.5m
AFB Rec A
Canyon 2.5m
Lake To *Fort Worth*
14m
To 306 190
San Antonio 35

Guest House ■
#15,508/9 Buses ⁙ Stanley
BQ ■   O Club Annex
Dickman   Shop   Hardee
          ■Gas   NCO Club
                 Schofield
O Club   Patch
        ■PX
        Snack ■ ■Burger
        #508 Bus Comm King
Frank Wilson

To Austin
159 35

	Break	Lunch	Dinner	Brun
O Club		M-F	Tu-Sa	Su
Annex	M-F	M-F		
NCO Club		M-F		
Snack	0600-1400 M-F			

Quarters:
BEQ: 4420/19 24h. Rate:
$10per.

BRAC 2005

181 5m 361 Ingleside
181 1069 4m
       ⊡M
To Corpus ●HQ
Christi
       ●BEO✚
       ●Galley
       USO

NS Ingleside
Ingleside, TX 78362
        (Corpus Operator)
861-1110   **361.961.2811**
776-xxxx   **776**-xxxx
     Menu **776.4774**

On Æ31, Air Force Circuit
On Æ78, Navy Circuit

Kelly Annex (to Lackland)
NAS Kingsville

Quarters:
   Distances walkable X to Kelly Annex.
Inns of Lackland: Availability ★ **5397, 3622**
24h. AETC FY 07/08 Rates: $24-42. Proto-
col 2423. E & retirees ★★★★ x ★ summer
4277,2550,2556 24h.
Golf: 3466/2517 **Holes:** 27 Gateway Hills
Golf Course 18; Gateway Valley Golf Course 9
RV: ★★★ **5179** 0800-1700 M-F, 0800-1130
SS, site C 5179, check in, pay at RV. RV ESW
$10,11, no dump.
Commercial: Motels on US90.
Ground Transport:
Shuttles: Base hrly 0500-2100 M-Th, 0900-

Lackland AFB   D-94
San Antonio, TX 78236
473-1110   **210-671**-1110

See Kelly Annex Æ31 for flight info.

	Break	Lunch	Dinner	Brun
O Club		M-F	Tu-Sa	Su
NCO Club		M-F	Tu-Sa	
Snack	7d	7d	7d	
Bowl	7d	7d	7d	
Rec C	7d	7d	7d	

Continued on following page

CONUS

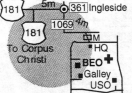

TEXAS (Continued)

Lackland AFB Continued from preceding page
2300 FSa, 0800-2100 Su, 3414. To Kelly from
Bank M-F. Courtesy van M-F from BOQ.
Commercial: #76 Bus near Gas, change to
#64 for downtown. #150 clockwise,
#151 counterclockwise loop around city 0619-
2147 M-F, 0716-2133 Sa. Limo 344-7433. Amtrak
north 0700 SuTT, east 0400 SuTT, west 0535
SuTT. Car rent at BX. Base commercial taxi 3555.

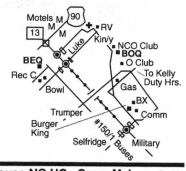

Quarters:
BQ: Availability
★★★★ x ★ week-
ends, drill, & NG
school periods.
Double occupancy
rooms, $12.00 Guest
quarters manager
512.782.5500.

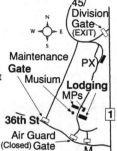

Texas NG HQ - Camp Mabry   D-80
Austin, TX 78763
954-5001 Operator (512) 782-5001

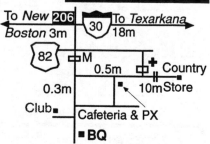

See Æ60, Sheppard AFB	**Lake Texoma Rec A**
On Æ34, Air Force Circuit	**Laughlin AFB**
On Æ55, Air Force Circuit	**Randolph AFB**

Distances short.
Quarters:
BQ: Availability
★★★★ 3227 0645-
1715 M-Th, for arrival other hrs, call, keys
left at main gate. Rates: $7sgl+$1per. Protocol **2316**
Elliot Lake Rec A:
★★★ 2254,2688 0715-1745 year round, reservations, check in Country Store. Rates: $35
cabin, no bedding, towels, Fully furnished
$75. RV EW $7d/35/w, ESW $10. Shelter W
$6, EW $10. Tent $2. No pets in cabins.
Commercial: Motels in New Boston.
Ground Transport:
Greyhound, Amtrak east 2012 SuTT, west
1039 SuTT in Texarkana.

Red River AD   D-8
& Lonestar Army Ammo Plant
Texarkana, TX 75501
829-4110   **903-334**-2141

	Break	Lunch	Dinner
Club		M-F	
Cafeteria		0600-1300 M-F	
Bldg 595		0630-1400 M-F	
		0930-1600 Sa	

| On Æ60, Air Force Circuit | **Sheppard AFB** |

157

San Antonio Area

	Page	D	C	Quarters Summary	
Brooks City B	54	240	210-536	1844 24h	■
Sam Houston	56	471	210-221	6125, GH 8744	■
Kelly Annex	31	945	210-925	1844 24h	■
Lackland AFB	56	473	210-671	O 3622, E 2556	■
Randolph AFB	55	487	210-652	1844 24h	■

Due to poor interface of city bus with Kelly, suggest inexpensive Randolph-Kelly connection: city bus from Randolph to downtown, get off near Marriott River Center, call commercial shuttle for trip from downtown to Kelly USA, as it will take you directly to Terminal or Inn. Shuttle Randolph-Kelly $45/$50, shuttle downtown-Kelly $12. MAC Shuttle 210-670-8855.

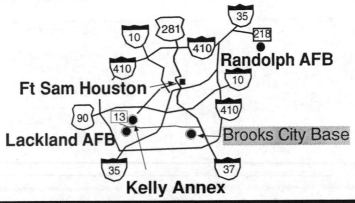

Randolph AFB

Ft Sam Houston

Lackland AFB

Brooks City Base

Kelly Annex

UTAH

DPG   Zulu-7
Distances short,
0.3m BQ-Bowl.

Quarters:
BQ: Antelope Inn Availability ★★★★ x ★ summer **2333** 0630-1800 M-Th, 0630-1600 F. For arrival other hrs, call, key at police. Rate: $22sgl+$3add per. O6 up thru protocol 3701.

Hill AFB
Carter Creek
SLC Airport
Tooele AD
Dugway PG

Dugway PG   D-8
(Michael AAF)
Dugway, UT 84022
789-1110   **435**.831.2151
↦↦↦↦ **Flights** ↦↦↦↦
Edwards   McChord
Hill   Travis

Chance of seat ★★★★
Flight Information:
OPS **5322** 0700-1730
M-Th

Comm
PX ■
Bowl
OPS ■
10m
Club ■
BQ
Gas ■
Police ■
M
80
77 To
35m
Salt Lake City 43m
To Tooele
199

	Break	Lunch	Dinner
Club		M-Th	M-F
Bowl	0600-2200 M-F		
	0900-2200 SS		

Facility is very remote and likely to close.

On Æ28, Air Force Circuit	**Hill AFB**
On Æ56, Air Force Circuit	**Salt Lake City Airport**

CONUS

Very Remote Facility.
Distances short.

Quarters:

BQ: Sunset Guesthouse
833.2056. Availability
★★★★ **2056** 0630-1700,
M-Th, other hrs security
2314.
Rate: $24.

RV: ★★★★ x ★ holiday **3301**
0800-1800 M-W, 0800-1900 Th, 0800-1230 FSa, reserve,
check in Service, other hrs try gym or fire house. RV EW $8.
Tent $2.

Commercial: Motels in Tooele.

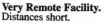

Tooele Army Depot D-8
Tooele, UT 84074
790.3211 **435.833**.3211

	Break	Lunch	Dinner
Club		MW	FSa
Bowl		1000-2200	

Zulu-5

VIRGINIA

For navy lodging information
about the Tidewater Area on the
Internet go to
www.nsa-norva.navy.mil.

Amtrak from Norfolk
(Newport News) 0845
xSa.

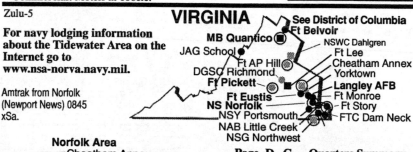

Norfolk Area

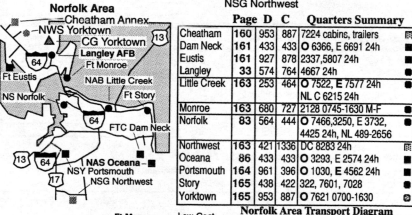

	Page	D	C	Quarters Summary	
Cheatham	160	953	887	7224 cabins, trailers	
Dam Neck	161	433	433	O 6366, E 6691 24h	■
Eustis	161	927	878	2337,5807 24h	■
Langley	33	574	764	4667 24h	●
Little Creek	163	253	464	O 7522, E 7577 24h	●
				NL C 6215 24h	
Monroe	163	680	727	2128 0745-1630 M-F	●
Norfolk	83	564	444	O 7466,3250, E 3732,	●
				4425 24h, NL 489-2656	
Northwest	163	421	1336	DC 8283 24h	
Oceana	86	433	433	O 3293, E 2574 24h	■
Portsmouth	164	961	396	O 1030, E 4562 24h	■
Story	165	438	422	322, 7601, 7028	●
Yorktown	165	953	887	O 7621 0700-1630	

Norfolk Area Transport Diagram

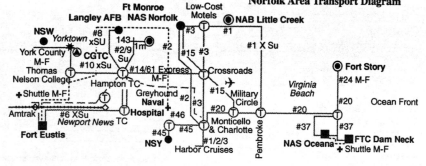

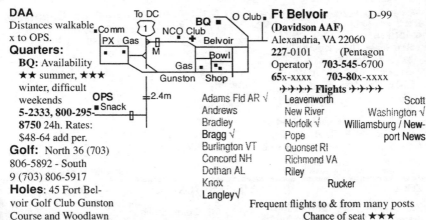

DAA

Distances walkable, x to OPS.

Quarters:
BQ: Availability ★★ summer, ★★★ winter, difficult weekends **5-2333, 800-295-8750** 24h. Rates: $48-64 add per.

Golf: North 36 (703) 806-5892 - South 9 (703) 806-5917

Holes: 45 Fort Belvoir Golf Club Gunston Course and Woodlawn Course

Ground Transport:

Post Shuttle M-F, does not go to OPS, 2375.
Commercial: City bus on post to PA Ave, Washington. Car rent 495-5116, will deliver to OPS. Taxi 781-7040.

Ft Belvoir   D-99
(Davidson AAF)
Alexandria, VA 22060
227-0101   (Pentagon Operator) **703-545**-6700
65x-xxxx   **703-80**x-xxxx
↦↦↦↦ **Flights** ↦↦↦↦

Leavenworth	Scott
New River	Washington √
Norfolk √	Williamsburg / New-
Pope	port News

Adams Fld AR √
Andrews
Bradley
Bragg √
Burlington VT
Concord NH
Dothan AL
Knox
Langley √
Leavenworth
New River
Norfolk √
Pope
Quonset RI
Richmond VA
Riley
Rucker

Frequent flights to & from many posts
Chance of seat ★★★

Flight Information:
OPS **6-7225** 7025/7026 24h Will manifest by phone.

	Break	Lunch	Dinner	Brun
O Club		M-F	Tu-Sa	Su
NCO Club		M-F	Tu-Sa	
Snack	0600-2000			
Bowl	0900-2300			

For Navy Tidewater Area Operator Assistance D 564.0111 C 757.444.0111

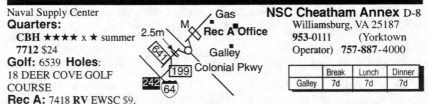

Naval Supply Center
Quarters:
CBH ★★★★ x ★ summer **7712** $24

Golf: 6539 **Holes**: 18 DEER COVE GOLF COURSE

Rec A: 7418 **RV** EWSC $9.
cabins, trailers ★★★★ x ★ summer 7224 0800-1530 M-F. Reservations up to 90d in advance, 1 week min summer (M to M). 2 night min winter. **Rates:** Summer: Cabin $35-75, trailers $35 depending on size and season, no pets.

NSC Cheatham Annex D-8
Williamsburg, VA 25187
953-0111   (Yorktown Operator) **757-887**-4000

	Break	Lunch	Dinner
Galley	7d	7d	7d

NDY
Naval Surface Weapons
Distances short.
Quarters:
BQ: Availability ★★★★ x Drill weekends. **7671** 24h. Rates: **O & E** $16+$8per, children +$2.

Golf: 3002 Holes: 9 Willow Oaks Golf Course

Ground Transport:
Base transport on call for duty to designated stops, **8751** 0700-1500 M-F.
Commercial: Greyhound stops on US301.

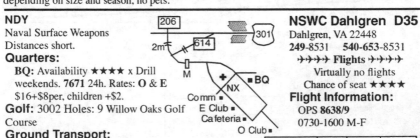

NSWC Dahlgren D35
Dahlgren, VA 22448
249-8531   **540-653**-8531
↦↦↦↦ **Flights** ↦↦↦↦
Virtually no flights
Chance of seat ★★★★

Flight Information:
OPS **8638/9**
0730-1600 M-F

	Break	Lunch	Dinner
O Club		M-F	F
CPO Club	M-F	M-F	
Cafeteria	M-F	M-F	

Fleet Training Center Distances walkable, 1m BOQ-BEQ.

Quarters:

Availability ★★★★ **BOQ Res 7014** 24h. Rates: $18sgl+$4add per, DV $26sgl+$6add per.
BEQ (no dependents) **6606, 6691** 24h. Rate E1-6 $5per, E7 up $10+$3add per.
Navy Lodge: 437.8100 Rate $63unit.

Ground Transport:

Base Shuttle: 0630-1600 M-F.
✚ **Shuttle:** Oceana 0905,1135,1350, 1540 M-F.
Commercial: #37 Bus to Oceana and Oceanfront, 1200-2400 xSa, 0930-0210 Sa. To NAS Norfolk transfer to #20 then #3/15, to Little Creek transfer to #20 then #1.

	Break	Lunch	Dinner	Brun
O Club		M-F	xSu	Su
NCO Club		M-F		
E Club		M-F	Sa	
Snack	0600-2300 xSu			
	0700-2300 Su			

FTC Dam Neck D-8

Virginia Beach, VA 23461
564-0111 (Norfolk Operator) **757-444**-0111
492.xxxx   **492**.xxxx

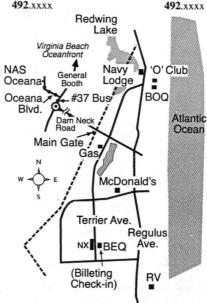

Dial 9 + seven digits on post.

FAF

Transportation Distances walkable x 3.3m BQ-OPS.

Quarters:

BQ: Availability ★★★
888.0968, 2337,5807 24h, assigned 1800. Rates: $28sgl +$7add per, DV $34sgl +$7add per. O6 up thru protocol 6030.
Golf: 0391/5598/1679 **Holes:** 27 The Pines Golf Course
Commercial: Motels on US60.

Ground Transport:

Post Shuttle 0650-1750 M-F, 4200.
✚ **Shuttle:** Langley-Portsmouth Naval ✚ 0730,1230 M-F 7866.
Commercial: #6 Bus to Newport News TC 0645 -2245 xSu. Greyhound on post. Amtrack at Lee Hall, to NY 0807, days of operation change seasonally.

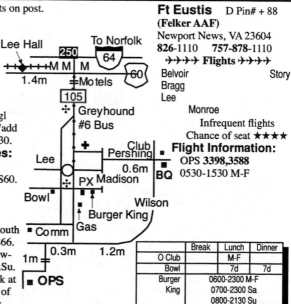

Ft Eustis D Pin# + 88

(Felker AAF)
Newport News, VA 23604
826-1110   **757-878**-1110
✈✈✈✈ **Flights** ✈✈✈✈

Belvoir	Story
Bragg	
Lee	
Monroe	

Infrequent flights
Chance of seat ★★★★

Flight Information:

OPS **3398,3588**
0530-1530 M-F

	Break	Lunch	Dinner
O Club		M-F	
Bowl		7d	7d
Burger King	0600-2300 M-F		
	0700-2300 Sa		
	0800-2130 Su		

CONUS (side tab)

APH
Subpost of Ft Lee, Res, NG
Distances short.

Quarters:
BQ: Availability ★★★★ x ★
during training **8335**, 0800-1630
M-F, other hrs SDO, **8201**. Rates:
$20sgl+$10add per.. Cottages
$20,39sgl+$10add per.

Rec A: ★★★★ x ★ summer **8219**, MWR **8367** 0800-2030
M-F+ SS summer, Check in Rec C. Cabin by pay grade, $25-
55unit, no pets. RV ESW $10, no dump, restroom,
shower. Discount Golden Age, Access.
Commercial: Motels in Bowling Green, Greyhound in Bowling Green.

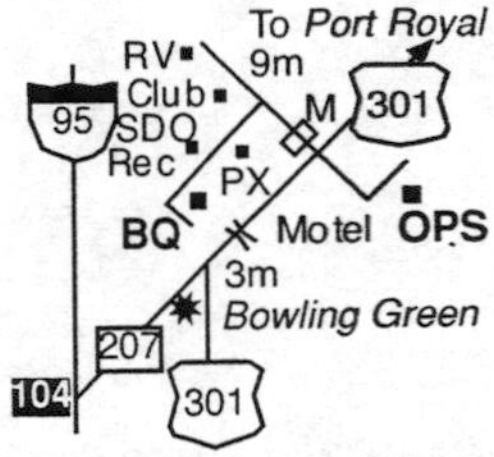

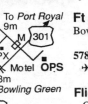

Ft A P Hill
Bowling Green, VA 22448
Ft. Lee Operator
578-8710   **804-633**-8710
➵➵➵➵ **Flights** ➵➵➵➵
Flights unlikely
Flight Information:
OPS **8290,8341**

	Break	Lunch	Dinner
Club		M-F§	
		7d¶	7d¶
		§ winter, ¶ summer	

On campus of University of Virginia
Quarters:
BQ: Availability ★ **C 6450/6334** 0750-
1650 M-F, other hrs SDO **C 6300**. Rates:
$20sgl, DV $25sgl, both +$5add per.
Ground Transport:
#2,5,9 Buses on Arlington, 0700-1700
xSu. In Charlottesville Greyhound,
Amtrak north 1711 SuWF 0648, west
1335 SuWF, south 2105.

JAG
Arlington

Judge Advocate General's School
Charlottesville, VA 22901
934-7115   **434.972**.6000
800.552.3978 then exten.

	Break	Lunch	Dinner
Club	M-F	M-F	M-F

On Æ33, Air Force Circuit	**Langley AFB**

Distances walkable.   On post dial last 5 of **C**

Quarters:
Billets: Availability ★★★★
Toll Free: 800.403.8533
Res: 804-733-4100 ex 5990
6694/8/9 24h. Rates: $36-
48sgl, DV 46sgl, both+$5dd
per. Guest House $46.
Protocol 1723,3565.
Golf: 734-2899/2402/1228
Holes: 27 Cardinal Golf Club
Ground Transport:
✚ **Shuttles** M-F to Walter
Reed 0500, Naval
✚ Portsmouth 0700, 7276.
Commercial: In Petersburg Greyhound, Amtrak
(north 1437,1022,1437 south 1342,1752,2333). Limo to
airport, 800-552-7911. Taxi 458-2535.

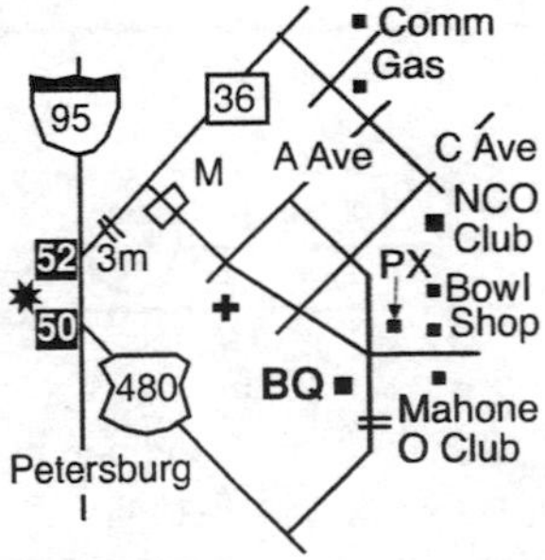

(Map: 95, 36, M, A Ave, Comm, Gas, C Ave, NCO Club, PX, Bowl, Shop, 52 3m, 50, 480, BQ, Mahone O Club, Petersburg)

Ft Lee   D-8
Petersburg, VA 23801
539-3000   **804-765**-3000
687-xxxx   **734**-xxxx

	Break	Lunch	Dinner
O Club		M-F	Tu-Sa
NCO Club		M-F	7d
Cafeteria	7d	7d	M-F

What Else Should Be Included?

As installations close, room becomes available
for more or expanded information. Should there
be something you would like to see added,
please let us know. Your suggestion will be carefully considered. Specifically this Handbook is
for data of immediate need such as the location
of the air terminal or some useful feature not
obvious without enquiry, for example ground
transportation. On the other hand all installations have post offices and seldom is their
location of immediate need. Including them
would add clutter. Definitely points of interest
accessible by public transport or shuttle will be
included if information is supplied.

Distances walkable, 1.2m O Billet-CPO Club.
Quarters:
  Availability ★★★ x ★ summer, Jan, Feb.
  BOQ 462.7522 24h. Rates: $18sgl+$5add per, DV
  $31sgl+$5add per. Protocol (D 564, C 444) 5901.
  CBO 318.2000 (no dep.) 24h. Rate: $6per.
  Navy Lodge: ★★★ x ★ summer, weekends, **C**
  464.6215 24h. Rate: $46unit.
  Golf: 462.8526 D 253.8526 **Holes**: 18 EAGLE
HAVEN GOLF COURSE
  RV Park ★★★★ 462.7282 0800-1700 M-F,
check in with host at Park, site 41. RV ESCW $10.
Tent $5.
Ground Transport:
  Commercial: #1 Bus at main gate to Norfolk
0645-1845 xSu, #8 Bus from Gate 12m W of Main
Gate 0532-2132 xSu ,-2032 Su, for NAS Norfolk,
transfer to #3, for Oceana, Dam Neck transfer to
#20 then #37.

NAB Little Creek   D-6
Norfolk, VA 23521
564-0111 (Norfolk Op.) **757-444**-0111

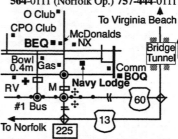

Retirees welcome at Navy Mess Hall.

	Break	Lunch	Dinner	Brun
O Club		W-Sa	Th-Sa	Su
CPO Club	Su	M-F	FSa	
Bowl		0800-2300		
McDonald's		0600-2300		

Headquarters
Distances walkable,
0.5m main gate-O Club.
Quarters:
  Billets: Availability ★★★ x ★
summer **2128** 0800-1645 M-F,
assigned 1400, Bldg T179.
Rates: $30sgl, $38family. O6
up thru protocol **3596** $38sgl,
$45family.
  Travel Park ★★★ **2384**
0800-1700 M-F check in Rec
Office. RV ESW $11 winter, $16 summer.
  Point Comfort Marina 788.4308
  Commercial: Chamberlin Hotel on post.
Ground Transport:
  #2/9 Buses 1m.

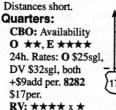

Ft Monroe
Hampton, VA 23651
680-2111 **757-788**-2111

Helicopters controlled
by Langley AFB Æ33.

	Break	Lunch	Dinner	Brun
O Club		M-F	WFSa	Su
Bowl		0700-2200		

BRAC 2005

On Æ122 DC	**Ft Myer**
On Æ83, Navy Circuit	**NAS Norfolk**

Distances short.
Quarters:
  CBO: Availability
  O ★★, **E** ★★★★
24h. Rates: **O** $25sgl,
DV $32sgl, both
+$9add per. **8282**
$17per.
  RV: ★★★★ x ★

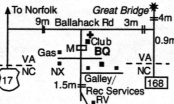

NSGA Northwest
Chesapeake, VA 23322
564-1336 **757-421-8**000
D thru operator

	Break	Lunch	Dinner
Club		M-F	xSu
Galley	7d	7d	7d

holiday **8264/0/1/2** 0730-1800 M-F summer, 0745-1615 winter, other hrs M gate, reservation, check in Rec Service, RV E $8. Tent $4. No dump, no water Nov-May.

On Æ85, Navy Circuit	**NAS Oceana**

BKT

Field training Distances long, 3m BQ-Club.

Quarters:
BQ: Availability ★★★★ x ★ summer **2443** 0730-1600 M-F. Rates: $8-18per, cottage $20sgl+$5add per. Protocol 2454. RV: Handled by BQ, other hrs MP, 8444, reservations. RV ESW $9. Tent $5. Firearms permitted. Discount Access.

Ground Transport:
Post Shuttle in summer.

Ft Pickett D-7
(Blackstone AAF)
Blackstone, VA 23824
438-8621   **434.292**.8621
→→→→ **Flights** →→→→
Belvoir   Willow Grove
Richmond VA

No flights late fall to early spring
Flight Information:
OPS **8461**,**8608**

	Break	Lunch	Dinner
Club			Tu-Sa
Snack		xSu	
Club 317		M-F	

Distances walkable.

Quarters:
BOQ: Availability ★★★★ **D 1030, C 398-8500** 24h. Rates: $12,19sgl +$4add per, DV $29sgl+$5add per. **BEQ 4562** (no dependents) 24h. Rate: $6per, $9suite.

Ground Transport:
#45 Bus to Norfolk. Transfer to #3 for other installations.

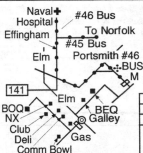

NSY Portsmouth D-8
Portsmouth, VA 23709
961-3000   **757.444**.0000

	Break	Lunch	Dinner
Club			xSa
Galley	7d	7d	7d
Bowl	1730-2000 T-T		
	0900-1600 Sa		
	1100-1700 Su		

On page Æ89, Navy Circuit
MB Quantico

Distances short.

Quarters:
BQ: Availability ★ **3371,4198** 0800-1900 M-F other hrs call, keys left with Security, 4000. Reservations accepted. Rates: $22sgl, $30family.

Ground Transport:
Buses on US1. Amtrak in Richmond.

DGSC Richmond
Richmond, VA 23297
695-1110   **804-279**-3861

Gas To Richmond 8m
Comm
Security
PX
BQ O Club   M

	Break	Lunch	Dinner	Brun
O Club		xSu	Tu-Sa	Su

Fly Space-A Without Waiting

A subject covered in Appendix A but summarized here. 1: Avoid bases where active duty flock. 2: Keep Handbook available at all times. 3: At first sign of jam check all alternatives. 4: Do not hesitate to back up. 5: Take first available useful flight. 6: Avoid popular destinations during spring break and Christmas. 7: When first arriving check for unusual destinations. 8: Before going to a base with few flights use DSN to check first. Watch for activity and ask.

VIRGINIA (Concluded)

Amphibious subpost of Ft Eustis   On post dial all 7 digits.

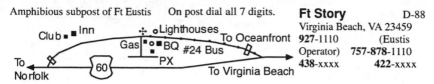

Ft Story   D-88
Virginia Beach, VA 23459
927-1110   (Eustis
Operator) **757-878**-1110
438-xxxx   **422**-xxxx

Distances long, 3m gate to gate.

Quarters:

BQ: Availability ★★★ x ★ summer **2337** 0730-1530 M-F, assigned 1600. Rate: $28sgl+$7add per.

Cape Henry Inn: ★★★★ x ★★★ **422.8818**. Rates: $29-65room winter, + $16 summer.

Travel camp: Trailers (on post) ★★★★ x ★ summer **7601** 0700-1700 M-F, 0800-1700 SS, no towels. Rates: Summer $40dbl+$7add per, winter $25dbl+$6add per. RV EW $14. Discounts Golden Age, Access.

Ground Transport:

#24 Bus to Virginia Beach, 2 morning, 2 afternoon M-F, 1 each SS. Transfer to #37 for Oceana and Dam Neck, to #20 for other installations and downtown Norfolk. Info 640-6300.

NWS Yorktown
Yorktown, VA 23691
953-4945 **757-887**-4000
Distances long,
1.5 main gate-BOQ.

Quarters:
Lodging: Availability ★★ x ★ **856.2378** May-Aug **7621** 0700-1630 M-F, reservations accepted. Rate: **E+O $24+6**& **DV**$28+6.

Golf: 887-4323 **Holes**: 9 Holly Oaks Golf Course

Ground Transport
York County Transport 0555-1821 M-F. CG Reserve Training Center Distances short.

Campground:
Gym 856.2128 reserve, check in at gym after 1200, max stay 1m. Rental tents. RV EW $10. Tent EW $5. No water Oct-April.

CGTC Yorktown
Yorktown, VA 23690
757.898.3500
Lodging 2120

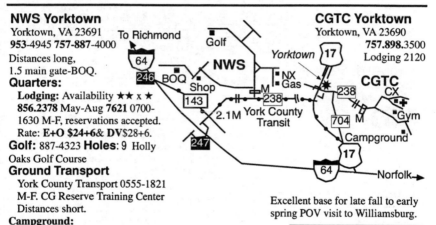

Excellent base for late fall to early spring POV visit to Williamsburg.

	Break	Lunch	Dinner
Galley	7d	7d	7d
Bowl		7d	7d

WASHINGTON

Zulu-8

Toll Free to
Navy MWR 888.463.6697.

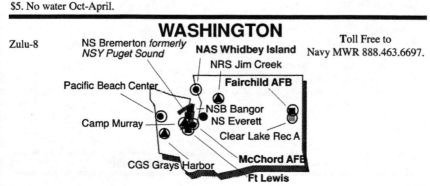

Subase. Distances walkable.

Quarters:
BOQ: Availability ★★★★
x ★★ summer, Res week-
ends **6581** 24h. Rate: $8per
+$4add per. Protocol 4949
BEQ: ★★★★ **4034/5/6**
24h. Rate: $4per. Reserve up
to 30d ahead for 1st night.
Navy Lodge: ★★★★ **C**
779-9100 24h. Rate: $45unit.
Commercial: Nearest motel
in Silverdale.

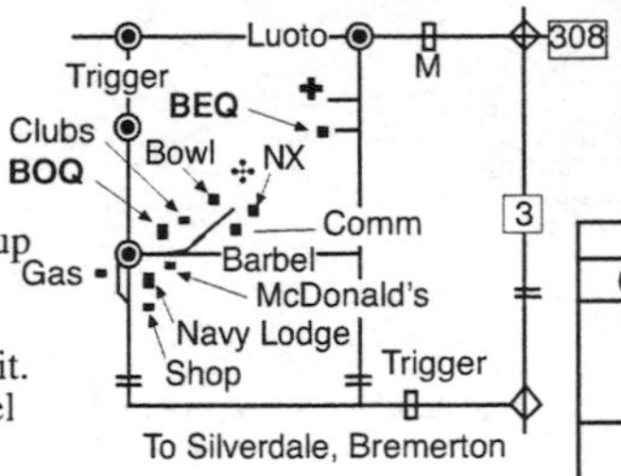

Ground Transport:
Base Shuttle 0600-1510
M-F. Bangor liberty bus starting 1330 M-F, 1020 SS.
Commercial: #34 Bus to Kitsap Mall 0738-2038 M-F, 0938-2138 Sa, 1038-1738 Su. 373-
2877. Limo to NSY, Sea-Tac Airport, Lewis, McChord 0400-2100, **800-562-7948** 0730-2130,
876-1737 24h, reservations required.

Naval Base Kitsap
(formerly NSB BANGER) D-88
Bremerton, WA 98315
744-1110 **360-396-6111**
322.XXXX 315.XXXX

Diagram labels: Luoto, Trigger, BEQ, M, 308, Clubs, Bowl, NX, BOQ, Comm, 3, Barbel, Gas, McDonald's, Navy Lodge, Shop, Trigger, To Silverdale, Bremerton

	Break	Lunch	Dinner
Clubs	Variable		
Deli	1030-1800 M-F		
	0930-1600-2200 Sa		
	1100-1600 Su		
Bowl	0700-2300 M-F		
	0800-2300 Sa		
	1100-1600 Su		
McDon	0600-2300		

Distances short.   On base dial **6+XXXX.**

Quarters:
Availability ★★★★
BOQ 475.3030 24h. Rates:
$10sgl DV $16, both +$2add
per.
BEQ 475.3035 24h. Rates:
E1-5 $5per, open bay; E6 & up
$10sgl+$2add per family. E7-9
suites $10.

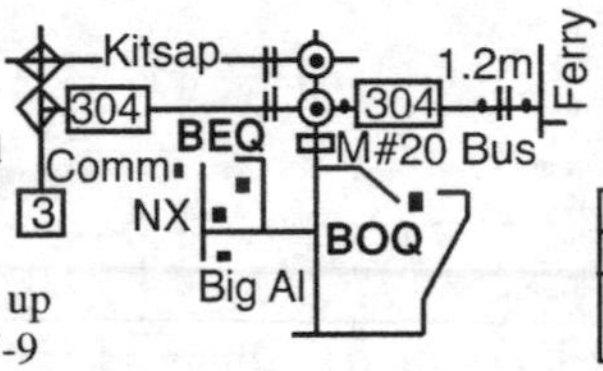

Ground Transport:
#20 Bus main gate to ferry 0615-2020 M-F, 0820-2200 Sa, 0820-1920 Su. Ferry station in
Seattle near Amtrak Station. Limo to Sea-Tac Airport, transfer at **airport** for Lewis, McChord
0435-2135, 876-1737 24h, 800-562-7930 0730-2130, reservation required.

Naval Base Kitsap D-8
**(formerly NSY Puget
Sound / NS Bremerton)**
Bremerton, WA 98314
439-2011   **360-476-3711**

Diagram labels: Kitsap, 304, 304, 1.2m, Ferry, Comm, BEQ, M#20 Bus, 3, NX, BOQ, Big Al

	Break	Lunch	Dinner
Galley	7d	7d	7d
Big Al	1000-2300 xSu		
	1200-2300 Su		

Quarters: On base dial 4+XXXX
BOQ: Availability ★★★★ x ★★
Res weekend, **4860** E7 up and **O**.
Rates: $8, DV $12, both $4add per.
BEH: 3111. Rates: E1-4 $6per, E5
up $10per (no dependents).

Ground Transport:
Shuttle: NS to Marysville Annex
M-F.
Commercial: #210 Bus Annex to
Everett. From Everett # 420 to Se-
attle, transfer to #300 to McChord.
#23 to Mulkito ferry and free bus
to Whidbey Island. Bus info **800-
562-1375.** Amtrak north 0834, south 0900,1535,2042, east 1150,1747. Car rent in Maryville.
Enterprise (watch forcing insurance) 360-653-2319. Airporter **Shuttle** to Whidbey Island, Sea-
Tac **800-235-5247.**

Marina:
C 425-304-3918 Everett Naval Station Marina

NS Everett   D-8
Everett, WA
727-3000 Menu **425-304-3000**
✈✈✈✈ **Flights** ✈✈✈✈
Navy flights from various NAS
utilize **Payne Field**, Snohomish
County Airport, **PAE** (6 miles SW
of Everett). Take Airport Road west
from I-5 and follow signs to field.
A/P will be on the left. There is no
source of military flight information.

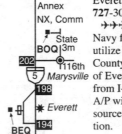

Diagram labels: Annex, NX, Comm, State, BOQ, 3m, 202, 116th, 5, Marysville, 198, Everett, 194, BEQ, Mainside

---

On Æ24, Air Force Circuit	**Fairchild AFB**

RV: Availability ★★★★ x ★★ FSS, No. to right, check in CG Station, season 1 March-31 Oct. RV EW $9. Tent $6.
Foot ferry to Ocean Shores 7 May-25 Sept, 1015-1545, 0047.

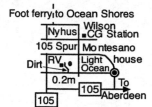

CGS Grays Harbor
Westport, WA 98594-0568
360-268-0121

RV: ★★★★ C 5315/5363 M-Th 8-1700, F 8-19, Sa 8-16, Su 10-1500 Reservations, limited service Oct-April. Max stay 2w. Check in Outdoor Rec. RV EWS $15. Tent $12, Cabins $20-25, 66 person Lodge $400/ night.

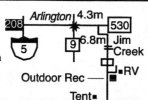

NRS Jim Creek   D-8
21027 Jim Creek Road
Arlington, WA 98223-8599
727.5301 (Op) **425.304.**5301
Within WA Toll Free
888.463.6697

GRF   Prefix 7 on post. Distances walkable x 3.5m BQ-✚.
Quarters:
   BQ: ★★★ x ★★ summer **967.2815/5051, 964.0211 24h.** Rate: $38-48+$5add per. Cancellations assigned 1800. Protocol 967.0144, 0136.
Golf: 6522/2786
Holes: 27 Fort Lewis Golf Course
   RV: ★★★ **7744** 0800-1700, reserve. RV EW $8, ETW $10,11. Tent $6. Free at outlying areas, self-contained only, NW Adventure Center C 967-7744.

Ft Lewis   D-88
(Gray AAF)
(Madigan Army Med C)
Tacoma, WA 98433
357-1110   253.967.1110
✈✈✈ **Flights** ✈✈✈

Cheyenne	Spokane
Fairchild	Whidbey Is
Helena	Yakima√
Peterson	
Portland	

Chance of seat ★★★★
Flight Information:
OPS **6628** 24h
Scheduling 4982

	Break	Lunch	Dinner	Brun
O Club		M-F	W-Sa	Su
Club	Su	Tu-F	F-Su	
Snack	0630-2200 M-F			
	0800-2200 SS			

Ground Transport:
Shuttle: 0600-1800 M-F, 0900-2200 SS, includes Madigan.
Commercial: #300 Bus to McChord and Tacoma 0541-2141 M-F, 0841-2147 Sa, 0841-2146 Su. #206 to Lakewood Mall 0536-2155 M-F, 0657-2157 Sa, 0757-2157 Su, 800-562-8109. Greyhound, Trailways on post. Airporter to Sea-Tac Airport, with a transfer at airport on to NSY and Bangor, 0600-1830 + 2230 xSa, reservations required 800-562-7948 0730-2130, 360-876-1737 24h. $11. All from post Bus Station . Amtrak in Tacoma south 0826,1056,1805, east 0826 MWSa. PX car rent 964-1331 0900-1800 M-F, 0900-1700 Sa, 1000-1500 Su. Less expensive than McChord. Taxi 582-3000, 472-3303.

On Æ42, Air Force Circuit	**McChord AFB**

For map see Ft Lewis above.
RV: ★★★★ **7610** 24h, reservations. RV $5, ESW $11. Tent $5. No dump.

Camp Murray
Tacoma, WA 98430
323-8000   253.512.8000

WA WASHINGTON (Concluded)

Quarters:

Availability ★★★★ x
★★ summer.
$65-85, houses $80-110,
motel $38-55, See hours
below, for check in during
other hrs, see bartender at
club or envelope on door
of office. Rates $35-105
depending on season, ac-
commodation, view, and rank.

RV: Considering the view, a contender for the title of best. RV: **CTV ESW** $15, Tent $7,
Dump, 20A E.

Ground Transport:

Bus from Pacific Beach to Aberdeen.

Hours: 15 May - 1 Sep: Su-Th 0800-2000, F 0800-2200, Sa 0800-2000
2 Sep - 14 May: Su-Th 0800-1800, F 0800-2200. Sa 0800-2000

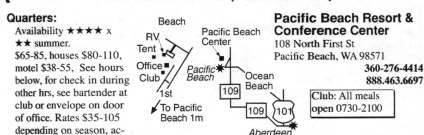

**Pacific Beach Resort &
Conference Center**
108 North First St
Pacific Beach, WA 98571

360-276-4414
888.463.6697

Club: All meals
open 0730-2100

On page Æ90, Navy Circuit   **NAS Whidbey Island**

WEST VIRGINIA

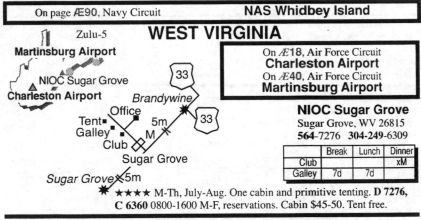

On Æ18, Air Force Circuit
Charleston Airport
On Æ40, Air Force Circuit
Martinsburg Airport

NIOC Sugar Grove
Sugar Grove, WV 26815
564-7276 **304-249-6309**

	Break	Lunch	Dinner
Club			xM
Galley	7d	7d	

★★★★ M-Th, July-Aug. One cabin and primitive tenting. **D 7276,
C 6360** 0800-1600 M-F, reservations. Cabin $45-50. Tent free.

WISCONSIN

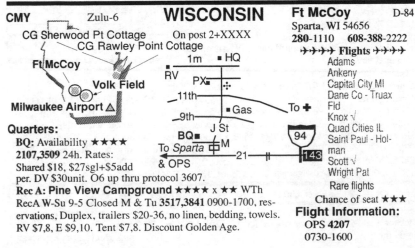

Ft McCoy   D-84
Sparta, WI 54656
280-1110 **608-388-2222**
↦↦↦↦ **Flights** ↦↦↦↦
Adams
Ankeny
Capital City MI
Dane Co - Truax
Fid
Knox √
Quad Cities IL
Saint Paul - Hol-
man
Scott √
Wright Pat
Rare flights

Chance of seat ★★★
Flight Information:
OPS **4207**
0730-1600

Quarters:

BQ: Availability ★★★★
2107,3509 24h. Rates:
Shared $18, $27sgl+$5add
per. DV $30unit. O6 up thru protocol 3607.

Rec A: Pine View Campground ★★★★ x ★★ WTh
RecA W-Su 9-5 Closed M & Tu **3517,3841** 0900-1700, res-
ervations, Duplex, trailers $20-36, no linen, bedding, towels.
RV $7,8, E $9,10. Tent $7,8. Discount Golden Age.

WISCONSIN (Concluded)

WI

On Æ45, Air Force Circuit — Milwaukee (Mitchell) Airport

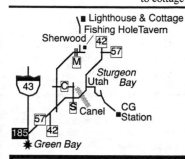

CG Rawley Point Cottage
Two Rivers, WI 54241

920.793-1304

Two units in town house. No linens, blankets, towels. Reservations 414-747.7185 Stays are minimum of 2 & maximum of 7 days. Check in at CG Station, Two Rivers M-F 0700-1130, 1230-1430. Cottage in Point Beach State Park, tell ranger going to cottage to avoid $3 fee. Rate: $25unit.

CG Sherwood Point Cottage
2501 Canal Rd
Sturgeon Bay, WI 54235

920.743.3367

One 2-bedroom cottage, no linens, blankets, towels. Reservations **414.747.7185**. Min 2d, max 14d. Check in CG Station, Sturgeon Bay 1200-2100. Rate $25unit.

CONUS

On Æ65 Air Force Circuit — Volk Field

WYOMING

Zulu-7

On Æ19, Air Force Circuit — Cheyenne Airport

FEW
Distances walkable, 1.2m BQ-Club.
Quarters:
Crow Creek Inn: Availability ★★★★ x ★★ July **1844,3077** 24h, children TLF only. AFSPC FY 07/08 Rates: **$25-44** O6 up thru protocol 2137.
RV: ★★★★ x ★★ summer **733.2988** 1000-1700 M-F, 0800-1200 Sa. RV $5, W $7, EW $10. Tent $5. No water Oct-April. Golf **773.3416**.
Golf: 307.773.3556 **Holes**: 18 F. E. Warren Golf Club
Ground Transport:
Base Shuttle 0600-1800 M-F.
Commercial:
Jitney from main gate. Greyhound and Powder Riverbuses are available. Car rent 632-2715. Taxi 635 5555.

Francis E Warren AFB   D-88
Cheyenne, WY 82005
481-1110   **307-773**-1110
At Airport, handled by Air **Freight** 3275 0730-1630 M-F.

⇥⇥⇥⇥⇥⇥ **Flights** ⇥⇥⇥⇥⇥⇥

Few Flights

Dining open to retirees.

	Break	Lunch	Dinner
Club	M-F	M-F	W-F
Bowl		7d	7d
Snack	0800-1600 M-F		

169

OUTSIDE CONUS

CONUS is contiguous United States (original 48). It does not include Alaska or Hawaii. With the exception active-duty dependents may travel in CONUS with sponsor on emergency leave and on a househunting trip incident to PCS, dependents can during a DOD test fly on a CONUS to CONUS flight. When accompanied by sponsor dependents can utilize a flight if point of origin or of destination (or both) for flight and dependent is outside CONUS (even if one or more additional CONUS points are transited). Should a dependent leave from a CONUS point and take advantage of an intermediate CONUS stop to get off there, that dependent will be billed a commercial fare. Active duty dependents may travel unaccompanied as Cat-V overseas when on a command-sponsored overseas assignment. Such travelers stationed overseas must have a letter from the sponsor's CO. This letter is valid for only one round trip. Under 18 cannot travel unaccompanied. Reports indicate these Cat-V may be all-but wiping out Cat-VI summer in Europe but not elsewhere.

A second distinction is "American territory" and "outside American territory", the latter also referred to as "foreign". Reserves, Guard, and their retirees not yet drawing pensions are restricted to American territory. Their dependents are not authorized Space-A air. Dependents, retirees, sometimes active duty, must meet passport/visa requirements of foreign countries. Under a law that became effective July 2, 2001 the **State Department requires both parents' consent** to obtain passports and visas for overseas travel of children under age 14. The intent of the law is to lessen the chance that parents can abduct their children and use U.S. passports to escape with them overseas; Brazil requires a visa even for an in-transit stop. These requirements are given in the headings of country listings. Except for active duty, Space-A passengers departing for American Territory from outside American territory can be manifested only to or thru installations or airports with immigration and custom facilities. **Ports of entry** include Andrews, Bangor, Charleston, Dover, Fairchild, Hickam, Homestead, Kelly, McChord, and Travis.

Closure of installations in American territory is subject to much political logrolling. Consequently notice almost always can be included in at least two editions prior to actual dates. Abroad closures of installations are not subject to whims of politicians so such closures can (and have) come virtually without notice. This also applies to services such as shuttles and facilities, e.g., clubs. A major problem is assuring an installation has, in fact, closed. For the purposes of this Handbook an installation is considered open if it provides any useful Space-A feature, in particular quarters (including camping) or flights and will continue to be included. To avoid removing possibly useful information, unless an installation is known to be gone, its details may be retained with a suitable note added. Readers should be aware that information presented on a base phasing down represents the most-favorable which can be expected. Travelers should use DSN to check ahead on matters of importance to them.

FLIGHTS

A **departure tax** is payable for AMC charter flights from commercial airports for outside-CONUS points, also at many foreign departure points. There is a $5 custom fee for AMC charter flights from outside USA territory to US airports. See Appendix D, Minimizing Expenses, for ways of avoiding these fees. Those traveling with dependents and starting from a CONUS point remote from the coast should consider tanker and ANG bases. They frequently originate flights to outside CONUS destinations. Most major CONUS installations with flights occasionally have flights to outside CONUS.

Ocean-crossing flights are difficult in summer. Starting trips at major bases with scheduled flights should be avoided unless there is specific news that a normally crowded base is moving retirees promptly. Do not overlook NAS. Scheduled C5 flights starting remote from coastal bases usually have excellent availability and offer through manifesting. The same is true for flights originating abroad from bases not heavily used. It is prudent to mail, E-mail, or Fax a remote sign up to all likely outward and return starting points. See "Remote Sign Up" *Æ243* in Appendix A.

ARRANGEMENT OF INFORMATION

OUTSIDE CONUS

Outside-CONUS installations and airports are placed in four geographical tabbed Sections. Within each Section installations are arranged alphabetically by state, island, or country. Each state, island, or country listing is headed by a map showing the general location of every installation or airport. Availability of ground transport is shown by map symbols described below.

Installation maps are provided in listings. Often exchanges, commissaries, and shoppettes cannot be used by all Space-A travelers due to status of forces agreements. When facilities cannot be used by all they do not appear on maps. Readers have reported entering such facilities despite restrictions but this Handbook is confined to authorized usage. As a general rule eating facilities, lodging, clubs, canteens, and banks may be used. Exceptions are noted, e.g., no facility other than the Passenger Terminal may be used in Australia. Because banks are important when arriving in a foreign county, location of usable on-installation banks are shown on maps and, where appropriate, convenient off-installation banks. Retirees may not have full usage of on-installation banks.

PASSPORTS, VISAS, AND SPECIAL PERMISSIONS

Requirements for passports or visas are given at the head of a country listing when they exist. Depending on status of forces agreements, such requirements may not apply to active duty. To keep this Handbook small, countries having difficult-to-obtain visas are omitted. The same is true of installations for which special permission is required to visit unless it is reasonable to obtain such permission. **One source of visas not requiring contacting embassies or consuls** is Visas A.S.A.P., 800-597-2727. 2505 N. Myers St., Burbank, CA 91504, Prices range from $115 to $195 + $16 return fee.

USE OF FACILITIES IN FOREIGN COUNTRIES

Restrictions on the use of facilities such as exchanges are given at the beginning of the country or island listing. Exceptions applying to a specific installation are in the details of that installation.

GROUND TRANSPORT

Public transport serving installations is far more prevalent abroad than in CONUS. As for CONUS, installations accessible by train or bus are designated by black quarters-availability symbol (■ ● ▲). Some walking is required. When access is only by car or taxi, quarters-availability symbol is gray (▨ ◉ △). Names of installations with flights are in bold, ● e.g., **Hickam**.

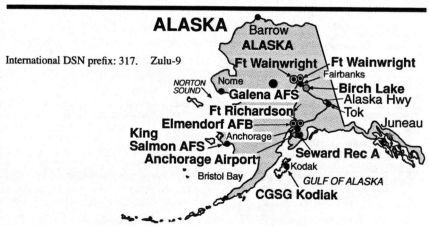

ALASKA

International DSN prefix: 317.   Zulu-9

Barrow
ALASKA
Ft Wainwright ● **Ft Wainwright**
NORTON SOUND   Nome   Fairbanks
● **Galena AFS** ● **Birch Lake**
Alaska Hwy
Ft Richardson Tok
Elmendorf AFB Juneau
Anchorage
King Salmon AFS
Anchorage Airport **Seward Rec A**
Kodak
Bristol Bay   GULF OF ALASKA
CGSG Kodiak

There are several scattered AFS. All can be reached from Eielson or Elmendorf and reported to have no readily available lodging. King Salmon and Galena do require prior permission. For permission for Eareckson call 392-3401, for other AFS 552-5453. Clear AFS 585-6519; Galena Airport 446-3405; King Salmon Airport 721-3492; Eareckson 392-3240. In winter heavy cold-weather gear is required.

ANC
176th WG
C130

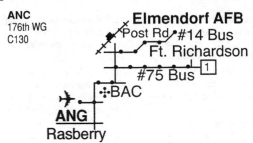

Elmendorf AFB
Post Rd #14 Bus
Ft. Richardson
#75 Bus [1]

:BAC

ANG
Rasberry

Kulis ANGB south side of Airport off Raspberry Rd.

Anchorage Airport
(Kulis ANGB)
Anchorage, AK 99502-1998
626-1144   **907-249**-1225
✈✈✈✈✈✈ **Flights** ✈✈✈✈✈✈
Hickam 2-3/y   Minneapolis
North Island 2-3/y   Minot
McChord 4/y
     No Pax to outside USA
     Chance of seat ★★★
Flight Information:
OPS **1225** Rec **1000**
0700-1700 M-F closed some F

EIL
168th ARW **KC135**
PACAF
Fairbanks
[3]✳ **Ft Wainwright**
     ● Eielson AFB
22m   ●Birch
38m 1m ⤢Lake
Mile 305 [2]

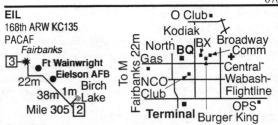

O Club ■ ✕
Kodiak
North BQ ■ BX Broadway
Gas   ⌐Comm
■NCO   Central
Club   Wabash-
              Flightline
Terminal Burger King ● OPS ■

Eielson AFB   D-88
Fairbanks, AK 99702
377-1110   **907-377**-1110
✈✈✈✈ **Flights** ✈✈✈✈

CONUS tanker bases
Elmendorf C-12   Mildenhall
March FSa A   Travis FSa A
McChord FSa A
     Chance of seat
     ★★★★ x ★★ summer
Flight Information:
Terminal **1250**
0730-1630 M-F
[Fax 2287, Bldg 1190,
Flightline Ave]. Recording
1623
OPS **1861** 24h
168ARG ANG KC135
1620.

Quarters:
Goldrush Inn: Availability ★★★ x ★ summer **1844** 24h.
PACAF Rates: $27-49 O6 up thru protocol 7686. TLF
$25unit.
Fam Camp: ★★★ x ★ summer **1232** 1100-1800 M-F,
1100-1700 SS May-Sept, 1839 off season. Check in at Rec
Issue Annex. RV ESW $7, no restroom, shower.
Birch Lake Rec A: Season June-Aug ★★★★ x ★ week-
ends, **1232,4214** 1000-1700 M-F, 1000-1600 SS, reserva-
tions 15 April to opening, at site C 488-6161, reservations
during season. Rates: $20-40 cabin, no linen, RV E $10. Tent
$6 No dump.

Ground Transport:
Shuttle: Base in winter 0600-0800, 1100-1300, 1530-1730, 1843. To Greely 1800, call
Greely motor pool 873-3228.
Commercial: RR in Fairbanks for Anchorage, Seward.

Aero Club: 1223 Eielson Flying Club

EDF   Prefix 2 on base.
AMC
     Distances long, 1.6m Terminal-BQ, 5m Terminal
to BQ at Richardson.

Quarters:
North Star Inn: Availability ★★★ x ★ summer
2454 24h, assigned 1700 summer. PACAF FY
07/08 Rates: $27-49. O 6 up thru protocol 3210.
Fam Camp: ★★★ x ★ summer **2023** May-Sept,
off season 4838. RV EW $10, Tent free.
Commercial: Motels in Anchorage, expensive,
Mush Inn lowest, 277-4554. Closest Sourdough
800-478-3030 $50unit.

Continued on following page

Elmendorf AFB   D-94
Anchorage, AK 99506
552-1110   **907-552**-1110
AF✈✈✈ **Flights** ✈✈✈ Army

Adak	Greely MWThF
Eielson	Wainwright MWTF
Juno	Posted at AMC
Kadena	C23 OPS **3337**
Kodiak	C12 OPS **3095**
March√ Sa A	0530-1830
Masawa	M-F
McChord Sa A	
Osan	
Travis√ Sa A	
Yokota√	

Elmendorf AFB continued from preceding page

Golf: 552.3821 1 April - 9 Oct **Holes**: 18 Eagle-glen Golf Course

Ground Transport:
Base Shuttle 0600-2100 M-F (0600-1800 summer), 1130-1830 SS.
Shuttle: To Ft Richardson Clinic.
Ft Rich shuttle reservations 384-0412
Commercial: #14 Bus to BAC in Anchorage, 0637-2055 M-F, 1020-1710 Sa, 343-6543. Taxi 552-2793, expensive. RR in Anchorage to Fairbanks, Seward. Taxi 563-5353, 276-1234.

Aero Club: 753.4167

Chance of seat
★★★★ x ★★ summer

Flight Information:
Terminal
552.8588, 4616,
24h. [Fax 3996, 632 AMSS/TROP 42525 Burns Rd]
Terminal open 24h Parking permit at Terminal.
Army C12 depart from Hanger 6 (M & Cedar Sts.) & land at Wainwright.
NOTE: Flights transiting Elmendorf en route from CONUS to CONUS require passenger's seniority on Elmendorf's sign up list to assure passage to following CONUS destination(s).

	Break	Lunch	Dinner	Brun
O Club		M-F	ThF	Su
E Club		M-F	7d	
Snack		0630-2200 M-F 0730-2100 Sa 1030-2100 Su		
Cafeteria		24h		

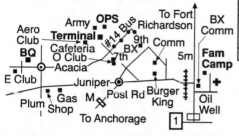

NOJ
Coast Guard Support
Quarters:
BQ: Availability ★★★★ x ★★ summer **5446** 0800-2200, reservations taken x PCS season. Rates: $28sgl, $38dbl, $44family.
Commercial: Buskin River Inn 800-544-2202.

Ground Transport:
Base Shuttle 0845-1545 M-F. Liberty bus to town, 5770. Car rent C 2261/64. Taxi 486-3100,3211.

CGSC Kodiak
Kodiak, AK 99619
487-xxxx   **907-487**-xxxx
No operator
➤➤➤➤➤➤➤ **Flights** ➤➤➤➤➤➤➤
Elmendorf Tu or W√   McClellan
Chance of seat
★★★ x ★ summer

Flight Information:
OPS **5158** 0900-1200 MTTF
Recording 5149

	Break	Lunch	Dinner	Brun
Club		ThF	§	Su
Galley	7d	7d	7d	

§ Sandwiches in lounge

FRN Army HQ for Alaska. Distances walkable.

Quarters:

BQ: Availability
I★★★★ x ★
summer **0421**
0600-2230 M-F,
1000-1745 SS.
For arrival other
hrs, call, keys left
with SDO, 2000.

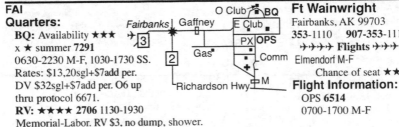

Rates: $25-25sgl+$7**add** per, DV $27sgl+$7add per. Protocol 2067.

Golf: 384-6675 **Holes:** 36 Moose Run Golf

RV: ★★★★ x ★ summer 1480, 1100-1800 M-F May-Sept, check in
Skeet   Range or with Host 1600-2000 W, 1100-1500 ThF, 1100-1600
Sa, RV ESW $10, Tent $5.

Commercial: Motels in Anchorage, expensive,
Mush Inn lowest, 277-4554.

Ground Transport:

✚ **Shuttle** to Elmendorf, contact BQ.
Commercial: #75 Bus to BAC in Anchorage,
transfer to # 14 to Elmendorf, #6 to Airport. RR in
Anchorage to Fairbanks, Seward. Taxi, expensive, 552 2793.

Ft Richardson   D-5
(Bryant AAF)
Anchorage, AK 99505
384-1110   **907**-384-1110
➤➤➤➤ **Flights** ➤➤➤➤
Helicopters

Chance of seat ★★
Flight Information:
OPS **4286,6333**,
C-12 **7889**
0730-1700 M-F
See Elmendorf for fixed-
wing flights. NG C12, D
4902, C 6904.

	Break	Lunch	Dinner	Brun
§ O Club		M-F	W-F	Su
NCO Club				
E Club			7d	
Cafeteria	7d	7d	7d	

§ Serves all ranks

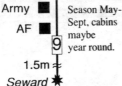

Army ■
AF ■
1.5m ⚡
Seward ✱

Season May-
Sept, cabins
maybe
year round.

Ground Transport:
Bus to downtown 7d during
summer. RR to Anchorage.

Quarters:
Availability ★★★,
motel $65-108unit, townhouse
$129-196. RV EW $19-25,
Tent $7-12, Yurt $18-24

Quarters:
Availability ★★★★
x ★ Th-Su. Rates: Cabins
$121-180, RV $16, Tent
$11

Seward Army Rec Camp
Seward, AK 99664
384-1649   **907**-384-1649
Above at Richardson. Sep 15-May
30 0700-1100 M-F, May-30-Sep
15 24H. Site C 224-2654/5559.
800-770-1858, Fax 0248.
Seward AF Rec Camp
Seward, AK 99664
552-5526   **907**-224-5425
Elmendorf PH: 907.753.2378

FAI

Quarters:

BQ: Availability ★★★
x ★ summer **7291**
0630-2230 M-F, 1030-1730 SS.
Rates: $13,20sgl+$7add per.
DV $32sgl+$7add per. O6 up
thru protocol 6671.
RV: ★★★★ **2706** 1130-1930
Memorial-Labor. RV $3, no dump, shower.

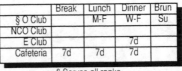

Ground Transport:
Shuttles: Eielson, Greely 1745, call Greely motor pool 873-3228.
Commercial: City bus on post, 264-6543.
Golf: 6223 **Holes:** 18 Chena Bend Golf Course

Ft Wainwright   D-99
Fairbanks, AK 99703
353-1110   **907**-353-1110
➤➤➤➤ **Flights** ➤➤➤➤
Elmendorf M-F

Chance of seat ★★
Flight Information:
OPS **6514**
0700-1700 M-F

Travis-Yokota Via Elmendorf

Most of the time it is easier as well as faster for a Cat-VI to fly via Elmendorf than via Hickam. In
winter many empty seats are the rule as well as available billets. M-F a tightly scheduled shuttle
keeps travelers out of the cold. Terminal is open 24h and has a cafeteria if worst comes to worst.

Alaska

HAWAII (Oahu)

Zulu-10, no daylight saving   International DSN Prefix 315

Installations on Oahu and interconnecting bus lines. Bus service is excellent but luggage must fit under seat or on lap, 848-5555. Bases with flights in **bold**. Occasional flights from Hickam, Kaneohe to other islands. **D (only) Operator Assistance to connect to any D or C on Oahu is 449-1110. Directory Assistance (i.e. information only) D & C 449.7110.**

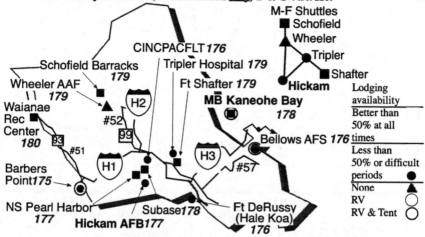

Oahu Quarters Summary, All accept reservations x Hickam, C Numbers.

Barbers Pt	175	Beach cott. 682-2019 0900-1700 MWF, 0900-1400 TuTh,Sa-1330	
Bellows	176	Beach cottages only, 259-8080 0800-2100	●
DeRussy	176	Hale Koa Hotel 955-0555 24h, 800-367-6027 0700-1745	●
CINCPAC	176	O only, 471-3041 24h	●
Hickam	177	448.5400 24h	●
Kaneohe	178	O,E6 up 257-2409; Beach cottages, TLF 254-2716	
Pearl Harbor	177	O 474-1201 24h, E 471-8053 (no dependents) 24h	
Schofield	179	624-9877 24h	
Shafter	179	DV 438-1685	■
Subase	178	BQ791.8300, E (no dependents) 471.9188 24h	
Tripler	179	839-2336 0630-2245 M-F, 0700-2000 SS, other hrs 6661	■
Waianae	180	Beach cottages only, 696-6783, list starts 1630, assigned 1930	

TLA apartment list at Hickam BQ. Most convenient in Area.

NAX C130, HH65

Beach cottages are controlled by Pearl Harbor MWR with on site management by Barbers Point *To Go* (ITT) Office **C 682.2019**, RV same office ★, **C 682-2019** Rate: $40-70 by grade. 0900-1700 MWF, 0900-1400 TuTh, 0900-1330 Sa, only for periods F-F, M-F, F-M, M-M. RV, Tent W $10,15. DV (O6 & up) $65 (Must call Flag Officer Cottage Reservations Manager @ **C 808.682.2206** or **D** 430.0111 EX: 474.8751.

Golf: 682-1911 **Holes:** 18 BARBERS POINT GOLF COURSE

Ground Transport:
   Commercial: #51 Bus to downtown on Route H1. For Hickam transfer to #47/9 then #19 in front of Airport.

Meals: Available at Bowling Alley, 19th Puka, Surfer Cafe, McDonald's, & Subway. Possibly CG Galley with prior arrangements.

CGAS Barber's Point D-94
(former NAS)
Ewa, HI 96862
484-xxxx   **808-684**-xxxx
✈✈✈✈ **Flights** ✈✈✈✈

Converted to Civilian Airport in 1999. Uncertain about possibility of Coast Guard Flights to CONUS.

Flight Information:
OPS **9295**

Barber's Point Map Index

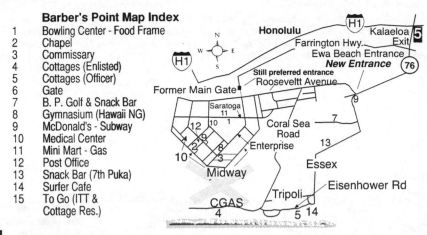

1 Bowling Center - Food Frame
2 Chapel
3 Commissary
4 Cottages (Enlisted)
5 Cottages (Officer)
6 Gate
7 B. P. Golf & Snack Bar
8 Gymnasium (Hawaii NG)
9 McDonald's - Subway
10 Medical Center
11 Mini Mart - Gas
12 Post Office
13 Snack Bar (7th Puka)
14 Surfer Cafe
15 To Go (ITT & Cottage Res.)

Honolulu
Kalaeloa Exit **5**
Farrington Hwy.
Ewa Beach Entrance
New Entrance **76**
Still preferred entrance
Rooseveltt Avenue
Former Main Gate
Saratoga 11
Coral Sea Road
Enterprise
Essex
Midway
Eisenhower Rd
Tripoli
CGAS 4
5 14

PACAF

Gas BX
■**Office**
Club
Waimanalo ⊟M (SS)
2.5m
M (M-F)
72 #57 Bus

Quarters:

BQ: Availability ★★ x ★ weekends, holidays, 0800-2100, **from mainland 800-437-2607**. Fax 4119. Call 1200 for cancellations. Reservations between Memorial Day & Labor Day: Active AF 90d, others 75d in advance. Rates: $55,back cabins; $60, beach cabins; $65 new(2002) cabins; RV, Tent $7. No dump, pets.

Ground Transport:

#57 Bus on Route 72. Transfer downtown to #19 to Hickam.

Bellows AFS

Waimanalo, HI 96795
808-259-8080

	Break	Lunch	Dinner
Club	7d	7d	7d

Distances short.

Quarters:

BOQ: ★ **3041** 24h (no children), assigned 1800. Call 1600 for no-shows. Rate: $20sgl+$5add per.

Ground Transport: Buses on Nimitz.

To Scholield, Barbers Pt, Waianae
AZ Memorial ⊚
Car Rental ■ ⊚
CINCPACFLT (Makalapa)
Subase
To Pearl Harbor **BOQ**
& Hickam AFB
Nimitz Hwy

CINCPACFLT 96818

471-xxxx   **808-471**-xxxx

Recreation Center

Quarters:

Hotel: Availability ★ **0555** 24h, outside HI 800-367-6027 0800-1600. Fax 800-425-3329. Reservations advised, accepted 1y ahead. Often short stays without reservations are possible if any open day(s) are acceptable. Rates: $67-$174 depending on grade and room location. Reservations closed on holidays. Internet reservations available.

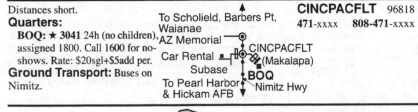

Kalakaua
#19 Bus
Kalia
Hale Koa   Army Museum

Ft DeRussy

(Hale Koa Hotel)
2055 Kalia Rd
Waikiki Beach, HI 96815
438.6739   808-955-0555

Ground Transport:

Parking $3, free transport from either parking by DeRoosy Caboosy.
#19 Bus outside hotel to Hickam 0500-2400 M-F, 0540-0010 Sa, 0540-2340 Su. Liberty bus Kaneohe 1900,2100,2400,0200.

HIK AMC PACAF
154th WG C130, KC130

Hickam AFB 96853 D-94

Info on D or C use 449.7111
Assistance on D 449.1110
449-xxxx   808-449-xxxx

Hickam Map Index

1 **Terminal**
2 Bowling Center
3 BX
4 Comm
5 **E** Club
6 Golf (9 hole lounge)
7 Gym, Fitness Center
8 Hawaii ANG
9 Library
10 **Lodging Office**
11 **O** Club
12 Operations
13 Post Office
14 Rec Equipment Issue

There are no fences between Hickam, Pearl
Harbor, or Subase.

Distances walkable on Hickam, 0.7m BQ
to Terminal

➤➤➤➤➤➤➤➤➤ Flights ➤➤➤➤➤➤➤➤➤

Andersen	March	Pago Pago MSa
Australia SuF	McChord	Travis√
Kadena√	Osan ThSu	Yokota√

Frequent flights to many destinations
Chance of seat fluctuates

Flight Information:

Terminal **808.449.1515** 24h. Temp. Recording 1854,6833. [Fax 808.448.1503, 635 APO/
TRO, 855 O'Malley] Tanker OPS 2052. ANG (C130) 9875. Army 0905. Terminal open 24h,
lockers, car rent, cafeteria 24h, BX. For Parking sign
log at Terminal, limit 60d. SATO 422.2729 provides
Electronic Travel Authority (VISA) for Australia in
less than ten minutes, $10.

	Break	Lunch	Dinner	Brun
O Club	xSu	M-F	Tu-Sa	Su
E Club		M-F	xM	Su
Cafeteria	0400-2000 M-F			
	0500-1900 Sa			
	0600-1300 Su			

Quarters:

Royal Alaka'i Inn:: Availability **O ★, E ★★★ D**
448.5400, C 448-5400/5500 24h O can use E quarters. Reservation extensions @ 0800.
PACAF FY 07/08 Rates: $27-49 per room. Motel hotlines in terminal.

Golf: 6490 / 448.2317 & Par 3 448.2318 **Holes:** 27 Mamala Bay Golf Course 18 & Par 3,
9 hole

Marina: C 449.5215 Hickam Harbor

Ground Transport:

Shuttles: Base 0700-17 M-F; Bus stop Vickers & 8th 0525-1535 M-F to
Wheeler 2739; ✚ **Shuttle:** To Tripler 0700-1515 M-F, 5123.
Commercial: #19 Bus from terminal to Airport, DeRussy 0630-0100 M-F, 0635-2315 SS.
Transfer in front of airport to #3 for Pearl Harbor or Subase, to Barbers point or Waianae
transfer to #47/9 in front of airport then to #51, for Schofield #52, for Tripler or Shafter
transfer to #31, for Kaneohe transfer to #56. Car rent 422-6915, 0700-2200. Taxi 533-4999,
422-22224. The Cab" 808-422-2222 is the only taxi service allowed on Oahu bases.

Distances short on NS, 1.8m BOQ to Hickam terminal.

Quarters:

Availability ★★★.
BOQ: 473-4165/5983, 474-1201 24h. Rate: $25sgl
+$5add per, DV $50per.
CPO: Rate $20+$5 per adult
BEQ (no dependents) **8053** 24h. Rate: $4per.
Navy Lodge on Ford Island 440.2290 421-6113
$80-100+   **Continued on following page.**

NS Pearl Harbor 96818
Info D or C   449.7110
Assist. D only   449.1110
471.xxxx   808-471-xxxx

	Break	Lunch	Dinner	Brun
Banyan Club		M-F	W	Su
CPO Club		M-F	Tu-Sa	
Club Pearl		24h		
McDonald's	0600-2400			

Hawaii

Golf: 471-0142 **Holes**: 18 & 7 Navy-Marine Golf Course 18, Ford Island Golf Course (free) 7

Ground Transport:
#3 Bus from to Airport, downtown, 531-1611. Transfer on Nimitz in front of Airport to #19 for Hickam and to buses to other installations, see Ground Transport for Hickam. Car rent.

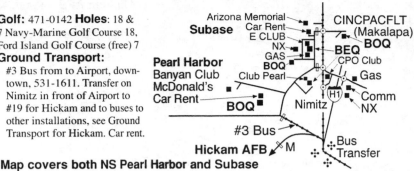

Map covers both NS Pearl Harbor and Subase

Distances short, 2.4m BOQ to Hickam terminal.

Subase   HI, 96818
471-xxxx   808-471-xxxx

Quarters:
BQ: ★★ 791.8300 Lockwood Hall EX: 1000, 24h, Rates: $16sgl, DV $30,35sgl, all+$6add per.
BEQ: ★★★★ (no dependents) 9188 24h. Rates: E $9per, E7up suite $15sgl +$10add per.

Ground Transport:
#3 Bus from to Airport, downtown, 531-1611. Transfer on Nimitz in front of Airport to #19 for Hickam and to buses to other installations, see Ground Transport for Hickam. Car rent 2592 0700-1545 M-F, 0800-1145 SS.

E Club	0600-2100 M-F

NGF
Marine Base
Distances long, 2m BQ-#56 Bus, 1.8m BQ-OPS.

Quarters:
BQ: Availability ★★★ E6 up & O 2409, 0730-2330. Rates: $25sgl, DV $35sgl both+$6add per.
TLF, beach cottages ★ C 254-2716 0630-1600 M-F, 0900-1800 SS. Rate: $55unit.
Camping: Reserve, check in, pay at Outdoor Rec 254-3230 0800-1630 Th-M, tent $8. No dump, pets.
Golf: 1745 **Holes**: 18 Kaneohe Klipper Golf Complex
Marina: C 808-254-7666 Kaneohe Bay Marina
Ground Transport:
Commercial: #70 Bus 0758-1337, at Kailua transfer to #56/7, return from Kailua 0737-1337. #56 Bus to Honolulu stops 1m from main gate. Use footpath between main gate and bus stop, not the expressway.

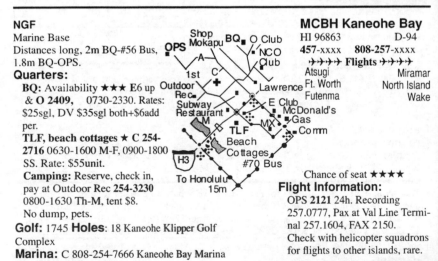

MCBH Kaneohe Bay
HI 96863   D-94
457-xxxx   808-257-xxxx

↣↣↣↣ **Flights** ↣↣↣↣

Atsugi	Miramar
Ft. Worth	North Island
Futenma	Wake

Chance of seat ★★★★

Flight Information:
OPS 2121 24h. Recording 257.0777, Pax at Val Line Terminal 257.1604, FAX 2150.
Check with helicopter squadrons for flights to other islands, rare.

	Break	Lunch	Dinner	Brun
O Club		M-F	WF	Su
NCO Club	Tu-Sa	Tu-Sa	F	
E Club	FSa		xSu	
Restaurant	0630-2100			
Subway	000-2200			

Hawaii

HHI

Distances walkable on each

Quarters:

BQ: Availability ★★★ **9650**, 800-490-9638 24h, reservations 45d in advance. Rates: $57-73dbl, suites $92dbl.

Commercial: Motel outside main gate.

Golf: Leilehua Golf Course 655-4653; Nagorski Golf Course 438-9587 **Holes**: Each has 18 **Ground Transport:**

Shuttle: Post 0630-1700. M-F: **S–W**–Tripler-Shafter, from **S** Conroy Bowl 0643,0918,1208,14231 M-F. From **W** 0649-1430. **W** to **S** 0850-1608, 438-2247. **W** to Hickam, call Hickam.

Commercial: Bus "Shuttle" on **S** to Wahiawa. Transfer in Wahiawa to #52 to Honolulu. For Hickam transfer again in front of Airport to #19. **W:** #52 Bus outside East Gate.

_S_ **Schofield Barracks**
Wahiawa, HI 96786   D-94
455-xxxx   808-624-xxxx

_W_ **Wheeler AAF** 96854
456-xxxx   808-656-xxxx
Flights moved to Hickam

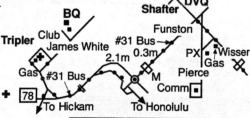

Car Rent — O Club — Snack — PX — Shop — Comm — Cafe — M — Shuttle Bus — To Trimble — Waianae — BQ — E Club — Gas — Wheeler Club — H2 — Kolekole — NCO Club 24h — Schofield — Kunai — Gas — PX — Cafe — Exit 17 — 99 — To Barbers Point — To Honolulu — Wahiawa — 452 Bus

		Break	Lunch	Dinner	Brun
S	O Club		M-F	W-F	Su
	NCO Club		M-F	Tu-Sa	
	E Club			xM	
	Cafeteria	0600-2400			
	Snack	0600-2200			
W	Club		M-F	W	
	Cafeteria	0630-1400 M-F			

Hawaii

Army HQ for Hawaii Distances walkable on each.

Quarters:

_S_: DVQ ★★

1685 0630-1700 M-F, 0800-1200 SS, reserve 72h in advance, max 7d. Check 1200 for cancellations. Protocol 16365. Rates: $26,29sgl+$5add per.

_T_: Guest House: ★★ 0630 2245 M-F, 0700-2000 SS,other hrs information desk in hospital 6661. Rate: $30unit shared bath, $47unit private.

Service reported excellent, inexpensive meals, retirees welcome.

Golf: see Schofield Barracks

Ground Transport:

Shuttles: M-F **S–T**–Wheeler-Schofield from theater 0807,1027,1317,1530, from **T** 0820,1040,1330,1543. **T** to Hickam ✚ 0940,1140,1340,1540.

Commercial: _S,T_, #31 Bus 0545-1815, transfer to #19 to Hickam, #3 to NS..

_S_ Ft Shafter   D-94
Honolulu, HI 96858
438-xxxx   808-438-xxxx

_T_ Tripler Army Med C
Honolulu, HI 96859
433-xxxx   808-433-xxxx

Club — DVQ — Shafter — Funston — BQ — Tripler — Club — James White — #31 Bus 0.3m — PX — Wisser — Gas — 2.1m — Gas — #31 Bus — M — Pierce — Comm — 78 — To Hickam — To Honolulu

		Break	Lunch	Dinner	Brun
S	Club		M-F	FSa	
T	Club		M-F	MF	Su

Visit KMC (Kilauea Military Camp) located within the Volcano National Park. This is the world's most active volcano.

HAWAII (Oahu Concluded)

Beach cabins Distances short.

Quarters:

Availability
★★★ C 6783
0800-2100,
reservations
(Oahu) 4158,
(other islands) 800-847-6771,
(CONUS) 800-333-4158,
0900-1600 M-F, active Army
90d ahead, other services and

**Waianae Army Rec C
[Renamed Pililaau
Army Rec Center]**
85-010 Army St
Waianae, HI 96792
808-696-6783

	Break	Lunch	Dinner
Club	SS	SS	FSS

retired 80d, Res 60d. In person list starts 1630, assigned 1930. Rates: $40-85 depending on rank and size. No pets.

Ground Transport:

#51 Bus to Barbers Point & Honolulu, transfer to #52 to Schofield, to Hickam transfer to #47/9 Bus, again in front of Airport to #19 (#3 to Pearl Harbor).

Low-Cost Commercial Quarters in Honolulu

Except when a major exercise is in progress, almost always quarters are available somewhere on Oahu. Hotels and models in the order of $50 are advertised in Hickam terminal, some pick up and return. Those on Waikiki do not. Close to the Hale Koa is the YMCA, 401 Atkinson, 941-3344, $30sgl, $43dbl no bath, $37sgl, $51dbl with bath. Closer is a hostal in the Hawaiian Colony, 1946 Ala Moana, 949-3382, $13sgl dormitory. Although the Hale Koa is a bargain for the lower ranks, for higher ranks quality hotels are available at a lower cost.

Waikiki
Atkinson
YMCA
Shopping Center
Hostel
Kalakaua
Ala Moana
Kalia
Hale Koa Resort

HAWAII (Island of Hawaii)

Cabins, availability
★★★ x ★
summer. Oahu
number for
reservations 0800-
1600. 90d in advance active, 60d retired, 45d NG,Res. 7d max stay, extensions if available. If willing to accept any available accommodations, usually possible to get in on short notice. Tours available. Those over 62 should obtain a Golden Age Passport to avoid paying park entrance fee. Rates: E1-5 $25-50dbl, E6-O3 $35-60dbl, O4 up $45-70dbl, all+5add per. Rate includes transport to/from Hilo Airport on 24h notice. No pets.

Gas Bowl
PX
Cafe
Park HQ
Office
1.1m
To Hilo 30m
Volcano House

Kilauea Military Camp
Hawaii National Park, HI 96718
Oahu Number: **808-438**-6707, Hawaii Number: **808-967**-8333, both 0800-1600.

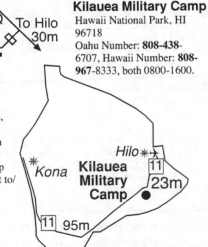

Kona
Hilo
Kilauea Military Camp
11 23m
11 95m

	Break	Lunch	Dinner
Cafeteria	7d	7d	7d
Blow		1500-2130	

HAWAII (Island of Kauai)

MBK
Distances long.
Quarters:
  BEQ: Availability ★ 383
0730-1600
M-F. Rate: Free.
  Beach cottages: H 752
0600-2100 M-F, 0900-1700
SS. For arrival other hrs,
call, make arrangements.
Rate: $50unit. Check in
Rec C. O6 up in HQ 255,
0730-1600 M-F. Reserve
3m ahead, call, key at main
gate. Rate: $55dbl+$5add
per. No pets. **Food off
station is expensive, but
meals are available at
Galley, NX, & Club.**

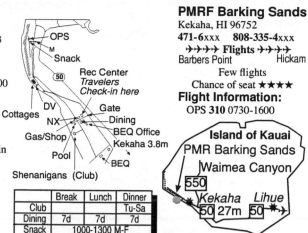

	Break	Lunch	Dinner
Club			Tu-Sa
Dining	7d	7d	7d
Snack	1000-1300 M-F		

PMRF Barking Sands
Kekaha, HI 96752
471-6xxx   **808-335-4**xxx
↦↦↦↦ **Flights** ↦↦↦↦
Barbers Point   Hickam
        Few flights
    Chance of seat ★★★★
Flight Information:
    OPS **310** 0730-1600

Island of Kauai
PMR Barking Sands
    Waimea Canyon
550
    Kekaha   Lihue
    50 27m 50 ⚔

ATLANTIC and CARIBBEAN

Installations and airports regularly served by Space-A flights in South and North America, also
on Atlantic and Caribbean islands excepting mainland US and the UK.

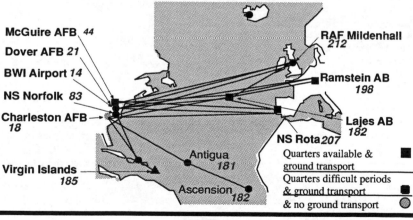

McGuire AFB *44*
Dover AFB *21*
BWI Airport *14*
NS Norfolk *83*
Charleston AFB
    18
Virgin Islands
    185

RAF Mildenhall
    212
Ramstein AB
    198
Lajes AB
    182
NS Rota *207*
Antigua
    181
Ascension
    182

Quarters available &   ■
ground transport
Quarters difficult periods ■
& ground transport
& no ground transport   ◉

Zulu-4

ANTIGUA

International DSN prefix 312

9m ●
Airport
St. John

SJH
NS has closed

Coolidge Airport
FPO AA 34054
854-1110   (Patrick
Operator)   **407-494**-1110
↦↦↦↦↦↦ **Flights** ↦↦↦↦↦↦
Ascension W   Patrick F
Charleston F

    Chance of seat ★★★★
Flight Information:
    x272 24h, at Charleston

Hawaii

AS ATLANTIC and CARIBBEAN
ASCENSION ISLAND (UK)

ASI
Prior permission required
for visiting or transiting, see
Patrick AFB.

Closing

International DSN prefix 312

Ascension Auxiliary AF
854-1110   407-494-1110
(Patrick Operator)
+·+·+·+·+·+ **Flights** +·+·+·+·+·+
Antigua WF   Patrick WF
Charleston WF

Chance of seat ★★★★
Flight Information:
Numbers above, ask for Ascension

Portugal Escudos obsolete

1 USD = 1127.732 PTE	1 PTE = 0.00603285 USD
1 USD = 0.637125 EUR	1 EUR = 1.56955 USD

Zulu-1

AZORES, TERCEIRA ISLAND (Portugal)

Passports required for dependents and retirees (usually stamped at Terminal for arriving and departing AMC flights but sometimes travelers must make own arrangements). Immigration at Airport open 24h. All facilities usable including Portuguese clubs. Lajes is an excellent alternative CONUS-Europe if direct flights are difficult. Calling Base Ops with Navy squadron numbers readily available can be most helpful in learning about Navy flights. Make arrangements with base community activities office for car rental just outside gate. Ask about flights don't depend on monitors.

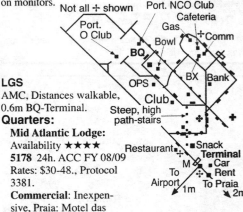

LGS
AMC, Distances walkable,
0.6m BQ-Terminal.
Quarters:
Mid Atlantic Lodge:
Availability ★★★★
5178 24h. ACC FY 08/09
Rates: $30-48., Protocol
3381.
Commercial: Inexpensive, Praia: Motel das
Nove Tihas, 53135,
Residencial Salles 53541.
Angra: Hotel de Angra
(about $50) 24041. "Rural
Salga"Bed & Breakfast
$30 (00351) 29590503.
Ground Transport:
Base Shuttle 0700-1730,
23151.
Commercial: Bus Praia-
Base to Praia 7d. Hrly bus
Praia-Angra 7d. Car rent
outside main gate, 52969,
0800-1600, M-F, 0900-
1200 SS. Taxi 3288. Hertz
Rental Car 885.3660.

Lajes AB APO AE 09720   D-94
535.1110   011.351.255.57.1110
Extensions thru operator
On base prefix 2.
AMC +·+·+ **Flights** +·+·+ **Navy**

Adana	Moron
Andrews Su	Naples
Aviano Sa	Norfolk Tu
Charleston SuTh	BWI SuTT
Dover√ Tu	Ramstein TuSa A
Keflavik Su	Rhein-Main
McGuire	Rota FSa
Mildenhall	Sigonella Su

Chance of seat ★★★
Flight Information:
Terminal **3227,3582** 24h [Fax
5110, 629 AMSS/TRP Bldg T612
Unit 7795]. Recording 3199.
OPS 4106 24h.

Corve
Santa Cruz
Flores
Graciosa   Terceira
Faila   **Lajes AB**
Praia da Vitoria
São Sebashão
Atlantic Ocean   Angra do Heroismo

Sao Miguel
Santa Maria

	Break	Lunch	Dinner	Brun
Club		7d	M-F	Su
Restaurant		M-F		
Bowl	0830-2230 M-F			
	1400-2100 SS			
Cafeteria	1100-2300			
	1600-2300 SS			
Terminal	24h			

Consider Portuguese clubs shown on map. Excellent
food, inexpensive. Portuguese money used.

182

NDW

Navy, AMC
Distances walkable to short drive from BQ to Marina, Pool, Food, NEXMart. Longer to Terminal-Shop.

NS Guantanamo Bay, Cuba

Quarters:

BQ: Availability ★ **2400** Fax: 2401 Rate: E-7 & up $12, DV $25.Located on Windward Point, off Sherman Avenue in Bldg. 1670 (Quarters currently assigned by CO's Secretary and difficult to obtain.)
Navy Lodge: Availability ★★★ before 911, 011.53.99.**7970.**

Attractions:

Boating, water sports, & golf. MWR **4360**

Ground Transport:

Rental Cars are available fromNEX at **4316**. Ground transportation is operated by K V Aerner Co. at **5210.**

NS Guantanamo Bay

PSC 1005 Box 1
FPO AE 09593-0100
723.3960   **011.53.99.**3960
➤➤➤➤➤ **Flights** ➤➤➤➤➤
C141 Su A
727 Jacksonville

Flight Information:

Terminal **6204** 1000-1700
Retirees are required a sponsor (can be anyone) living at GTMO. Sponsor must request permission through the Air Ops Dept and should allow one week for processing. Send request to Air Operations Department, PSC 1005 Box 35U, FPO AE 09508

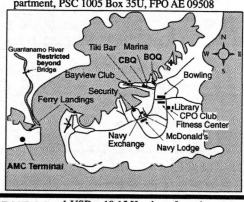

PLA Zulu-5 Distances short. **HONDURAS**   1 USD = 19.15 Honduran Lempira
1 Honduran Lempira = 0.051 USD

Quarters:

BQ: ★★★★
(Radio Bedrock).
4450, 6745. If arriving late, have gate make radio contact. Rate: Free. Honduran representative 4116,4235. Dining, cafeteria usable, not BX. Joint Task Force B protocol **D** 449.4177.

White House:

Comayagua
7m
M Van Stop
   Dining
1
BX Rec
     C
56m
BQ■Army   **Terminal** ■
(White House)
Tegucigalpa
AF
BQ

Soto Cano AB   D-94

APO AA 34042
449.4000/1/2 **011.504.234.**4634
➤➤➤➤ **Flights** ➤➤➤➤
Charleston Tu
Chance of seat ★★★★

Flight Information:

6632/29 [Fax 6663]
C 011.504.237.8833

To leave base and return apply 5d in advance for base pass at terminal, by phone 37-8833 x4116, or send copy of both sides of ID to PSC42 by mail or Fax x4765.

No retirees [La Casa Blanca]Residence, a safe house in Tegucigalpa, run by JTF-Bravo's liaison office to the embassy. The White House is not a hotel, so take toiletries and a towel. Located at Colonia Loma Linda Norte, #299, Avenida F.A.O. If emergency assistance is needed call the liaison in Tegucigalpa at 232.0712. JTF-B Protocol: **D 4177**

Commercial: Inexpensive hotels in Comayagua, 720332, 720, 215, 721210. Check MWR for Tegucipalpa.

Continued on following page.

Ground Transport:

Shuttles: To Comayagua 24h. To Tegucipalpa: Lv Soto Cano 0900 M-F, 0800 SS, Airport 1300 M-F, 1000 SS, Ar White House 1145 M-F, 1030 SS. Lv White House 1315 M-F, 1045 SS, Airport 1430 M-F, 1545 SS, Ar Soto Cano 1600 M-F, 1715 SS. All military buses are free. **Commercial:** Trailiasa bus stops at AB, 7538. Taxis inexpensive.

PUERTO RICO (US)

Zulu-4 No daylight saving

BQN

Quarters:

BQ: Availability ★★X★ weekends (C 890) **8492** 0800-1630 M-F, other hrs club (C 890) 2581. Rates: newly proposed rates $60-120. No pets.

Ground Transport:

Publicos. Car rent at airport.

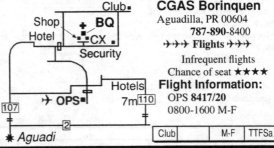

CGAS Borinquen

Aguadilla, PR 00604

787-890-8400

⇥⇥⇥ **Flights** ⇥⇥⇥

Infrequent flights

Chance of seat ★★★★

Flight Information:

OPS **8417/20**

0800-1600 M-F

Club		M-F	TTFSa

Distances walkable, 0.6m BQ-main gate.

Quarters:

BQ: Availability ★★★ x ★ summer **3821** 0630-1800 M-F, 0800-1700 SS, reserve. Rate: $18-36dbl+$5add per. DV $55dbl+$10child. Protocol 3240.

Ground Transport:

Post Shuttle: 0730-1630 M-F, from BQ every :30. **Commercial:** Buses outside main gate, #19 to Rio Piedras.

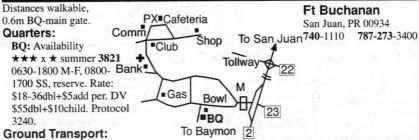

Ft Buchanan

San Juan, PR 00934

740-1110   **787-273**-3400

	Break	Lunch	Dinner	Brun
Club		M-F	TTFSa	Su
Cafeteria	M-F	M-F		
Snack	xSu	7d	7d	
USO			7d	

SJU
156th AW
C-130
Transient flights.

Cafe 0600-1300 M-F

To San Juan

⇥ BX / Cafe

1.5m OPS

McDonald's

Muñiz ANGB   D-88

San Juan Airport

860-9219 **787-253-5**129

Weekly flights

Chance of seat ★★★★

Flight Information:

OPS **129** 0730-1600 M-F

Every Saturday morning a C130 Air National Guard or Air Force unit departs for its home base and that afternoon another arrives. Check with ANG & AF C130 for their rotation dates to and from this facility. No lodging. Western U.S. C130 units frequently RON at Kelly Annex (TX) while flying home.

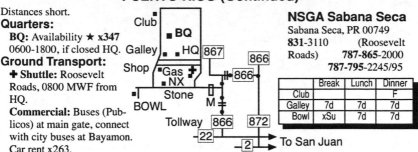

Distances short.

Quarters:
BQ: Availability ★ x347 0600-1800, if closed HQ.

Ground Transport:
✚ **Shuttle:** Roosevelt Roads, 0800 MWF from HQ.
Commercial: Buses (Publicos) at main gate, connect with city buses at Bayamon. Car rent x263.

NSGA Sabana Seca
Sabana Seca, PR 00749
831-3110 (Roosevelt Roads) **787-865**-2000
787-795-2245/95

	Break	Lunch	Dinner
Club			F
Galley	7d	7d	7d
Bowl	xSu	7d	7d

SOUTH AMERICA and ADJACENT POINTS

Required for Space-A: V Visa. T Tourist Card. P Passport. C Country Clearance.

Argentina	BUE	Buenos Aires	P	Equador	QIO	Quito	P
Bahamas	NAS	Nassau		Guatemala	GUA	Guatemala City	T
Belize			P	Haiti	PAP	Port au Prince	P¶
Bolivia	LPB	La Paz	P or T	Honduras	TGU	Tegucigalpa	P¶
Brazil	RIO	Rio de Janeiro	PV§	Jamaica	KIN	Kingston	
"	BSB	Brasilia	PV§	Nicaragua			PVC
Chile	SCL	Santiago	PT	Paraguay	ASU	Asuncion	PV
Columbia	BOG	Bogotá	PC	Peru	LIM	Lima	P(V or T)C
Costa Rica	OCO	San Jose	P	Uruguay	MVD	Montevideo	PV
Dominican Rep.	SDQ	Santo Domingo	P	Venezuela	CCS	Caracas	P(V or T)
El Salvador	SAL	San Salvador	PVC				

§ Includes transiting. ¶ Or proof of US citizenship. Lead time for country clearance 30d x Columbia 10d.

Table above lists airports occasionally served by flights from Charleston. For departures from these airports, contact Military Attache, US Embassy. Years ago embassy flights left weekly. Although it is still easy to board when a plane is known, flights are no longer scheduled well in advance. Once in South America it is difficult to plan a return by Space-A. Check for latest requirements.

Atlantic

VIRGIN ISLANDS (US)

STX Zulu-4, no daylight savings
ANG

St Croix Airport
(Alexander Hamilton)
St Croix, VI 00850
860-9228 **809-778**-3299
↣↣↣↣↣↣ **Flights** ↣↣↣↣↣↣
Isla Grande Airport, San Juan
St Thomas
Chance of seat ★★★
Flight Information:
OPS **C 2165,3299** duty hrs

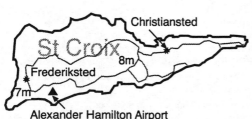

SA ATLANTIC and CARIBBEAN

VIRGIN ISLANDS (US) (Continued)

STH

Harry S. Truman Airport

Charlotte Amalie

St Thomas Airport
(Truman)
St Thomas, VI
340.860-9165
➔➔➔➔ Flights ➔➔➔➔
Isla Grande Airport, San Juan
St Croix
ANG C130 Units from CONUS

Chance of seat ★★★
Flight Information:
Number above, duty hrs

No planes-stationed, call St Croix for ANG, Roosevelt Roads for Navy. Airport tower C 340.774.1836 knows of flight 10min before landing. Jet Center C 777.9177, FAX 8889 and Alliance Aviation C 777.4646, FAX: 4545 handle passengers. Go to Crash Shack on apron to board, C 340.774.1809. Bus "City" to downtown 0600-2100 7d.

Military Exchange Privileges

	Retiree from U.S.	Ret. Depend. from U.S.	AD & Dep on LV from another country
PACIFIC			
Guam	Yes	Yes	Yes
Korea	Yes (Note 3)	Yes (Note 3)	Yes (Note 3)
Japan/Okinawa	Yes (Note 8)	Yes (Note 8)	Yes (Note 4,5,6,7)
ATLANTIC			
Belgium	(See Note 1)	(See Note 1)	No
Germany	(See Note 3)	(See Note 3)	(See Note 2)
Greece	No	No	(See Note 4)
Italy	(See Note 6)	(See Note 6)	(See Note 5)
Netherlands	No	No	No
Norway	No	No	No
Puerto Rico	Yes	Yes	Yes
Saudi Arabia	No	No	No
Spain	No	No	No
Turkey	No	No	No
United Kingdom	No	No	No

NOTES

1. Privileges may be granted on a case-by-case basis by the Commander, NATO/SHAPE Support Group, in coordination with the US Ambassador to Belgium.
2. Only personnel stationed in Europe and North Africa.
3. Must be ordinarily resident or be visiting in Germany for a period of 30 days or more. Rationed items may not be purchased. All purchases are subject to the payment of a fixed rate tax to German customs. Entry to commissary and exchange facilities requires DD Form D (Retired) or DD Form 1173, and a German Customs Certificate.
4. Only personnel stationed in the NATO are. Personnel may not purchase controlled items (e.g. electronic and other expensive items.)
5. Personnel stationed in NATO countries may purchase rationed items.
6. May purchase non-rationed items only.

Atlantic

186

MAJOR TRAVEL HEALTH ISSUE
Deep Vein Thrombosis

Deep vein thrombosis (DVT) is a serious medical condition which can be caused by extended inactivity, including that endured on long trips. In layman's terms, DVT is a blood clot in a vein deep inside your body.

This is a process for formation of thrombi that either partially or completely block circulation in a deep vein, generally in the lower extremities.

Deep veins bear primary responsibility for returning deoxygenated blood to the heart. Unlike the superficial veins, deep veins are surrounded by powerful muscles that contract to force blood back to the heart. Efficient and quick return of blood to the heart by the power of our leg muscles is a crucial phase of the circulatory process. Inactivity slows down blood circulation and creates a tendency for clot formation.

DVT can occur in almost anyone; most patients are over 60 years of age. However, pregnant women are 5 times more likely to develop DVT than nonpregnant women. Oral contraceptives or replacement estrogens may also increase the risk of clotting, particularly when combined with other risk factors like obesity, smoking, or hypertension. Whenever we remain relatively immobile for hours°, we become candidates for acquiring DVT.

Simple precautions may help prevent DVT.

- Getting up to stretch your legs at least once every hour is important.
- While seated, stretch your legs occasionally, flex and extend your ankles and lift your legs.
- From time to time take slow, deep breaths.
- Before traveling speak with your doctor about wearing elastic support hose during your trip. These are available for both men and women, but may require a prescription from your healthcare provider.

Consent to Obtain Passports

Under a law that became effective July 2, 2001 the **State Department now requires both parents' consent to obtain passports** and visas for overseas travel of children under age 14.

Money Exchange Rates

Exchange rates at the time an edition goes to press are given in details where they apply. This provides a jump start when entering a new country. But without question it is better to consider money as a native rather than translating to US$.

Proposed Map Changes

Check facility maps for replaced or additional building locations. If we are missing landmarks, traffic lights, or anything else which will benefit future travelers, please submit detailed information. Provide specifics as to where changes belong.

EUROPE and WESTERN ASIA

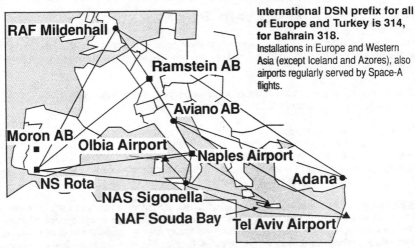

International DSN prefix for all of Europe and Turkey is 314, for Bahrain 318.

Installations in Europe and Western Asia (except Iceland and Azores), also airports regularly served by Space-A flights.

BAH   Zulu+3   **BAHRAIN**   1 USD = 0.371125 Bahraini Dinar
                                              1 Bahraini Dinar = 2.69451 USD

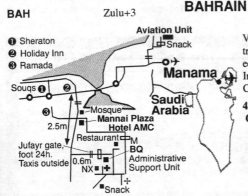

❶ Sheraton
❷ Holiday Inn
❸ Ramada

Visa and passport showing no Israel entrance required for dependents and retirees. 72h Visas available on arrival, BD10. International telephone prefixes: D 318, C 973.

FPO AE 09834
439.4332 Operator 09773-331-868

Charters ↣↣ Flights ↣↣ Cargo

Naples	Dover
BWI	Lajes
Rota	Norfolk
Sigonella	Rota
	Sigonella

Distances on Administrative Support Unit short, all others long. AT&T direct at ASU.

Quarters:

BQ: **4241** 24h. On ASU availability ★★. Rates: **O** $4per, **E** $2per. Mannai Palace Hotel **C 727-762** ★★★.

Commercial: Many western-style hotels.

Ground Transport:

AMC provides transport for charter flights, show at AMC. Show at Aviation Unit for cargo flights, transport not provided.

Shuttles: From ASU to hotels 0620-1935, to Aviation Unit 0525-1840, from Aviation Unit 0625-1905, 4263.

Commercial: There are city buses but are not needed. Agree on price before entering taxi, Airport-ASU≈BD4 ($12). International driver's licence required.

★★★ Chance of seat ★★★★
Flight Information:

C 727-347,368 | Aviation Unit
0730-1600 Sa-W | C 33-1868,5250
Show time 2200 SuW | 0600-1800

72h visa (BD5≈$15) is adequate and can be extended if necessary (additional fee). 7d visa can be obtained in one vis∞it to Brahrain Embassy, Bombay. Space-A to Bahrain is unclear due to varying requirements for visas imposed for manifesting.

	Break	Lunch	Dinner
Restaurant	7d	7d	7d
ASU Snack		1100-2300	

Europe

1 USD = 0.637125 EUR   1 EUR = 1.56955 USD

BELGIUM

Zulu+1

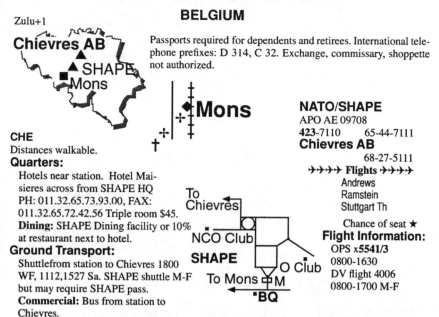

Passports required for dependents and retirees. International telephone prefixes: D 314, C 32. Exchange, commissary, shoppette not authorized.

CHE
Distances walkable.
Quarters:
Hotels near station. Hotel Maisieres across from SHAPE HQ PH: 011.32.65.73.93.00, FAX: 011.32.65.72.42.56 Triple room $45.
Dining: SHAPE Dining facility or 10% at restaurant next to hotel.
Ground Transport:
Shuttlefrom station to Chievres 1800 WF, 1112,1527 Sa. SHAPE shuttle M-F but may require SHAPE pass.
Commercial: Bus from station to Chievres.

NATO/SHAPE
APO AE 09708
423-7110   65-44-7111
Chievres AB
68-27-5111
✈✈✈✈ **Flights** ✈✈✈✈
Andrews
Ramstein
Stuttgart Th

Chance of seat ★
Flight Information:
OPS x**5541/3**
0800-1630
DV flight 4006
0800-1700 M-F

Consent to Obtain Passport

Since July 2, 2001 the State Department requires both parents' consent to obtain passports and visas for overseas travel of children under age 14.

Travel Notes

Europe

EUROPE and WESTERN ASIA
GERMANY

1 USD = 0.637125 EUR   1 EUR = 1.56955 USD

Zulu+1

Passports required for dependents and retirees. Exchange and commissary not usable unless stationed in Germany. Installations without significant use to travelers are omitted.

International telephone prefixes: D 314, C 49. **C Nos. ending 113 are directory assist, substitute 0 for operator assist.** C Numbers are: City Code-Military Access Code-Extension.

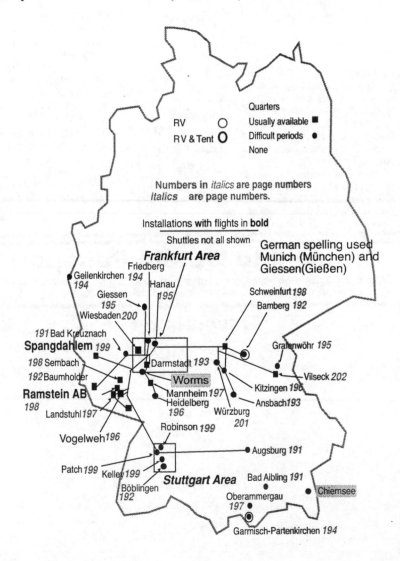

Europe

Distances short on each kaserne.

Quarters:
BQ: Availability ★ 1700,2812

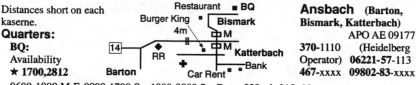

Ansbach (Barton, Bismark, Katterbach)
APO AE 09177
370-1110 (Heidelberg Operator) 06221-57-113
467-xxxx 09802-83-xxxx

0600-1900 M-F, 0900-1700 Sa, 1000-8900 Su. Rate: $28sgl+$15add per.

Ground Transport:
Shuttles: Post connects all kasernes 7d. **R-M M-F:** (From Barton) Nürnberg, Kitzingen, Würzburg, Hanau, Rhein-Main 0700, 468-7880. Motor pool 8457. Car rent C 1621, 1000-1800 M-F, 1000-1600 Sa.

German shuttle information has not been updated, request that travelers submit updated information. Thank you.

	Break	Lunch	Dinner	Brun
Restaurant		M-F	Tu-Sa	Su
Burger King	7d	7d	7d	

Distances walkable, 1.2m BQ-main gate, 1 (2m main gate-RR.

Quarters:
BQ: Availability ★ M-F, Octoberfest, ★★★★ SS **1700** 24h. Rates: $43gl+$6add per communal facilities, Suite $55sgl, $70dbl.

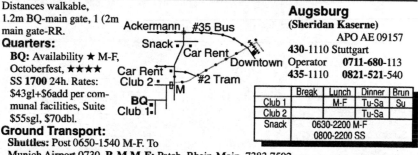

Augsburg
(Sheridan Kaserne)
APO AE 09157
430-1110 Stuttgart
Operator 0711-680-113
435-1110 0821-521-540

Ground Transport:
Shuttles: Post 0650-1540 M-F. To Munich Airport 0730. **R-M M-F:** Patch, Rhein-Main, 7383,7502.

	Break	Lunch	Dinner	Brun
Club 1		M-F	Tu-Sa	Su
Club 2			Tu-Sa	
Snack	0630-2200 M-F			
	0800-2200 SS			

DOD

Quarters:
BQ: Availability ★ D 3893, C 5778/9/3445 0700-2100 M-F, 0800-1600 SS. Rate $66sgl, DV $60sgl, both + $12add per. O6 up thru protocol D 3820, C 5745.

Bad Aibling
APO AE 09098
430-3893 (Stuttgart Operator) 08061.38.3000
441-xxxx 08061-38-xxxx

Ground Transport:
RR to Munich in Bad Aibling.

	Break	Lunch	Diner
Club	M-F	M-F	M-F
Snack		M-F	

Distances walkable, 0.7m BQ-main gate.

Quarters:
BQ: Availability ★ 1700 0730-2300 M-F, 0700-1500 SS. Rates: $33sgl, $43dbl, DV $55sgl, $70dbl. Protocol 6466.

RV: ★★★★ x ★★ summer **6498** 1000-1800 M-F, reserve, check in RV. Rates: RV EW $10, Tent $5.

Ground Transport:
Commercial: #1 Bus 0611-2007 xSu, 0837-2007 Su.

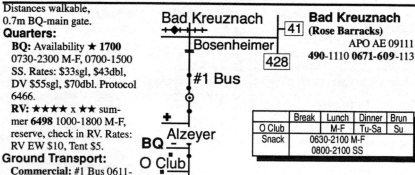

Bad Kreuznach
(Rose Barracks)
APO AE 09111
490-1110 0671-609-113

	Break	Lunch	Dinner	Brun
O Club		M-F	Tu-Sa	Su
Snack	0630-2100 M-F			
	0800-2100 SS			

Distances short,
0.6m Club-Snack1.

4, 22 | 26 | 505

Zollner Berliner Ring Club BQ

1m #1 Bus
Car Rent Bank
Quarters: Snack 1 Cafeteria

Bamberg
APO AE 09139
(Warner Barracks)
469-7777 0951-300-7777

BQ: Availability ★★★
1700 0800-1730 M-F,
1030-1430 SS, make arrangements for arrival other
hrs. Rate: $35sgl shared bath, $45sgl private bath,
both +$5add per. DV $55+$15add per.
RV: ★★★★ 1100-1800.
Golf: Holes: 9 Bamberg Golf Course
Ground Transport:
Erlangen, Nürnberg Airport 0610. **✈ Shuttle:** Würzburg 0645 M-F, returns 1800. Motor
pool 7427.
Commercial: #1 Bus to RR, frequent service. Taxis outside club gate.

	Break	Lunch	Dinner	Brun
Club		M-F	Th§	Su§
Snack1		Tu-Su	Tu-Su	
Snack2	7d	7d	7d	
Cafeteria		0800-1900 M-F		
		0900-1800 SS		

§ = twice monthly

Distances walkable,
0.6m BQ-Shuttle.
Quarters:

RV ✈ Baumholder
School

Baumholder
(Smith) APO AE 09034
485-1110 0678-36-113

BQ: Availability ★★★★
1700 0730-2000 M-F,
1000-1800 SS. Rate:
$30sgl+$17add per. DV
$30,32per.
RV: 7182 1100-1800 M-W,
1200-2000 ThF, also 0900-
1800 SS summer,
reservations, RV or tent $8, E $10. No water Nov-April. **Commercial:** In Baumholder.
Golf: DSN 485-7299 or C 06783-6-7299 **Holes:** 18 Rolling Hills Golf Course
Ground Transport:
Shuttles: Post 0700-1700 M-F; **R-M M-F:** Bad Kreuznach, Wiesbaden, Rhein-Main 0630 ,
6430,7217/98. **✈ Shuttle:** Landstuhl 0755,1035 M-F, 7273.
Commercial: Bus in Baumholder. Car rent C 3-5446 0900-1700 M-F.

	Break	Lunch	Dinner	Brun
O Club			Tu-F	Su
NCO Club		M-F	Tu-Sa	
Snack		0700-2000 xSu		
Bowl		1100-2300		

Distances short.
Quarters:

81 To Stuttgart
831
BQ ■
O Club
0.4m Taxi
Snack M
Bank ✚

Böblingen
(Panzer Kaserne)
APO AE 09046

430-1110 (Stuttgart
Operator) 0711-680-113
431-2xxx 07031-25-xxx

BQ: Availability ★ summer
D 401, C 432 0900-1700 M-F,
handled by Club for arrival other
hrs, call. Rates: $35sgl+$15add
per, $95suite.
Ground Transport:
Shuttles M-F: To Patch, Robinson Barracks 0555-2030.
Commercial: Bus outside gate.

	Break	Lunch	Dinner
O Club		M-F	
Snack			

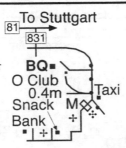

Europe

Distances short .

Quarters:

BQ: Availability ★★★ D 1700, C 06151.69-1700 or 06151-69-7520 Reservations: 06151-69-1700/7520. 0730-2100 M-F, 1300-2100 SS. Rates: $30, DV $40sgl, both +$15add per. Reserve 30d in advance for up to 5d.

Ground Transport:

Shuttles: Between kasernes, 0600-1840 M-F. **R-M:** Rhein-Main 0900; Mannheim, Heidelberg, 1350 M-F, 6428,7396. **Commercial:** Frequent tram service between kasernes, RR, downtown. #12 S-Bahn to Frankfurt. Air-Liner Bus to Frankfurt Airport starts 0415, 20min run, DM11. Car rent 1000-1800 M-F.

Darmstadt
(Cambrai-Fritsch)
APO AE 09175
370-1110   (Heidelberg
Operator) **06221-57**-113
348-xxxx **06151-69**-xxx

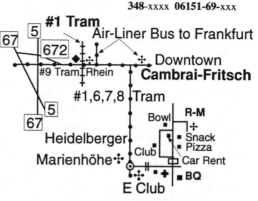

	Break	Lunch	Dinner	Brun
Club	7d	M-F	Th	Su
E Club		M-F	7d	
Cafeteria	0800-1500 M-F			

Frankfurt Area Quarters Summary

	Page	D	C	
Darmstadt	193	348	06151-69	D 1700, C 430 0730-2100 M-F, 1300 SS
Friedberg	194	324	06031-81	1700 0800-1630 M-F
Giessen	195	343	0641-402	1700 0800-2000 M-F
Hanau	195	322	06181-88	1700 0600-2200 M-F, 0730-1630 SS
Landstuhl	197	486	06371-86	8342 24h
Ramstein	198	480	06371-47	O 2228, E 5529, DV 7411, 24h
Sembach	198	496	0630-267	7588 24h
Vogelweh "K Town"	196	489	0631-536	7190 24h
Wiesbaden	200	338	06121-34	D 1700, C 38650 24h

Europe

German Golf Clubs

Edelweiss Resort Alpental Golf Course		C 08821-2473	9 hole
Eifel Mountain **Spangdahlem**	D 452-6821	C 06565-61-6821	9 hole
Grafenwöhr Golf Course	D 475-8535	C 09641-838535	9 hole
Heidelberg Golf Course	D 379-6139	C 06202-53767	18 hole
Kitzingen **Larson Barracks**	D 355-1550/8373	C 09321-4956	9>18 hole
Woodlawn GC **Ramstein**	D 480-6240	C 06371 47 6240	18 hole
Rheinblick, **Wiesbaden**	D 336-2816	C 0611-420675	18 hole
Rollings Hills, **Baumholder**	D 485-6172/7182	C 06783-66172	9 hole
Stuttgart Golf Club		C 07141-879151/150	18 hole
Whispering Pine, **Bamberg**	D 469-7583	C 0951-300758	9 hole

Frankfurt Area

Wiesbaden • **Frankfurt** — Friedberg — Hanau — Rhein-Main AB (255, 5, 3, 45, 66, 66, 8, 643, 3, 5, 3)

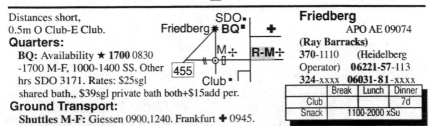

Distances short,
0.5m O Club-E Club.
Quarters:
BQ: Availability ★ **1700** 0830
-1700 M-F, 1000-1400 SS. Other
hrs SDO 3171. Rates: $25sgl
shared bath,, $39sgl private bath both+$15add per.
Ground Transport:
Shuttles M-F: Giessen 0900,1240. Frankfurt ✚ 0945.

Friedberg
APO AE 09074
(Ray Barracks)
370-1110   (Heidelberg
Operator)   **06221-57**-113
324-xxxx   **06031-81**-xxxx

	Break	Lunch	Dinner
Club			7d
Snack	1100-2000 xSu		

Rec A   Distances walkable.
Quarters:
BQ: ★★ **873** 0800-1700 M-F. Reserve 7d ahead, up to 3d,
sponsor required. Rate: $35sgl+$4add per.
Hotels: ★★★★ x ★ Patton C **0882l-79-08** summer, reserve
D 695 C 79091 0800-1700 M-F. **Reserve** 800-462-7691. C
08821-72981 (from CONUS 011-49-8821-72981), D 440-2575 Fax 3942. Without reservations contact hotels 24h. Sheridan Kaserne **Rates:** Patton Hotel $67 E1-6; $82 E6-O3; $92 O4-O6; $99 O7 & up; Patton Hotel Suite $123. Prices are single/double & children 17 and under are free in parents' room on available bed space.
Vacation Village: ★★★★ x ★ holiday D 848, C 535-54 0800-2100 summer, Rates: Delux Cabins $1001 per week; Rustic Cabins
$399 per week RV $17-27 Gravel Site
w/W (1-4 people), Tent $13-17(per tent).
Commercial: Many hotels, economical
pensions.
Ground Transport:
City buses connect all.

Garmisch-Partenkirchen
Unit 24501 APO AE 09053
430-1110   (Stuttgart
Operator) **0711-680**-113
440-2xxx   **08821**-xxx

NATO AB
Distances walkable, 1 (2m BQ-Bus.
Quarters:
BQ: Availability ★ **4962** 0800-
1700
M-F. Rates: **O, E** with dependents
DM40sgl
+DM10add per, DV
DM60sgl+DM10add per, NCO
(no dep) DM25per. Sponsor
required.
Ground Transport: #91 Bus to
RR 0631-1937 M-F, 0642-1437 Sa.

Geilenkirchen AB
APO AE 09104
606-7172, 02451-63-xxxx
tone, then 229-0111, request 4962

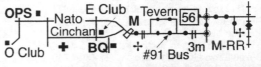

	Break	Lunch	Dinner	Brun
O Club		M-F	W-F	Su
E Club	0715-2100 M-F			
	0930-2100 SS			

Europe

Distances short, 0.6m BQ- snack bar.

Quarters:
BQ: Availability ★★★★ **1700** 0800-1930 M-F, 0900-1630 SS. Rates: $25sgl shared bath, $39sgl private bath. DV $45sgl, all +$15add per.
Commercial: In Giessen.

Ground Transport:
Shuttles Kirchgöns, Friedberg 0630 M-F. R-M 0820.
Commercial: #1,5100 Buses 0522-2235.

Giessen (Gießen)
(Rivers)
APO AE 09169
370-1110   (Heidelberg
Operator)   **06221-57**-113
343-xxxx   **0641-402**-xxxx

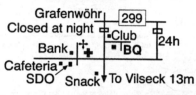

	Break	Lunch	Dinner
Restaurant	M-F	M-F	
Bowl		1100-2300	
Burger King		0730-2100	

Training Area. Distances short.

Quarters:
BQ: Availability ★ **1700,6182** 0600-2200 M-F, 0700-1700 SS. For arrival other hrs, call with credit card, keys left with SDO, 8302. Rates: $32,42sgl+$4,6add per. $49sgl+$6add per.
DV $42sgl+$6add per. Reservations 3d ahead. Protocol 6221,7145. TLF $52room, $30 onetime charge for pets.
Commercial: In Grafenwöhr.
Golf: 09641-838535 **Holes:** 9 Grafenwöhr

Ground Transport:
Shuttle to Vilseck from tower 0723.1327. Motor pool 8304. Check for ✚ shuttle.

Grafenwöhr
APO AE 09114
475-1110   **09641-83**-113

Grafenwöhr
Closed at night
Bank
Cafeteria
SDO   Snack ▼ To Vilseck 13m
299
•Club
■BQ 24h

	Break	Lunch	Dinner
Club	M-F	M-F	ThF
Snack	7d	7d	7d
Cafeteria	7d	7d	7d

Distances walkable, 0.8m O Club-E Club.

Quarters:
BQ: Availability ★ May-Sep & Holiday Weekends, ★★ other times. **D 1700/8357** 0600-2200. Reservations taken 5d in advance. Handles quarters at Argonner, Gelenhausen and Pioneer. Gelenhausen is 14m east of Hanau on Route 66, direct trains from Hanau. Rates: $50sgl+$5 add per, **DV** $60+5 per. .

Ground Transport:
Shuttles M-F: R-M: Rhein-Main 0900, 8042,8394,8952.
Commercial: #6,14 Buses.

Hanau
(Argonner, Pioneer)
APO AE 09165
370-1110   (Heidelberg
Operator)   **06221-57**-113
322-1110   **06181-88**-113

Commercial
Out of Country
Lodging PH: 011-49-6181-9550
Lodging Fax: 011-49-6181-955197
In Country
Lodging PH: 06181-9550
Lodging Fax: (+49)6181-955195/197

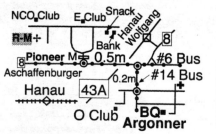

	Break	Lunch	Dinner	Brun
O Club		Tu-F	Tu-F	Su
NCO Club	M-F	M-F	M-F	
E Club		M-F		
Snack		1300-2200 M-F		
		1000-2000 SS		

Europe

Distances short on each.

Quarters:
BQ: Availability ★★★ x ★ summer
1700 24h. Reserve up to 2w ahead for
FSa with credit card 0730-1630 M-F.
Res.**C** 06221.338.9387 List starts
0730, call, assigned 1500. Rates:
$50sgl, $80dbl, weekends $14room.
DV $60sgl, $90dbl. O6 up thru protocol 8707.

Ground Transport:
Shuttles: PHV-✚-Patton-Shopping
0620-1650 M-F, 0820-2300 Sa, hrly.
R-M M-F: From PHV to Mannheim, Darmstadt, Rhein-Main 0735,
6711,7687.
Commercial: Trams and buses from
all x PHV to RR and downtown.
Shopping Center closest shuttle stop
to RR, Patton to tourist area. A Tram
to Mannheim.

Heidelberg
(Patrick Henry Village)
(Patton Barracks)
APO AE 09102
370-1110 **06221-57**-113

	Break	Lunch	Dinner	Brun
PHV O Club	Tu-Sa	Tu-F	Tu-Sa	Su
NCO Club			xWSu	Su
Snack	7d	7d	7d	
Patton Club	M-F	xSu	xSu	Su
Cafeteria	7d	7d	7d	

Distances walkable in each area. All Space-A facilities in
Vogelweh. Three kasernes on east side useful only as shuttle
stops.

Quarters:
Ramstein Inns (Vogelweh): Availability ★★★★
7190,7641 24h. USAFE Rates: $32-48.
Commercial: In Kaiserslautern.

Ground Transport:
Shuttles: Kasernes 0800-
1430 M-F. Ramstein 0612-
1949 M-F, 0749-1549 SS.
R-M M-F: From BQ: Rhein-Main 0600,1300,1825,
Ramstein 1305,1550,2155.
Commercial: City bus to kasernes, downtown, RR.
Einsedlerhof RR station. Car rent Bldg 3050, 59881,
1000-1800 M-F, 1000-1400 Sa.

Kaiserslautern
(Vogelweh)
APO AE 09094
483-1110 **0631-411**-113
489-xxxx **0631-536**-xxxx
Often called K-Town

	Break	Lunch	Dinner	Brun
Club 1			xTu	
Club 2			W-Sa	Su
Snack	0600-2400			

Distances walkable.

Quarters:
BQ: Availability
★ **600** 0900-1630
M-F. For arrival
other hrs, call, make
arrangements
for keys. Rates:
$25,40,45sgl+$10add per.
Golf: 09321-4956 **Holes:** 18 Golf Course Kitzingen

Ground Transport:
Shuttles: Harvy-Larson 7d; **R-M M-F:** Würzburg,
Rhein-Main 0800, 2677,2787.
Commercial: Bus to RR 0552-1847.

Kitzingen
(Harvy Barracks)
APO AE 09031
(Würzburg
350-1110 Operator) **0931-899**-113
355-8xxx **09321-305**-xxx

	Break	Lunch	Dinner
Woodland	7d	7d	7d
Cafeteria	7d	xSu	xSu
Bowl	1100-2300		

Europe

2d General Hospital
Distances short.

Quarters:
Ramstein Inns (Landstuhl):
Availability ★★★★ x ★★ summer **8342** 24h. USAFE Rates: $30-49
Commercial: Hotels in Landstuhl.

Ground Transport:
Shuttles: Ramstein 0630-1855 M-F, 0900-1500 Sa. **R-M**
M-F: K-Town, R-M 0800, Pirmasens 1600.
✚ **Shuttle:** Pirmasens 0700-1600 M-F x 1300,1600 Th.
Check motor pool at Pirmasens to assure a particular run is operating.
Commercial: Taxi 3851/2.

Landstuhl Med Cen
APO AE 09180
483-1110 (Kaiserslautern
Operator) **0631-411**-113
486-xxxx **06371-86**-xxxx

	Break	Lunch	Dinner
Club		Tu-Sa	Tu-Sa
Dining	7d	7d	7d
Snack	0630-1700 M-F		
	0930-1300 SS		

Distances short.

Quarters:
BQ: Availability ★★★★
1700,8118 0600-2400
M-F, 0800-2030 SS,
assigned 1800. Rates:
$40sgl, DV (O5 up)
$50sgl, both +$20add per.

Ground Transport:
Shuttles M-F: R-M : Darmstadt, Rhein-Main,
0640; Heidelberg, 6232,6802.
Commercial: A Tram: Heidelberg RR
0457-2301; Mannheim RR 0457-0116 xSu,
0616-0116 Su.

Mannheim
(Benjamin Franklin Village)
APO AE 09086
370-1110   (Heidelberg
Operator)   **6221-57**-113
380-xxxx   **0621-730**-xxxx

	Break	Lunch	Dinner	Brun
O Club		M-F	xSu	Su
NCO Club	SS	M-F	7d	
Snack	0600-2100 M-F			
	0800-2100 SS			

NATO School, Euro used.
Distances short, 1m BQ-RR.

Quarters:
BQ: Availability ★ x
★★★★ FSa, school
holidays (Xmas, Easter,
August) **08822-1830,4616**
0700-2200 M-F, 0700-1000
Sa, 0730-1000 Su.
Commercial: Many in
town.

Ground Transport:
Hrly RR. #1084,9606/21
Buses RR-BQ.

Oberammergau
APO AE 09172

0882-6751

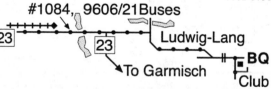

	Break	Lunch	Dinner
Club	7d	7d	7d

Ramstein Area

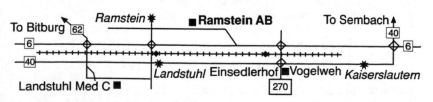

Shuttles connect Landstuhl, Ramstein, Sembach and Vogelweh

	Page D		C	Quarters Summary	
Landstuhl AMC	197	486	06371-86	8342 24h	■
Ramstein AB	198	480	06371-47	O 2228, O6 7411, E 5529, all 24h	■
Sembach AB	198	496	06302-67	7588 24h	■
Vogelweh "K-Town"	196	489	0631-536	7190 24h	■

RMS On base dial all seven digits.
USAFE - AMC Distances walkable, 0.9m
VQ-Terminal. AT&T Direct at O Club.

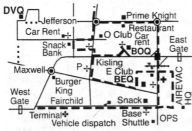

Quarters:
Ramstein Inns: Availability ★★★ (**E**
with dependents) **D 480.4960 Res: 4920**
24h. USAFE Rates: $32-48. Protocol
480.7558/6854 (if arriving before 1600).
Southside Billeting: 480.4940 24h.
Rates: $12per, suite $118per.
Prime Knight (Officers quarters): As-
signed 1800, check out 0700, **480.4950**
(no children).
Nearby BQs at Vogelweh, Landstuhl, Sembach.
Commercial: Hotels in Landstuhl, Ramstein.

Golf: 480.6240 **Holes: 18** Woodlawn Golf
Course
Ground Transport:
Shuttles: Base M-F at Terminal 0645-0745, 1045-
1245, 1615-1715, Sa 0545-1630. Landstuhl 0530-
1610 M-F, 0545-1630 Sa. Vogelweh 0530-1610
M-F, 0545-2230 Sa. Sembach 0620-2230 7d. Info
5961. Schedules reported a 'mess!'
R-M: From O BQ, Terminal to Vogelweh,Sembach,Rhein-Main 0535,1217,1800, 5373/4.
Check with Pax Terminal for Army's shuttle schedules.
Commercial: Bus to Landstuhl RR. Kaiserslautern. Taxi 12604,50510. **Retirees can no lon-
ger rent cars from AAFES due to change in Status of Forces Agreement, Hertz is ok.**

Ramstein AB   APO AE 09009
480-1110 Operator 0.69.371.47.1113
C from U.S. 011.49.6371.**DD**.xxxx
'**DD**' if DSN is 480 use 47, if 479 use 46
➤➤➤➤➤➤➤➤➤➤➤ **Flights** ➤➤➤➤➤➤➤➤➤➤➤➤

Andrews	Mildenhall √ 2-3d
Aviano	Naples MW √ 2-3d
Bahrain	Olbia √ 2-3d
Charleston 4/w	Rhein-Main 2-3/w
Dover SuTh √ 1/d	Rota 4/w
Izmir	Sigonella 4-5/w
Jackson 2/W	Souda Bay 1/2w
Kelly Annex 1/m	Travis 2/w
Lajes 1/m	Westover 2/w
McGuire 2/m	

To get to Rota, Sigonella, Naples and, Souda Bay use Norfolk.
Frequent flights to many destinations
All space-a entering GE thru Ramstein required to
clear GE customs.
Chance of seat ★★★★ x ★★ CONUS
Flight Information:
Terminal 479.4440/4299/2120 24h. [Fax 2364.
623AMSS/TROP] Recording **480.5364/2433**.
Schedules for next day **2100**. Airevac
479.2245,2345. **ATM in terminal.**

	Break	Lunch	Dinner	Brun
O Club		M-F	xSu	Su
E Club §	xSu	xSu	7d	Su
Dining	7d	7d	7d	
Terminal		24h		
Burger		0600-2200 M-F		
King		0700-2200 SS		

§ Does not serve **O**, nonclub members

Distances short on each.
Quarters:
BQ: Availability ★★★★ Conn Guest House **1700** 0800-
2300. For arrival other hrs, call, keys left with SDO, 6288.
Rates: $29,44,49+$10,15add per, DV
Ground Transport:
Shuttles: Conn-Ledward 0630-1800 M-F, 0900-1600 SS.
Conn-Ledward-Bad Kissingen 0530-1715 M-F, 0915-1500
SS. ✚ **Shuttle:** Würzburg 0745,1000,1300 M-F; **R-M**
M-F: From Conn: Bamberg 1500; Rhein-Main 0735.
Commercial: Bus on Route 303.

Schweinfurt
(Conn, Ledward Bks)
APO AE 09226
350-1110   (Würzburg
Operator) **0931-889**-113
354-xxxx **09721-96**-xxxx

	Break	Lunch	Dinner
Burger		0630-2100 M-F	
King		0800-2100 SS	

Continued on nest page.

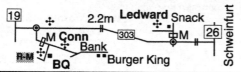

	Break	Lunch	Dinner
Burger King	0630-2100 M-F		
	0800-2100 SS		

SEX

Distances short 0.5m BQ-O Club.

Quarters:

Ramstein Inns (Sembach): Availability ★★★★ **7588** 24h. Assigned 1400. USAFE Rates: $32-48. Protocol 6102.

Commercial: In Sembach.

Ground Transport:

Shuttles: Base 0650-1700 M-F. To Ramstein 0740,1205,1635, info 5961 Ramstein. To Ramstein,Vogelweh if Pax for Sembach 1240,1530,2130, 480-5373/4.

Commercial: Bus at main gate

Bowl

Bank

Cafeteria R-M

Sembach BQ Club
M

4m 48
6
40
Kaiserslautern

to Sembach town, K-Town RR 0700-1906 M-F, 1310 Sa, 1217,1926 Su, some enter base, schedules at Rec C. 1000-1800 M-F, 1000-1400 Sa. Taxi 7658.

Sembach AB
APO AE 09099
496-1110   **06302-67**-113

	Break	Lunch	Dinner	Brun
Club	M-F	M-F	7d	Su
Bowl	SS	7d	7d	
Cafeteria	0600-1500 M-F			
	0800-1300 Sa			

SPA
USAFE

Distances walkable, 0.5m BQ-OPS.

Quarters:

Eifel Arms Inn: Availability ★★★ **5159** 24h. USAFE Rates: $30-48. Protocol 6434. TLF at Bitburg.

Golf: 06565-61-6821 **Holes:** 9 Eifel Mountain

Ground Transport:

Shuttles: Bitburg housing 0615-2030 M-F, returns 35min later. **R-M:** Bitburg housing, Rhein-Main 0600, info 6645.

Commercial: Bus from main gate to Trier 0627-1705 xSu, also to Bitburg. Car rent, Hertz 6629 0900-1700 M-F, Taxi C 951010.

Budget · Popeye's
Burger King
Spangdahlem
E Club
To Bitburg   M   Hertz
50   O Club
50   R-M   Terminal
BQ   OPS Snack

Spangdahlem AB
APO AE 09123
452-1110   **06565-61**-113
✈✈✈ **Flights** ✈✈✈
CONUS (ANG)
Dover√   McGuire
Chance of seat ★★★★

Flight Information:
OPS **6633** 0600-2200 M-F, 0800-2000 Sa, 1200-2000 Su. Terminal 8866/8867/7209, 0700-1600 M-F. Flight info from OPS, manifest at Terminal.

	Break	Lunch	Dinner	Brun
O Club		M-F	Tu-F	Su
Club		M-F	7d	
Burger King	0600-2100 M-F			
	0700-2200 Sa			
	0800-2100 Su			

STR

Distances short on each.

Quarters:

Kelley: ★★ D 4212-815/304, C 049-11-711-7292-815 0800-1600 M-F. Rate: $40-50+$4add per.

Patch: ★★ x ★★★ FSa C 0711.680.**7181**/ **7137** 24h, E7 up and O only. Rates: $35gl, DV $47sgl. both+$4add per. O6 up thru protocol 4186.

Robinson: ★★ (**D 420,** C 9814-100) **6209** 24h. Rate: $35sgl+$5add per. Club only other facility open.

Golf: 07141-879151 **Holes**: 18 Stuttgart Golf Course

Stuttgart
APO AE 09131
430-1110   **0711-680**-113
✈✈✈✈✈✈ **Flights** ✈✈✈✈✈
Chievres MT   Naples√
Heidelberg Th   Northolt Th
Mildenhall MTh   Ramstein Th
Chance of seat ★★

Continued on facing page

Europe

Ground Transport:
3 daily local shuttles connect all installations and Böblingen.
Commercial: City buses serve all x AAF.

Flight Information:
OPS **D 421-4218, C 0711-729-4218/78** 0730-1630 M-F
Call duty day before.

AAF	Break	Lunch	Dinner	Brun
Snack		Machines		
K O Club		M-F	F	Su
Snack	0700-1900 M-F			
	1000-1900 SS			
P O Club		Tu-F	Tu-F	Su
NCO Club		xSu	xSu	
Snack	0700-1700 M-F			
	0900-1400 SS			
Robinson		Tu-Sa	Tu-Sa	

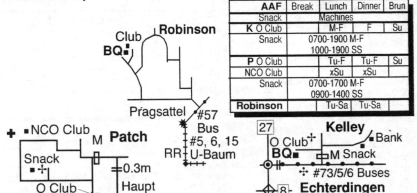

Distances short, 0.5m BQ-Club.

Quarters:
BQ: Availability ★★★★
x ★ when classes are large **1700,2555**
0700-2300. Rates:
$59db shared bath, DV
$42sgl+$6add per. Protocol 1500/10.

Ground Transport:
Shuttles: Grafenwöhr from PX 0946,1550. 2831.
M-F: R-M: Hoenfels,Rhein-Main 0450, 3100,3199. ✚
Shuttle: Würzburg 0630.

Vilseck APO AE 09112
475-1110 (Grafenwöhr
Operator) 09641-**83**-113
476-xxxx 09662-83-xxxx

	Break	Lunch	Dinner
Club		M-F	xSa
NCO Club			Sa
Cafeteria	0700-2030 M-F		
	0830--1600 SS		

On Æ196, in Kaiserslautern   **Vogelweh**

Quarters:
Hotel: Availability ★★ x
★★★ FSS American Arms **D**
1700, C 38650 24h, assigned
1800 Rates: $50sgl+$20add per.
DV $60sgl +$25add per. Reserve
14d ahead.
Golf: D 336-2791 011-49-0611-
420675 **Holes**: 18 Rheinblick Golf
Course
Ground Transport:
Shuttle: R-M M-F: Rhein-Main 0840; Bad Kreuznach,
Baumholder 1445 if Pax for Wiesbaden, 7212.

Wiesbaden
APO AE 09096
370-1110 (Heidelberg
Operator) 06221-**57**-113
338-7493 0611-**343**-664

	Break	Lunch	Dinner
Arms	7d	7d	7d

EUROPE and WESTERN ASIA
GERMANY (Concluded)

GE

Distances walkable.

Quarters:
BQ: Availability ★ **1700** 0700-2300 M-F, for arrival other hrs, call, keys left with SDO. Rates: $40sgl+$10add per, DV $60sgl+$15 add per. O6 up thru protocol 7241/5.
List of hotels available.

Ground Transport:
Shuttles: R-M M-F: Rhein-Main 0905, Kitzingen, Ansbach 1445.
✚ Shuttle: Bamberg, Kitzingen 0850-1750; Schweinfurt 0900,1110, 1520, Vilseck.
Commercial: City buses nearby.

Würzburg (Leighton)
APO AE 09244
350-1110 **0931-889**-113

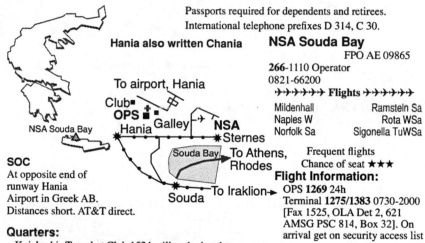

	Break	Lunch	Dinner
Club		M-F	W-F
Cafeteria		1000-2200	
Snack		0630-2100 M-F 0730-2100 SS	

Zulu+2

GREECE

1 USD = 0.637125 EUR   1 EUR = 1.56955 USD

Passports required for dependents and retirees.
International telephone prefixes D 314, C 30.

Hania also written Chania

To airport, Hania
Club■
OPS ■
Hania Galley ↦ NSA
NSA Souda Bay
✱Sternes
Souda Bay To Athens, Rhodes
✱ To Iraklion→
Souda

SOC
At opposite end of runway Hania Airport in Greek AB. Distances short. AT&T direct.

NSA Souda Bay
FPO AE 09865
266-1110 Operator
0821-66200
↣↣↣↣↣ Flights ↣↣↣↣↣

Mildenhall	Ramstein Sa
Naples W	Rota WSa
Norfolk Sa	Sigonella TuWSa

Frequent flights
Chance of seat ★★★
Flight Information:
OPS **1269** 24h
Terminal **1275/1383** 0730-2000 [Fax 1525, OLA Det 2, 621 AMSG PSC 814, Box 32]. On arrival get on security access list

Quarters:
Kyiakaskis Travel at Club 1524 will make hotel or car rent reservations. Royal Sun Hotel, Lena Beach (w/balconies overlooking Med, big pool $68. Money exchange at finance or club. Aircrew stay at Kydon Hotel.

	Break	Lunch	Dinner
Club	xSu	7d	7d
Galley	7d	7d	7d

Ground Transport:
To return to base assure name is added to Access List at main gate before leaving NSA. If arriving by ground, contact Security, preferably before arrival, to get name on Access List. This probably cannot be done Su.
Shuttle: Hania Express morning, afternoon M-F. Morning pick up 0635 at Sameria Hotel (bus station) 0635 M-F. Check by phone first. Local area shuttle including Sternes 0530, 0815, 2000. Shuttles from Quarterdeck, schedules there and at terminal. Ride to Hania usually available at gate.
Commercial: Bus Hania-Sternes M-F. Bus Hania to Iraklion. Ferry to Athens port 2030 from Souda. Car rent 40810,45161,50510, 54454,57444, 93776 gas coupons at NX, about 25% of outside price. Taxi 98700/1, $15 to Hania.

Europe

201

TLV   Zulu+2
International C prefix
972. Passport required.
**On arrival request
immediately passport
not be stamped.** AT&T
direct.

▲ Tel Aviv

1 USD = 3.44202 ILS   1 ILS = 0.290527 USD
Israil New Shekels ILS

Tel Aviv Airport (Ben Gurion)
OL-A, 621 AMSG (AMC), Unit 7228, Box 7
APO AE 09830-7228
Comm. 972 3 977-4333 Fax: 972-3 972-1989
➤➤➤➤➤➤ **Flights** ➤➤➤➤➤➤
Ramstein (approx 2/m)
Sigonella (when ships in port)
Chance of seat ★★★

Quarters:
Commercial only, expensive, particularly in Jerusalem,
YMCA $70sgl. See Government information or Chris-
tian guest house office inside Jaffa Gate for lower-cost
quarters. Palace Hotel 74-2798 (and others) in Bethlehem
good, $30 or less. Maxim, Tel Aviv near Opera Tower
good, $40sgl. All listed hotels have private facilities.

Flight Information:
Nos. above, Lefur, 0800-1700
Su-F. Call to determine flight.
Report to Lefur.
[Fax 1989, OL-A, 621 AMSG
Unit 7228, Box 7]. Departure fee
$34, not charged on AMC.

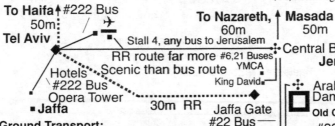

Ground Transport:
Inexpensive. Buses go to every point of interest. Essentially
do not operate F afternoon-Sa afternoon. Frequent trains
Tel Aviv-Haifa, recommended over buses. 0835 train from
Jerusalem makes connection for Haifa. Tour buses operate
primarily from Jerusalem and Tel Aviv. In areas of frequent
bus service the relatively high cost of tours can be saved by
using buses with the advantage of being able to advance as
desired rather than by tour schedule.

ITALY

AVB Distances short x 3m   Zulu+1
BQ-Terminal. AT&T direct
in Rec C.

1 USD = 1.56955EUR   1 EUR = 1.20855 USD
International phone prefixes D 314, C 39.
All facilities usable by retirees and leave.

Quarters:
Mountain View Lodge: Availability ★★ x
★ April, Oct **5041, 5722** 24h. USAFE Rates:
$32-48 O6 up thru protocol 001-39-0434-30-
4704/4705/4706.
Commercial: BQ has list of hotels. Domino
lowest 65-1256. Currency exchange at BX.
Golf: C 011-39-0434-667386 **Holes:** 9
Alpine Golf Course
Ground Transport:
Shuttles: Base from dining 0622-1727, from
terminal 0645-1746, 2667.
From Vehicle Ops to Marco Polo Airport 2

Aviano AB   APO AE 09601
632-1110 Operator   **011.39.434.66.711**
➤➤➤➤➤➤ **Flights** ➤➤➤➤➤➤

Adana WSa A	Naples Su
BWI 4F, 1,3,5Sa 2Su	Olbia M A
Dover MWF	Ramstein TuF√
Incirlik W	Rota M A
Ismir	Sigonella 2&4Th
Lajes 4F, 1,3,5Sa 2Su	Souda Bay Tu
Mildenhall F√	

Frequent flights to many dest.
Chance of seat
★★★ x ★★ CONUS

Flight Information:
Terminal **0434.667.520,7680,7782**
0600-2100 xSu, 0800-1700 Su. [Fax
7782, Det 3, 721 AMOG, Unit 6165
Box 215, APO AE 09601-5000]]
Recording **7520**. OPS **7222** 24h
For Parking contact Security 7200.

shuttles per day. Aviano USA Base - M.Polo Airport:
single ticket € 16,20, Aviano USA Base - M.Polo
Airport: return ticket (valid 7 days) € 24,40
Shuttle: Vicenza 0745 TWF, returns 1500, sign up day
before 7695 0730-1630 M-F. Base taxi may be utilized
after normal duty hrs, 7666/8.
Commercial: AAFES TAXI 0434.652922. Bus from
town square (tower) to flight line gate and Pordenone
0605-1930 xSu, 0900-1830 Su. Purchase ticket at
Centrale before boarding. Not open for early bus. Six
daily trains to Sacilie for connection to trains on Udine-
Pordenone-Sacile-Venice line 0637-2937 x Su, 0856-
1930 Su. BX car rent 99-660287, D 8719 1000-1630
M-F, 1000-1530 Sa. Commercial taxis not permitted
on base. Taxi 99-65109,651268. Three airports in the
area: Venice (Marco Polo) 1.5 hour by car; Treviso
1.5 hour by car; & Trieste (Ronchi dei Legionari) 1.5
hour by car. Train, taxi, or bus will take you to any of
these three airports.

	Break	Lunch	Dinner
Club		M-F	
Dining	7d	7d	7d
Burger King	0700-2100 M-F		
	0800-2100 SS		
FL Snack	0600-1700 M-F		
	0800-1300 Sa		

Europe

Distances short, 0.5m BQ-main gate. AT&T direct.
Quarters:
BQ: Availability ★★★ x ★ summer **C**
39.05.054.7225/7221/7448 0700-2100 (24h summer), reservations. Rates: (+$5 summer) Lodge
$36sgl, $46dbl, $51three. Cabin $45unit, no linens. RV W $10-12, EW $12-16.
Ground Transport:
Shuttle 7d. Frequent trains summer to Tombolo
from Pisa, Livorno. Buses at RR. Infrequent buses
to Darby. PX Car Rent.

Camp Darby
APO AE 09613
633-1110   **050-54**-7111

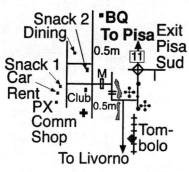

	Break	Lunch	Dinner	Brun
Club		M-F	W-F	Su
Dining	7d	7d	7d	
Snack1	0700-1900 xSu			
	0900-1700 Su			
Snack2	1000-2300 xSu			
	1600-2300 Su			

Distances short, 0.5m BQ-main gate. AT&T direct.

Quarters:

BQ: Availability ★★★ x ★ summer C
39.05.054.7225/7221/7448 0700-2100 (24h summer),
reservations. Rates: (+$5 summer) **Lodge** $36sgl, $46dbl,
$51three. Cabin $45unit,
no linens. RV W $10-12,
EW $12-16.

Ground Transport:
Shuttle 7d. Frequent
trains summer to Tom-
bolo from Pisa, Livorno.
Buses at RR. Infrequent
buses to Darby.
PX Car Rent.

Camp Darby
APO AE 09613
633-1110   **050-54**-7111

Snack 2 | •BQ
Dining | To Pisa Exit
| 0.5m | Pisa
Snack 1 | | Sud
Car
Rent | Club
PX | 0.5m
Comm
Shop | Tombolo
To Livorno

	Break	Lunch	Dinner	Brun
Club		M-F	W-F	Su
Dining	7d	7d	7d	
Snack1	0700-1900 xSu			
	0900-1700 Su			
Snack2	1000-2300 xSu			
	1600-2300 Su			

NAP   Naval support AT&T direct at USO.
Divided into 6 separated areas.

Quarters:

BQ: CAPO Inn Availability ★★★★ 5250, 4336
24h, assigned 1830. Rate: $30per night, confirma-
tion one day at a time. **Carney Park**, 5m from
NSA, C 0867-1579, cabins, trailers, **no** bedding.
RV ESW $15, Tent $10. No dump, **pets. E** only.
Navy Lodge: C **081-509-71201/2/3**, NW of
Naples, Hotel Costa Bleu, Pinetamare. Cannot be
reserved via 800-Navy Inn. Rate: $105, going up.
Commercial: For inexpensive hotels **contact** Infor-
mation in Central Station.

Golf: 081-526-4296 **Holes:** 9 Carney Park

Ground Transport:

Shuttles: NAF-NSA-✚-AF South 0600-0105.
NSA-Fleet Landing 0700-2400 when fleet is in.
[NSA-Carney Park 1000-2035
1 June-15 Sept.] Pinetamare-NAF, **Pintemare**-NSA.
NSA-AF South.

Commercial: #3S Bus from Central Station to
NAF. **Buy bus ticket before boarding**, available at

Naples   FPO AE 09622
(Capodichino Airport)
626-1110 Operator   **081-568**-0021
✈✈✈✈✈✈✈✈ **Flights** ✈✈✈✈✈✈✈✈
Adana   Olbia MTh
Aviano Tu   Ramstein√ ThSa
Bahrain W   Rota√
Charleston   Sigonella√
Dover   Souda Bay Sa
Mildenhall Su
Norfolk Sa
Frequent flights to many dest.
                Chance of seat ★★★★

Flight Information:
Terminal **5283** 0600-2200 xSu
0830-1430 Su.
[Fax 5259, Passenger Terminal]

NAF	Break	Lunch	Dinner
Galley	7d	7d	7d
Cafeteria	0630-1800 M-F		
	0600-1300 Sa		

booths in front of Central Station, at newsstand at Airport, bars, and tobacco stores. Subway
Central Station-AF South. Car rent **at** Airport.

12m NAS to NAF
E Club• NX Comm   Airport Terminal BEQ
Scarfiglio   NX Galley
NSA   E Club BX Q Club   M
AF South (NATO)   ←12m→   0.3m 0.4m
                            Cafeteria
Domizina   3m #14 Bus   NAF
Delle Acacie   Mergellina
Pinetamare   Central   5m
NSA Agnano S. Marco   Station
Navy Lodge   10 Calata   2m
AF South   USO, E Club   Fleet Landing

SIZ

Distances short NAS1, walkable NAS2, 0.5m O BQ-Terminal. AT&T direct.

Quarters:

BQ: O ★★ 2300, 5585, 5853 24h. Rates: $10per, DV $25per. Protocol 5313. **E ★★★ 5467** 24h, office in Terminal. Rates: $5per, E9 suite $15per.
Navy Lodge: D 4082, C 011-3995-713-0190.24h Not reservable by 800-Navy Inn. Rate: $63room,
Commercial: Sigonella Inn, a modern hotel 0.5m from main gate NAS1, expensive 713-0002. Inexpensive hotels in Catania. TLA Stars & Stripes 308-565.

Ground Transport:

Shuttles: NAS1-NAS2 0600-0100, at NAS2 16min later outside main gate than at Terminal. Shuttle from E Club NAS1 to Fleet Landing, Catania when ships are in port, scheduled by ships. Shuttles to housing area Motta and TLA.
Commercial: Bus outside main gate NAS1 to Catania RR xSu 0650,0710,0745,0855,0900,12 50,1400,1515,1715, From Catania RR xSu, Etna (Red) 0600-1800; AST (Blue) 0620-1900. Car rent in Terminal 5468 0830-1700 xSu. Taxis outside main gate NAS1.

NAS Sigonella FPO AE 09627
624-1110 Operator **095-86**-1110
NAS1 **56**-xxxx

✈✈✈✈✈✈ **Flights** ✈✈✈✈✈✈

Adana MW	Olbia M
Aviano Th	Ramstein MThSa
Bahrain WSu	Rota√
Lajes Tu	Souda Bay TuSa
Naples√	Tel Aviv §
NorfolkTu	

§ When fleet in port
Frequent flights to many destinations
Chance of seat ★★★

Flight Information:
Terminal **5575/6** 24h. [Fax 5211. Det 2 608 APS/TRO, PSC 812 Box 3030]. P3 5338. Terminal open 24h, snack bar, car rent.

	Break	Lunch	Dinner
NAS1 Galley	7d	7d	7d
NAS2 Galley	7d	7d	7d
BOQ		7d	7d
Terminal		24h	

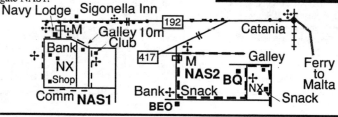

Distances short, 0.6m BQ-main gate.

Quarters:

BQ: Availability ★ x ★★ Nov, Dec. **8034** 24h, list starts 0600, assigned 1800. Rates: $42sgl+$10add per, DV $52sgl+$10add per. O6 up thru protocol 7712 0800-1700 M-F.
Travel Camp 7094, check in Outdoor Rec, RV EW $13. Tent $7. No dump.
Commercial: Nearby economical hotels, BQ has list.

Ground Transport:

Shuttle: Post 0830-2300 xSu, 4 runs to RR.
✚ **Shuttle:** Aviano approx 1500 TuWF.
Commercial: #1 Bus main gate to RR. **Purchase ticket before boarding.** Ticket booth opposite RR station, also at bars and tobacco shops. ITT has books of 10 tickets. PX car rent C 505916.

Vicenza APO AE 09630
(Caserma Ederle)
634-1110   **0444-517**-111
Check ✚ for A flights W to Adana, and Aviano.
Helicopter to Aviano

	Break	Lunch	Dinner	Brun
Club	M-F	M-F	7d	Su
Dining	7d	7d	7d	
Burger		0700-2100 M-F		
King		0800-2000 SS		

EUROPE and WESTERN ASIA

JORDAN

Zulu+3

1 USD = 0.707300 Dinar   1 Dinar = 1.41383 USD

Amman Airport

▲ Amman Airport

AMM

International phone prefix: C 962.

Passport, visa, and diplomatic permission required.

Amman Airport
(King Abdullah)
APO AE 09892
64-4371
↷↷↷↷ **Flights** ↷↷↷↷
Ramstein
Chance of seat ★★★★
Flight Information:
x263

Zulu+1

1 USD = 0.637125 EUR   1 EUR = 1.56955 USD

NETHERLANDS

Passports required for dependents and retirees.

Commissary, exchange, shoppette not usable by leave or retirees.

International phone prefix D 314, C 31.

	Break	Lunch	Dinner
O Club	7d	xSa	M-F§
Dining	M-F	M-F	M-F
Cafeteria	0800-1500 M-F		
§ Jacket, tie req.			

AFCENT

Quarters:

BQ: Availability

★★ **3188** 0730-2200 M-F. Reserve 2022 0800-1700 M-F. For arrival other hrs, call, make arrangements. Protocol handles all billets. Rates: $42sgl w/shared bath, $50dbl. No pets. **No U.S. money, Credit Cards are accepted.**

Ground Transport:

#35/6/7 Buses to RR 0604-2343 M-F, 0747-0043 Sa, 1004-2343 Su. #69 Bus in front of O Club, infrequent. Frequent trains to Maastrict, Amsterdam.

AFNORTH
360-1110   045.526.2222

M⌂ Dining
Cafeteria
Bank ▪ 0.1m
0.4m
BQ⌂
O Club

#35/6/7
Buses

Heerlen
In de Cramer Exit

76 28 **Located in town**
76   **of Brunssum**

SAUDI ARABIA

Sun time, approx Zulu+3

1 USD = 3.75000 Riyals   1 Riyals = 0.266667 USD
Saudi Arabia Riyals

Although there may still be flights to Dhahran Airport (DHA) and Jedda Airport (King Abdul Aziz JDW), the required visas are so difficult to obtain detailed information is not included.

SPAIN

Zulu+1

1 USD = 0.637125 EUR   1 EUR = 1.56955 USD

Moron AB
NS Rota

Passports required for dependents and retirees.

Shoppette can be used by retirees and leave but not exchange or commissary.

International phone prefixes D 314, C 34.

When arriving by air at Rota get papers required at that base before leaving by land. Check procedures upon arrival.

Recommended that travelers do not drive into Gibralter, park and walk. Spanish Customs are known to delay drivers up to an hour.

EMO

Distances walkable.
AT&T direct.

Quarters:

BQ: Hotel
Frontera
Availability
★★★★ x ★ during exercises
8098 24h. Rates: $10per, DV $12per.

Meals: Available at Dining Hall

Ground Transport:

Shuttles: Car rental at Gas Station 955.822.022 is the same company as Rota. If you want to drop car at Rota ask when renting. To Sevilla (Cruzcampo, in front of brewery) 0800,1500,2400, from Sevilla 0700,1000,1500,2300 7d. Check for medical transport to Rota.

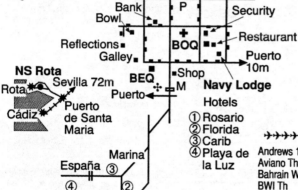

Moron AB

APO AE 09643
722-1110   **95-584-8111**
↣↣↣↣ **Flights** ↣↣↣↣
Rota

Germany
CONUS

Many flights between CONUS & Iraq, uncertain as to space-a availability.

Normally few flights, no aircraft stationed
Chance of seat ★★★★

Flight Information:
OPS **8382/8100/1**
0800-1700 M-F

RTA   AT&T direct.

Naval Station and NAS
Distances walkable, 0.6m
BEQ-Terminal.

NS Rota   D-94

FPO AE 09645
727-1110 Operator **956-82**-3000

Quarters:

Availability ★★★★ x ★ summer.
Billeting Office is at Pax Terminal. BOQ desk, subject to availability, will extend stay without checking out. **BOQ: 1750/1** 24h List starts at 0800, assigned 1800, rooms vacated daily. Rates: $15sgl DV $18,25sgl both +$4add per. Protocol 2795.
BEQ: 2460 24h. Rate: $4-8per.
Navy Lodge: ★★ x ★ summer **2643** 24h. Cannot reserve via 800-Navy Inn. Rate: $57unit.
Commercial: Low-cost hotels, Playa de la Luz 99-81-0500 best, recommended for those with dependents. Carib 956.81.0700, Rosario 956.81.0600 $34. All ★ summer, particularly August.
Golf: C (34) 956 82 2260, **D** 727 2260 **Holes**: 18
Ground Transport:

↣↣↣↣↣↣ **Flights** ↣↣↣↣↣↣↣↣

Andrews 1/w
Aviano Th A
Bahrain WSa
BWI Th
Charleston
Cheery Pt
Dover 2-3/w
Lajes 1/w
McGuire W
Mildenhall Tu A

Naples√
Norfolk Su
Olbia Th A
Quantico
Ramstein 3/w
Sigonella 3/w
Souda Bay
Westover

Frequent flights to many dest.
Chance of seat ★★★

Flight Information:
Terminal **2834,2411** 24h. [Fax 2968, Air Terminal SP819 Box 7] Terminal open 24h, cafeteria, lockers, car rent.
24h pass on arrival issued by Navy, must be renewed each 24h at main gate. Leave-enter 0800-2400. Arriving by ground without pass one will be issued at gate on showing ID.

Europe

Shuttles: Restaurant2- main gate-Puerto Gate 1630-2030 xSu. Shuttle from commissary to Moron 1430 M-F, call Vehicle Ops, Moron by 1600 day before. Check for possible medical transport to Moron.

	Break	Lunch	Dinner	Brun
Restaurant1		M-F	W-Sa	Su
Restaurant2		M-F	M-F	
Galley	7d	7d	7d	
Cafeteria		24h		

Commercial: Bus station in old RR station outside main gate 81-0499, to Cádiz, Puerto de Santa Maria, Sevilla. All trains Cádiz-Sevilla-Madrid stop at Puerto, 7m from Rota. RR & bus schedules at Terminal. Car rent at Terminal 2675 0900-2000 M-F, 0900-1700 Sa. Taxis inexpensive, 2929. Crown car rental in terminal reported also being open Su 0830-2200.

TURKEY

1 USD = 1.24950 TRY   1 TRY = 0.800320 USD

Zulu+2   Turkey New Lira

Passports, visa (obtained on arrival $45 & good for 3 months) required for dependents and retirees, also some active duty. International drivers license required. Exchange, commissary not usable. Taxis inexpensive. International prefixes D 314, C 90. No off-base passes or gas to retirees.

Istanbul
Izmir
Adana
Diyarbakir

ADA   Prefix 6 on base.
AMC Distances walkable, 0.5m BQ-Terminal.

Terminal Snack
Security
Cafeteria

Gate passes required for entering, exiting base, **24h at Turkish Duty Office, longer at Pass & ID, Bldg 833.**

BQ

Club
M Adana 8m

AT&T direct.

Adana (Incirlik AB)

APO AE 09824
676-1110   90-322-316-1110
C extensions thru operator.
✈✈✈✈✈✈ **Flights** ✈✈✈✈✈✈
Aviano FSa   Istanbul Tu/W
Diyarbakir W   Ramstein MTh A
Dover Th

Frequent flights to many dest.
Chance of seat ★★★
Flight Information:
Terminal **6424/5** 0600-2000
[Fax 3420, 628 AMSS/TRO, Bldg 518].

Quarters:
Hodja Inn: Availability ★★★ x ★ summer **6113,9357/8** 24h, reservation 9353, assistance for commercial if no quarters. USAFE Rate: $30-49. O6 up thru protocol 8352.

	Break	Lunch	Dinner	Brun
O Club	xSu	M-F	xSu	Su
NCO Club		xSu	xSu	Su
Cafeteria		0630-2130		
Snack		0600-1800		

Commercial: Inexpensive hotels in Adana, BQ has list.

Ground Transport:
Base Shuttle 0715-1730 M-F.
Commercial: Bus to Adana 0730,0900,1100,1300,1500,1700,1900,2100,2300 M-F, 1300,1500, 1600 SS, from Adana RR & bus station 0630,0815,1015,1215,1410,1810,2010. 2215 M-F, 1000,1400,1700 SS. Car rent in Adana. Taxis marked "Gate" permitted on base, 333-01-469-26.

Europe

IGL

No AMC counter at Airport. Passenger Service meets all flights, has transport to Izmir. AT&T direct.

Quarters:
Grand Mercure Hotel, free if available. Other quarters through Military Lodging at Mercurie.

Ground Transport:
Shuttle 7d.

Izmir Airport (Cigli)

APO AE 09821

675-1110 Operator   4844-5360

➔➔➔➔➔➔➔➔ **Flights** ➔➔➔➔➔➔➔➔

Adana ThSu A	Istanbul Tu
Aviano MTh A	Ramstein ThSu A

Chance of seat ★★★

Flight Information:
Terminal **3248,3442** 0730-1630
M-F, 0930-1130 SS
[Fax C only 90-233-2441-7044,
425 Airborne Sq LGTA Unit 6870
Box 105].

UNITED KINGDOM

Zulu

1 USD = 0.504285 £ (pound)	1 £ (pound) = 1.98301 USD
1 USD = 0.637125 EUR	1 EUR = 1.56955 USD

International telephone prefixes: D 314, C 44

Dependents, retirees require passports. Use of exchange, commissary, and shoppette without ration card requires purchase of $36) book of tax coupons (not available to retires not living in the UK. All installations are served by public transport. Intercity, local buses are called coaches, buses respectively. B&B (Bed and Breakfast, room in home or inn) is economical when quarters not available. In details London terminals of rail lines are given.

UNITED KINGDOM

Alconbury
Lakenheath
Mildenhall
Scheduled
Transport
Heathrow
Gatwick
Menwith Hill Station
RAF Croughton
RAF Alconbury
RAF Fairford
RAF Lakenheath
RAF Mildenhall
London Airports

DSN access to CONUS is obtained from Lakenheath and Mildenhall, possibly other installations by prefixing 88-312.

RAF Alconbury

APO AE 09470

268-1110   **01480-84**-3000

Distances short.

	Break	Lunch	Dinner	Brun
Club		M-F	xSu	Su
Burger King	0700-1900 M-F			
	0800-1900 Sa			
Bowl	0600-2300 M-F			
	0900-2300 SS			
Pizza	1030-2000			

Quarters:
Britannia Inn: Availability ★★★★ **6000** 24h.
USAFE Rates: $30-49
Commercial: Country Hotel 0.5m from main gate, 56927.

Ground Transport:
Shuttles: Molesworth 0645-2300. Upwood (✚) 0630-1615 M-F. 2214 24h. ✚ **Shuttle:** Lakenheath, call 4506 for seat. Occasional transport to Mildenhall, 2877.
Commercial: #350/1 Buses xSu, to Peterboro 0654-2139, to Huntington 0722-2054. Car rent 59191 0830-1739 M-F, 0839-1200 Sa. Taxi 2556.

Peterborough

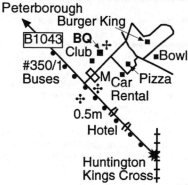

Burger King
B1043 **BQ**
Club
#350/1
Buses
Bowl
Car
M   Pizza
Rental
0.5m
Hotel
Huntington
Kings Cross

Europe

Quarters:

Shepherd's Rest Inn: Availability ★★★★ **8394** 0700-1700 M-F. 0800-1800 SS. USAFE Rates: $32-48. After hour keys @ 'LE' Desk. See security at village gate for directions to 'LE' desk.

Ground Transport:

✚ **Shuttle:** Lakenheath, call day ahead 8227. Bus on route 4031.

	Break	Lunch	Dinner
Club		Tu-F	FSa
Bowl		7d	7d

FFD Prefix 72 on base. Distances walkable, 1.1m BQ-OPS.

Quarters:

The Stirling House: ★★★★ **4272,4784** 0700-2300 M-F, 0800-1500 SS. For arrival other hrs, call, make arrangement for key. USAFE Rates: $30-48. O6 up thru protocol 4200.

Commercial: Hotels and B&B in Fairford, BQ has list. Bull expensive.

Ground Transport:

Check Vehicle OPS 4210,4614, 4898 0700-1630 M-F.

Commercial: #75 Bus to Swindon from main gate 0930, to Fairford 1422. #77 bus Fairford square to Cirencester 0745-1826 M-F, 0815-1826 Sa, to Swindon 0708-1818 M-F, 0750-1801 Sa, others from town. Car rent in Swindon. Taxi 810085.

Ground Transport:

Shuttles depart both airports 7d to Lakenheath,Mildenhall.
From Gatwick: 0930,1200 (D, near Stall 8, Coach Station, South Terminal, RR from Victoria Station, London).
From Heathrow: 1000,1230 (Terminal 3 arrival level. Picadilly subway from London).

Shuttles depart Lakenheath 0500,0730, Mildenhall 0530,0800 to both airports.

RAF Croughton
APO AE 09494
236-1110 **01280-70**-8055
Retired Activities 8182

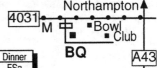

	Break	Lunch	Dinner
Club			
Bowl			

RAF Fairford
APO AE 09456
247-1110 **01285-71**-4000
Limited Base

	Break	Lunch	Dinner
Rec C		M-F	
Bowl		1600-2200 M-F	
		1000-2200 SS	

London Airports
(**LGW** Gatwick,
LRH Heathrow)
238-2281 **01638-54**-2281
No Space-A flights
Nos. above 3d AF Transport
at Mildenhall

Getting Around the UK

Mildendhall is the only point of entry for those requiring passports. Lodging there is on-off. If arrival is before noon, get on DSN and check other installations. Alconbury has good quarters availability and convenient bus connections to mainline trains. Once a billet is found check ground transport availability, in particular for transport meeting arriving Pax. **Do not overlook the chance that Navy might have a useful flight.** Keep a RR system map on hand (available at stations). Trains are virtually everywhere, routes are known with frequent service, comfortable, and fast. Buses, however, are cheaper.

Europe

London Military Clubs

British military clubs in London can be used by Space-A travelers. Union Jack Club is across Waterloo Rd. from Waterloo Station. Victory Services is just north of Marble Arch, very close to an underground station. Both welcome US active and retired. Not low cost but considering their convenient locations are reasonable by London standards. Victory requires membership, £1 per night Active, £12+£8add add per per year. Both have single and double rooms with and without bath. Double with bath is £59 (Victory) and £63 (Union Jack).

Union Jack Club:
Sandell St., London
SE1 8UJ, 0171-928-4814.
OH:+44(0) 207 928 6401
(Mon - Fri 8.30am - 5.00pm,
Sat 9.00 - 2.00pm

Victory Services Club:
63-79 Seymour St.,
London W2 2HF,
+44 (0)20 7723 4474,
Fax: +44 (0)20 7402 9496

Menwith Hill Station

Communications. Distances short, 0.1m
main gate-BQ.

Quarters:

BQ: Availability ★ **C 7711,7895** 0800-
0100, if no answer 7897. Reservations,
call, can reserve entire weekend after
1200 F. Rate: $30per. DV $33per.
Commercial: In Harrowgate.

Ground Transport:

Pay shuttle to Harrowgate RR 0900-1940
M-Th, 0900-2400 FSa, tickets at Club or
exact change.
✚ **Shuttle:** Lakenheath weekly. Occasional transport to other installations,
x271.
Commercial: Bus xSu outside main gate
to RR.

Menwith Hill Station
APO AE 09468
262-1110 **01423-77**-0421
D thru operator

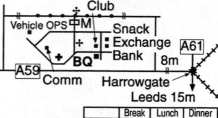

	Break	Lunch	Dinner
Club	7d	7d	7d
Snack		7d	7d

West of London Clubs

WestRoyal Sailors home
Queen St. C **0170**-5824231, Fax 5293496
£22sgl, £47dbl, most with bath. After 2000
£13sgl, £25dbl. **E** only.

Royal Fleet Club
2-12 Morice Sq, Plymouth. C **01752**-562723,
Fax 550725. £17sgl, w/o bath, £22sgl w/b.
Double £35-44.

NOTE: Your input is needed.

Printed flight schedules provides considerable input value to future editions. If possible, please verify with terminal staff which flight destinations have regular flights and note these on the back of the schedule. AMC Grams are most frequently dated information and normally provide minimum to no value. *Verified* terminal e-mail and web site addresses have considerable traveler value, if possible submit these via e-mail to publisher@spaceatravel.com. All changes on base maps are important. **Copies of current maps showing facility locations are since '911' increasingly helpful.**

If you obtain information helpful to campers, please forward this information and if possible mail a detail map of the region. Travelers sharing information support each other by continuing this publication as the most comprehensive and accurate military travel handbook ever written.

Europe

M **MHZ**   AMC, Distances walkable
0.2m BQ-Terminal. AT&T direct.
L **LKZ**   Distances walkable.
In summer direct flights to/from CONUS may be
difficult. Viable alternative routes from CONUS are
via Lajes or Germany. To CONUS viable alternatives are via Lajes, Spain, or Italy. Germany is not
recommended unless known to be moving Cat-VI.
Heavy usage by Cat-V in summer has made it extremely difficult in summer for Cat-VI to Germany
or CONUS.

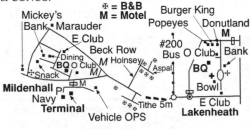

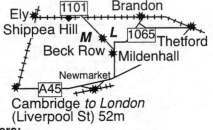

Cambridge *to London*
(Liverpool St) 52m

M **RAF Mildenhall**   D-88
                              APO AE 09459
238.1110   **01638-54-**3000
L **RAF Lakenheath**   AE 09464
226-1110   **01638.52-**3000

AMC →→	Flights →→	Navy
Adana		Naples
Atlanta Tu		Ramstein
Aviano M		Scandinavia
BWI Su		Stuttgart
Charleston√		
Dover√		UK flights
Lajes		not posted
McConnell		at AMC
McGuire		Terminal.
Ramstein√ TuF A		Sign up,
Travis		board at
		Navy.

Frequent flights, many destin.
                Chance of seat
★★★ x ★ summer   ★★★
Flight Information:
Terminal 2248,2526   OPS
0530-2230 xSu,   **2142**
0600-2230 Su, [Fax   0730-
2250, 627 ALSS/TRO   1630 M-F
Unit 4875]OPS **2929**

M Retirees cannot eat in Dining
Hall, but can at *L* hospital.
Terminal:
Lockers, motel & car rent
hotlines. Food machines.

Quarters:
M **Gateway Inn** ★ **2203,2407,6001** 24h, list starts 0100, assigned 1815. Reservation
2655,2965.
   Protocol 2777 (O7 up). USAFE Rates at both $32-49
L **Liberty Lodge** ★★★ X ★ summer **01638-52700 6700, 3217** 24h. Protocol 2444.
   USAFE Rates at both $32-49
Commercial: Many B&B, hotels in area,
   some pick up, information at Terminal. Of Beck Row motels, Smokehouse is the better. Use
   caution for Fairlegh House.
Golf: L D 226-3551, **C** (01638) 52-3551/2223 **Holes**: 9 (18 Tee) Breckland Pines Golf
   Course
Ground Transport:
M-L **Shuttle:** From *M*: 0630-1800 M-F, 1000-1730 SS; From *L*: 0655-1825M-F, 1023-1753
   SS.
Gatwick,Heathrow Shuttles: Four leave *L* 0500, 0730, *M* 0530,0800.
L ✚ **Shuttles:** Afternoon, check with sending installations.
About 2000 transport leaves *M* to some installations. Trucks from *M* freight terminal about
1200 M-F, 2069. Vehicle operation *L* 1843, *M* 2339. Transportation in Terminal. If arriving
on a flight, check with passengers for possible transport.
Bus: *M* Schedules at Mickey's Tea Bar and Rec C, stop across from Mickey's. #200Note:
The bus 'shelter' is across from Mickey's but the buses don't stop there; they come from the
left (east), then circle the roundabout then stop on the way back east. Bus xSu Mickey's east
to Mildenhall, Lakenheath (towns), Brandon,Thetford, 0747-1901, east to Newmarket 0702-
2024, all with B&B and, x Mildenhall, RR. To Mickey's,Lakenheath from Newmarket

Europe

RAF Mildenhall, Lakenheath continued from preceding page

0716-1830, (1242,1442 stops only at Lakenheath), from Thetford 0614-1935 (1206,1404 stops only at Lakenheath). #347 § Mickey's to Cambridge,Newmarket 1110, from Cambridge 1735, from Newmarket 1800, to Brandon 1830, from Brandon 1015. #495 § to London Victoria Coach Sta 0855, from London 1800. #496 § Mildenhall town to London Victoria Coach 1210, from London 1500. Neals M-F Mickey's to Mildenhall town 0752-1753, From King St, Mildenhall village to Mickey's 0740-1740. #155 to Bury St. Edmunds 0936,1302 M-F, 0909 Sa, RR, from Bury 1215,1745 M-F, 1200 Sa. § indicates tickets must be purchased in advance, ITT 0800-1730 M-F, 0800-1200 Sa, 2630,4103.

		Break	Lunch	Dinner	Brun
M	O Club		M-F	xSu	Su
	E Club	7d	7d	7d	
	Dining	7d	7d	7d	
	Snack	0600-2300			
	Bowl	1000-2230			
	Marauder	1100-2130 M-Th			
		1100-2300 FSS			
	Terminal	0530-1900 M-F			
	Snack	0630-1900 SS			
L	O Club		M-F	M-Th	
	E Club		M-F	xSu	Su
	Bowl	0630-2245 M-W			
		24h Th-Su			
	Burger	0600-2200 M-F			
	King	0700-2200 SS			

RR: Shippea Hill, 5m to **M**, platform only, 2 trains, taxi difficult after dark. RR-bus connections at Brandon,Newmarket, xSu Thetford,Bury St Edmunds. B&B between at all. Arriving late consider these B&B then bus in morning, reverse if arriving late by air for RR next day. For Scotland Brandon-Thetford line to Peterborough or military transport to Alconbury then bus to Peterborough.

Car Rent: Auto Rent near traffic circle 717717. Mildenhire at Bird in Hand 718288, does accept credit-card damage coverage. Car rent office in terminal and at Lakenheath only for those stationed in UK. **Save by calling CONUS to make reservations with US companies.** Lakenheath AAFES car rental 011.44.1638.523050 **Taxi:** At **M** BQ, 712261.

Travel Notes

Europe

PACIFIC and EASTERN ASIA

Pacific installations useful to Space-A travelers and airports regularly served by Space-A flights. Country and island listings follow in alphabetical order. Okinawa is listed under Japan.

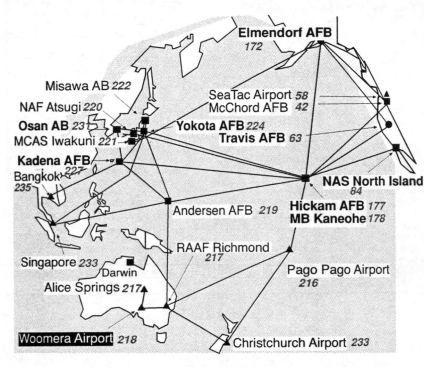

- **Elmendorf AFB** *172*
- Misawa AB *222*
- NAF Atsugi *220*
- SeaTac Airport *58*
- McChord AFB *42*
- **Osan AB** *23*
- MCAS Iwakuni *221*
- **Yokota AFB** *224*
- **Travis AFB** *63*
- **Kadena AFB**
- Bangkok *235*
- **NAS North Island** *84*
- Andersen AFB *219*
- **Hickam AFB** *177*
- **MB Kaneohe** *178*
- RAAF Richmond *217*
- Singapore *233*
- Darwin
- Alice Springs *217*
- Pago Pago Airport *216*
- Woomera Airport *218*
- Christchurch Airport *233*

AMERICAN SAMOA

Zulu-11

International prefix: D 315

PPG
Pronounced Pango Pango.

Quarters:
Herb and Sal's Motel, 633-5413, 9m. Le Apiolefaga 699-9124, 3m. **Barry's B&B**, [samoa@samoatelco.com] PO Box 5572, Pago Pago, ZIP 96799, 684.688.2488 or 699-5113, recommended by readers.

Ground Transport:
Bus to town. Car rent at Airport, usually not open when plane arrives. Taxis. Scheduled flights make approx 2h refueling stop. Cafeteria open when passengers are in terminal.

Pago Pago Airport
684-449-1515
✈✈✈✈ **Flights** ✈✈✈✈✈

Alice Springs Su
Christchurch
Hickam Su
Richmond SuM
Travis Su
Woomera M

★★★ west, ★ east

Flight Information:
1515 0600-1600 M-F
0600-1000 Sat.
Fax 011-684-699-9991.

Pago Pago
Tutulia Island
9m

PACIFIC and EASTERN ASIA
AUSTRALIA

Visa free to AAA members

1 USD = 1.41102 Australian Dollar
1 Australian Dollar = 1.11495 USD

Free Electronic Travel Authority in lieu of visas are available thru travel agencies and air lines for commercial travel only. In Honolulu Consul, 545-5423, is at Bishop and S. King on route of #19 Bus from Hickam. In DC 1601 Mass Ave, 20036, in LA 2049 Century Park E. 90067. Visa is free, limit 1y. Australian info 800-433-2877.

Australian Departure Tax A$27 payable at terminal during processing. Few facilities other than terminals are available but some use of E quarters at Richmond and clubs has been reported.

International telephone prefixes: D 312, C 61.

Scheduled flights to RAAF Richmond originate at Travis and are heavily used by active duty with dependents to Hickam. Normally retirees find availability better at Hickam although there are extended periods when few seats are released. During such times it is particularly important to keep close check with the terminal as there are occasional unscheduled flights. Taking a Pago Pago flight usually is desirable as many on Australian flights get off there.

Due to cargo being primarily outbound, returning to CONUS is less of a problem than going except April, May. Rare flights serve RAAF Amberley Field (near Brisbane). Military Attache, US Embassy, Canberra knows of these flights. Arrangements to board are made thru Richmond. Starting a return trip to CONUS from Pago Pago can be difficult.

ASP Zulu+9.5
Quarters:
Many lodges, motels, hotels.
Ground Transport:
Ansett, CATA buses meet all scheduled commercial flights. Long-distance buses, airlines, RR to Adelaide and Sydney. Many car rent agencies.

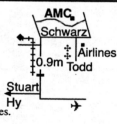

Alice Springs Airport
APO AP 96548
011-61-089-530-570
✈✈✈✈✈✈ **Flights** ✈✈✈✈✈✈
Richmond Tu

Chance of seat ★★★★
Flight Information:
530-570 0730-1600 M-F. [Fax 89-530-382]. Cannot return on same plane.

Sign up at AMC by 0900 day of flight. Call at 1200 to confirm. Normal departure time 1605. Contact customs at Airport for AMC representative.

RCM Zulu+10
AMC, Main access to Australia. Distances short.

H = Hotel M = Motel

Richmond — 3.6m
Bank | Terminal
Marsh — Clarendon/Windsor — Bank

Quarters:
BQ: E at NCO Club, 2442, availability questionable. Rate: A$3per.
Hotels and motels in Windsor and Richmond, Windsor more convenient. Peter White @ Richmond. Coach House Inn, has excellent relations with the military 221 Richmond Rd., Clarendon NSW 2756 Tel: 02 4577 7754 Fax 02 4577 2299

RAAF Richmond
APO AP 96554
C From U.S. 011.61.2.45-87-1652
C In Country 02.45-87-1652
✈✈✈✈✈✈ **Flights** ✈✈✈✈✈✈

Alice Springs Tu	McChord W
Christchurch 2-3/y	Pago W
Hickam W	Travis W
§ Only if cargo	Woomera §

Chance of seat ★★★★
Flight Information:
Sign up at US Hangar (Bldg 308) next to RAAF Terminal. 011.61.02.4587.1653 [Fax 011.61.45.87-1663, Det 1, 615 AMSG Unit]

Continued on following page

Pacific

215

PACIFIC and EASTERN ASIA
AUSTRALIA (Concluded)
RAAF Richmond continued from facing page

Ground Transport:

Windsor-Richmond bus at main gate. Clarendon RR Station 1.1m from main gate, frequent service, 1.5h to Sydney. Clarendon Hotel (pub type) near station. Taxis come on call by AMC, take to bank in Richmond, wait for money exchange, then take to Richmond RR Station. Taxi 13-147.

Flight Information: (continued)

11028] Recording 3879. Call in 0800-0900 day prior to flight. Call back 0930 for final disposition of request. Manifesting is completed day prior to flight. In-flight meals Changes in procedures have been frequent, check.

Peter White @ Richmond. Coach House Inn, has excellent relations with the military 221 Richmond Rd., Clarendon NSW 2756 Tel: 02 4577 7754 Fax 02 4577 2299

UMR   Zulu+9.5

Quarters:

In Woomera, Eldo, (has restaurant), Road House.

Ground Transport:

Stateline bus at theater, Woomera, 2230 to Alice Springs, 0530-2310 to Port Augusta. Ansett buses in Pimba. Call Port Augusta, 42-2611, x227 to stop train at Pimba.
Opal Air at Airport M-F.

Woomera Airport

APO AP 96552

D 730-1350 x438

C 011-61-08-8678-2438

→→→→ **Flights** →→→→

Alice Springs   Richmond

Chance of seat ★★★★

Flight Information:

Snack bar at Airport open when plane is in.

To Alice Springs 4m | Woomera
5m
Pimba
To Port Augusta 100m

Officially Closed Dec. 99 contact RAAF Richmond for possibility of unscheduled flights.

GUAM (US)

Zulu+10, no daylight savings

Andersen AFB *219*

NCTAMS *219*

Micronesia Mall

Yigo

3

NS Guam

218

Dedado

4 *Agana*

1

2

Nimitz Hill Top O' The Mar Club

2

4

International telephone prefix: D 315. Operator assist for all Navy: D 322-1110, C 355-1110.

When direct flights are difficult, via Guam is a viable alternative but number of flights has been dwindling as well as availability of billets. Spring of 2000 contract flights to and from Diego Garcia, via Singapore, were stopping at Anderson.

Camping permitted on beaches, free, no hookups.

Guam Mass Transit buses have been an on and off thing. At time of writing they were not operating.

Many hotels, expensive, $45 (Maile Garden 472-7173) up. Taxis expensive, unreliable, arrange with gate for admission. 477-8620; 565-5963; 646-1155,4070,6390,9240; 649-4119,5711,6842.

Pacific

UAM AMC   Dial 7 digits on base.
Distances walkable x to M gate. 1m
BQ–Terminal.

Quarters:

Andersen Lodge: Availability
★★ 362.2801/444/2981 24h. PACAF Rates: **$27-49.**
Protocol 1320. **E** $10per. Camping on beach $5. No
commercial close, check NCTAMS **Æ219**

Golf: 671.366.4653 Palm Tree Golf Course

Dive Shop: 6975

Ground Transport:

Beach Shuttle from Club 1800-2400 F, 1200-2400 Sa,
1200-1700 Su.

Commercial: National car rent in Terminal 362-2181
0800-1800. On-base taxi 8144. Taxi from Agana,
expensive, unreliable.

Andersen AFB   D-94
Guam APO AP 96543
366-1110   **671-366**-1110
↣↣↣↣↣ **Flights** ↣↣↣↣↣
Hickam W√   Travis
Kadena 4/w   Yokota A TuF
Osan

Seat availability fluctuates
Flight Information:
362.2801, 366.8144/4444 24h.
[Fax 3984, 734 AMSS/TRP Unit
14008].
Terminal open 24h, lockers, 24h
cafeteria, car rent.

	Break	Lunch	Dinner
Club		Tu-F	TFSa
Dining	7d	7d	7d
Bowl	0700-2130		
Golf	0700-1400 M-F		
	0630-1530 SS		

To NCTAMS 5.5m Car Rent
M   24h Cafeteria   Comm
    Terminal 7th BX
Main To Beach Perimeter
Gate   Chicago Bonins
to   Carolines 4th Bowl Dining
Terminal 2.2m   Club
              Gas   **BQ**   Golf

Distances long. 1.4m BQ-M Gate.

Quarters:

BQ: Availability ★★★★ x ★
conferences **5259,7224** 24h,
handles quarters near All Hands
(formerly O) Club **901.**873.3630 on
Nimitz Hill. No commercial close.
Rates: **O** $8sgl+$4add per. Nimitz Hill
$20sgl+$10add per. DV $15per, **E** (no
dependents) $4, $25sgl+$10add per.

Golf: 344.5838/39 **Holes:** 18
Admiral Nimitz Golf Course

Ground Transport:

Commercial: National car rent 564-
1870, 0800-1700 xSu, 0900-1600 Su.

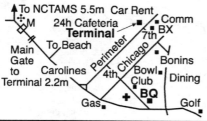

BQ Shop
Gas
E Club   McDonald's
              M
Comm   NX To
          Agana
          Nimitz
          Hill

NB Guam
(Orote Point)
Orote Point, Guam 96630
339-xxxx   **671-339**-xxxx

Agana
Pitti
USO   Nimitz Hill
Top O'The Mar Club

	Break	Lunch	Dinner	Brun
O Club		TTF	TTF	Su
E Club		M-F	xSu	
McDonald's	0530-2200			

Master radio station
Distances short.

Quarters:

BQ: Availability ★★★★ **5793**
24h. Rates: **O** $8sgl+$2add per, DV
$20sgl+$4add per. O6 up thru protocol 5311. **E**1-6 $4sgl+$2add per, E7 up
$6sgl+$2add per. No commercial close.

Ground Transport:

National car rent, 632-0111/2, 0800-1700 M-Th , 0800-
1800 F, 0900-1600 Su.

NX
Snack
BQ   Shop
     Galley
1/4m
To Andersen
M   5.5m

NCTAMS
Guam 96910
355-xxxx   **671-3**55-xxxx

	Break	Lunch	Dinner
Galley	7d	7d	7d
Snack	0900-2200		

Pacific

Zulu+7 (No daylight savings time.)

DJK

INDONESIA
1 USD = 9,037.65 Indonesian Rupiah
1 Indonesian Rupiah = 0.000110648 USD

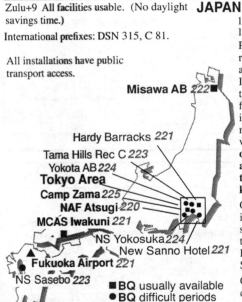

▲ **Jakarta Airport**

Java

International prefix: C 62

Jakarta Airport (Halim)
OMADP, Box 2, Unit 8133
APO AP 96520-8133
011-6221-360-360
➤➤➤➤➤ **Flights** ➤➤➤➤➤
Kadena 2/m Tu
Chance of seat ★★★★
Flight Information:
x2920 0730-1600 M-F
[Fax 6221-372-518]

Zulu+9 **All facilities** usable. (No daylight savings time.)

International **prefixes**: DSN 315, C 81.

All installations have public transport access.

JAPAN

1 US Dollar = 99.5950 ¥(Yen)
1 Japanese ¥(Yen) = 0.0100407 USD

Passports required for dependents and retirees, limit 90d without visa. Yokota and Kadena are major points of entry but Iwakuni and Misawa also have immigrations and customs. Other installations with flights, particularly Atsugi, are useful for intra-Japan flights. On arrival passports must be stamped. AMC provides this service. **It is the passenger's responsibility on leaving Japan to obtain an exit stamp after being assigned a seat. At Atsugi this means going to Immigration at Yokohama.**

Okinawa is as much Japan as the main islands but for Space-A purposes is treated separately. Okinawa map Æ225 and details follow details for the main islands. International drivers license required, SOFA, to rent at Navy.

Civilian hotels and restaurants have become very expensive in Japan. In terms of US$ this is due in part to the long-term decline in the $ vs the ¥ but far more impor-

Misawa AB 222 ■

Hardy Barracks 221

Tama Hills Rec C 223
Yokota AB 224
Tokyo Area
Camp Zama 225
NAF Atsugi 220
MCAS Iwakuni 221
NS Yokosuka 224
New Sanno Hotel 221
▲ Fukuoka Airport 221
NS Sasebo 223

■BQ usually available
●BQ difficult periods
▲BQ not available

tantly to increases in ¥ prices. Unfortunately low-cost hotels do not have beds or toilets acceptable to most Americans. Hardy Barracks Æ221 is the low-cost choice for visiting Tokyo. Quarters are usually available Su-Th, It has a one-zone subway fare to anywhere downtown and is 1.1m from dining facilities at the New Sanno Hotel,

---

NJA
Distances walkable, Terminal-BOQ 0.5m, -BEQ 0.8m.
Quarters:
Availability ★★★★ x ★ when carrier is in.
BOQ: 3696 24h. Rates **O** $8per, DV $10per. Protocol 3674.
BEQ: 3698 24h. Rates: E1-6 $3per, E7 up $10per.

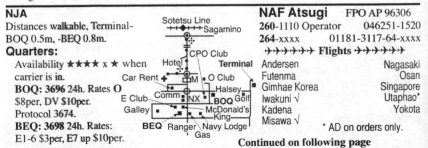

Sotetsu Line
Sagamino
CPO Club
Hotel
Terminal
Car Rent
O Club
M
Halsey
E Club Comm
NX BOQ Golf
Galley
McDonald's
BEQ Ranger Navy Lodge
Gas
King

NAF Atsugi FPO AP 96306
260-1110 Operator 046251-1520
264-xxxx 01181-3117-64-xxxx
➤➤➤➤➤ **Flights** ➤➤➤➤➤

Andersen	Nagasaki
Futenma	Osan
Gimhae Korea	Singapore
Iwakuni √	Utaphao*
Kadena	Yokota
Misawa √	

* AD on orders only.

Continued on following page

Pacific

NAF Atsugi continued from preceding page

Golf: 3779/3788 **Holes:** 18 Whispering
Pines Golf Course
Navy Lodge: ★★★ 6880 24h. Rate: $40,48unit.
Not reservable via 800-Navy Inn.
Commercial: Hotel outside main gate.

Ground Transport:
Shuttles: Station 0645-1645 M-F. Yokota, Yokosuka TT. Occasional transport 6248.
Commercial: Bus outside main gate to Sagamino Station. Car rent 3726 0800-1700 xSu.

Sangamino ← → Atsugi Soutetsu Line
Ishikawa-cho
Yokohama Kelhin-Tohoku Line
Canal
Motomachi Shopping St. ■
25-min walk   Bund Hotel
Immigration ■

Frequent flights to many dest.
Chance of seat ★★★★
To stamp out, go to Immigration,
Yokohama 0830-1145, 1300-1645.

Flight Information:
3118,3803 0600-2200. Recording 3801
[Fax 3149, PSC 477, Box 13]. **To stamp
out, go to Immigration, Yokohama
0830-1145, 1300-1645 M-F.**

	Break	Lunch	Dinner	Break
O Club		Tu-F	Th-Su	Su
CPO Club		xSa	7d	
E Club		7d	7d	
Galley	7d	7d	7d	
MacDonald	0700-2100			
Golf	0630-1900 xTu			
Terminal	0600-1800 M-F			
	0600-1400 Sa			

FUK
At West Gate off Route 3 bypass opposite side of
runway from Airport terminal.

Ground Transport:
Shuttle to Sasebo from #3 Terminal parking 1100,1700,2015,2230.

Fukuoka Airport
225-2438   092-451-2558
✈✈✈✈✈✈ **Flights** ✈✈✈✈✈✈
Iwakuni Tu   Yokota Tu
Kadena Su
Chance of seat ★★★★
Flight Information:
Nos. above 0730-1600 M-F,
1300-1900 Sa

Quarters:
BQ: *H* Availability ★★★★ x ★ weekends 3270,
3345 24h, Rm 413A. Rate: $17sgl+$2add per shared bath,
suite $20sgl, $25dbl private bath. Reservations. Check in
1400-1600. Certainly the best bargain, especially for retirees, near downtown Tokyo.
S Availability ★★★★ x ★ summer,weekends 7231,7220 24h.
Reserve 7121 0800-1900. After 1800 ★★★★ due to no-shows. Rates: E1-5 $29sgl, E6-O3 $38sgl, O4 up $44sgl all
+$11dbl. Retirees $63sgl, $77dbl, $95suite. Unaccompanied
dependents not permitted.
Ground Transport:
Shuttle *S* to Yokota 1330,2130, also 2230 FSS. To Misawa
0900 TuSu $45, pay driver.
Commercial: # 97 Bus connects *H*, *S*, and Subways. One-zone subway fare anywhere in downtown area.

H Hardy Barracks
S New Sanno Hotel
Unit 45003 APO AP 96337
229-8111   03.3440-7871
C to Front Desk
011.81.33440.7871

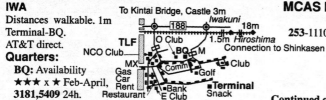

H Cafeteria, Breakfast, Lunch M-F

IWA
Distances walkable. 1m
Terminal-BQ.
AT&T direct.
Quarters:
BQ: Availability
★★★ x ★ Feb-April,
3181,5409 24h.

To Kintai Bridge, Castle 3m
188 *Iwakuni*
18m
TLF   O Club   1.5m *Hiroshima*
NCO Club   BQ M   Connection to Shinkasen
MX   Comm   ■Club
Gas   Golf
Car
Rent
Bank   ■**Terminal**
Restaurant   E Club   Snack

MCAS Iwakuni
FPO AP 96310
253-1110   0827-21-4171
C thru operator

Continued on following page

Pacific

list, call, assigned 1900. Rates: **O** $10per. DV $15,18per. O6 up thru protocol 4211. E1-5 $5per, E6 up $10per. Except for **DV**, Space-A only when TLF is full or closed. **TLF: ★★★★ x ★** May-Oct, **3221**, 0800-2200. Rate: $30,40dbl+$2add per.
Commercial: Hotels in Iwakuni.
Diving: 253.6058 Scuba Locker (IronWorks)
Golf: 253-3402 / 3187 Holes: Torii Pines
Marina: 253-3691
Ground Transport:
Shuttle 0700-2200 7d. Taxi Service (On Base Only) 253-5954 or 090-2000-8545
Commercial: Bus 0656-2225 outside main gate to Iwakuni **RR** To atomic bomb memorial train to Nishi Hiroshima then #3 tram or walk. This exhibit is remarkable for being fair unlike politically correct exhibits in the US. Shinkansen (Bullet) at Hiroshima **Sta** or Bus from Iwakuni 0600-1900 to Shin Iwakuni. To walk to castle, follow W bank to low-level bridge then E bank. MWR car rent 3186. Taxi 99-21-1111.

→→→→→→ Flights →→→→→→

Atsugi	Misawa
Fukuoka	Nagasaki
Futenma	Osan
Kadena√	Yokota
Kunsan	

Chance of seat ★★★★
Flight Information:
5509, 3947 0600-2200.
Recording 1854 [Fax 3301, Passenger Terminal]. Has customs and immigration.

	Break	Lunch	Dinner	Brun
O Club		M-F	7d	Su
NCO Club	Sa	M-F	7d	Su
E Club	Sa	7d	7d	Su
Club	1630-2130 M-F			
	1000-2100 SS			
Restaurant	0900-2200			
Golf	0600-2400			
Terminal	1000-21000 xFSa			
	1000-2400 FSa			

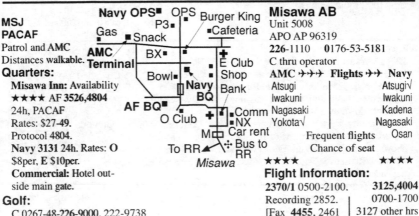

MSJ
PACAF
Patrol and AMC
Distances walkable.
Quarters:
Misawa Inn: Availability ★★★★ AF **3526,4804** 24h, PACAF
Rates: $27-49.
Protocol 4804.
Navy 3131 24h. Rates: **O** $8per, **E** $10per.
Commercial: Hotel outside main gate.
Golf:
C 0267-48-**226**-9000, 222-9738
Holes: 18 Gosser Memorial Golf Course
Ground Transport:
Shuttle 4062. Pay shuttle to New Sanno, Yokota $60.
Commercial: Bus to RR (Misawa Eki) outside main gate. Taxi 5438/9.

Misawa AB
Unit 5008
APO AP 96319
226-1110   **0176-53-5181**
C thru operator
AMC →→→ Flights →→ Navy

AMC	Navy
Atsugi	Atsugi√
Iwakuni	Iwakuni
Nagasaki	Kadena
Yokota√	Nagasaki
Frequent flights	Osan
Chance of seat	

★★★★   ★★★★
Flight Information:
2370/1 0500-2100.   3125,4004
Recording 2852.   0700-1700
[Fax **4455**, 2461   3127 other hrs
PSE 76, Box   P3 3017/55
7733].

	Break	Lunch	Dinner	Brun
O Club		M-F	Tu-Sa	Su
E Club	xSu	M-F	7d	Su
Cafeteria	0630-1300 M-F			
	0800-1300 Sa			
Burger K	0600-2000			
Bowl	24h			

PACIFIC and EASTERN ASIA
JAPAN (Continued)

JA

NB Sasebo
FPO AP 96322
252-1110   0956-24-6111
2476-00-252-xxxx

	Break	Lunch	Dinner
Club	7d	7d	7d
Snack		0700-1830	

Distances short, 0.8m BOQ–main gate.
AT&T direct

Quarters:
Availability ★★.
BOQ: 3794
24h. Rates:
$15per, DV
$20,25per. O6 up thru
protocol 3020.
BEQ: 3413 24. Rate:
$5per (no dependent).

Car Rent M Comm NX Shop Gas Bank Snack Hotels 35 Sasebo BEQ Shop Navy Lodge BOQ Club

Navy Lodge: ★★ **0322** 0630-2230 **C** (011) 0926240173. Rate: $49unit. Not reservable 800-Navy Inn.
Commercial: Hotels in Sasebo.
Marina: C 011-81-95-62-4611Sumay Cove Marina/Clipper Landing
Ground Transport:
Shuttle to Fukuoka Airport from Gas 0500,1000,1400,1645, also ✚ shuttle to Airevac MTh, 3326.
Commercial: RR Station (Sasebo Eki) 1m from main gate. Buses on Route 35.

Distances short.
Quarters:
BQ: Cottages, lodge, ★★★ x ★★ summer, Nos. above
24h. Reservations 0800-1600 M-F 60d ahead. Rates:
Lodge $25sgl, $35suite, cottages $35-150.
RV: 3412 0800-1700, reserve 3m in advance. RV, Tent
W $1per. Pets only in cottages.
Golf:
C 042-374-2811D 224-3426 **Holes:** 18 Tama Hills Golf
Course
Ground Transport:
Minami Tama station 0.3m from main gate, change at
Tachikawa for all other installations..

Tama Hills Rec Center
224-3421   0423-77-7009
APO 96328-5119
Nambu Line   Minami Tama
0.3m
Shop   Restaurant
Office

	Break	Lunch	Dinner
Lodge	xTu	xTu	xMTu

Tokyo Area

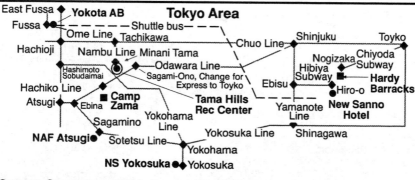

East Fussa — Yokota AB — Shuttle bus — Tachikawa
Fussa — Ome Line — Chuo Line — Shinjuku — Toyko
Hachioji — Nambu Line Minani Tama — Nogizaka Chiyoda Subway
Hashimoto Sobudaimai — Odawara Line — Hibiya Subway — Hardy Barracks
Hachiko Line — Sagami-Ono, Change for Express to Toyko — Ebisu — Hiro-o
Atsugi — Ebina — Camp Zama — Tama Hills Rec Center — Yamanote Line — New Sanno Hotel
Sagamino — Yokohama Line
NAF Atsugi — Sotetsu Line — Yokosuka Line — Shinagawa
Yokohama
NS Yokosuka — Yokosuka

Pacific

Quarters Summary
DSN, for C see installation details   Availability

NAF Atsugi	220	264	**O** 3696, **E** 3698,3793 24h	●
Hardy Barracks	221	229	3270,3345 24h	■
New Sanno Hotel	221	229	7231 24h	■
Tama Hills	223	224	3421	●
NB Yokosuka	222	243	**O** 7317 24h, **E** 7777 24h, Navy Lodge 6708 24h	●
Yokota AB	224	225	7712 24h	●
Camp Zama	225	263	4474 24h	■

221

Distances walkable.
AT&T direct.

Quarters:
Availability
★★★★ x ★ when
fleet is in,
**Central
Billeting/BEQ
243-5569**
BOQ:
D 243-5685/7317
24h. Call for rates.
O6 up thru
protocol 7601.

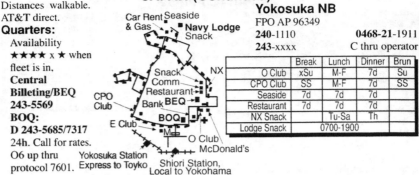

Car Rent Seaside
& Gas
■Navy Lodge
Snack

Snack
Comm
Restaurant
CPO
Club
Bank BEQ
E Club
BOQ
Mc
NX
O Club
McDonald's
Yokosuka Station
Express to Toyko
Shiori Station,
Local to Yokohama

Yokosuka NB
FPO AP 96349
240-1110
243-xxxx

0468-21-1911
C thru operator

	Break	Lunch	Dinner	Brun
O Club	xSu	M-F	7d	Su
CPO Club	SS	M-F	7d	SS
Seaside	7d	7d	7d	
Restaurant	7d	7d	7d	
NX Snack		Tu-Sa	Th	
Lodge Snack		0700-1900		

Navy Lodge ★★★ x ★
summer **6708** 24h, list starts 0700, assigned 1800. Rate: $49unit. Not reservable via 800 Navy Inn.

Marina: C 011-81-468-96-2067/ 011-81-468-16-4155 Green Bay Marina

Ground Transport
Shuttle 0630-1800 7d. Shuttle TT Atsugi, Yokota. Unscheduled runs, 6812/3.
Commercial: RR outside main gate, taxi 4444.

OKO AMC Distances walkable, 0.4m BQ-Terminal. AT&T direct.

Quarters:
Kanto Lodge:
Availability ★ 24h, list starts at 0001, assigned . Visit or call front desk **224.2000/2** before 1800 and hold with Credit Card. Unfunded waiting list rooms are released at 1800. Extensions 0930. PACAF FY 07/08 Rates: $27-49.
Protocol 4141. Travelers' Lodge in "Sip & Surf" Cafe rents lounge chairs $5 for overnight sleeping; located next to BX.
Commercial: Sanko Plaza Hotel 52-1101. Morikawa Hotel 52-0711.
Golf: 011-81-425-52-2510 ext: 5-7455

Ground Transport:
Base Shuttle 0600-2300 7d, :01 from Terminal, 9121. Navy shuttle Atsugi, Yokosuka 0830 Tu, 1200 Th. Check at Army and Navy desks in Terminal for unscheduled transport. From BQ: New Sanno Hotel shuttle 0930 returns at 1330, also 1600 FSS 1015. $24 shuttle to Narita 000,1100,1300, 7720,9519. Misawa $45 shuttle 1130 SuTh.
Commercial: East Fussa RR station close to main gate, Fussa station 1m. Car rent 8070 0930-1730 xSu, 1000-1600 Su. Taxi 5901/2/3 0400-2400 M-F, 24h SS.

Morikawa Hotel
Immigrations
Gas
Car Rent
Bank
BX
Comm
Plaza Hotel
Hachiko
Line
East Fussa
0.5m
Fussa
Ome Line
■Terminal
Cafeteria
O Club
■BQ
Burger
King
NCO
Club
To
16

Yokota AB
APO AP 96328
225-1110
81.3117.55.1110
All extensions thru operator

⇥⇥⇥⇥⇥⇥ **Flights** ⇥⇥⇥⇥⇥⇥

Andersen
Atsugi
Elmendorf
Fukuoka
Hickam
Iwakuni
Kadena ThF

Kunsan
McChord
Misawa√
Nagasaki
Osan MWF
Singapore MTTF
Travis

Frequent flights to many dest.
Chance of seat
★★★ x ★ summer to CONUS

Flight Information:
5661/2 0400-2200. Recording 7111. [Fax D 9768, 630 AMSS/TRP]. OPS 7006. Terminal open 24h, lockers, Cafeteria, BX. Parking across Route 16 from Terminal. Immigration 7816/8 0500-1700. Retirees must go off base and check in with Japanese immigrations and obtain a 90 day visa.

	Break	Lunch	Dinner	Brun
O Club		Tu-F	Tu-Sa	Su
NCO Club	xSu	xSu	7d	Su
Term. Cafe.		24h		
Burger King		0600-2200 M-F		
		0700-2200 Sa		
		0800-2200 Su		

PACIFIC and EASTERN ASIA
JAPAN (Continued)

JA

Army HQ
Distances walkable
including to RR,
0.8m BQ-OPS. AT&T direct.

Camp Zama
(Rankin AAF)
APO AP 96337
263-1110   46251-1520
51-1788-xxxx

Quarters:
BQ: Availability ★★★★
F-Su, ★★★ M-Th **3830** 24h.
Reservations for weekend
1200 Th. Rates: $14sgl, $18dbl
communal, $14sgl private. DV
$25sgl +$5add per. Protocol O7 up 4019.
Commercial: Hotels at RR.
Golf: D: 263-4224 **C:** 046-251-1788-263-4975
Holes: 18   Zama Golf Course
Ground Transport:

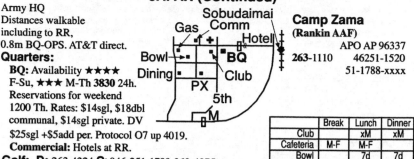

	Break	Lunch	Dinner
Club		xM	xM
Cafeteria	M-F	M-F	
Bowl		7d	7d
Snack		7d	7d
Dining	SS		

Shuttle M-F, 4 trips. Shuttle to Airport 0900-1900. Check motor pool for unscheduled transport 3772,4053.
Commercial: Sobudaimai RR Station (Eki), Odawara Line. Change to express at Sagami Ono for Tokyo, change at Ebina for Atsugi. Taxi 74-0596.

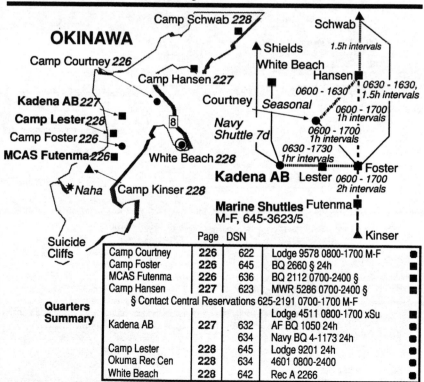

Quarters Summary

	Page	DSN		
Camp Courtney	226	622	Lodge 9578 0800-1700 M-F	■
Camp Foster	226	645	BQ 2660 § 24h	■
MCAS Futenma	226	636	BQ 2112 0700-2400 §	■
Camp Hansen	227	623	MWR 5286 0700-2400 §	■
			§ Contact Central Reservations 625-2191 0700-1700 M-F	
Kadena AB	227	632	Lodge 4511 0800-1700 xSu	●
		634	AF BQ 1050 24h	●
			Navy BQ 4-1173 24h	●
Camp Lester	228	645	Lodge 9201 24h	●
Okuma Rec Cen	228	634	4601 0800-2400	●
White Beach	228	642	Rec A 2266	●

Although Okinawa is part of Japan and shares the same passport rules, for Space-A travel it is treated separately. Okinawa is another of those crossroads which are viable alternatives when direct flights are difficult. Except for Kadena AB and two Rec C, all installations are Marine.

Pacific

223

The quarters summary on the preceding page gives all the installations having Space-A lodging on a formal basis. When Central Reservations is open it should be contacted first to obtain billets at Foster, Futenma, and Hansen (does not apply to lodges). Almost always quarters are available somewhere on the island. Distances short.

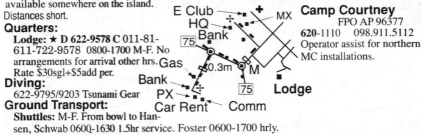

Quarters:
Lodge: ★ D 622-9578 C 011-81-611-722-9578 0800-1700 M-F. No arrangements for arrival other hrs. Rate $30sgl+$5add per.
Diving:
622-9795/9203 Tsunami Gear
Ground Transport:
Shuttles: M-F. From bowl to Hansen, Schwab 0600-1630 1.5hr service. Foster 0600-1700 hrly.
Commercial: Buses outside main gate.

Camp Courtney
FPO AP 96377
620-1110   098.911.5112
Operator assist for northern MC installations.

Distances walkable.
Quarters:
BQ: ★★★ x ★★ summer , Central Reservations 645.2455, C from U.S. 011.81.611.745.2455 0800-1630 M-F. Rates: O $19sgl+$10 add per, DV $30sgl+$10 add per. Protocol 7274. E 1-5 $10per, E 6-9 suites $12sgl+$10add per.
Golf: 3752 Holes: 18 Awase Meadows Golf Course
Diving: 4206 Tsunami Gear
Ground Transport:
Shuttles: M-F. Post 0540-1725. Lester, Kadena 0630-1730 hrly service. Courtney, Hansen 0600-1700 hrly service. Schwab 0630-1630 1.5hr service. Futenma, Kinser 0700-1700 2hr service. Vehicle Dispatch 3623/5.
Commercial: Buses on Routes 58, 330. Car rent 635-4577, 1000-1800 xSu.

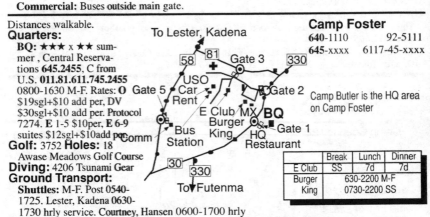

Camp Foster
640-1110   92-5111
645-xxxx   6117-45-xxxx

Camp Butler is the HQ area on Camp Foster

	Break	Lunch	Dinner
E Club	SS	7d	7d
Burger King		630-2200 M-F	
		0730-2200 SS	

NFO   AT&T direct
Marine tankers (KC130)
Distances short x to Terminal.
Quarters:
BQ: Availability ★★ 2112 0700-2400, when open contact Central Reservations first, 2191, 0700-1700 M-F. Rates: O $19sgl, $30dbl, E 1-5 $10per, E6 up $12sgl+ $10add per.
Ground Transport:
Shuttles: Station 0630-1635 xSu. M-F 2hr service Foster 0630-1615. Kinser 0715-1715.
Commercial: Buses on Route 58. Car rent Bldg 243, 631-4549 0900-1700 xSu.

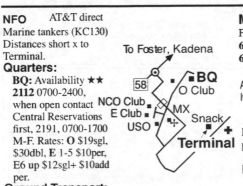

MCAS Futenma
FPO AP 96372
640-1110   (Foster)   92-5111
636-xxxx   C thru operator
↣↣↣↣↣↣↣ Flights ↣↣↣↣↣↣↣
Atsugi   Osan
Iwakuni   Yokota

Infrequent flights
Dependents with command sponsorship papers can fly on Marine flights.
Chance of seat ★★★★
Flight Information:
3039/410630-2100 xSu.

	Break	Lunch	Dinner	Brun
O Club		M-F	Th-Sa	Su
NCO Club		M-F	xMSa	

Distances walkable. AT&T direct.

Quarters:

Availability ★★★.

BQ: 4522/4860 0700-2400, when open contact Central Reservations first 2191, 0700-1700 M-F Rates: O $19sgl, E6 up $12sgl, E1-5 $10sgl, all +$10 add per.

Hansen Lodge: 011-81-611-723-4511 0800-1700 xSu. Rate $10per.

Diving: 623-7717 Tsunami Gear

Ground Transport:

Shuttles M-F (from USO): Foster 0600-1700 hrly service. Courtney, Schwab 0645-1717 1.5hr service,

Commercial: #23/2 Buses outside gates. Car rent 5092, 1000-1800 xSu.

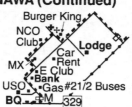

Camp Hansen

620-1110

623-XXXX C 972-7200 then, after dial tone enter on base seven digit number. **From US:** 011.81.611.7xx.xxxx (last six digits of number you are calling)

	Break	Lunch	Dinner
NCO Club	SS	M-F	7d
Burger King	0600-2200 M-F		
	0730-2200 SS		

DNA

Distances walkable x to Navy. 1.5m BQ-Terminal. AT&T direct.

Quarters:

BQ: Shogun Inn. Availability AF: ★★★ 632-1010/50 24h. Rates: O $12per. DV $22per. O6 up thru protocol 634-1808. TLF $35unit.

Navy: ★★★ 634.0677 Front Desk, 1173 Res. 24h. Rates: O1-4 $8sgl+$3add per, O5 up $12sgl+$5add per. DV $25sgl+$5add per. Protocol 634.8241. E $4sgl+$2add per.

Commercial: Hotels outside gates 2 & 4.

When billets are full: Because terminal is closed at night, no billets can be a disaster (particularly with an early show time when it is cold). Gym is open 24h, also FSa Bowl. At Navy billets 0.6m away from terminal quad billets share lounges unused at night. Get in late and out early.

Aero Club: D 634-5758 Kadena Aero Club

Golf: 634-3900 **Holes:** 9 Chibana Golf Course, 18 Banyan Tree Golf Course

Marina: (Navy) PH: C 011-81-98-892-5111 Sea Side Marina, White Beach Recreation Area; (AF) PH: C 634-6344 Kadena Marina

Diving: PH: C 634-6344 Kadena Marina

Ground Transport:

Shuttles: M-F AF BOQ shuttle on call. From bus station M-F Lester,Foster 0700-1800 hrly. From USO, BX Navy shuttle to Camp Shields 1800-2200 M-F, 0900-2200 SS. Seasonal Navy shuttle to White Beach. Naha Airport from terminal 0900,1100, 2120, returns from domestic

Kadena AB   APO AP 96368

630-1110   098-938-1111

63x-xxxx   C:011.81.611.7xx. xxxx (last six digits of number you are calling) **Now from off base call Kadena numbers starting with:**

630- = 098-960-	645- = 098-970-
632- = 098-962-	622- = 098-954-
633- = 098-959-	646- = 098-971-
634- = 098-961-	623- = 098-969-

AMC ✈✈✈ **Flights** ✈✈   Navy

Alaska	Manila	Atsugi√
Andersen	Misawa	Iwakuni
Hickam	Osan	Misawa
Jakarta	Yokota√	

Frequent flights to many dest.

★★★   ★★★

Flight Information:

634-2159 0600-2200 [Fax 4-4221, 633 AMSS/TRO Unit 5190 Box 20]. Cafeteria, USO, lockers, Terminal open 0600-2200 M-F, 0800-2000 SS. Transport provided to immigration on arrival, passenger must stamp out when leaving.	634-6406/7 0600-2200 M-F 0600-2000 SS Not posted at AMC P3 Mission Control 634.8354 Quarterdeck 634.8356

Customs

634.4398/2217

Pacific

Continued on facing page

	Break	Lunch	Dinner	Brun
O Club	M-F	M-F	xSu	Su
NCO Club	M-F	M-F	7d	Su
E Club		7d	7d	
Restaurant		M-F	xTu	
Cafeteria	0600-2000 M-F			
	0800-2000 SS			

terminal 1100,1300,2300, info 4505.
Ground Transport (con't):
Commercial: Buses outside all gates. Car rent
633-0007, 0830-1730 xSu, 1000-1600 Su. Taxi
99-937-2467.

Distances walkable.
Diving: 637-2027 Tsunami gear
Ground Transport:
Shuttle: M-F Futenma,Foster 0700-
1700 2h service.
Commercial: Buses on Route 58.
Car rent Bldg 1227, 3834, 1030-
1930.

NCO Club To Foster, Kadena
USO
O Club 58

Camp Kinser
640-1110   911.5111 then,
after dial tone enter on base
seven digit number.
637-xxxx C thru operator

	Break	Lunch	Dinner
O Club			
NCO Club		7d	7d
Cafeteria	7d	7d	7d

Hospital Distances short.
Quarters:
Lester BOQ 2455
Kuwae Lodge: Availability ★★★★ x
★ May-Oct **9201/9102/7719** 24h, Rates:
$32sgl+$5add per.
Ground Transport:
Shuttles: Stop at Lodge, ✚. M-F Kadena
0640-1740, Foster 0715-1815 hrly.
Commercial: Buses on Route 58. Car rent, Bldg
400, 633-1607 0800-1700 xSu.

To Kadena
✚ Kuwae Lodge
Shop
58   Gate 2
Gate 1

Camp Lester
FPO AP 96362
640-1110 098.911.5111
then, after dial tone enter on
base seven digit number.
645-xxxx   C From US:
011.81.611.7xx.xxxx (last
six digits of number you are
calling)

	Break	Lunch	Dinner
Snack	7d	7d	7d

Route 58, 50m north of Kadena, off Route 58 west of Hentona
Quarters:
Availability ★ x ★★★ Nov,Dec. Nos. above at Okuma 0800-
2400. Reserve 1m in advance, pay at Kadena Rec C, 0730-1730 M-F,
0800-1530 Sa. D 634-4322, C **631.2300/1850.** Rates: $20 Cabins to $135
Five bedroom Bungalow $145. Tent $8.
Ground Transport:
#20 Bus (Kadena Gate 1) to Nago, transfer to #67 Bus to Hentonia, #69
Bus Hentonia to Okuma (1.5m west of Hentonia).

Okuma Rec Facility
634-4601 098-041-5164
631.2300/1850

■Office
✚ M
Restaurant

Distances walkable.
Quarters:
Cottages at Oura Wan
745-2455
Diving:
625-2691 Tsunami gear
Ground Transport:
Shuttle: From USO M-F
Foster,Hansen,Courtney 0600-1630 1.5h service.
Commercial: Buses outside main gate, #22 to Naha.
Car rent 3830, 1000-1800 xSu. Taxi 2492.

329 M
To USO
Kadena ✚ NCO Club
Gas Car Snack
Rent ✚ ■MX
O Club
E Club

Camp Schwab
620-1110 098.972.6700
625-xxxx C From US:
011.81.611.7XX.XXXX (last six
digits of number you are calling)

	Break	Lunch	Dinner
Clubs	7d	7d	7d
USO	0900-2300		
Snack	0700-2400 M-Th		

Quarters:
Reserve at Kadena **642-2264/6** up to 30d in advance. Availability
★★ winter, ★ summer. Cottage $40, trailer $30, RV W $4, Tent
W free. No pets.
Ground Transport
Seasonal Navy shuttle from Kadena. Driving follow Route 8 to
end. Shuttle to Kadena summer. #27 Bus from Koh-Kuutai Iriguchi bus stop near Gate 2,
Kadena, to Heshikiya bus stop. Continue toward beach.

White Beach Rec A
FPO AP 96378
642-2264/66 **Admin /
Marina; Manager** 642-
2311/2353; **Rec Services**
642-2252

Pacific

Zulu+9
International telephone prefix: D 315; C 82.
Passports (visas for more than 15d stay) required for dependents and retirees. Ration card needed for exchanges and commissaries. International drivers license required.

Operator Assist:
Army   D **723**-1110 (Yongsan) C 7913-1110
AF   D **784**-4110 (Osan) C 011-82-333-661
There are Army installations in addition to those shown on map to left. All have clubs and snack bars but no known Space-A quarters on a formal basis.

Buses and trains are fast, clean, inexpensive. Blue trains are excellent. RTO and TMO are in all major stations and will purchase tickets at a discount.

International ferries: From Pusan to Shimonseki, 7d, $55-90; Osaka WSa, $100-250, Kobe MF, $100-225; Hakata TTSa, $55-110. From Inch'on: To Tanjin (near Beijing), every 5 days, $100-250; Wehai MTh, $90-250; Chingttao alternate Sa, $100-300. Cheju ferry to either Pusan or Mokpo 6d/w.
China: USO has tours to China. Visa requires 1 week. Embassy in Seoul is on street just south of Main Post Office, Near Myong-dong station on Blue Line, hours 0900-1200 M-F.

1 USD = 992.615 South-Korean Won
1 South-Korean Won = 0.00100744 USD

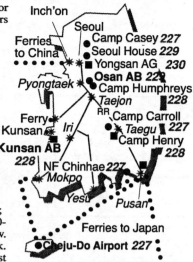

Quarters:
BQ: Availability ★★★★ numbers to right 0600-2300.
Ground Transport:
Shuttle to Camp Henry 0700-2200.

Camp Carroll
APO AP 96260
765-7822/3   0545-970-7822/3
Meals at club.

Quarters:
BQ: Casey Lodge Availability ★★★★ numbers to right 0600-2300. Rates: $30,40sgl+$10add per.
Ground Transport:
1.2m from Tong Du Choen RR station.
Golf: C 351.869.1110 D 730-4884

Camp Casey
APO AP 96224
730-4247   0351-869-4247
Meals: Club, Popeyes, Burger King.

CJU
Training and Lodge, 25m from Airport
Quarters:
BQ: ★★★★ x ★ July, Aug, ★★ Nov-Feb **3330** 0800-1700 M-F, other hrs 3305. Rates: 4-person room $6per, 2-person room $10per.
Ground Transport:
Military transport meets flights, BQ will arrange pay ($25) transport for commercial flights.

Cheju-Do Airport
APO AP 96220
763-3305   064-94-9672
→→→→→→→ Flights →→→→→→→
Osan
Chance of seat ★★★★
Flight Information:
No. above, 24h
Airevac 3005.
Reported Space-A not accepted

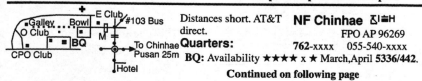

Distances short. AT&T direct.
Quarters:
BQ: Availability ★★★★ x ★ March,April **5336/442**.

NF Chinhae 실▄H
FPO AP 96269
762-xxxx   055-540-xxxx

Continued on following page

Pacific

NF Chinhae continued from preceding page

0800-1700 M-F (Supply Office). Other hrs OOD 5110.
Rates: O1-4 8per, O5 up $15per. DV $25sgl+$5add per.
E $4,6 per (no dependents}.
Commercial: Gum Gahg Hotel 0.5m from gate.

Ground Transport:
Mail truck to Hialeah 0430 xSu 5304,5803.
Commercial: #103 Bus at main gate. Taxi to bus station under $1. To Pusan RR, Express Bus to Pusan Bus Station then #201 Bus to RR.

	Break	Lunch	Dinner
O Club		7d	7d
CPO Club		7d	7d
E Club			7d
Galley	SS	SS	SS
Bowl	1000-2200		

Distances short. AT&T direct,

Quarters:
BQ: Availability ★★★★
7040/7459 24h. Rate:
$30sgl+ $5add per. DV
$40sgl+$10add per. O6 up
thru protocol 8949.
Ground Transport: Bus
outside Gate 2 to RR.

Dining(O)
To RR, AB
NCO Club
Dining(E)
Snack
Bank
Gate 2   Gate 1
BQ

Camp Henry
Taegu   APO AP 96212
768-xxxx   **053-470**-xxxx

	Break	Lunch	Dinner
NCO Club	7d	7d	7d
Dining (O)	xSu	xSu	xSu
Dining (E)	7d	7d	7d
Snack	0630-2100 M-F		
	0830-1730 SS		

Distances short.

Quarters:
BQ: Availability ★★★
7355 0800-1700 M-F,
0800-1200 Sa. Rates:
$13sgl communal,
$20,25sgl private bath, all
+$5add per.
Commercial: None close.

Water Tower
Bank
Bus
BQ
Comm
PX
Club
Burger King

Camp Humphreys
APO AP 96271
753-1110 **333-690**-1110

	Break	Lunch	Dinner	Brun
Club		M-F	Tu-Sa	Su
Burger K	0630-2200			
PX	0600-2200 M-F			
	0730-2200 SS			

Ground Transport:
Post shuttle 0600-2200. Kimpo shuttle 0530,1200 M-F. Mung Jin Bus to Osan, Yongsan, 0550-1900 M-F, 0620-1900 SS. $2.10 to Osan, 7354.

KUZ   AT&T direct.
Distances long, 1.9m BQ-Terminal. 1.4m BQ-Airport.

Kunsan AB   APO AP 96264
782-1110 011.82.63.470.1110/0100

Quarters:
BQ: Availability ★ **4604** 24h. Rates: $10sgl, DV
$16sgl, both +$5add per. Protocol 5270.
Commercial: 12m to nearest (Kunsan).

Ground Transport:
Shuttles: Base 0600-1980 M-F, 5317. Pay shuttle
(Wolf Pack Wheels) to Osan 0800 + 1800 F, $10.
Returns
1600 + 1800 SS. Tickets at Rec C 24h 3w in advance. M-F 0800 and return usually available,
weekends and holidays normally sold out, 1800 F
to Osan usually booked. However 6-8 no shows are

Ferry Terminal
Air Base Bus Route
City Hall   Kuns
Seoul Express
Red Stripe
Hotel
12m
Restaurant
BQ
Golf
E Club
BX   Rec C
        Burger King
Shop   Bank
Comm
OPS   Terminal

	Break	Lunch	Dinner	Brun
E Club	xSu	xSu	7d	Su
Burger K	1000-2200			
Restaurant	1100-2230			
Rec C	24h			
Golf	0700-Dusk			
Bowl	1100-2300 Su-Th			
	24h FSa			

Continued on next page

Kunsan AB continued from facing page

customary.

Commercial: Red/Blue Bus to Kunsan, time from Rec C 0600-2310, from City Hall 0535-2245, frequent service, W600. AAFES Taxi $20. From Kunsan: Seoul Express Bus 0600-2220, return 0600-1930, W6300 (W9500 Deluxe). To Osan or Seoul: Ferry 0620-2200, half-hrly service to Changhang, train 0730-1940. To Osan or Seoul: Red Stripe Bus to Iri 0530-2230 every 3-5 minutes, W1,100. To Taegu, Pusan, Red Stripe Bus to Taejon 0735-1920 W3,500, then train. Taxi 4318.

↦↦↦↦↦↦ Flights ↦↦↦↦↦↦

Fukuoka	Misawa MWF
Iwakuni	Osan
Kadena	Yokota MWF

Chance of seat ★★★★

Flight Information:
Terminal **4666** 0830-1730 M-F, 0800-1600 Su, other hrs recording. [Fax 5616, Passenger Terminal]. OPS 4707 24h.
KAL commercial flights to Kimpo Airport, 1200,1800, $30.

Quarters:
Annex of Osan O Club
Availability ★★★ 5 rooms for Nos. above, reservations 0700-1600.
Rate: $40,50unit.
Ground Transport:
Subway 0.8m away. Many buses.

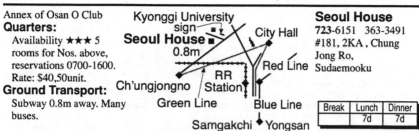

Seoul House
723-6151   363-3491
#181, 2KA , Chung
Jong Ro,
Sudaemooku

Break	Lunch	Dinner
	7d	7d

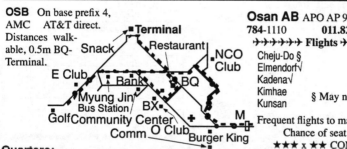

OSB On base prefix 4, AMC AT&T direct. Distances walkable, 0.5m BQ-Terminal.

Osan AB APO AP 96278   D 194
784-1110   **011.82.31.661**.1110
↦↦↦↦↦↦ Flights ↦↦↦↦↦↦

Cheju-Do §	McChord
Elmendorf√	Travis
Kadena√	Yokota√
Kimhae	
Kunsan	§ May not take Space-A

Frequent flights to many dest.
Chance of seat
★★★ x ★★ CONUS

Flight Information:
1854 0630-2100, recording other hrs. [Fax 4897, 631 AMSS/TRP Unit 2073]. Recording 6809.
Terminal open 0600-2100.

Quarters:
Turumi Lodge: Availability ★★ **1844,4597** 24h, Rates: $12per, DV $22per. O6 up thru protocol 5669. TLF $35unit.
Commercial:
Hotels outside main gate, some pick up, info 782-5213, Tours, Community Center.
Golf:
The Lakes at Osan 784-4128
Aero Club: C & D 4424
Ground Transport:
Airport Shuttle Bus: Osan to Incheon Departs Leisure Travel Services (Bldg.924) 0600, 0700, 1000, 1200, 1500, 1700 **Incheon to Osan Departs** from the USO Counter (Gate 14) See Osan Driver 0830, 1000, 1530, 1830, 2000, 2230 (If there are no delayed arrivals the bus will depart at 2230.) **Fare:** Leisure Travel: $25 Official Travel: $35 (TDY/PCS status) Contact Leisure Travel Services at 784-4254 for details.
Commercial: Myung Jin pay shuttle ($3.60) from bus station to Yongsan and ($2.10) to

Continued on following page

Pacific

RK

PACIFIC and EASTERN ASIA
KOREA (Concluded)
Osan AB continued from preceding page

Camp Humphreys, frequent service. K55 Bus W600 thru base via main gate to Pyongtaek RR. To Camp Henry: train to Taegu, To Camp Hialeah or NF Chinhae: train to Pusan. To Kunsan AB: train to Changhang then ferry to Kunsan and Red/Blue Bus to AB, train to Iri then Red Stripe Bus to Kunsan and Red/Blue Bus to AB. BX taxi 4121 0600-2330, $1.30 on base.

	Break	Lunch	Dinner	Brun
O Club		M-F	xSu	Su
NCO Club		7d	7d	
E Club	7d	M-F	7d	
Restaurant		7d	7d	
Terminal	0800-2000 M-F, -1800 SS			
Community	24h			
Golf	0600-2130			

Distances walkable, 0.6m BQ–Bus Station.

Quarters: AT&T direct.
Army Hotel: Dragon Hill Lodge: Availability ★★ D **738-2222,** C (82-2) 2071-2200 request front desk, 24h. From CONUS 01-82-2790-0016. Fax 1576. List, call, 1300, assigned 1800. Rates: E1-5 $55-100, E6-O3 $65-110, O4 up & Retirees $75-120, all +$15 add per. DV $140,160unit. Protocol 3315,8208.
Walker Center (open bay) ★★★★ x ★ exercises. **736-1047** 24h. Rate: Free.
Religious Center ★★★★ x ★ during retreats **7314,7593** 0800-1700 M-F, double-bed room, communal. Rate: $10unit.
Coiner Dorm ★ **724-8830** 0900-1800. Rates: $25sgl+$17add per, $50,60room.
Commercial: Several outside hotels with post phones. Lodge has list.

Ground Transport:
Shuttle 0610-1730. Airport shuttle 0600-1500 M-F, 0700-1900 SS. Myung Jin pay shuttle ($3.60) to Osan, continues to Camp Humphreys 0550-2100 M-F, 0700-2100 SS.
Commercial: #78 Bus to Religious Center. Blue Line subway to downtown and Seoul House. To Osan Myung Jin Bus, or train to Pyongteak then K55 Bus. To Camp Henry train to Taegu. To Camp Hialeah or NF Chinhae train to Pusan. To Kunsan, Myung Bus to Osan then Wolf Pack Wheels, or train to Changhang then ferry to Kunsan and bus to AB, or train to Iri then Red Stripe bus to Kunsan, or Seoul Express Bus (Ho Nam Express Bus Terminal) to Kunsan.

Yongsan Garrison
APO AP 96204
723-1110   **011.82.2.7913**.1110

	Break	Lunch	Dinner	Brun
Embassy		xSu	xSu	Su
Main Club		M-F	7d	SS
Oriental		7d	7d	
Lodge	7d	7d	7d	
Burger K	7d	7d	7d	
Bus	0700-2100			
Cafeteria	24h			

NEW ZEALAND

International telephone prefixes: D 315, C 64.

1 US Dollar = 1.26710 New Zealand Dollar
1 New Zealand Dollar (NZD) = 0.789204 US Dollar

Passport required for active duty not on official orders, dependents, and retirees, visa for more than 89d stay. From USA to Christchurch, New Zealand it is easier to depart from Hickam rather than from CONUS. Christchurch is not served unless there is cargo and stop is on the return from Richmond, AU.

Pacific

CHC
NAF Harwood, Antarctic Support
Quarters:
Hotels and motels close to airport with courtesy phones and pick up. More in town.
Airport Plaza Christchurch Hotel (@ Airport) PH: 64.3.358.3139
Commodore Airport Hotel (3m from Airport) PH: 64.3.358.8129
Airport Gateway Motor Lodge (5m from Airport) PH: 64.3.358.7093
Ground Transport:
Bus to town 0630-2030, 30min service.
Taxis at airport.
Recommend glass insurance be purchased when renting auto.
Airport Rentals Ltd. PH: 64.3.359.5123
Thrifty Car Rentals (@ Airport) PH: 64.3.358.7533
Budget (@ Airport) 64.3.358.7488
Hertz (@ Airport) PH: 64.3.358.6730
Avis (@ Airport) 64.3.358.9661.

Christchurch Airport
AMC Flt. Ops., PSC 467 Box 214, APO AP 96531-1034
From within NZ address: AMC Flight Ops, Private Bag 4747 Christchurch, NZ

C 011.6.43.358-1455 EX: 5069/5457 (International)
C 03.358.1455 (from within NZ, drop 03 if in CC)
After hours recorder 011.64.3.358.1455
FAX: **C** 011.64.3.358.1458

↦↦↦↦↦↦↦ **Flights** ↦↦↦↦↦↦↦

Hickam	Richmond
	Travis

Chance of seat
★ west, ★★★★ east

Flight Information:
1455 24h. [Fax 1458]. Sign up at AMC, Orchard Rd 0900-1200,1300-1700 M-F. Check in at Quantas. AMC personnel in terminal only for check in. In-flight meal not available. Check by phone, 1457, after 1700 day before flight.

Not served if no cargo, westbound flights infrequent. Only about 12 flights per year. Most missions are between Sept & March for Operation Deep Freeze.

Auckland
North Island
NEW ZEALAND
Greymouth
Stewart Island / Wellington
Christchurch
South Island

AMC Terminal, Bank
(Depart @ Counter 32)
To Christchurch 5m
Memorial Dr.

Motels ■⋅❖
Orchard Rd
Antarctic Exhibit
Gate 3
AMC Office

SINGAPORE
SGP

Johor Baharu, Malaysia
Navy Port
Zulu +8
#170 Bus
Sembawang
RSAF Paya Lebar
5m ▲ ✈
MRT RR
MRT
✈*Singapore*

Paya Lebar is not an airline airport.

Flight Information
No. above 0730-1630 on days of flights.
[Fax C 382-3614, US DOD AMC Air Movement Center, Bldg 30, Eastern Link Rd, Paya Lebar AB]. Call day ahead of flight.

1 USD = 1.38490 Singapore Dollar
1 Singapore Dollar = 0.722074 USD
Passports required, visas also for stays of more than 15d, no problem as it is easy to go to Malaysia.
International telephone prefix: C 65.

RSAF Paya Lebar
FPO AP 96534
AMC Ph **D** 315.370.2745
AMC FAX **D** 315.370.29622
C Ph (65) 280-0624
C Fax (65) 382-3614

↦↦↦↦ **Flights** ↦↦↦↦
Diego Garcia M-F   Yokota MThSa

No Cat 6 to Thailand even if seats are available because a/c goes via Utapaho Thai AB, due to no customs at base.

Chance of seat ★★★★ x ★
spring break, Christmas.

Snack	0800-1615 M-F

Pacific

Day & Zimmerman (D&Z) has a seven-year contract that began 1 Sep 2001 to operate the AMC facility. **Arriving passengers should call AMC Terminal Paya Lebar at least one day in advance** with names and passport numbers so that USAF can arrange base clearance with Singapore base security. Traveling dependent passport numbers are required! **Departing passengers are requested to give one week advance notice of departure via fax (including same information).** Passengers changing flights should give one day advance notice. [Note: NO Space-A passengers are permitted to travel TO Diego Garcia. All travelers (military and civilian) MUST be on official orders. Passengers may transit THROUGH Diego Garcia if they are manifested through by Yokota, Japan. Check with Yokota to see if they'll do this.]

Only S$ used, obtain some before arriving, especially S$1 bills. Some travelers have reported obtaining Singapore money from snack bar at Paya Lebar. Others have been unable to get it there. Singapore moving in the opposite direction from the phasing down affecting so many installations. Flights have become very regular. If heading for Kuala Lumpur or Bangkok, consider going directly to Johor Bahru and making RR or bus reservations there.

Quarters:
Billets: Availability ★★ 711-6848 0730-1630 M-F, at Navy Port, commercially operated in Sembawang Housing. Locally called Sembawang.
Commercial: Economical and good are YMCA. Rates for double with private bath: Palmer Rd $47 222-4666 (singles w/o bath), Orchard Rd 337-3444 $56US single, Strand Hotel on Bencoolen St (across the street) $40US. Stevens Rd (least convenient) 737-7755. Many hotels convenient to public transport. Particularly if continuing north consider hotels in Johor Bahru. New Mayfair Hotel (near National Museum) under $20. Several in the $20 range near the RR station and bus terminal.

Ground Transport:
The Singapore public transit system is a strong contender for best in world. Subways (MRT) and buses are fast, clean, run on time, and most-often are not crowded except rush hours. Mulitple travelers can cut cost by sharing taxi.
Buses require exact change (available at all MRT stations). There are no transfers between buses nor between MRT and buses. Transfer among MRT lines is free. The highest bus fare is S$1.60. Bus fares are paid on board, MRT tickets are obtained from machines at stations. The highest MRT fare is S$1.60. Transitlink Guide (S$1 at MRT stations) is invaluable. For taxi to AMC, Paya Lebar 254-1117, 293,5545,481-6696. Fare to Palmer Rd ≈S$10. Bus stops are outside main gate of Paya Lebar.

Singapore is an excellent gateway to eastern Asia or to round-the-world trips. Travel agents sell discounted tickets to just about anywhere. For globe circling, head for Bahrain. Even greater savings are in Malaysia and Thailand.

Suggested that travelers be prepared for heat and carry water.

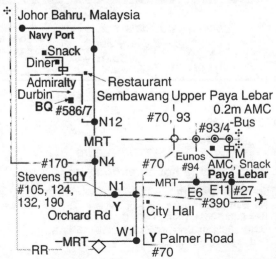

Pacific

BKK Zulu+7

Airport 10m NE of Bangkok. AT&T direct at GPO.
Passport required, visa also for more than 30d
International telephone prefix: C 66-2

Bangkok

RR
Hotel
#4, 20, 109 Buses
Rama IV
GPO Silom
Sathom Nua
Sathorn Tai
1m
Water Taxis
(buses)

Standard Chartered Bank
1.8m
Expressway
Car Rent

JUSMAG
YWCA
Budget
Hotels YMCA
King Hotel
Christian Guest
Convent Road

1 US Dollar = 31.2405 Thai Baht
1 Thai Baht = 0.0320097 USD

Bangkok Airport (Dong Muang)
JUSMAG-THAI
AMC Representative
APO AP 96546-5000
Thailand address
L 7 Santhorn-Tai, Bangkok 10102
PH: 662.287.1036 EX: 166 or 167
Cellular: 661.640.8940

➤➤➤➤➤➤➤➤ **Flights** ➤➤➤➤➤➤➤

Kadena C130 2/m
Chance of seat ★★★★

Flight Information:
0700-1600 M-F. [Fax 1027, Rm D-114].
Sign up, check in JUSMAG. Reconfirm
4d before flight. Check in 0715. Bus
from JUSMAG 150 baht. No other access to plane.

Restaurant	0600-1800 xSa

Quarters:
Commercial only: All with bath except budget.
YWCA 286-1936, $23sgl, has Hostel. YMCA
287-1900 $52sgl, excellent. Christian Guest
House 233-6303, $26sgl, breakfast. King Hotel $20sgl. Budget hotels under $10. Because
Space-A life centers on JUSMAG and all classes of hotels are nearby, there is little reason to
stay in another area with one exception: If taking an early train or commercial flight consider
staying the night before at the hotel just west of the RR station to avoid traffic jams.

Ground Transport:
Buses everywhere, cheap, but bus-stop signs are not reliable. Most buses on Rama IV take the
overpass at Sathorn. Use stop before or after overpass. Consider tours rather than self guided
except to Grand Palace and Emerald Buddha. These are directly accessed by water taxi. Water
taxis (really water buses) make many stops along river and are cheap. Most taxis metered and
so marked. Because there are only 2 planes/m to Bangkok, retirees living in Thailand tend to
return via Singapore and take the train north.

Unless intention is to visit Singapore before traveling north, consider going directly from Paya
Lebar Airport to Johor Bahru by train, Bus, RR or MR. Train is easiest particularly at the border.
There are many low-cost hotels in vicinity of bus and RR stations. It is much cheaper and more
convenient to make train reservations and purchase tickets in Johor Bahru than in Singapore. $1
= Maylay ringglt 3.78. Most of the time it is possible to make reservations day of travel but there
are periods of great demand including Christmas, Chinese New Year, and end of Ramadan. Dong
Muang RR station is a full-service station, all trains stop, at least three per hour in both directions.

Some readers prefer the bus but horror stories tell of locked lavatories and no stops (particularly
in Thailand). Trains are so inexpensive, especially in Malaysia for those over 65, why not buy
both births in a 1st-class sleeper?

Although Bangkok itself is an interesting objective, Space-A travelers use it as a low-cost base to other countries. Kula Lumpur is
far easier to reach and offers air fares almost as low as Bangkok.
The Thai Air Force will take US Space-A to destinations in Thailand. Information from JUSMAG-Thai in Bangkok.

Kuala Lumpur

RR Sambanthan
YMCA
Low-cost hotels

Bangkok continued on next page

Pacific

PACIFIC and EASTERN ASIA
THAILAND (Concluded)
Singapore-Bangkok by Train

Singapore	lv 0730	1425	2000§	2230§	0830	1140	1715
Johor Bahru	lv 0754	1448	2027	2255	Commuters to Johor		
Kuala Lumpur	ar 1350	2055	0510	0605	Horizontal line = change train		
	lv1415	2200§	0730	2030§	§ 1,2 class sleepers, ¶ 2 class only.		
Butterworth	ar 2210	0555	1410		Buy tickets in Johor. 50% discount		
	lv1340¶				for those over 65.		
Hat Yai Jn.	ar 1752			0915	In Malaysia 2nd-class coaches are excel-		
	lv 1810§	1840¶	1555¶	1705¶	lent. 1st-class sleepers are recommend-		
Bangkok	ar 1930	1035	0835	1000	ed. In Malaysia for those over 65 it is so		
					cheap consider buying both berths.		
Bangkok	lv 1330¶	1435§	1515§	1550¶			
Hat Yai Jn.	ar 0603	0634	0653	0844	Northward get enough bahts at the bor-		
	lv		0720¶	1550§	der station.		
Butterworth	ar	1240			There are express buses paralleling this		
	lv0730	1435	2200§		rail service.		
Kuala Lumpur	ar 1410	2115	0625	0545			
	lv1430	2225§	0725	2100§			
Singapore	ar 2110	0650	1340	0600			

US OUTLYING ISLANDS

Flights are available to islands listed below. Facilities are limited. Special permission may be required to visit but not necessarily to transit. Passports are not required.

NKW	Diego Garcia 370-0111	PNI	Ponape
JON	Johnston 441-3330	SPN	Saipan
KOR	Koror, Palau	TKK	Chuuk (Truk) 322-1110, request 339-1195
KWA	Kwajalein 480-1110	SWK	Wake 424-2101,2429
MDY	Midway 430-0111	YAP	Yap

RESERVIST FLIGHTS

Charleston-MacDill-Homestead-Patrick-Jacksonville-Charleston F1st 3 weekends
Charleston-Jacksonville-Patrick-Homestead-MacDill-Charleston S1st 3 weekends
Charleston-Robins-Dobbins-Pope-Charleston 1st,3d weekends.
Ft Worth-Ellington-Bergstrom-Ft Worth 4th weekend.
Ft Worth-Kirtland-Bliss-Ft Worth 3d weekend.
Ft Worth-Tinker-Tulsa-Ft Worth 1st weekend.
March-Nellis-Phoenix Airport-March twice a month.
McChord-Portland-Eugene-Fairchild 1st weekend, sometimes 2/m.
Norfolk-MacArthur Airport, LI, NY. handled by Hudson General. 516--588-2111
North Island-Davis Monthan-Phoenix-North Island 3/m. Su
North Island-Phoenix Airport-Davis Monthan-North Island 3/m. Su
Travis-Davis-Monthan-Kirtland-Travis Su.
Travis-Kirtland-Davis-Monthan-Travis F.
Whidbey Island-Portland-Whidbey Island 1st weekend FSu

Flights pick up reservists on F then return them on Su. They are particularly useful for Space-A as their days of operation are known in advance and they usually have seats particularly on the way to picking up and returning after dropping off. In some cases, particularly Navy, the plane will be provided by an installation other than the originating or terminating point listed below. In such cases the plane will go directly to the first pick-up point and will return to its home base after the last drop-off point,

This Section lists likely origins of flights **to** installations and airports shown in **bold**. Most-likely origins are checked, e.g., Travis√. Especially for bases with many flights, example Andrews, this Section can be used as a more-inclusive listing of destinations **from** than those given in details. Exceptions are Airevac flights on circular routes. Days of operation of Airevac flights and other scheduled flights are noted. CONUS NAS are likely destinations from all other CONUS NAS.

Aberdeen PG
Andrews
Bragg
Martin State

Adana
Aviano
BWI F
Dover
Izmir
Lajes
Mildenhall
Naples
BWI
Ramstein√
Sigonella√

Altus
Dover
Elmendorf
Fort Worth
Hickam
McChord
Peterson
Randolph
Travis√

Anchorage
Dobbins
Hickam
Minneapolis
Minot

Andersen
Fairchild
Grand Forks
Hickam√
Kadena√
McConnell
Minot
Travis√
Yokota√

Andrews
Adams Fld AR
Albany NY
Arnold
Atlanta
Atlanta - Fulton Co
Atlanta - Hartsfield
Barksdale
Beaufort
Belvoir
Benning
Bradley A/P CT
Bragg
Buckley
Burlington VT
Gordon
Campbell
Charleston
Cherry Point
Columbia SC
Dallas Love Fld
Davis Monthan
Dobbins
Dover
Drum
Eglin
Fort Worth
Harrisburg
Hurlburt
Jacksonville FL
Johnstown PA

Kansas City MO
Keflavik
Kelly
Kirtland
Knox
Lajes
Langley √
Las Vegas
Leavenworth
Little Rock Adams
MacDill
Maxwell √
McGhee Tyson
McGuire
Millington TN
New London
New Orleans
New River √
Norfolk √
North Island
Offutt
Orlando FL
Patrick
Patuxent
Pensacola
Peterson √
Pope √
Quonset RI
Randolph √
Redstone
Richmond VA
Robins √
Savannah
Scott √
Shaw
Sill
Stewart
Tampa FL
Tinker
Travis
Tyndall
Whidbey Island
Whiteman
Willow Grove √
Wright Pat √
Youngstown

Antigua
Ascension
Patrick

Ascension
Antigua
Charleston√
Patrick

Atlanta
Andrews
Belvoir
Fort Worth
Jacksonville √
Key West
Langley
Maxwell
Mayport
Minneapolis
New Orleans √
Norfolk √
North Island
Pensacola
Scott
Whidbey Island

Atsugi
Iwakuni
Kadena√
Misawa√
North Island
Kaneohe Bay
Wake
Yokota

Aviano
Adana
BWI
Dover
Izmir
Lajes
McGuire
Mildenhall
Naples
Ramstein√
Sigonella
Souda Bay

Bahrain
BWI
Dover
Naples
Norfolk
Rota
Sigonella

Bangkok
Kadena√
Yokota

Bangor
Augusta ME
Belvoir
Drum

Barking Sands
Hickam√

Barksdale
Andrews√
Dover
Ft Worth
Hickam
Wright-Pat

Beale
Peterson

Beaufort
Cherry Point
New River
Norfolk
Washington
Willow Grove
Yuma MC

Belvoir
Albany NY
Andrews
Bangor ME
Benning
Bradley CT
Bragg
Burlington VT
Cherry Point
Columbia SC
Concord NH
Dobbins
Drum
Eustis
Harrisburg
Holloman
Huachuca
Hunter

Knox
Lakehurst
Langley √
Leavenworth
Little Rock Adams
McGuire
New London
New River √
Norfolk √
Pickett
Pope
Quonset RI √
Raleigh-Durham
Richmond VA
Redstone
Riley
Robins
Rucker
Scott
Smyrna
Stewart
Washington √
Willow Grove √
Wilmington
Wood
Yuma PG

Benning
Andrews √
Atlanta
Beaufort √
Bragg √
Campbell √
Cherry Point
Rucker √
Dobbins
Knox √
New River
Norfolk
Pope
Wright Pat

Birmingham
Andrews
Bradley CT
Bliss
Peterson
Hood
Scott
Boise
Helena

Bragg
Aberdeen PG
Andrews
Atlanta - Hartsfield
Belvoir
Benning
Dobbins
Johnstown PA
Knox
Langley
Lewis
New River
Norfolk √
Washington
Willow Grove

Brunswick
Ft Worth
Jacksonville√
Norfolk√
North Island

Patuxent
Rota
Whidbey Island
Willow Grove

Campbell
Andrews
Beaufort
Belvoir
Benning
Charleston
Dover
Knox
McGuire
Rucker
Travis
Willow Grove
Wright Pat

Charleston
Andrews
Antigua
Ascension
Cherry Point
Dobbins
Dover√
Dyess
Homestead
Jacksonville
Keesler
Lajes
MacDill
March
McChord
McGuire
Mildenhall√
Norfolk√
Oceana
Patrick
Ramstein
Robins
Rota
Scott
Selfridge
Soto Cano
Willow Grove
Wright Pat

Charleston WV
Andrews
Charleston√
Charlotte
Pope√
Travis
Wright-Pat

Charlotte
Beaufort√
Charleston WV
Pope√
Cheju-Do
New River
Osan
Beaufort√
Charleston WV
Pope√

Cheju-Do
New River
Osan
Yokota

Cherry Point
Andrews √
Beaufort √

235

Belvoir
Charlestown
Jacksonville
Langley
McGuire
Minneapolis
New Orleans
New River √
Norfolk √
North Island
Pax River
Pope
Quantico
Scott
Washington √
Yuma MC
Cheyenne
Helena MT
Peterson √
Chievres
Andrews
Ramstein
Stuttgart
China Lake
Edwards
Fallon
Point Mugu
Christchurch
Hickam
Pago Pago
Richmond
Travis
McChord
Columbus
Corpus Christi
Andrews
Ft Worth√
Jacksonville
Los Alamitos
Mayport
Meridian
New Orleans
Norfolk
Pensacola
Willow Grove
Wright Pat
Davis Monthan
Andrews
Peterson √
Scott
Wright Pat
Daggett
Andrews
Dobbins
Yuma
Dobbins
Andrews
Charleston√
Minneapolis
Pope
Robins
Savannah
Scott
Dover
Adana
Altus
Andrews
Aviano
Bahrain
Barksdale
Campbell
Charleston√
Jackson
Kelly
March

McChord
McGuire
Mildenhall√
Norfolk
Ramstein√
Rota
Scott
Tinker
Travis√
Westover
Willow Grove
Wright Pat
Drum
Albany
Andrews
Bangor
Belvoir
Bradley
Burlington VT
Norfolk
Willow Grove
Dugway
Edwards
Hill
McChord
Travis
Dyess
Benning
Charleston
Eielson
Hickam
March
Mildenhall
Norfolk
Pope√
Travis
Edwards
Miramar
North Island
Wright Pat
Eglin
Andrews √
Dobbins
Kelly
Kirtland
Langley
Maxwell
MacDill
McConnell
New Orleans
Oklahoma City
Peterson
Quonset Pt
Randolph
Redstone
Robins
Scott √
Shaw
Wright Pat √
Eielson
Barksdale
Dyess
Elmendorf√
Fairchild
Grand Forks
Little Rock
March
Minot
El Centro
Ft Worth
Fairchild
Kingsville
Lemoore
Meridian

North Island √
Oceana
Peterson
Whidbey Island √
Elizabeth City
Gander
Ellington
Ft Worth
Ellsworth
Elmendorf
Grand Forks
MacDill
McChord
Mildenhall
Minot
Mt Home
Nellis
Offutt
Travis
Elmendorf
Altus
Eielson√ F
Kadena
Knoxville
Kodiak
Little Rock
March
McChord√ F
Osan
Travis√ F
Yokota√
Eustis
Belvoir√
Bragg
Story
Fairchild
Andersen
Eielson
Hickam
March
McChord
Mildenhall
Portland
Fallon
China Lake
Kelly
Lemoore √
Miramar
Norfolk
North Island √
Oceana
Whidbey Island √
Yuma MC
Forbes
Andrews
Hickam
McConnell
Offutt
Peterson
Riley
Fort Worth
Atsugi
Andrews√
Bliss
Brunswick
Corpus Christi√
Davis-Monthan
El Centro
Ellington
Fallon
Hood
Kelly
Kingsville
Kirtland
Miramar

New Orleans √
Norfolk
North Island
Pensacola
Randolph √
Rota
Scott
Sigonella
Tinker
Washington
Willow Grove
Wright Pat
Fukuoka
Misawa
Yokota√
Futenma
Atsugi
Iwakuni
Kaneohe Bay
Osan
Yokota
Gordon
Andrews
Norfolk
Rucker
Scott
Gowen Field
Grand Forks
Andersen
Eielson
Ellsworth
Hickam
Mildenhall
Travis√
Greely
Richardson
Wainwright
Griffiss
Grissom
CONUS ANG
Hanscom
Andrews
Burlington VT
Langley
Otis
Scott
Washington
Wright Pat √
Harrisburg
Andrews
Belvoir
Burlington VT
Pittsburgh
Willow Grove √
Hickam
Altus
Andersen
Richmond
Barking Sands
Christchurch
Dyess
Fairchild
Forbes Field
Grand Forks
Grissom
Kadena√
Kelly
Knoxville
March
McChord
McConnell
Milwaukee
Minot
Oklahoma City
Osan√

Pago Pago
Phoenix
Pittsburgh
Richmond
Rickenbacker
Salt Lake City
Travis√ W
Westover
Yokota√
Hill
Andrews
Boise
Dugway
Fairchild
Fallon
Grand Forks
Helena
Kirtland
Minot
Scott
Travis
Whidbey Island
Wright-Pat
Holloman
Belvoir
Benning
Davis Monthan
Huachuca
Peterson
Rucker
White Sands
Yuma PG
Homestead
Charleston
Jacksonville
Hood
Bliss
Carson
Corpus Christi
Fort Worth
Kelly
Peterson
Polk
Riley
Scott
Sill
Huachuca
Miramar
Peterson
St Joseph
Yuma
Hunter
Andrews
Belvoir
Key West
Redstone
Rickenbacker
Rucker
Hurlburt Field
Dyess
Little Rock
Quonset Pt
Scott
Indian Springs
Indiantown Gap
Wilmington
Irwin
Carson
March
Peterson
Riley
Iwakuni
Atsugi
Futenma
Kadena

Misawa
Osan
Sea-Tac
Yokota
Izmir
Adana√
Aviano W
Ramstein
Jackson
Andrews
Dover
Ramstein
Scott
Jacksonville
Andrews√
Atlanta√
Atsugi
Brunswick
Charleston
Cherry Point
Homestead
Keesler
Lajes
Norfolk √
Oceana
Patuxent
Pensacola
Rota
Sigonella
Washington
Whidbey Island
Willow Grove √
Jakarta
Kadena
Kadena
Andersen√
Atsugi
Bangkok
Elmendorf
Fukuoka√
Hickam√
Iwakuni
Jakarta
Kelly
Kunsan
March
Manila
Osan√
Sea-Tac
Travis√
Yokota√
Kaneohe Bay
Fort Worth
Kelly
Miramar
North Island
Yuma MC
Kansas City
Ellsworth
Kelly
Peterson
Riley
Scott
Warren
Wood
Keflavik
Andrews
Lajes
McGuire
Mildenhall
Norfolk√
Kessler
Andrews √
McGuire
New Orleans

Peterson
Randolph
Scott
Shaw
Travis√
Tyndall
Kelly
Andrews √
Barksdale
Fort Worth
Langley
Offutt
Peterson
Scott √
Wright Pat
Andrews
Cannon
Davis-Mon
Eglin
Ellsworth
Kaneohe Bay
Kansas City
Keesler
Kirtland
Laughlin
Little Rock
Luke
Maxwell
McConnell
Mildenhall
Minneapolis
Miramar
Moody
Nellis
Norfolk
Peterson
Pittsburgh
Polk
Ramstein
Riley
Scott
Sill
Tinker
Travis
Warren
Wood
Wright-Pat
Key West
Andrews
Atlanta
Bragg
Cherry Point
Corpus Christi
Ft Worth
Hunter
Mayport
Miramar
Norfolk √
North Island
Oceana
Pensacola
Peterson
Willow Grove √
Kingsley
Kingsville
Ft Worth
El Centro
Meridian
Pensacola
Kirtland
Andrews√
Eglin
Ft Worth
Hill
Offutt

Peterson
Randolph
Travis M
Wright Pat
Knox
Andrews √
Belvoir
Benning √
Capital City KY
Dobbins
Hunter
Indianapolis
Langley
Little Rock -Adams
Jefferson City MO
Langley
Leonard Wood
McCoy √
New Orleans
New River
Norfolk
Peterson
Pope
Rucker
Scott √
Smyrna
Stewart
Willow Grove
Wright Pat
Knoxville
Eglin
Elmendorf
Hickam
MacDill
Moron
Nashville
Spangdahlem
Kodiak
Elmendorf
Kunsan
Iwakuni
Kadena√
Osan√
Sea-Tac
Yokota√
Lajes
Adana
Andrews MF
Brunswick
BWI
Charleston
Jacksonville
Keflavik
McGuire√
Mildenhall√
Norfolk
Ramstein
Rota√
Sigonella
Lakehurst
Belvoir
Drum
Stewart
Langley
Andrews √
Atlanta
Belvoir √
Bliss
Charleston
Cherry Point
Eglin
Hanscom
Knox
Leavenworth
Maxwel

New River
Norfolk √
Offutt
Peterson
Pope
Randolph
Riley
Scott √
Shaw
Tyndall
Wright-Pat
Laughlin
Leavenworth
Andrews
Belvoir√
Carson
Knox
Langley
Peterson
Scott
Sill
Leonard Wood
Wright Pat
Lemoore
Fallon √
Fort Worth √
Miramar
Norfolk
North Island √
Whidbey Island
Yuma MC
Leonard Wood
Belvoir
Forbes
Knox
Scott
Lewis
Cheyenne
Helena
Reno
Spokane
Whidbey Island
Yakima √
Lincoln
Little Rock
Eielson
Elmendorf
Hurlburt
MacDill
McChord
Nashville
Patrick
Pope
Los Alamitos
Fresno
Miramar
North Island
Phoenix
Mather
Yuma
Los Angeles
Andrews
Peterson
Louisville
Andrews
Belvoir
Charleston
Offutt
Luke
North Island
Mac Dill
Andrews
Belvoir
Bragg
Charleston

Dobbins
Eglin
Langley
Little Rock
Maxwell
New River
Pittsburgh
Pope
Scott
Washington
Wright Pat
Malmstrom
Mansfield
March
Andersen
Barksdale
Charleston
Dover
Elmendorf√
Hickam√
Kadena
Mather
Minot
Travis√
Martinsburg
St Croix
Maxwell
Andrews√
Bragg
Dobbins
Langley
MacDill
Randolph
Rucker
Tyndall
Wright-Pat
Mayport
Atlanta N
Corpus Christi
Key West
Norfolk√
Oceana
Pensacola
McChord
Altus
Andrews
Benning
Charleston
Christchurch
Dover√
Dugway
Eielson
Elmendorf√
Fairchild
Gowen Field
Hickam
Little Rock
March
Minneapolis
Niagara Falls
Osan
Pago Pago
Portland
Richmond AU
Scott
Tinker
Travis
Whidbey Island
Yokota√
McConnell
Andersen
Elision
Grand Forks
Hickam
Mildenhall

237

Minot
Robins
McCoy
Ankeny IA
Indianapolis
Knox
Lansing MI
Little Rock Adams
Madison - Truax
Offutt
Quad Cities IL
St Paul - Holman
Scott
Springfield IL
Wright Pat
McGee-Tyson
Andrews
Beaufort
Cherry Point
Little Rock Adams
Smyrna
McGuire
Albany NY
Andrews √
Belvoir √
BWI
Charleston√
Cherry Point
Dover
Keflavik
Lajes√
Lansing MI
Mildenhall√
Naples
Norfolk√
Pope
Ramstein
Rota
Scott √
Travis
Willow Grove
Wright Pat
Memphis
Meridian A
Meridian N
El Centro
Corpus Christi
Ft Worth
Kingsville
Norfolk
North Island
Pensacola√
Mildenhall
Adana
Aviano
BWI
Charleston√
Dover√
Dyess
Fairchild
Grand Forks
Keflavik
Kelly
Lajes√
McConnell
McGuire√
Milwaukee
Naples
Pease
Ramstein√
Rickenbacker
Rota
Souda Bay
Stuttgart
Travis

Milwaukee
Hickam
Minneapolis
Anchorage
Andrews
Atlanta
Cherry Point
Chicago O'Hara
Dobbins
Kelly√
McChord
Norfolk
North Island
Robins
Travis
Whidbey Island
Willow Grove
Minot
Andersen
Eglin
Eielson
Ellsworth
Hickam
March
Mildenhall
Miramar
Pendleton √
Edwards √
Fallon
Fresno
Jacksonville
Kaneohe
Key West
Lemoore
Long Beach
Mather
Nellis
North Island
Pendleton √
Peterson
Point Mugu
Travis
29 Palms
Whidbey Island
Yuma √
Misawa
Atsugi√
Fukuoka
Iwakuni
Sea-Tac
Yokota√
Mobile
Moffett
Andrews
Mather
Moody
Moron
Knoxville
Lajes
Rota
Travis
Mt Home
Fairchild
Naples
Adana
Aviano
Bahrain
McGuire
Mildenhall
Norfolk
Olbia
Ramstein
Rota√
Sigonella√
Souda Bay

Stuttgart
Nashville
Knoxville
Little Rock
Nellis
Scott
Tyndall
Nellis
Davis-Monthan
Dyess
Fallon
Kelly
Kirtland
March
Nashville
Phoenix
Point Mugu
Scott√
Travis
New Orleans
Andrews√
Atlanta
Corpus Christi
Ellington
Ft Worth√
Maxwell
Norfolk
North Island
Pensacola√
Peterson
Randolph
Scott
Stafford VA
Washington
New River
Andrews √
Beaufort
Benning
Belvoir√
Charleston
Cherry Point √
Boston - Logan √
Knox
Langley
New Orleans
Norfolk √
Pax River
Pope
Quantico
Washington √
Niagara Falls
MacDill
McChord
Pope
Travis
Norfolk
Andrews √
Atlanta
Atsugi
Bahrain
Beaufort
Belvoir √
Bragg √
Brunswick
BWI
Charleston
Columbia SC
Dobbins
Dothan AL
Drum
Ft Worth
Knox
New London
Jacksonville√
Jacksonville FL

Keesler
Keflavik
Key West
Langley √
Lemoore
March
Mayport
McGuire
Meridian
Naples
Nellis
New Orleans
New River √
North Island
Palm Beach FL
Patuxent
Pensacola
Peterson
Pope
Richmond VA
Rota
Schenectady NY
Scott
Sigonella
Washington √
Whidbey Island √
Willow Grove
Wright Pat
North Island
Andrews
Atsugi
Beaufort
Davis-Monthan
Pendleton
Edwards
El Centro √
Fallon √
Ft Worth√
Fresno √
Kaneohe
Langley √
Los Alamitos
Las Vegas
Lemoore√
Meridian
Minneapolis
Miramar
Monterey
Nellis
New Orleans
Norfolk
Oceana
Phoenix
Peterson √
Point Mugu √
Rota
San Clemente
Sigonella
Travis
29 Palms
Washington
Widbey Island √
Willow Grove
Yuma √
Oceana
Atlanta √
Charleston
Cherry Point
El Centro
Fallon
Jacksonville
Key West √
Mayport
Norfolk
North Island √

Pensacola
Whidbey Island
Willow Grove √
Offutt
Andrews √
Ankeny IA
Buckley
Cheyenne
Ellsworth
Forbes
Grand Forks
Hill
Kirtland
Kelly
Langley
Maxwell
McConnell
Mildenhall
Minot
McGhee Tyson
Norfolk
Peterson √
Randolph √
Scott
Tyndall
Vandenberg
Wright Pat
Oklahoma City
Eglin
Hickam
St Croix
Travis
Olbia
Aviano M
Naples M
Ramstein M
Sigonella M
Osan
Cheju-Do
Elmendorf
Hickam√
Iwakuni
Kadena√
Kelly
Kunsan
McChord
Sea-Tac
Travis√
Yokota√
Otis
Andrews
Barnes MA
Hanscom
Little Rock Adams
Savannah GA
Pago Pago
Christchurch
Hickam√
McChord
Richmond
Travis
Patrick
Andrews√
Antigua
Ascension
Charleston√
Little Rock
McGuire
Willow Grove
Wilmington
Patuxent River
Andrews√
Brunswick
Cherry Point
Jacksonville

Destinations

New River
Norfolk
Willow Grove
Pease
Pendleton
March
Miramar
North Island
Point Mugu
29 Palms
Yuma √
Pensacola
Andrews √
Beaufort
Cherry Point
Corpus Christi√
Ft Worth
Jacksonville
Key West
Kingsville
Mayport
Meridian
Miramar
New Orleans
Oceana
Norfolk
Rucker
Scott
Washington
Whidbey Island
Willow Grove
Wright Pat
Peoria
Peterson
Alexandria LA
Andrews √
Bliss
Buckley √
Eglin
Helena
Hood
Irwin
Kelly
Kirtland
Lewis
Long Beach
Los Angeles
Las Vegas
Miramar
Maxwell
Norman OK
Oceana √
Offutt
Phoenix
Randolph √
Hood
Salt Lake City
San Antonio
Scott √
Travis
Tucson
Vandenberg
Warren
Wright Pat √
Phoenix
Andrews
Davis-Monthan
Hickam
Huachuca
March
Nellis
North Island
Peterson
Point Mugu
Travis

Pittsburgh
Hickam
Kelly
MacDill
Pope
Westover
Point Mugu
China Lake
Elmendorf
Hickam
Kelly
Miramar
Nellis
North Island
Pendleton
Phoenix
Polk
Hood
Randolph
Pope
Andrews √
Belvoir
Benning
Charlotte
Cherry Point
Dobbins
Dyess
Hurlburt
Keesler√
Langley
Little Rock
MacDill
McGuire
Niagara Falls
New River
Norfolk
Pittsburgh
Raleigh-Durham
Robins
Rucker
Scott
Sill
Travis
Portland
Fairchild
McChord
Whidbey Island
Providence
Quantico
Beaufort
Cherry Point √
New River √
St Croix
Washington √
Quonset
Albany
Andrews
Belvoir
Bradley
Bragg
Brunswick
Eglin
Hurlburt
Norfolk
St Croix
Scott
Washington
Ramstein
Adana√
Amman
Andrews √
Aviano
Charleston
Chievres
Dover√

Izmir
Kelly
Lajes
McGuire
Mildenhall√
Naples
Rota
Sigonella
Souda Bay
Spangdahlem
Stuttgart
Tel Aviv
Tinker
Travis
Randolph
Andrews √
Eglin
Fort Worth √
Keesler
Kirtland
Langley
Maxwell
New Orleans √
Offutt
Peterson √
Polk
San Antonio
Scott √
Sheppard
Tyndall
Vance
Wright Pat √
Redstone
Andrews
Benning
Hunter
Wright-Pat
Richardson
Greely
Wainwright
Richmond AU
Hickam
McChord
Pago Pago
Travis
Rickenbacker
Akron-Canton
Hickam
Indianapolis
La Crosse WI
Little Rock Adams
Mildenhall
Toledo OH
Dulles √
Riley
Belvoir√
Carson
Hood
Irwin
Langley
Sill
Robins
Andrews √
Beaufort
Belvoir
Charleston
Dobbins √
Knox
Langley
McConnell
Mildenhall
Minneapolis
Pope
Scott √
Shaw

Willow Grove
Wright Pat √
Youngstown
Rota
Aviano
Bahrain
Charleston
Dover
Jacksonville
Lajes
McGuire
Mildenhall
Moron
Naples√
Norfolk√
Olbia
Ramstein
Sigonella√
Willow Grove
Rucker
Atlanta Hartsfield
Campbell
Belvoir
Benning √
Bragg
Hood
Hunter
Knox
Pope
Salt Lake City
Hickam
Savannah
Andrews
Atlanta
Campbell
Dobbins
Hurlburt √
Knox
Mildenhall
Otis
Scott√
Wright-Pat
Schenectady
Scott
Little Rock Adams
Andrews √
Benning
Bliss
Charleston √
Cherry Point
Columbus OH √
Dallas Love
Davis Monthan
Belvoir
Dobbins
Eglin
Fort Worth
Knox
Grand Forks
Hanscom
Hurlburt
Jefferson City MO
Kansas City MO
Kelly
Langley √
Leavenworth
Lincoln
MacDill
Maxwell √
McConnell
McGuire √
Nellis √
New Orleans
Norfolk
Offutt √

Panama City FL √
Peterson √
Pope
Randolph √
Richmond
Robins
San Antonio
Sill
McCoy √
Tinker √
Washington √
Willow Grove
Wright Pat √
Sea-Tac
Iwakuni
Kadena
Kunsan
Misawa
Osan
Yokota
Selfridge
Charleston
Norfolk√
Scott√
Willow Grove
Yuma MC
Seymour J
Shaw
Andrews √
Burlington VT √
Cherry Point
Washington
Wright Pat
Sheppard
Andrews
Keesler
Peterson
Randolph
Sigonella
Adana√
Aviano
Bahrain
BWI
Lajes
Naples√
Norfolk
Olbia
Ramstein
Rota√
Souda Bay
Tel Aviv
Sill
Bragg
Carson
Cherry Pt
Hood
Keesler
Leavenworth
Norman OK
Norfolk
Peterson
Riley
Singapore
Yokota
Andersen
Soto Cano
Charleston
Tegucigalpa
Souda Bay
Aviano
Mildenhall
Naples
Ramstein
Sigonella

Destinations

S America	Christchurch	Little Rock	Miramar	Travis	Patuxent
Charleston	Davis-Mon	Lewis	North Island	**Whidbey Island**	Pensacola
Spangdahlem	Dover√	Los Alamitos	Nellis	Andrews	Pope
CONUS ANG	Dugway	March	Offutt	Atlanta	Rota
St Croix	Fairchild	Mather	Peterson	Beaufort √	Scott √
Martinsburg	Fallon	McChord	Travis√	Brunswick	Sigonella
Norfolk	Grand Forks	McConnell	**Volk**	El Centro √	**Wilmington**
Oklahoma C	Hickam√	Mildenhall	**Wainwright**	Fallon √	Indiantown Gap
Quonset P	Kadena√	Minneapolis	Greely	Hill	McGuire
St Thomas	Kelly M	Miramar	Richardson	Jacksonville	Patrick
Oklahoma C	Kirtland	Moron	Warfield	Lemoore	**Wright-Pat**
Quonset P	Little Rock	Niagara Falls	Aberdeen	Lewis	Andrews√
St Thomas	Malmstrom	Norfolk	Charleston	McChord	Barksdale
Warfield	March	North Island	Little Rock Adams	Miramar	Charleston
St Joseph	McChord Sa	Peterson √	Scott	Nellis √	Dover
Huachuca	McConnell	Scott√	St Croix	Norfolk √	Eglin
St Thomas	Mildenhall	Offutt	St Thomas	North Island √	Hanscom
St Croix	Minneapolis	Oklahoma City	Warren	Pensacola	Kelly
Warfield	Minot	Osan√	**Washington**	Portland	Kirtland
Stewart	Moron	Peterson √	Andrews	Whiteman	Langley√
Suffolk	Niagara Falls	Pope	Beaufort	Jefferson City MO	Maxwell
Lajes	Norfolk M	Ramstein	Belvoir √	Scott	Peterson
Albany	Offutt	Richmond	Bragg	**White Sands**	Randolph
Andrews	Oklahoma City	Scott√	Burlington VT	Holloman	Redstone
Belvoir	Osan√	Tinker	Cherry Point	Yuma PG	Scott
Lakehurst	Peterson	Vandenberg	Gordon	**Whiteman**	Travis
Quonset	Pope	Westover	Hanscom	**Whiting Field**	**Yokota**
Story	Ramstein	Whidbey Island	Jacksonville FL	**Willow Grove**	Andersen√
Eustis	Richmond	Yokota√	Jacksonville NC	Andrews √	Cheju-Do
Stuttgart	Scott MSa	**Tyndall**	Langley √	Atsugi	Elmendorf√
Chievres	Tinker	Keesler	MacDill	Beaufort √	Fukuoka
Mildenhall	Vandenberg	Nashville	Millington	Belvoir √	Hickam√
Naples	Westover	Shaw	New Orleans	Bragg √	Iwakuni√
Ramstein	Whidbey Islan	Randolph	New River √	Brunswick	Kadena√
Syracuse	Yokota√	Andrews √	Norfolk √	Chicago -	Kelly 1-3/m
Tel Aviv	**29 Palms**	Langley √	North Island	Waukegan	Kunsan
Ramstein	Altus	Offutt	Pensacola	Corpus Christi	McChord
Sigonella	Andersen√	Peterson	Peterson	Drum	Misawa
Tinker	Andrews √	Randolph	Quantico	Ft Worth	Nagasaki
Andrews	Bliss	Hood	Quanset	Harrisburg √	Osan√
Randolph	Charleston	Scott	Richmond	Jacksonville	Sea-Tac
Scott	Davis-Monthan	St Augustine FL	Shaw	Key West	Travis√
Wright Pat	Dover√	Willow Grove	Willow Grove √	Lajes	**Youngstown**
Travis	Dugway	Wright Pat	Wright Pat √	Langley √	Andrews√
Travis	Fallon	**Vance**	**Westover**	McGuire	Oklahoma City
Altus	Fresno √	Randolph	Dover	Millington	Quonset P
Andersen√	Hickam√	**Vandenberg**	Hickam	Norfolk √	
Andrews Sa	Kadena√	Edwards	Niagara Falls	North Island	
Bliss	Kelly	Los Alamitos	Pittsburgh	Oceana √	
Charleston	Kirtland	March	Ramstein	Patrick	

Unaccompanied Dependents of Deployed Military Members

Unaccompanied dependents of deployed military members, including Reserve and Guard personnel, when the deployment order is for at least 120 consecutive days, are authorized to travel space-available, unaccompanied in Category IV. This includes Navy personnel assigned to a deployed ship with Permanent Change of Station orders. This authorization is only valid for the duration of the deployment period of the military member.

Space-A travel is authorized to/from CONUS and OCONUS locations, between CONUS locations, and within/between OCONUS theaters. All travel will be on a noninterference (nonreimbursable) basis.

Eligible dependents may sign-up for Space-A travel no earlier than 10 days prior to the military member's deployment. In addition, dependents are eligible to commence travel effective on the first day of military member's deployment. Space-A travel must be complete by the last day of the military member's deployment.

Eligible dependents must present to the air terminal personnel a verification letter signed by the member's commander verifying the member's deployment. The documentation must be in the dependents' possession during travel.

Non-Command Sponsored Dependent Travel

Non-command sponsored dependents of active duty members serving unaccompanied permanent change of station (PCS) overseas tours may travel as Space-A Cat III accompanied, Cat V unaccompanied to and from the members overseas tour location. Dependents restrictions on CONUS to CONUS is enforced.

Combatant commanders are responsible for deciding their participation in this Space-A travel initiative, length of stay, limits on number of trips allowed, and any other stipulations deemed necessary. Diego Garcia and Korea do not participate in this initiative.

Travel is in accordance with DOD 4515.13-R (Air Transportation Eligibility) Chapter 6.

Prior written approval must be obtained from the installation commander or their designee. Dependents must provide to the Air Terminal a copy of the approval letter signed by the active duty member's unit commander. At a minimum, the letter must include the sponsor's name/rank and the approved unaccompanied PCS tour location, sponsor's contact information, dependent name(s), and current residence information, the length of stay authorized, and the time frame for which the approval letter is valid. Additionally, required travel documents (passport, visa, etc.) and sponsors must ensure dependents have sufficient funds to pay for commercial transportation if space-a transportation becomes unavailable. Dependents under age 18 must be accompanied by an eligible parent or guardian. If dependents are traveling on a non-U.S. passport be sure to check with terminal staff prior to anticipating space available travel.

Category	Priority	Principal Group
I	A	Active Duty and dependents on emergency leave, those in lower categories who have been upgraded, to Category I, Active Duty dependents with family emergencies. Some with Space required option.
II	B	Active Duty and accompanied dependents on Environmental and Morale Leave (EML).
III	C	Ordinary leave and accompanied dependents. Medal of Honor.
IV	D	Unaccompanied dependents of deployed members including reserve and guard when deployed at least 120 consecutive days. Unaccompanied dependents on EML.
V	E	Unaccompanied dependents to and from members PCS overseas tour location. Unaccompanied students. Permissive TDY. Unaccompanied dependents abroad.
VI	F	Retirees and accompanied dependents. 1. Reservist, National Guard. 2. U.S. Territory. Advanced ROTC. 3. CONUS only.

1. Those not drawing pension require letter of elegibility and are limited to U.S. territories, no dependents.
2. Completed DD Form 1853 required. (Form available on web site Links page.)
3. Letter of authorization from ROTC professor required.

A APPENDIX A, SPACE-A FLIGHTS

Space-A Flight Eligibility

Those eligible to travel Space-A are divided into Categories as shown in table on the preceding page. Each Category corresponds to a Priority Letter used on AMC Terminal computer printouts (alone or as first letter). DOD Directive 4515.13R gives complete details.

Those drawing 100% disability VA pension or dependents without a sponsor, e.g., widows, cannot travel Space-A. Dependents of active duty can travel within CONUS. Such dependents can travel without sponsor between CONUS and outside CONUS and between outside CONUS points when on a command-sponsored overseas assignment. Travelers stationed overseas must have a letter signed by the sponsor's CO verifying command sponsorship. Dependents under 18 cannot travel unaccompanied.

Overview of Procedures

Sign-Up and Show

First action toward taking a Space-A flight is to "sign-up". At bases not following AMC (Air Mobility Command) procedures, this may be for a specific flight. In many non-AMC cases sign-up must be done in person but some installations will place on list by phone. At installations following AMC procedures sign-up can be done in person and often by Fax, E-mail, web sites, or mail. AMC sign-up establishes a date-time controlling priority within category for 60 days to any destination on any flight. The 60 days cannot be extended but a new sign-up can replace an old to obtain a later expiration date. It is prudent to sign-up early although most of the time everyone waiting gets a seat.

At a time specified for a given flight (show time) those signed up and present are selected (to the limit of available seats) according to categories and positions on sign-up list. Rank plays no part. If would-be Pax do not respond when called, they must wait until the entire list is finished and restarted. It pays to be at least one to two hours early as posted show time can be advanced without warning and need for additional time to clear security screening. Always make a check as late as feasible for an early-morning show.

Check In and Boarding

At non-AMC installations baggage check and other matters may be handled at the same location as show, boarding passes often are not issued, and boarding is informal. At AMC terminals, once selected the normal procedure is to go to a luggage check-in point where bags other than carry-on are checked, money for meals (if desired) and other charges taken, and a boarding pass issued. Never leave the terminal once this is accomplished; boarding time can be advanced.

AMC Sign-Up Procedure

For an originating point:

In person:

If Space-A counter is manned, in most cases data is entered directly into the computer. Information necessary: Sponsor's name, rank, SSN, branch of service, category, number of seats required. If there are accompanying dependents, their names and SSN.

Dependents need not be present at sign-up. Destinations desired (up to 5, one should be "All"). ID(s) and, when required, passports, visas, and country clearances. Active duty must present leave or other orders. On-leave sign-up cannot be prior to date leave is effective. Reserve, NG, retirees not yet drawing pension, and ROTC must submit the data listed under the diagram on page 241. Date-time will be assigned when data is entered. Date is Julian (days of year numbered consecutively, e.g., Feb 28 is day 59). Sign-up is good until 2400 on the 60th day following date-time or until leave expires. If a call starts before 2400 on last day, sign-up is valid for that entire call. In the past some bases considered date of sign-up as the first of 60, others started day following.

Once signed up, sponsor is given a sign-up sheet containing as a minimum the date-time but often complete sign-up data. Retain this sheet for submission at show time and to carry forward initial date-time through intermediate points. If not given such a sheet to keep, try to get one. Keep all paperwork including boarding passes until reaching final destination.

Some bases maintain a self-service sign-up. This consists of an automatic time-date stamp, a supply of forms or blank paper, and a place to put completed sheets. Forms call for the necessary information. If paper is blank, supply data given above. Stamp and sign the sheet keeping a copy. In most cases self-service is available at all times when the terminal is open. It may be accessible even when terminal is closed. When Space-A counter is crowded, using self-service can save time.

Remote Sign-Up

Many bases with AMC procedures accept sign-up by Fax, Web Site, E-mail, or mail. Information so submitted is identical to that required for in-person sign-up and now includes Social Security Number of each person. Internet sign-up links are available at spaceatravel.com. Remotes must be signed before being sent. Date-time is when a request is processed at the terminal. **For other than retirees drawing pension, copies of any required orders, DD Form 1853, or letters must be transmitted with the sign-up request.** Once posted by the terminal a remote sign-up becomes identical to an in-person sign-up. It is possible to check that a remote sign-up has been received by calling the terminal to which it was sent. Some bases, even ones not accepting remotes, will send Fax remotes at no charge if possible by DSN. Keep a copy of a Fax. Many bases will accept the copy should the original not be received. When submitting request via Internet carry a dated printout with you.

It is convenient for retirees to print post cards with the necessary information as indicated below. Emphasize last name. Hopefully this

---

Maximum 4.25"

Space-A Travel Remote Sign Up

Name: **Jones,** John P.
        Last
SSN: 000-00-0000

Address: Street, Apartment Number
         City, State, ZIP Code

Grade: E7   Retired, Cat-VI, Navy

Number of seats required: 2

Destinations:
1.   All   2. CONUS   3.
4.   5.

Dependent name(s):   Maria Jones
Dependent SSN: 000-00-0000

All necessary travel documents are on hand.
Dependent traveling on Mexican passport

Signature: _____

Maximum 6"

---

will prevent having name entered backward. For added insurance print return address and the bold label on the reverse side of the card. Carry some of these cards on trips. One use is to drop a remote off on departure to establish a new date-time in the event return is via that base and no carry-forward date-time is on hand.

Active Duty on leave cannot sign-up before leave is effective so, to obtain best-possible position on the list, Fax requests just after midnight beginning day leave starts. In contrast retirees can mail their requests well in advance of the proposed trip. Keep in mind sign-up must still be valid if carried forward to an intermediate stop. It is prudent to allow sufficient days of validity for reasonable contingencies. For example, for a 30d visit abroad, mail outward requests 30d in advance and return requests just before departing outbound. Either in-person or remote request is for a one-way trip from originating point to furthest selected destination.

Remote requests can be sent to as many bases as desired. Consider sending a request to every likely starting point (outward and return) as well as those where a layover or change of direction is possible.

For an Intermediate Point:

Immediately upon arrival take all sign-up sheets and boarding passes so far used on the trip to obtain a new sign-up. Assure original date-time is carried forward. If the flight is continuing but not toward your final direction, your manifested destination must the intermediate point or a new sign-up date-time may be required. Regulations are clear that departure toward final destination must be on first available flight. So far heavy-traffic bases have not enforced this requirement. As a precaution Fax, E-mail, or mail a remote to key intermediate points in case the originating base denies it received the Fax or letter or if the intermediate base considers your trip is being broken by a layover. If date-time of a remote is earlier than that carried forward, it can be used instead. Note the turnaround point is not an intermediate point; it is the final destination. Original sign-up date-time is purged on turn around.

Some travelers have reported problems with terminals claiming their trip had terminated and a new sign-up was required. In general date-time carry-forward appears to be applied liberally but things at time of writing were still muddy on this point. What is clear is, if manifested on a flight, when a traveler leaves the manifest by choice to take another plane, a new sign-up is required.

Once manifested from an intermediate or originating point, existing date-time for all directions of travel is eliminated but some terminals, e.g. Hickam, Kadena, and Yokota, permit a new in-person sign-up to be made after boarding pass is issued. Others, e.g. Travis, do not allow this. If such sign-up is useful but cannot be made in person, drop a mail remote off before leaving.

There is no list in this Handbook of Fax numbers, Internet addresses (available at spaceatravel. com), or special mail addresses of all installations or airports to which remote requests can be sent. Rather Fax numbers are in the details of each base offering such sign-up and appear following the main flight-information telephone number: [Fax: XXXX]. Unless otherwise specified the Fax number is combined with the DSN or commercial prefixes of the base and the mail address combined with that of the base. Internet Sign-Up is available on our Web Site. For mail it is advisable to write in large letters on the address side of the envelope or post card "Remote Sign-Up".

Terminating base does not have to be AMC. Carry forward starts at the first AMC base. For example a trip starting at Luke to Scott and on to Europe would carry forward date-time from the Scott sign-up as Luke does not follow AMC procedures. Date-time is carried forward by a sign-up sheet from originating or intermediate AMC bases or by manifest of arriving flight. It should also be on the boarding pass but in the past this was not the case at all bases. It is important that Pax arriving at an intermediate AMC base go immediately to the Space-A counter and obtain a new sign-up sheet (check that the original date-time is on the new sheet). This applies even if arriving at one of paired installations. It is advisable to carry all sign-up sheets through to final destination.

In the case when remote sign-ups were sent to two AMC bases and the trip starts at one then passes through the other, the traveler has the option at the second base of either carrying forward the starting date-time or using the date-time of the intermediate stop.

Not resolved at the printing was what happens if a trip involves transferring between two non-paired bases, for example a trip from Travis (final destination Europe) to McGuire then Greyhound to Dover to resume the trip. Somewhat similar is a trip from Travis to Scott with the intention of continuing east from Scott but being bumped at Peterson. Travis date-time would not be accepted at Peterson. The traveler proceeds by the next available flight eastward to an AMC base. Would that base accept the date-time from the Travis sheet? Travis terminal says yes but readers reports will be awaited on experiences with this type of flight. At date of publication this whole area of trips other than routine AMC was fraught with unknowns. As information comes in from those actually traveling in such a manner, their experiences will be reported in Space-A Travel Update.

Many AMC terminals post daily computer printouts showing standings of all signed up. There are variations among terminals but the figure shows information appearing in one form or another. It indicates that 119 Space-A seats have been requested ahead of Col Smith for Italy and 209 for Spain. The second line for Maj Jones shows he added Spain to selected destinations on day 35 at 0741. Specifying destination "all" eliminates the need to add or change destinations.

Check printout day after sign-up to assure entry is proper. Number showing position on list is of little significance as many sign-up with no intention of showing soon. At Hickam number to CONUS is often over 2,000 but typically it is possible to leave any selected day. As a general rule all Cat-VI go or no Cat-VI goes. Although position on list is not important most of the time, it is prudent to get on list early.

Non-AMC Procedures

The majority of installations offering Space-A flight opportunities do not follow AMC sign-up procedures. These include some major installations handling many Pax such as NAS North Island. As far as is known all assign seats according to categories. At those maintaining a list it is for a specific flight. Some allow being on more than one list. Many accept only in-person sign-up. A few will list by phone. Few accept remote sign-up, apparently not carry-forward of date-time either. Some start lists only on the day of the flight, those arriving before that time keep track of their order of arrival and enter list accordingly. Keeping track of arrival order is the rule when no list is established prior to show time. At installations handling only occasional Pax, there may be no sign-up as such, a would-be passenger waits at a place designated until crew arrives. It is up to Pax to enquire what procedure is being used.

Show Time

To be assigned a seat on a desired flight based

Name	Grade	Priority	Seats	Date-Time	Destinations
SMITH,J	COL	R	4	32 1214	IT 120 SP 210
JONES,T	MAJ	R	1	32 1304	IT 124
≡≡≡					
JONES,T	MAJ	R	1	35 0741	SP 234

on date-time or order on a list sponsor must be present at "show time", usually called "show". This may be as simple as waiting at a designated place starting no later than a specified time. Show time is often 1.5 to 3 hours before departure time depending on terminal and type of plane. It pays to be present at least 30 minutes before time posted as show time can be advanced without warning. Show for a previously unposted flight may be immediately after flight is known. Show times can be advanced or delayed. It is good practice to check for a change in show time, in particular a late check for an early-morning flight. At Scott habitually posted show times for Airevac flights are very early, but changed to a later time before flights are called.

With AMC procedures, at show time names are called in order of category and date-time within category until available seats are filled. If there are ample seats, call may be omitted. The same is true if names had been entered on a list. Should a Pax not respond when applicable date-time or name is called (regardless of category) that passenger must wait until all further down have been served and call restarted. If arriving too late to sign-up before call has started (including Pax manifested to the base in question and wishing to be remanifested), should seats remain after all on list have been served seats will be offered to those not signed up (or not signed up to destination of flight). In the case of Airevac some installations treat those off the plane and those previously waiting as a single group and select on the basis of category and date-time. Others place those off the plane behind those waiting. When seats remain, most terminals will accept Pax up to the time plane is loading, particularly if passenger has no baggage to check. Some small terminals have been known to accept a single passenger after plane was loaded and ready to taxi out. If not selected for desired flight, remain in terminal until plane has left. It is not unusual for more seats to be offered. When arrival time at intermediate stop is after show time of a desired continuing flight but ahead of departure time, request plane crew to radio ahead and ask if paperwork can be completed to enable quick transfer. Traveling without checked baggage greatly facilitates such rapid transfers.

At large terminals selected travelers proceed to another counter (usually) where boarding passes (if used) are issued, money for meals (if available and desired) and, sometimes for overseas flights involving commercial airports customs or other fees (check OK with the exception of some foreign departure fees). Generally luggage must be checked at this time. Not having baggage readily available is risky. Once selected, do not leave terminal before boarding plane. Planes can be boarded when crew is ready regardless of posted boarding times.

When selected for a flight, sponsor's name will be removed from priority list for all destinations regardless of direction of flight. If flight is delayed, sponsor may have the choice of remaining on the manifest or leaving it to try for another plane. Check carefully before doing so as this can result in losing carry-forward date-time.

Category-VI travelers (often called Cat-VI), have problems when higher priorities come filling every plane. Arriving at a terminal determine quickly if flights are leaving without taking all higher priorities . Should there be a back up, find out how long travelers have been waiting and if they are pressing for any flight or just making show times for scheduled flights. If higher priorities overflow all flights, there is no practical alternative for a Cat-VI other than selecting another route or continuing to visit the local area. When there is not an overflow of higher priorities actually in the terminal at all times, a Cat-VI has a reasonable chance, even in the summer, of moving when many seats are available during a short period or when an unexpected flight appears.

Bumping

Space-A passengers may be bumped due to load, weather, dangerous cargo, space-required, etc., but one Space-A passenger will not be bumped for another Space-A passenger regardless of category (with the exception of funded emergency cases). When required, those with most-recent sign-up times in lowest-priority category are bumped first. Bumped passengers are entitled to original sign-up date-time when placed on list for continuing flight. Assure this is accomplished. There is no entitlement to original sign-up date-time at non-AMC procedure intermediate stops to which passenger is manifested. Bumping is infrequent but its possibility should be considered when transiting bases with a heavy space-required demand or bases with low probability of continuing flights.

Passports and Visas

Error on the side of having passports and visas unnecessarily. There is wrong advice travelers do not need them due to status of forces agreements, transiting, or stays of short duration. Even if visas are not necessary when transiting,

Space-A travelers can always be bumped. Get multiple-entry visa if at all possible and assure that visa is good for entering via military base, the latter apparently not a difficulty today. Of all avoidable Space-A travel problems, the worst is being without a valid visa when such is required. Whether visas are needed is noted in details of installations or airports requiring them. Also assure passports are stamped in and out when that is required. **Upon entering Israel immediately specify passport should not be stamped.**

Luggage

On large planes AMC permits each Space-A traveler two pieces of checked luggage with a maximum combined weight of 140 lbs (no excess allowed, usually interpreted to mean a maximum of 70 lbs each piece) and maximum dimensions each piece of 62" combined width, length, and depth; plus one carry-on which will fit under a seat. Navy may restrict checked luggage to 40 lbs and carry-on to 10 lbs. The 10 lb restriction has been applied regularly at some NAS. Over 30 lbs combined weight of all luggage may exclude T39, C12, or C21 flights. There are great advantages in holding luggage to a carry-on. The most-frequent contributor to this Handbook makes three or four Space-A trips a year with durations up to two months, total weight 18 lbs in a small pack carry-on.

Put all essentials (particularly prescription medicines) in carry-ons. It may be necessary to do without checked luggage for weeks. Prescriptions should be in their original containers, not mixed together (customs regulations). Packs are better than grips of any type including bags with straps as considerable walking may be required. Because planes can be cold, a warm coat also serving as a rain coat is desirable. A lightweight air mattress comes in handy when it is necessary to sleep in a terminal and may be used on planes when there is room. Regulations state there is no passenger access to checked luggage during flight.

Reserve and Air National Guard Flights

At AMC bases Reserve (Res) and ANG flights are the same as other flights but there may be useful training flights which do not appear on terminal board. Often Res and ANG flights are known well in advance by units. This permits definite plans for the start of a Space-A trip. Known ANG and Res units offering Space-A are listed in details of installations.

Another form of Res flights, called Reservist flights, are those which take Reservists to their weekend training sites. Such flights start and return to base providing plane on F and Su one, two, or three times a month. These flights are very useful to Space-A travelers as they are scheduled well in advance and virtually always take everyone waiting. Known Reservist flights are listed Æ234. For Navy reservist flights an NAS other than the one to which the reservists are being taken may supply the plane so it will originate at that NAS and return to it.

P3 Flights

P3 (sub hunter) flights do not take dependents but are otherwise very useful. Although P3 flights sometimes appear on terminal boards, more often it is necessary to contact patrol squadrons separately. At NAS with more than one squadron, one is designated as host squadron. It will know of any transient P3 flights but it is often necessary to contact each of the home squadrons to learn of their flights. Terminal or OPS can supply P3 phone numbers and such numbers are given in details of installations.

Upgrade to Category I

If an emergency arises at home during a Space-A trip, Active duty should contact home unit to request orders upgrading them to Category I. Retirees should request Red Cross to verify emergency then request upgrade from installation CO or CO's representative. It is essential that report state immediate presence is required. Authority for such upgrading is in Chapter 4, paragraph 4-3, DOD Regulation 4515.13R.

Common Avoidable Problems

Tight Schedules

Such schedules are incompatible with Space-A travel but not impossible. If starting time can be set to coincide with departure of a plane from a base with excellent availability of seats, outward travel by Space-A is feasible even for tightest of schedules. Travelers with must-return dates should be prepared to continue commercially. Many installations offering flights have a **SATO** (Scheduled Airlines Ticket Office). SATO can provide information about commercial flights, make reservations, and sell tickets. In a few cases SATO offices are open whenever there is a large incoming flight but most operate limited hours. Within CONUS call 800-872-7286 if local SATO office is closed or nonexistent. Abroad discounted tickets often are available thru travel agents at prices far less than at SATO. Keep in mind experienced travelers taking what the system gives and having information about alternative routes seldom encounter significant delays using Space-A flights. The most-frequent contributor to this Handbook has taken many must-arrive-by trips since 1982 and only once switched to commercial.

Preselected Itineraries

Insisting on a specific route such as returning to CONUS from Germany can result in days of waiting which could be avoided by going via Rota. A sad example occurred in 1995. A retiree went to Hickam to catch a flight to Australia and awaited a direct flight meanwhile passing up several flights to Pago Pago because he feared getting stuck there. He gave up and returned to Travis. However Samoans get off westward flights at Pago Pago consequently it is easy to get to Australia from there.

High-Demand Periods

For those taking two or less trips per year it is easy to avoid rush seasons. England is great in Oct or Nov but difficult earlier. Unless constrained, say by wanting to see the midnight sun, stay away from July to October, especially to Europe, the far east, and Alaska. Nevertheless these broad peaks do not block Cat-VI. Just more care is required to keep moving. It is the short peaks such as spring break and Christmas that can completely bar routes, for example to Singapore.

Driving to Starting Base

Driving to a base to start a Space-A trip by air requires a return to that base, convenient or not. A retired couple from NJ driving to Travis for a flight to Hawaii could not effectively use a Hickam to McGuire flight on returning. By contrast, if a traveler must return to the starting base in any event, there is no problem caused by driving to that base.

Loss of Documentation

Difficulties caused by loss or theft can be minimized by carrying in a money belt copies of retirement order, marriage certificate, front and back of ID, first page of passport, and a second credit card.

Lack of Information

The most-prevalent avoidable problem is traveling without up-to-date and complete information. You have the best, also the most-current, information available at the spring of 2006 but nothing is more certain than change. Keep your copy of the Handbook up to the moment by sending in any changes you may note.

Getting There Quickly and Easily

For overseas flights, particularly in summer, avoid, if practical, bases with regularly scheduled flights, e.g., Dover, as these are used extensively by space-required and high-priority Space-A. This applies particularly to retirees as they can be blocked indefinitely should active duty or Cat-V stream in but it also applies to active duty. Cat-III (ordinary leave) can move up the priority list and eventually go as there are not enough Cat-I and Cat II to block them but it may take days. Nevertheless, if Cat-III go where Cat-VI find it easy, they will be out on the first flight. Flight Destinations, Æ235-240 lists many possibilities for reaching desired destinations.

Send remote sign-ups as early as practical to every base which could be useful for starting out or for coming back. There are times, even midsummer, when difficult bases such as Charleston move everyone every day. But do not go there unless it is known such is the case or it is convenient to stop by and check on the way elsewhere. For example, if driving south anyway, stop at McGuire or Dover, maybe you will get out. Use DSN or cell phone to find a base away from the high-priority rush having a flight. It is easy to determine if Cat-VI are moving. That is the key question to ask even for active duty. At the worst of times, difficult bases are seldom backed up on all routes. It is almost-always possible to reach a point on the southern route in Europe, say Sigonella or Rota. The impact of Cat-V in the summer on that route is not yet known. Retirees with dependents should consider bases with tankers or ANG as dependents can fly from them to outside CONUS without having to get to the coast.

Take what the system gives. Board first available flight in a useful direction. That is nicer, later flight may be cancelled, release zero seats, or get filled. Transferring to a base with quarters from one without makes life easier. It is necessary to avoid going to a base where continuing flights are unlikely without knowing there is a suitable flight out; but going to a base with a reputation for good access to flights is the right way of playing the odds. When anxious to move and all viable routes are blocked, haunt terminal or OPS. Flights appear with no advance notice. Keep luggage at hand. It may be necessary to run for a flight. At bases with ANG, Res, or Navy, check with them. It is not unusual to find flights which never appear on the terminal board and unknown at OPS until too late. Watch for activity. Ask those appearing to be passengers about their flights. There may be a seat available unknown to the terminal. Look at the field for Space-A type planes. If there are any, find out when and to where they are going. Contact every available source of information, not just the terminal. When learning of, or just suspecting, a useful unposted flight, contact its crew.

If return may be via the same base within 60d, when possible sign-up for a return flight and proceed forward either by another base or on a flight which will not remove name from list. An example of the former is to sign-up at Rhein-Main and depart from Ramstein, of the latter sign-up at Mildenhall and depart by an in-country Navy flight. Another possibility is to drop off a mail remote just before leaving. When manifested through an intermediate stop it is usually possible to sign-up for return as manifests are not checked against the list. Some bases using AMC procedures allow another sign-up after boarding pass is issued.

APPENDIX B, SPACE-A QUARTERS

There are no priorities for Space-A quarters except as established by sign-in time when lists exist. In general BOQ and BEQ cannot be reserved other than by active duty on PCS or TDY. Nevertheless AF policy is Space-A can make a tentative reservation day before, with some permitting up to three days advance reservation with a credit card. BOQ and BEQ offices are designated **BOQ** and **BEQ** respectively. Offices serving both **O** and **E** are designated **BQ**. Guest houses, Hostess Houses, Navy Lodges, and the like often can be reserved by those on leave and by retirees as can Recreation Areas (Rec A). Special reservation information is given in installation details. For most CONUS Navy Lodges early reservations are made via **800-628-9466** (800-Navy Inn), from Europe D **565-2027**. Outside US territory Lodges could not be so reserved although the

stated intention is to extend this service to all Navy Lodges. In CONUS the lodges at Fallon and El Centro also are excluded. For last-minute arrival use local number given in details. Active duty and reservists on orders can reserve up to 60d in advance, all others up to 30d.

Army central reservation number, **1.800.462.7691** (800-GO-ARMY-1), from Germany 0130-81-7065, from Italy 168-70555, from Korea 077-811-893-0828. These numbers do not include NG. Primarily for active duty but some posts will handle retirees.

AF Central Reservation for CONUS and Hickam: **1.888.235.6343** (888-AF-LODGE) After prompt dial first three digits of base name.

Navy Lodge Central Reservation: **1.800.628.9466** (1-800-NAVY-INN).

Military accommodations are listed directly under **Quarters:**. Quarters data are in following order: 1: Expected availability by stars, ★ = 0-25%, ★★ = 25-50%, ★★★ = 50-75%, ★★★★ = 75-100%. This is the same star system used to show expected availability of seats on planes but flight categories do not apply to quarters. 2: Front-desk phone number. 3: Hours phone is answered. 4: Charges per night in the form $8per ($8 per person), $8sgl, $12dbl ($8 single, $12 double), $25unit ($25 for room, cabin), +$5add per (plus $5 for each additional person). Rates are rounded to nearest dollar.

Unless otherwise specified, quarters are available for all ranks and for dependents. Restrictions are noted, e.g., (no dependents). Number of rooms not given as 5 rooms with a demand for 1 are better than 50 rooms with a demand for 100. If feasible, go to the lodging office rather than call. It is easier to say 'no' over the phone. Unfortunately there are many installations, particularly those with flights, which do not give out all available quarters to Space-A preferring to turn away travelers in order to hold empty rooms 'just in case'. AF policy is that Space A can call the day ahead and receive a (credit card) confirmed reservation on available rooms. Rooms not held for confirmed reservations will be given out when ready.

DV quarters (usually O6 and up) may be available only thru protocol. If so, details say 'O6 up thru protocol'. Call protocol. If it cannot be reached, call billeting and ask them to contact protocol. Should DV quarters be available directly from billeting, details still give protocol numbers. It is best to contact protocol first. If protocol does not handle Space-A billets, its number does not appear or there is a note.

Military quarters appear in the following order: BOQ, BEQ (BQ, CBQ, CBH if combined), TLF, Guest House, Navy Lodge, Army Hotel, Rec A suitable for overnight accommodations or with RV or tent sites. See Æ93, 263-265 for more information on RV and tent.

If, in addition to military quarters or RV and tent facilities, hotels, guest houses, and the like are nearby or on shuttle or bus route, that information follows under the heading **Commercial:** (this heading omitted if no military quarters exist). Rates for commercial generally are not noted. Exceptions are when they are unusually expensive or inexpensive, when no military quarters are available and low-cost commercial facilities exist , or when lower-cost or more convenient commercial are available than on-installation quarters.

TLA (Temporary Living Allowance) apartments exist, notably Hawaii. As these cater to the military, they are convenient to use. Lodging offices and terminals often have lists of such facilities, also of motels offering military discounts, and, in some areas, of B&B (Bed & Breakfast).

Meals

Dining facilities are shown by meal diagrams in installation details. See Æix for diagram explanation. In the past many dining halls and galleys would not accept Space-A, particularly retirees, or applied a large surcharge.

Clubs serving meals are always included. They honor memberships in other Clubs but may deny service or impose a surcharge to those not members of any club. If all meals are covered by facilities on diagram, other meal facilities may exist.

Number of Rooms Versus Availability

This Handbook has always reported on the availability of quarters, RV spaces, etc., not on their number as 10 rooms with a demand for 5 are better than 50 rooms with a demand for 100. Nevertheless one reader insisted the number of rooms should be reported as then he could tell whether of not he could get in. He was asked if there were two bases each with 50 rooms but one had a demand for 80 and the other a demand for 30, in which one he most-likely would find an available room.

APPENDIX C, TRANSPORT

The best-kept secret at many passenger terminals is availability of low-cost commercial transportation and military shuttles. Indeed enquiry often leads to denial that transport exists when it does but more often to incomplete or erroneous information. To a large extent this is due to Space-A travelers being willing to jump into a taxi rather than attempting to use low-cost or free transport. True, taxis are convenient but so is commercial air. It seems pointless to save money by using Space-A air then dissipate that saving on taxis. Consequently under **Ground Transport:** installation details report all known free or low-cost transport in the following order, each with hours operated and phone numbers: • On-installation shuttles (free unless otherwise indicated). • Interinstallation shuttles (free unless otherwise indicated). • Hospital shuttles (✚ **Shuttle** in details). • Other military transport. Following **Commercial:** are bus, RR, limo, car rent, and last taxi. Generally omitted here as not being ground transport is Army air.

On-Installation Shuttle

All known on-installation shuttles are noted even if of no significant help to travelers. When known, times of first and last runs are given. Shuttle routes are shown on map if such is useful, shuttle stops may be, ✚ (combined Bus,

Shuttle stop ✤). Special information is noted, e.g., at North Island, "Red route to Terminal".

Inter-installation and Off-Installation

All known inter-installation and off-installation shuttles are noted even of no significant help to travelers. When there are more than three runs per day, time of first and last runs are given, for three or less, time of each run. When a network of shuttles exist, a transport diagram is provided. Off-installation shuttles primarily interconnect installations or go to nearest town or airport. Particularly useful are Marine Shuttles on Okinawa. They connect most installations on the island and offer a zero-cost sight-seeing tour.

Hospital Shuttle

✚ Shuttles operate from an outlying installation to a major hospital. In some cases major hospital knows schedules of these shuttles, others have no knowledge. Some desire Space-A travelers to sign up at the hospital but at most travelers just board shuttles. Most outlying hospitals (clinics etc.) know the shuttles serving them, some require

Appendix

signing up for a seat. At others the shuttle simply pulls up to its stop and boards those waiting, the hospital not knowing if it came. If difficult to get precise information at hospital, check with originating motor pool.

Couriers

When installations are relatively close as in England and Germany, couriers may operate between them. Some are scheduled, most are not. Check with Motor Pool for couriers or unscheduled transport. Enquire if there is some other office which controls couriers.

Bus and RR

Buses and, to a lesser extent, RR serve many installations. They are very economical compared to taxis. Retirees with Medicare cards ride virtually free (sometimes free) in many areas. Where buses or trains serving an installation are infrequent, stopping times are given. Intercity bus info **800-231-2222**. Do not overlook Amtrac when arriving at Andrews and going toward New York. It is cheaper and usually quicker than taking a commercial flight (**800-USA-RAIL**). Unless trains are frequent, schedules serving installations are given. When significant, bus stops are shown on maps as ❖ (combined bus-shuttle stop as ✚).

Airline 800 Numbers

Aero California	800.237.6225	Delta (domestic)	800.221.1212	(domestic)	800.225.2525
Aero Mexico	800.237.6639	(international)	800.241.4141	(international)	800.447.4747
Airtran	800.247.8726	Gulf	800.553.2824	Philippine	800.435.9725
America West	800.235.9292	Frontier	800.432.1359	Qantas	800.227.4500
American	800.443.7300	Iberia	800.772.4642	Scandinavian	800.221.2350
Austrian	800.843.0002	Japan	800.525.3663	Southwest	800.435.9792
British	800.247.9297	KLM (see Northwest/KLM)		Sun Country	800.752.1218
BWIA	800.538.2942	Korean	800.438.5000	SwissAir	800.221.4750
Canadian	800.426.7000	Lufthansa	800.645.3880	Thai	800.426.5204
Cathay Pacific	800.233.2742	Mexicana	800.531.7923	TWA	800.221.2000
China	800.227.5118	Midwest Exprs.	800.452.2022	USAir	800.428.4322
Continental	800.525.0280	Northwest/KLM		United	800.241.6522

Car Rent

Many Space-A travelers use rental cars. On-installation car rent is shown on maps and local phone numbers are given. References to agencies known to attempt forcing unwanted insurance carry note 'watch forcing insurance'.

Car Rental 800 Numbers

Advantage	800.777.5500	Kemwel Holiday Auto	800.678.0678 •
* Alamo	800.327.9633	*** National	800.227.7368
*** Avis	800.831.2847	RentAWreck	800.535.1391
** Budget	800.527.0700	* Thrifty	800.367.2277
** Dollar	800.800.4000	• US # Reported best price in Germany	
••** Enterprise	800.325.8007		
*** Hertz	800.654.3131	•• Watch for forcing insurance	

Composite Travelers' Rating
*** Excellent
** OK
* Leaser

CONSIDER PURCHASING TRAVEL INSURANCE
It Can Save Your Life!

APPENDIX D, MINIMIZING EXPENSES D

Space-A travel is so economical compared to commercial travel that some disregard possibilities of minimizing expense. This Appendix is for those to whom cost is important. It is also for those who regard Space-A as a fascinating game in which winning or losing is determined not only by rapidity of travel but also by money spent.

Taxis and Transport Choices

Taxis are a major expense almost always avoidable. This is covered in Appendix C preceding. Sometimes a choice is available among shuttles and commercial transit. Coming in to McGuire heading for New York City it costs several times more to take a limo than the #317 Bus. Even two rail routes can be different. Arriving at Willow Grove heading for NYC, taking SEPTA to Trenton then NJ Transit rather than Amtrak saves more than half. One thing which works quite well when going from an installation is to get to the main gate and ask the guard to help get a ride. Obviously all these money-saving expedients work better as weight of luggage decreases. Indeed heavy luggage eliminates many cost-savings entirely.

Airport and Customs Fees

These fees may be avoided by using military planes and military installations.

Quarters

Available quarters range from free to well over $60sgl. Navy, AF, and Coast Guard are usually considerably less than Marine and especially Army. TLF, Guest Houses, and particularly Army Hotels are more expensive than BOQ-, BEQ-type quarters on the same installations. When there is a choice, as on a POV trip or when installations are close together, use DSN to determine most economical selection. When no quarters are available, check possibilities of getting to an installation with them before opting for commercial. For example Rhein-Main rarely had available lodging but many different quarters were reachable by shuttle. Staying in quarters usually is less expensive, nicer, and more convenient that using commercial accommodations but not always, a major reason for including rates starting with the Fifth Edition. For example, driving by El Paso on I10 in 1992, a good motel room with convenient access to the Interstate could be had at Van Horn for ≈$15sgl. The Army Hotel at Ft Bliss charged ≈$25sgl.

Rental Cars

Rates for rental cars vary widely. Exchange-franchised agencies tend to be economical but not necessarily lowest. It is best to shop around, particularly abroad. Car-rent numbers are given in installations details but this does not guarantee they are the most-economical available although, if known (in particular from reader reports), that determines numbers to be listed when there is a choice. Frequent reports indicate it is cheaper to reserve a car calling a company's US number than to rent the same car abroad.

A saving not to be overlooked are credit cards which insure if all coverage by agencies is refused. This is significant as rental agencies vastly overcharge for insurance. Beware, some agencies, particularly if a renter has no viable alternative, will refuse to rent a car unless overpriced insurance is purchased thereby voiding all coverage by the credit-card company. Sometimes this disreputable practice is applied independently by local agencies but it seems to be overall company policy by some. Many agencies of Enterprise, also Mildenhire in England, were reported to be forcing insurance in this manner. Some credit-card companies have discontinued covering car-rental insurance. Even when so covered the general practice seems to be the renter must pay for any damage then recover it from the card issuer. Particularly abroad a traveler may wish to avoid hassles by buying the overpriced insurance but that should be the choice of the renter, not dictated by rental companies.

Another ploy to avoid is the fuel purchase option permitting a car to be brought back portant. Luggage small enough to fit on lap or under seat permits buses in Hawaii to be used. Beginning travelers especially tend to take far too much luggage. As a practical example, the following is a list of everything carried in or on a skiing pack by a frequent Space-A traveler for making trips up to 1.5 months long. On pack: trench coat with extra liner; plastic poncho; gloves and knit hat in pockets of trench coat, jacket. In pack: 2 pajamas, 3 trousers, 5 shirts, 3 pairs of socks, 2 handkerchiefs, 2 underwear tops, 5 bottoms, slippers, toilet articles, alarm clock, magnifying glass, original copies of all precriptions, emergency towel and wash cloth, toilet paper, spare glasses and pens, medical adhesive tape (the universal repair material), a copy of this book, maps and money for countries to be visited, medicines. Weight of pack without trench coat 18 pounds.

Although travel light is the most-common advice sent in, for this edition a reader challenged the

Appendix

251

APPENDIX D, MINIMIZING EXPENSES (Concluded)

above contending at age 70 he needed to carry more. This contention was put to the 80-year-old traveler referenced above who replied he knew he could get along with less but saw no point in that in the past but, with advancing years, 18 pounds has become too much. Weight will be reduced for future trips.

Be Patient

Do not jump for a commercial flight unless up tight against a must-return date. Explore alternative routes and position yourself to take advantage of unexpected flights. Many a tale is told of those giving up and going commercial only to find others with patience arriving at the same time or even earlier.

Low-cost Air Fares

Abroad, when necessary or desirable to take commercial air, shop around. The range of prices is great. In late 1994 at Singapore one way to Bahrain was quoted from $600 to $1200. **Almost always quotes from SATO abroad can be beaten.**

When commercial air is included, as by a retiree flying around the world, go for low-cost countries. For example Bangkok to Bahrain quotes ranged from $380 to $700. Buy through tickets when there is a planned stop over, e.g., Bangkok-India-Bahrain. Use trains to bridge between flights, e.g., Bangkok-New Delhi, Punjab Mail to Agra (Taj Mahal), Punjab Mail to Bombay-Bahrain.

In India (and most such countries) rail fares are so low that trying to save additional money by traveling lower than 1st class is questionable. Although a few readers have written they prefer buses to trains, many horror stories have reported long rides without rest stops with the on-board lavatory locked.

APPENDIX E, AIREVAC (MEDIVAC)

Specially equipped C9 AIREVAC A/C & missions have retired. Now medical transportation is provided on an as need basis. Commonly used aircraft within CONUS are C17, C130, and C135.

Flights may stop, remain overnight, or over fly normal destinations. Common cross country destinations from Andrews are Scott, Peterson, Miramar, Travis, and McChord. Miramar is commoning reached on the return from Travis. C17 aircraft depart their home base, start AIREVAC missions at Andrews, fly to Ramstein AB, Germany and return with mission passengers and commonly carry space available travelers. Aircraft then return to their respective home base.

APPENDIX F, NAVY SHIPS

There is no Space-A travel as such on Navy ships. Nevertheless there are opportunities. One possibility is a formal cruise arranged by the Navy, often in conjunction with an organization such as the Navy League. A second is on invitation by a member of the ship's complement. Both require advance planning and formal action. The remaining possibility is to request passage of the ship's commander. This requires locating a ship with a suitable destination and determining if there is available space sufficiently in advance of sailing to obtain permission and prepare the necessary papers.

Prior to 1990 about three reports were received of retirees traveling on Navy ships. None were firsthand and none were detailed. Since then only rumors have been heard. This is not to say such travel cannot be done or even that it is difficult but clearly it is not widespread. If any reader can supply definite information, it will go out in the first-available Space-A Travel Update.

APPENDIX G, TELEPHONE

There are two types of telephone numbers included in this Handbook: 1. DSN (Defense Switched Network, D), the primary telephone link between most military installations. 2. Commercial, C.

DSN (Previously called Autovon, in Europe ETS)

When dialing between major areas DSN numbers are preceded by a 3-digit international prefix, e.g., 312 for CONUS. Out of CONUS prefixes

APPENDIX G, TELEPHONE (Concluded)   G

are given at head of country or island listing. Next (or first if no international prefix is needed as when dialing between two points in the same major area) is the DSN prefix for the particular installation or airport in **bold**, commonly 3 digits, then the extension, commonly 4 digits. When an installation or airport has DSN, its main DSN number is to the left under installation name. When there is an operator assist the main number will for the operator and, should there be room, the word Operator will appear in the details. Should there be a common DSN operator assist for several installations that assist number may appear in heading for the area. For example, C & DSN 449.7110 is the Operator Assistance number for all military listings on the island of Oahu, HI. [NOTE: You must use 449.7110 for *Directory Assistance* with either DSN or Commercial for all military listings in Hawaii.] More commonly the regular DSN operator for an installation may serve as DSN operator (& directory) assist for one or more other installations. In such cases the common assist number appears as the main number directly under the address and the installation providing the operator name. If the operator is at a different installation, that installation will be named.

In most cases for direct dialing to the desired extension on the called installation, the DSN prefix given in the operator assist number is dialed followed by the extension number. Should a prefix other than that of the operator be required for direct in dialing, that prefix will be given either directly under the operator number (485-xxxx, xxxx representing extension number), or with the extension, the latter when there

Commercial

Commercial numbers are given to the right or below DSN numbers or, when necessary for clarity, preceded by **C**. The same technique as described above for DSN applies to commercial. International country prefixes are given at the heading of country or island listing. If part of the commercial operator-assist number is used together with the extension for direct in dialing, that part is in **bold**, e.g., **081-568-0021** for Naples. Commercial-only extensions (preceded by C) often can be reached thru DSN assist **When calling from abroad to USA, arrange to pay in the US. It is cheaper.** Most US long-distance carriers have access codes which reach an operator in the US directly instead of using foreign operators. With a phone card it is often possible to dial directly to phone desired. More convenient are dedicated phones at many installations going directly to the US. Because most such phones on installations are by AT&T, 'AT&T direct' is used as a symbol in installation details to indicate direct access to a US operator but such service may also be available via other US companies.

Telephone Rates

When planning your trip compare carrier rates and taxes for calls between countries. Rates within foreign countries and between countries vary. Check telephone credit cards and be sure their rates outside CONUS are what you want.

If possible, assure that billing will be done from the US. **Toll free information calls by dialing 1.800.373.3411**

APPENDIX H, O6 UP & E9

To keep Handbook size small, special information pertaining only to O6 and up is limited to protocol numbers and rates for DV (Distinguished Visitor) quarters when such exist. Nevertheless it was called to the attention of the publisher in 1988 that some O6 and up traveling Space-A for the first time were not aware of facilities available to them. Starting with the 3rd Edition this Appendix was added. At installations were DV applies to other than O6 and up, the difference is noted, e.g., O7 and up or O5 and up. If DV quarters are not being used by the designated ranks, many installations will release them to lower ranks.

Special Category Lounges

Most installations with significant flights have a special-category lounge (may have another name such as DV Lounge) available, usually in terminal or OPS but sometimes elsewhere. Many of these lounges are kept locked when not in use. Either a key will be supplied or the lounge unlocked upon request. Most are available for use by O6 or up, active or retired, but some do not accept retirees and Navy at Andrews requires Flag rank. Luggage may be left in the majority of

253

DV lounges but Rhein-Main only permits hand carried. Although most lounges are open when the buildings they are in are open, some are not. Lounges are particularly useful when they are in buildings open when terminal is closed. Enquire of OPS or Terminal. Permission may be granted for use by lower ranks. Unauthorized travelers using a DV lounge run the risk of being placed on the Space-A blacklist.

Protocol

Most large installations have a protocol office. The protocol extension is probably the most-regularly changed phone number. At small installations this task is often handled as an extra duty. At Navy stations frequently the secretary of the CO serves this function. In most cases protocol is not open 24h, the most-prominent exception being when handled by the SDO. Protocol may have quarters directly under its control are not available from the lodging office. Should arrival be outside protocol hours, it may be necessary to make advance arrangements as the lodging office frequently cannot give out protocol-controlled quarters even if unoccupied. At other installations lodging offices handle DV suites when protocol is closed. At AFCENT all officer quarters are controlled by protocol. At some installations as noted in details O6 up must go through protocol when that office is open rather than apply directly to the lodging office (noted as 'O-6 up thru protocol'). At others lodging will contact protocol. At still others, Hickam for example, protocol is not involved with quarters for Space-A. Some protocol offices do not handle retirees. When such limitations are known, they appear in the details of the installations involved. Protocol numbers are given in details but, in general, the lodging office can provide the protocol telephone number or will contact them. When quarters will

be available but assigned later at a stated hour, protocol often can release a lodging earlier. At some installations protocol will handle O5. On installations with one or more major commands there may be a separate protocol office for each command as well as for the installation itself. It appears best to contact the installation protocol first.

Because some LTC refer to themselves as Col, it simplifies matters when contacting either protocol or lodging for a Col to say O6 rather than Col.

In general protocol cannot make reservations for Space-A travelers but often they can assist. Plane crews may be able to radio ahead to request quarters. As a rule, it is best to try protocol first.

Flights

As a matter of routine, obtaining a seat on a Space-A flight has nothing to do with rank. Once selected for a seat, O6 up may be provided some amenities. Among these are being informed personally that the flight is ready to board (do not rely on such notification), being first onto or off of the plane, and radioing ahead to make arrangements.

Duty Driver

At installations where duty drivers are not available on a regular basis, they may be provided to O6 and up including retirees. This is particularly true at Navy.

E9 Protocol

Some facilities now provide protocol lodging and access to DV lounges to personel in paygrade E9. This is reflected within listing.

APPENDIX I, STATE, COUNTRY ABBREVIATIONS

Standard US Post Office 2-letter codes are used for states. Below are 2-letter codes for countries, islands, and territories as used in this Handbook.

AI	Azores	BZ	Belize	GR	Greece	JA	Japan	SA	Saudi Arabia
AN	Antigua	CH	Chile	GT	Guatemala	JM	Jamaica	SG	Singapore
AG	Argentina	CL	Columbia	GU	Guam	JO	Jordan	SP	Spain
AU	Australia	CN	Canada	HA	Haiti	NT	Netherlands	TH	Thailand
BA	Bahrain	CS	Costa Rica	HO	Honduras	NZ	New Zealand	TU	Turkey
BE	Belgium	DR	Dominican R	IC	Iceland	PE	Peru	UG	Uruguay
BH	Bahamas	EC	Ecuador	IE	Indonesia	PG	Paraguay	UK	United Kingdom
BO	Bolivia	ES	El Salvador	IS	Israel	PN	Panama	US	United States
BR	Brazil	GE	Germany	IT	Italy	PR	Puerto Rico	VE	Venezuela
						RK	Korea	VI	Virgin Islands

APPENDIX J, SPACE-A MILITARY PLANES J

Below are common aircraft offering Space-A seats. Maximum Pax numbers are nominal only. There are variations among different models of the same type. The number of seats offered depends on many factors including cargo, duty Pax, weather, and length of mission.

Cargo and Passenger Planes

C5   High-wing, 4 fan jets, 73 reclining seats in main passenger compartment on upper deck. There are a few more seats behind cockpit which are sometimes used.

C9   Low-wing, 2 jets DC9 airline-type seats. Navy transports equipped to carry a variable number of cargo pallets, up to 100 Pax.

C12   Low-wing, 2 turboprops, 7 Pax, 30lb baggage limit may be imposed.

C17   High-wing, 4 jets, Pax depending on configuration. Uncomfortable seats.

C20   Low-wing, 2 jets, 24 Pax, 30lb baggage limit may be imposed.

C21   Low-wing, 2 jets, 7 Pax, 30lb baggage limit may be imposed.

C22   Boeing 727.

C23   High-wing, 2 turboprops, usually equipped with 6 Pax seats which are folded up if there are 3 cargo pallets.

C26   Low-wing, s turboprops 10-14 passenger seats.

C40   Boeing 737 2 jet up to 130 passenger seats.

C121   Low-wing, 2 jet, 6 Pax.

C123   High-wing, 2 turboprops, troop seats, probably no longer carrying Space-A.

C130   High-wing, 4 turboprops, poor lavatory except for latest model, troop seats, up to 60 Pax nominally.

Tankers

KC10   Low-wing, 3 fan jets, tanker version of DC10, reclining seats. Max Pax depends upon seats installed.

KC130   Marine tanker version of C130, no dependents, no Pax on refueling mission, troop seats, Pax depends on load, 20 nominal. AF HC130 similar.

KC135   Low-wing, 4 jet, tanker version of 707, troop seats, Pax depends on load, 20 nominal.

Miscellaneous

P3   Antisubmarine patrol plane, low-wing, 4 turboprop, no dependents, up to 10 Pax.

T39   Low-wing, 2 jet, 7 Pax, 30lb baggage limit may be imposed.

T43   Low-wing, 2 jet, 60 Pax.

U21   Low-wing, 2 props, 4 Pax.

APPENDIX K, PERSONAL FUNDS

Space-A travelers have means of obtaining funds not available to those traveling commercially. For members of any club, clubs usually will cash checks to a specified limit, often $50 to $200, abroad in either foreign or US currency. Clubs frequently will exchange currencies. Banks on installations normally honor checks but abroad there may be restrictions on use of banks by retirees. Facilities such as exchanges may cash checks of amounts greater than costs of purchases.

For those who travel extensively and may not be home to pay bills on time, a credit card which draws directly on a checking account is extremely convenient. Such cards are often called debit cards. Not all companies offer them. Those that do may not offer them in every state. Debit cards frequently are issued with nominal limits too low to cover contingencies. For a single traveler $1,500 appears to be sufficient and can be arranged. Because of problems in reporting loss of a credit card, it is recommended that only two (with different expiration dates) be carried, one for convenient access, another in a money belt. One can be a combined credit-phone card such as the AT&T Universal card. For travel abroad, choose a card widely accepted such as Visa.

Money belts are advisable not only for an extra credit card but also for passport when it is not in constant use, cash, and, for retirees, a copy of retirement orders and, when appropriate, marriage certificate. The latter are needed to obtain a replacement ID. Possibly not legal, a copy of front and back of ID and of first page of passport in the money belt could prove invaluable.

Many travelers find it more convenient to draw cash (usually in the currency of the country) from time to time rather than bothering with travelers checks. It is always convenient, often all-but-vital, to have some native currency on arrival (coins as well as bills). Therefore holding a reasonable amount of foreign currency rather than exchanging all when leaving a country to which return is likely should be considered. The most-frequent contributor to this Handbook maintains two sacks of money, one for the Pacific and one for Europe. Also consider carrying a sufficient number of US bills in the money belt as they work when all else fails. $500 appears to be an appropriate amount. Twenties are more useful than larger bills.

ATM (Automatic Teller Machines) have prolifer-

ated around the world including on installations. A suitable credit card to which a PIN (Personal Identification No.) has been assigned to access either checking or savings accounts is required. On installations ATM will provide either US$ or local currency and will accept either to credit to accounts. There may be a significant charge to use ATM. Further in some foreign countries a credit card may be retained by the machine if operated incorrectly.

APPENDIX L, LOCATION IDENTIFIERS

The 3-letter location identifiers for installations and airports included in this Handbook are given below in alphabetical order. A 4-letter location identifier exists but is not used for Space-A.

ABQ	Kirtland AFB	NM	DPG	Dugway PG	UT	LFI	Langley AFB	VA
ADA	Adana	TU	DYS	Dyess AFB	TX	LGF	Yuma PG	AZ
ADW	Andrews AFB	MD	ECG	Elizabeth City CG	NC	LGS	Lajes AB	AI
AFF	Air Force Academy	CO	EDF	Elmendorf AFB	AK	LIM	Lima	PE
AHC	Sierra Army Depot	CA	EDW	Edwards AFB	CA	LKZ	Lakenheath, RAF	UK
AMM	Amman Airport	JO	EFD	Ellington Field	TX	LMI	Kingsley Field	OR
ANB	McClellan, Ft	AL	EIL	Eielson AFB	AK	LPB	La Paz	BO
ANC	Anchorage Airport	AK	EMO	Moron AB	SP	LRF	Little Rock AFB	AR
APG	Aberdeen PG	MD	END	Vance AFB	OK	LSF	Benning, Ft	GA
APH	Hill, Ft	VA	FAF	Eustis, Ft	VA	LSV	Nellis AFB	NV
ASI	Ascension Aux. AF	AS	FAI	Wainwright, Ft	AK	LTS	Altus AFB	OK
ASP	Alice Springs Airport	AU	FBG	Bragg, Ft	NC	LUF	Luke AFB	AZ
ASU	Asuncion	PG	FCS	Carson, Ft	CO	MBK	Barking Sands, PMR	HI
ATA	Istanbul Airport	TU	FFD	Fairford, RAF	UK	MCC	McClellan AFB	CA
ATL	Atlanta Airport	GA	FFO	Wright-Pat AFB	OH	MCF	MacDill AFB	FL
AVB	Aviano AB	IT	FHU	Huachuca, Ft	AZ	MCY	McCoy, Ft	WI
BAB	Beale AFB	CA	FLV	Leavenworth, Ft	KS	MDT	Harrisburg Airport	PA
BAD	Barksdale AFB	LA	FME	Meade, Ft	MD	MDY	Midway Island	US
BAH	Bahrain Airport	BA	FMH	Otis ANGB	MA	MEI	Meridian Airport	TN
BED	Hanscom AFB	MA	FNJ	Gordon, Ft	GA	MEM	Memphis ANGB	TN
BGR	Bangor Airport	ME	FOE	Forbes Field	KS	MFD	Mansfield Airport	OH
BIF	Bliss, Ft	TX	FOK	Suffolk Cnty Airport	NY	MGE	Dobbins AFB	GA
BIG	Greely, Ft	AK	FRF	Rhein-Main AB	GE	MHZ	Mildenhall, RAF	UK
BIX	Keesler AFB	MS	FRI	Riley, Ft	KS	MIB	Minot AFB	ND
BKF	Buckley ANGB	CO	FRN	Richardson, Ft	AK	MKC	St Joseph Airport	MO
BKK	Bangkok Airport	TH	FSI	Sill, Ft	OK	MKE	Milwaukee Airport	WI
BKT	Pickett, Ft	VA	FTK	Knox, Ft	KY	MOB	Mobile, CGATC	AL
BLV	Scott AFB	IL	FUK	Fukuoka Airport	JA	MRB	Martinsburg Airport	WV
BNA	Nashville Airport	TN	GFA	Malmstrom AFB	MT	MSJ	Misawa AB	JA
BOG	Bogotā	CL	GSB	Seymour Johnson	NC	MSP	Minneapolis Airport	MN
BOI	Gowen Field	ID	GTB	Drum, Ft	NY	MTC	Selfridge ANGB	MI
BQN	Borinquen, CGAS	PR	GUA	Guatemala City	GT	MTN	Warfield ANGB	MD
BSB	Brasilia	BR	GUS	Grissom ARS	IN	MUI	Indiantown Gap, Ft	PA
BSM	Bergstrom ARS	TX	GVW	Richards-Gebaur	MO	MUO	Mountain Home AFB	ID
BUE	Buenos Aires	AG	HGT	Liggett, Ft	CA	MVD	Montevideo	UG
BYS	Irwin, Ft	CA	HIF	Hill AFB	UT	MXF	Maxwell AFB	AL
CBM	Columbus AFB	MS	HIK	Hickam AFB	HI	NAP	Naples, NAF	IT
CCA	Chaffee, Ft	AR	HLR	Hood, Ft	TX	NAS	Nassau	BH
CCS	Caracas	VE	HMN	Holloman AFB	NM	NBC	Beaufort, MCAS	SC
CEF	Westover AFB	MA	HRT	Hurlburt Field	FL	NBG	New Orleans, NAS	LA
CHC	Christchurch Airport	NZ	HST	Homestead AFB	FL	NCA	New River, MCAS	NC
CHE	Chievres AB	BE	HUA	Redstone Arsenal	AL	NCO	Atlanta, NAS	GA
CHS	Charleston AFB	SC	IAB	McConnell AFB	KS	NDW	Guantanamo Bay	CU
CJU	Cheju-Do Airport	RK	IAG	Niagara Falls Airport	NY	NDY	Dahlgren, NSWC	VA
CLT	Charlotte Airport	NC	IGL	Izmir Airport	TU	NEL	Lakehurst, NAEC	NJ
COF	Patrick AFB	FL	ILG	Wilmington Airport	DE	NFG	Pendleton, Camp	CA
COS	Peterson AFB	CO	INS	Indian Springs AFS	NV	NFL	Fallon, NAS	NV
CVS	Cannon AFB	NM	IWA	Iwakuni, MCAS	JA	NFO	Futenma, MCAS	JA
CWR	Charleston Airport	WV	IWO	Iwo Jima, CGLS	JA	NFW	Ft Worth, NAS	TX
CYS	Cheyenne Airport	WY	JAN	Jackson Airport	MS	NGF	Kaneohe Bay, MCAS	HI
DAA	Belvoir, Ft	VA	JOH	Johnston Island	US	NGP	Corpus Christi, NAS	TX
DAG	Daggett Airport	CA	KEF	Keflavik, NS	IC	NGU	Norfolk, NAS	VA
DIA	Peoria Airport	IL	KIN	Kingston	JM	NHK	Patuxent, NAS	MD
DJK	Jakarta Airport	IE	KOR	Koror Island	US	NHZ	Brunswick, NAS	ME
DLF	Laughlin AFB	TX	KUZ	Kunsan AB	RK	NID	China Lake, NWS	CA
DMA	Davis-Monthan AFB	AZ	KWA	Kwajalein	US	NIP	Jacksonville, NAS	FL
DNA	Kadena AB	JA	LAC	Lewis, Ft	WA	NJA	Atsugi, NAF	JA
DOV	Dover AFB	DE	LAX	Los Angeles Airport	CA	NJK	El Centro, NAF	CA
			LCK	Rickenbacker ANGB	OH	NKT	Cherry Point, MCAS	NC

NKW	Diego Garcia		PLA	Soto Cano	HO	SPN	Saipan Island	US
NKX	Miramar, MCAS	CA	PNI	Ponape Island	US	SPS	Sheppard AFB	TX
NLC	Lemoore, NAS	CA	POB	Pope AFB	NC	SSC	Shaw AFB	SC
NMM	Meridian, NAS	MS	POE	Polk, Ft	LA	STH	St Thomas	VI
NOJ	Kodiak, CGSC	AK	PPG	Pago Pago Airport	US	STR	Stuttgart	GE
NPA	Pensacola, NAS	FL	PSM	Pease ANGB	NH	STX	St Croix	VI
NQA	Memphis, NSA	TN	QIO	Quito	EC	SUU	Travis AFB	CA
NQI	Kingsville, NAS	TX	RCA	Ellsworth AFB	SD	SVN	Hunter AAF	GA
NQX	Key West, NAS	FL	RCM	Richmond, RAAF	AU	SWK	Wake Island	US
NRR	Roosevelt Roads, N	PR	RDR	Grand Forks AFB	SD	SZL	Whiteman AFB	MO
NSE	Whiting Field	FL	RIO	Rio de Janeiro	BR	TBN	Wood, Ft Leonard	MO
NSF	NAF Washington,DC	MD	RIV	March AFB	CA	TCM	McChord AFB	WA
NTD	Point Mugu, NAWC	CA	RME	Griffiss AFB	NY	TGU	Tegucigalpa	HO
NTU	Oceana, NAS	VA	RMS	Ramstein AB	GE	TIK	Tinker AFB	OK
NUQ	Moffett Airport	CA	RND	Randolph AFB	TX	TKK	Chuuk Island	US
NUW	Whidbey Island, N	WA	RNO	Reno Airport	NV	TLV	Tel Aviv Airport	IS
NXX	Willow Grove, NAS	PA	RTA	Rota, NS	SP	TNP	Twenty-nine Palms	CA
NYG	Quantico, MB	VA	SAL	San Salvador	ES	TYS	Knoxville Airport	TN
NZY	North Island, NAS	CA	SAV	Savannah Airport	GA	UAM	Andersen AFB	GU
OCO	San Jose	CS	SCH	Schenectady Airport	NY	UMR	Woomera Airfield	AU
OFF	Offutt AFB	NE	SEA	Seattle Airport	WA	VAD	Moody AFB	GA
OKC	Oklahoma C Airport	OK	SCL	Santiago	CH	VBG	Vandenberg AFB	CA
OKO	Yokota AB	JA	SDQ	Santo Domingo	DR	VPS	Eglin AFB	FL
OLB	Olbia Airport	IT	SEA	Sea-Tac Airport	WA	WRB	Robins AFB	GA
OQU	Quonset Point Airport	RI	SGP	Paya Lebar Airport	SG	WRI	McGuire AFB	NJ
OSB	Osan AB	RK	SIZ	Sigonella NAS	IT	WSD	White Sands MR	NM
OZR	Rucker, Ft	AL	SJH	Coolidge Airport	AN	WSP	Stewart Airport	NY
PAM	Tyndall AFB	FL	SKA	Fairchild AFB	WA	XLE	Benning, Ft	GA
PAP	Port au Prince	HA	SKF	Kelly AFB	TX	XRW	Campbell, Ft	KY
PDX	Portland Airport	OR	SLC	Salt Lake C Airport	UT	YAP	Yap Island	US
PHX	Phoenix Airport	AZ	SLI	Los Alamitos AFRC	CA	YNG	Youngstown Airport	OH
PIE	Clearwater, CGAS	FL	SOC	Souda Bay, NSA	GR	YUM	Yuma, MCAS	AZ
PIT	Pittsburgh Airport	PA	SPA	Spangdahlem AB	GE			

COMMERCIAL DISCOUNTS

There are many budget travel companies in Europe that retirees can use. Fly to Britain Space-A and then spend one to two weeks in Southern Europe from Portugal to Turkey or in North Africa for between $400 to $700 U.S. with Thomson Tours, Greater London House, Hampstead Road, London NW1 7SD, phone London 0171-707-9000.

The lowest prices are in April & May, the best time for Space-A travel.

Discount Airfares:
Club Med 800.247.6578
Cheap Tickets 800.377.1000
Global Discount Tickets 888.777.2222
Discount Trip Europe:
New Frontiers 800.366.6387
Jet Vacations 800.538.0999

Long Stay Vacations:
Go Ahead Vacations 800.242.4686
Sun Holidays 800.243.2057
Two weeks to one month in the Algarve in Portugal or in the Costa-del-Sol in Spain.
Budget Cruises: Cruise World 800.588.7447
Liberty Travel 800.270.7245

OBTAINING A NEW HANDBOOK

To save money, ask exchanges or overseas Bookmarks for additional copies of new editions. If not in stock, tell them our **AAFES CRC# is 5440602.** AAFES orders this title under their STOVES contract program.

Whenever possible, direct Visa, MC, AE, or Discover orders should be placed on the Internet at www.spaceatravel.com. Credit card orders must have a United States billing address. APO/FPO, PR, Am VI, AS, & Guam are all U.S. addresses. Regulations prohibit processing credit cards with non-United States addresses. Payment of non-U.S. orders must be by money

order or certified check in the amount of $34. If access to the Internet is unavailable call 888-277-2232 0800-1700 Central Time (orders only, no Space-A travel information at this number). With check or money orders use order blank or separate sheet with complete information and payment. Handbook price to U.S. addresses is $25.00 plus $5 S&H. Texas addressees add $2.06 sales tax. Unless otherwise instructed, then-current edition will be sent. Include clearly printed e-mail address with your order. Updates are available via Internet when e-mail address is provided.

Appendix

Insurance... Who Should Be Contacted

Do you have travel health insurance to cover medical expenses when away from home? Will it provide your spouse and you a prepaid medical flight home? In an emergency good travel insurance can save you tens of thousands of dollars.
Who should be contacted in case of a medical emergency? Family member(s), friends, etc. Where are their telephone numbers when you travel?

What is the name of your primary medical provider, and how can he/she be contacted?

Enter "ICE" on cell phones.

ICE have become a quick way for emergency service personnel to learn who to contact in the event of an emergency. Enter close relative or friend's number under 'ICE' in case some needs to reach next of kin, etc.

Travel Kit using compact well built backpack.

Passport w/current visas
Latest edition - Worldwide Space-A Travel Handbook
Camera with adequate film, digital memory
Compact sound source / radio w/headset(s) chargers &/or fresh backup batteries
Extra shoelaces
Band-Aids
Elastic support hose - very important preventive medicine contact doctor before buying.
ZipLock bags for clothes, medicines, etc.
Chewing gum and/or Breath Mints
Diary or logbook
Pens / pencils
Inflatable pillow &/or mattress w/patch kit
Phone numbers for bank, family, friends, credit card company
Compact pen light w/ fresh battery
Hat, compact umbrella, poncho
Sunglasses
2 small sealed packages of laundry soap
Limit clothing - wash at lodging facilities
> Extra underwear
> Extra socks
> Long pants
Plan clothing for laying to accommodate local conditions
Jacket

Compact Overnight (Toiletry) Kit

Soap in small ZipLock bag
Disposable razor & shaving cream in small container
Prescriptions & letter(s) from doctors & eyeglass prescription
Prescriptions in smallest possible pharmacy bottles
Anti-acid (Gas-X type pills)
Hairbrush & comb
Compact tooth brush & small toothpaste
Mini deodorant

Checked Baggage Can Get Lost So...

Prior to traveling consider using the Internet for your benefit by scanning important papers like ID cards, drivers licenses, insurance papers, eye glass and medical prescriptions, passport pages, important telephone numbers, etc. and e-mail them to yourself.

Know how to download your e-mail from a public computer in the event of needing any of this information.

Be sure to pack **in your carry on backpack** adequate supply of medicines in their original containers. Considerations should be made to have a few extra days of medicines with you in event of an unscheduled delay in your return home.

Safe Driving Ideas

Avoid Hydroplaning

Tires must cut through water to maintain contact with the road. Too much water on the road or if you are traveling too fast, your vehicle may start to hydroplane on top of the water.

Don't drive with bald or badly worn tires.
Ensure your tires are properly inflated.
Slow down when rainfall is heavy or water is standing on the road.

Turn Cruise Control Off

When the road is slippery, turn off your cruise control system. Snow, ice, slush or even rain can cause wheel-spin and loss of control.

Immediately reducing power is the only way to stop wheel-spin and to maintain control. An activated cruise control system continues to apply power, thus keeping wheels spinning. By the time your cruise control can be disengage, you may have lost control.

When your brakes get wet

A puddle can be deeper than it looks. After driving through water up to the wheel rims or higher, test your brakes on a clear patch of road at low speed. If wet breaks are not stopping the vehicle as they should, dry them by pressing gently on the brake pedal with your left foot while maintaining speed with your right foot.

Pre-Travel Notes

Pre-Travel & Driving

ABOUT THIS HANDBOOK

There is no reference material on this page.

This Handbook had its inception in 1985 when its original publisher asked an experienced Space-A traveler why he carried a notebook instead of one of the then-published books. Answer: No book covered both flights and billets. None had installation maps. None were complete. None were accurate. None covered ground transport or meals. Obviously a single book accurately reporting all essentials on every installation having either quarters or flights was needed. The publisher offered to issue the notes in book form. But, at that time, less than 300 installations were covered. It took over a year to gain data on the remaining installations. First edition appeared in December 1986. Five thousand copies were printed.

It was obvious, keeping the Handbook up to date and accurate was a major challenge. Other publishers attempted this by mail questionnaires, also done for the Handbook, sometimes with notable success. Unfortunately about half the installations do not respond to a mail request. Even when they do, it is unreasonable to expect the person replying to know of all matters needed by travelers. Accuracy and completeness depend on contributions by travelers. Fortunately for many years the original compiler of the notes remained an active traveler and enjoyed digging out changes. This passed time rapidly while waiting for a flight. Although he remained a prolific contributor, many others now have joined in and they are the hope for the future. As stated elsewhere, the publisher would like to pay some active travelers to get the new information but, because Space-A travelers sign statements they are not using Space-A for personal profit, that is impossible.

Prior to publication of the Handbook, some other Space-A books were only issued every four years, far too long a period to keep books current. It was, therefore, intended to have new editions of the Handbook annually. That was done up to the Gulf War. The war essentially froze changes but it was clear great changes would take place once the war was over. Indeed they did. It was judged mid-spring 1992 was as early as a 5th Edition could be issued containing the bulk of expected changes. Advantage was taken of this extra time between editions to reformat the entire Handbook in response to readers' suggestions. The most-obvious change was going from the original objective of producing the smallest and lightest book practical yet containing all essential information on all installations to meeting requests for larger type and presenting information in a less cryptic fashion. Larger type and spelling out rather than abbreviating of necessity increased number of pages. The format for the 5th Edition proved so acceptable to readers it was carried over succeeding editions. Nevertheless each new edition is revised for improved access to information and to expand on that information. Starting with the 10th edition a new publisher took over.

The Handbook remains the smallest Space-A travel book which even starts to give details on all bases with Space-A facilities and it covers billets, flights, golf courses, marinas, Aero Clubs, RV and camping. Each of the other books available cover just one of these three major subjects.

Any delay between closing an edition and issuing it is an enemy of accuracy. With conventional publishing techniques this period can easily be months. For the Handbook all changes were entered into computer files as received. Once the decision to go with a new edition was made, it took a laser printer about 10 hours to produce camera-ready copy then it is taken to the printer to shoot and run. Beginning with the 12th edition, technological changes eliminated producing hard copies, negatives, and printing plates.

New information does not stop flowing in once an edition is closed. It is placed in the computer files ready for the next edition. To make this new information available to purchasers of the just-published edition, a four page newsletter, Space-A Travel Update, was started in July 1989. Although its primary mission was to distribute change information quickly, there is almost always room for in-depth information and for tales of Space-A travel submitted by readers. With the release of the 11th edition, Space-A Travel Updates became part of travelers' Handbook purchase.

SPACE-A TRAVEL UPDATES

Checking information never ceases. Changes and new information are entered into computer files immediately so the next edition always includes everything known up to press time. Nevertheless, the continuous nature of checking and information-gathering guarantees important developments of use to travelers will be discovered immediately after releasing an new edition.

Space-A Travel Update brings to subscribers quickly developments and changes affecting Space-A travel. Particular attention is given to reporting changed DSN or commercial area codes and facility prefixes and changes of flight information and lodging numbers. An important item is timely information on base closings including additions to or removals from the closure list, changes in closure dates, and how closing is progressing, e.g., when flights stop at a base still open for billeting. This information includes not only permanent changes which will be in the next Handbook edition but also temporary conditions expiring before next edition is published. Such transitory conditions can seriously impact travel. The reverse side of the coin is that changes not affecting Space-A travel in a significant way are not reported both to avoid wasting space and to avoid clutter. An example is a BQ rate change.

Primary mission of **Worldwide Space-A Travel Handbook** is to contain all essential travel information on every installation or airport offering flights, quarters, RV and tent spaces, or ground transport useful to Space-A travelers in the smallest and lowest-cost book feasible. **Space-A Travel Update** has the same primary mission. Nevertheless there is much nice-to-know beyond must-know. Because habitually more room exists in an Update issue than is needed for essential information, remaining room is devoted to nice-to-know. Subjects include the following:

1. Use of quarters as bases for visiting points of interest on foot, by shuttle, or by low-cost public transport.
2. Space-A experiences readers wish to share with others.
3. Particularly useful flights.
4. Desirable commercial lodging, particularly where no quarters exist,
5. Minimizing wait for flights.
6. Alternative routings.
7. Money saving.
8. Special conditions of installations.

Readers are encouraged to assist by contributing information useful to other travelers. They are credited for anything published in **Space-A Travel Update** and on the acknowledgment page of **Worldwide Space-A Travel Handbook** (unless contributor otherwise instructs). Whenever possible information should be provided via either e-mail or our web site. Providing source references is beneficial; if obtainable, include e-mail addresses to your source. If submitting map changes or other information via mail, please put your name on the first sheet. It certainly helps if ZIP+4 is complete and legible. **Mail submissions to:** spaceatravel.com, PO Box 55, Hurst, TX 76053-0055 or Fax 817.282.5900. Because travelers attest they are not using Space-A for personal profit, there can be no payment for information.

Space-A Travel Updates are normally provided via the Internet. Electronic Updates are downloadable as files and printable on computers in libraries, USOs, and terminals. For those with full Internet access, Updates are provided electronically. Those without full Internet access can receive hard copy Updates.

If Handbooks are not available in your AAFES exchange, AAFES contract information is found in the front of this book. If a Navy Exchange doesn't have copies please obtain the manager's name & telephone number and call us toll free at 888.277.2232. The easiest and most efficient way to obtain copies is ordering from our secure Internet web site with Visa, MC, AE, or Discover cards. Personal information is not shared or released. To place a telephone order call 888.277.2232 0800-1700 Central (orders only, no Space-A information at this number). With all orders please include your pay grade, birth year, and service & status. Requested demographic information is obtained for statistical research. If you have an e-mail address, clearly print this within your order to assure that you will have access to electronic *Space-A Travel Updates*. Whenever possible, place orders on Internet at spaceatravel.com.

SPACE-A TRAVEL UPDATES (Concluded)
CONTRIBUTIONS

For the next Handbook edition, data on permanent changes are key. Nevertheless temporary conditions terminating before the next edition, such as billet rehabilitation or runway repaving, can have a serious impact on Space-A travel for many months. Such news will appear in Space-A Travel Update so please submit it.

If at all possible, using e-mail is a tremendous help to the publisher. If e-mail isn't available, please put your name on any loose sheet or on the first sheet when more than one are stapled together. **Send to:** spaceatravel.com, PO Box 55, Hurst, TX 76053-0055 or Fax 817.282.5900.

Items of No Value

AMC pamphlets. Any old publication. General instructions on Space-A. Materials outside scope of the Handbook. Published lists of DSN or remote sign-up Fax numbers unless changed numbers are so indicated.

Valuable Contributions

Any changes from data published in the current edition. If new telephone extensions are submitted, please state whether they are in addition to published extensions, e.g. BQ also 1234, or are replacements, e.g., 9876 instead of 6789. Many DSN prefixes and commercial area codes are changing. This information is very important as are the projected change dates.

Any map changes. Such changes are difficult to obtain by mail. Frequently even a new map published by an installation is in error. Almost never do they include traffic lights serving as useful landmarks. Specifically, when reporting a new location of a facility, please indicate where the new location is on the map in the Handbook, e.g., just under B in BQ or by drawing or copying a segment of the map. In most cases giving a building number does not help. Be specific. For example writing that a new Burger King has opened across the street from the PX does not permit that facility to be placed on the map if the PX is at a corner of two streets.

A current list of flights from any installation is valuable. Current and late are emphasized. These are published in *Space-A Travel Update* as well as being placed in the computer file for the next *Handbook* edition.

Any changes in shuttle service (including hospital shuttles) on or between installations. This includes hours and days shuttle operate and info phone numbers. Similar information on commercial bus lines serving an installation including any change in route number or telephone number for bus information. Such information is virtually impossible to gain by mail. Indeed, even when visiting a base, often availability of shuttles and buses will be firmly denied even when such facilities exist.

Any change in car rent, taxi availability, or applicable phone numbers is important. These tend to come and go. For example Travis AFB and NAS Jacksonville lost car rent offices in their terminals. Both were reported by readers. Specific reports on car rent, good and bad, are needed covering quality of service, rates, and forcing of insurance. Many readers have great interest in renting cars. The only source of reliable, up to date information are readers who rent cars.

ACKNOWLEDGMENTS

Accuracy and completeness is due in large part to traveler contributions of new or changed information, also of calling attention to errors, and suggesting improvements. A general thank you is directed to all contributing to this and prior editions. Due to file destruction while making 15th edition our list will be restarted in subsequent editions. An apology to those contributing but not listed in this edition. With abnormal delays, our efforts were focused on providing this edition. Those who contributed are very important and it will be our continued effort to provide full recognition in future editions.

RV and Tent

Information Applicable Unless Otherwise Stated in Details

Year-round. No reservations. Site equipped with sewage dump (called dump in details), restroom, shower, Pets allowed but must be restrained. Firearms prohibited or, if permitted, secured. Size of RV not a problem. If arriving after check-in point is closed, select site and check in later. No restrictions on who can use facilities other than those also applying to quarters.

Types of Accommodations

Trailer refers to an on-site equipped unit. May be of any form including mobile home. RV is a privately owned unit of any type brought to the site by a traveler. On maps RV applies either to office handling sites or to sites themselves. Number of sites is not given unless of special significance as 5 sites with a demand for 2 are better than 20 with a demand for 40. Expected availability on driving up without a reservation is given by the same star system used for quarters or flights, *=<25%, **=26-50%, *** =51-75%, **** ≥76%. Cottages, trailers, and other fixed units are equipped with linens, blankets, electricity, sewage, and water (ESW) unless otherwise stated.

Rates

Rates are per unit per day and follow hookup letters: E=electricity, S=Sewer, T=cable television, W=water. If more than one letter applies they are in alphabetical order. Example: RV $5, EW $9. Tent $3 means RV space without hookups $5, with EW $9, and tent space without site facilities $3. Rates are rounded to nearest dollar. Dry or primitive means no central water.

Maps

The quarters symbol marking locations of installations are surrounded by light circles if there are RV sites but none for tents, by heavy circles if there are both tent and RV spaces. There is only one installation know for tents only. Should an installation without BQ have cottages or other permanent facilities in its FamCamp or Rec A, the quarters symbol will so reflect.

For list of installations with any RV, tent, or similar facility alphabetical by state, see Æ264 & 265.

Golden Passports to US National Parks and Monuments

Entrance permits for free admission, valid for all in car. Age for those over 62. Access for medically determined disabled. Both are free, lifetime, and obtained in person at the facility. Eagle is annual, costs $25, and obtained by mail or in person. Some installations offer discounts at camp grounds or Rec A as stated in details.

Disabled Veterans

Those drawing 100% disability VA pensions with less than full military retirement benefits are NOT enitiled to fly Space-A.

Space-A Travel For Long-Term Care

In a test that began Feb. 1, 2000 U.S. Transportation Command allows military members to travel space-available from their permanent duty station on temporary duty to accompany their dependents to and from long-term care providers in the continental United States.

Want something added?
Tell us.

RV & Tent

Rec Areas, Camp Grounds, and RV in CONUS

Specific data of facilities are in installation details.

C = Cabin, Cottage; **H** = Hotel, Motel; **L** = Lodge; **O** = Off main installation; **R** = RV Spaces; **T** = Tent Spaces; **Tr** = Trailer Spaces

Alabama
103   Dauphine Island: RT
41   Maxwell AFB: RT, O: RTTr
104   Redstone Arsenal: RT
104   Rucker, Fort : RT

Arizona
19   Davis-Monthan AFB: R
105   Gila Bend AFAF: R
105/6   Huachuca, Fort: CRT
37   Luke AFB O: CHT
106   Yuma PG: R
92   Yuma, MCAS: ORCT

Arkansas
106   Chaffee, Fort: R
35   Little Rock AFB: R

California
109   Barstow, MCLB: R
16   Beale AFB: R
81   Big Bear Rec A: CRT
109   Channel Islands, CG: R
109   Coronado, NAB: R
22   Edwards AFB: R
74   El Centro, NAF: R
110   Irwin, Fort: RT
111   Lake Tahoe: CH
111   Hunter Liggett, Fort: RT
81   Miramar, MCAS: R
87   Pendleton, Camp: CRT
114   Petaluma, CGTC: RT
88   Point Mugu, NAWC: CTR
110   Defense Language Inst.: OCM
114   Roberts, Camp: RT
115   San Diego, NS: OR
117   San Luis Obispo: RT
117   Stockton DDRW: R
63   Travis AFB: RT
65   Vandenberg AFB: R

Colorado
118   AF Academy: RT,ORT

Florida
122   Blanding, Camp: LRT
123   Blue Angel Park: RT
126   Destin Rec A: CRT
23   Eglin AFB: RT61
77   Jacksonville, NAS: RT
78   Key West, NAF: RT
41   Lake Pippen Rec A: CRT
38   MacDill AFB: RT
124   Marathon Rec, CG: C

124   Panama City: RTTr
51   Patrick AFB: RT
87   Pensacola, NAS: CRT
64   Tyndall AFB: CRT

Georgia
20   Atlanta, NAS: OCRT
126   Benning, Ft: CRT
20   Dobbins ARB: R
127   Gordon, Ft: CRTTr
127   Hunter AAF: RTTr
128   McPherson, Ft: OCRT
128   Stewart, Ft: RT

Idaho
47   Mountain Home: RT,ORTTr

Illinois
57   Scott AFB: RT

Indiana
130   Atterbury, Camp: RT
130   Crane, NWSC: RT

Kansas
43   McConnell AFB: R

Kentucky
131   Campbell, Ft: CR
132   Knox, Ft: CRT

Lousiana
15   Barksdale AFB: RT
82   New Orleans, NAS: RTr
133   Polk, Ft: R ORTTr

Maryland
134   Aberdeen PG: ORT
13   Andrews AFB: RT
136   Naval Academy: RT
86   Patuxent River, NAWC: RTTr
136   Solomons, NRC: CRTTr

Massachusetts
137   Cuttyhunk Island,C: M
27   Hanscom: RT OCRT

Michigan
137   Grayling, Camp: RT
137   Point Betsie, Rec Cottage: C

Mississippi
138   Shelby, Camp: R
31   Keesler AFB: R

Missouri
139   Leonard Wood, Ft: OCRT

Rec Areas, Camp Grounds, and RV in CONUS

Specific data of facilities are in installation details.

C = Cabin, Cottage; H = Hotel, Motel; L = Lodge; O = Off main installation; R = RV Spaces; T = Tent Spaces; Tr = Trailer Spaces

Montana
39	Malmstrom: RT OM

Nebraska
49	Offutt ARF: RT

Nevada
75	Fallon, NAS: CRT
48	Nellis AFB: RT

New Hampshire
140	New Boston: RTTr

New Jersey
140	Dix, Ft: OR
44	McGuire: R
141	Picatinny Arsenal: RT

New Mexico
28	Holloman AFB: R
32	Kirtland AFB:
142	White Sands MR: R

New York
143	Drum, Ft: RT
144	Academy, Military : RT

North Carolina
145	Bragg, Ft: R OTr
145	Elizabeth City, CG: R
146	Fisher, Ft Rec A: CLRT
146	Lejeune, Camp: O Aparts., Tr
82	New River, MCAS: RT
59	Seymour Johnson: RT

North Dakota
26	Grand Forks AFB: RT

Ohio
67	Wright-Patterson: RT

Oklahoma
13	Altus AFB: RT
147	McAllester AAP: RT
62	Tinker AFB: RT

Pennsylvania
150	Tobyhanna: C
91	Willow Grove, NAS: C

South Carolina
145	Bragg, Ft Rec A: R OTr
18	Charleston AFB: RT
152	Short Stay Rec A:

South Dakota
24	Ellsworth AFB: RT

Tennessee
152	Arnold EDC: RT
153	Mid-South, NSA: RT

Texas
154	Bliss, Ft: Rt
154	Brooks City Base: RT
74	Corpus Christi, NAS: RT
155	Goodfellow AFB: ORT
154	Hood, Ft: CRT
156	Sam Houston, Ft: OCRT
78	Kingsville, NAS: CRT
156	Lackland AFB: R
60	Lake Texoma: CRT
34	Laughlin AFB: R ORTTr
55	Randolph AFB: R
157	Red River AD: CRT

Utah
159	Tooele AD: RT
28	Hill AFB: R OCLRTTr

Virginia
160	Cheatham Annex: CR
162	A.P. Hill, Ft: CR
163	Little Creek, NAB: RT
163	Monroe, Ft: R
163	Northwest, NSGA: RT
164	Pickett, Ft: RT
89	Quantico: RT
165	Story, Ft: RTTr
165	Yorktown, CGRTC: RT

Washington
24	Fairchild: R OCRTTr
167	Grays Harbor, CG: RT
167	Jim Creek, NRS:
167	Lewis, Ft: RT
42	McChord AFB: RT
167	Murray, Camp: RT
168	Pacific Beach: MRT

WestVirginia
168	Sugar Grove, NRS: CT

Wisconsin
168	McCoy, Ft: CRTTr
169	Rawley Point, CG: C
169	Sherwood Point, CG:

Wyoming
169	Warren AFB: CRT

United Service Organizations' U.S List

The USO is a private, nonprofit organization whose mission is to support the troops by providing morale, welfare and recreation-type services to our men and women in uniform. The original intent of Congress — and enduring style of USO delivery — is to represent the American people by extending a touch of home to the military. The USO currently operates more than 130 centers worldwide, including ten mobile canteens located in the continental United States and overseas. Overseas centers are located in Germany, Italy, the United Arab Emirates, Japan, Qatar, Korea, Afghanistan, Guam, and Kuwait. Service members and their families visit USO centers more than 5.3 million times each year. The USO is the way the American public supports the troops.

ANDREWS AFB   301/981-1854
BELLEVUE FSS COMMUNITY CENTER
                     202/404-6404
BOSTON   617/720-4949/4531
BWI AIRPORT   410/859-4425
CHARLOTTE DOUGLAS AP
                     704/359-5581
CHICAGO MIDWAY AIRPORT
                     773/582-5852
CHICAGO NAVY PIER
                     312/923-7070
CHICAGO O'HARE IAP
                     773/686-7396
CLEVELAND HOPKIINS IAP
                     216/433-7313
CORPUS CHRISTI, NAS
                     361/776-4779
DALLAS/FORT WORTH IAP
                     972/574-
8182/8183
DENVER IAP   303/342-6876
DOVER AFB   302/677-6905
DRUM, FORT   315/774-0356
DULLES IAP   703/572-4876
FORT BELVOIR FAMILY SUPPORT SER-
VICES   703/805-2464
FORT BLISS   915/569-5644
FORT EUSTIS MWR LEISURE CENTER
                     757/878-2415
FORT HOOD   254-768-2771
FORT MYER FAMILY PROGRAMS OF-
FICE   703/696-7798/0958
GREAT LAKES NTC   847/688-5591/5593
GULFPORT, NCBC   228/575-5224
HAMILTON, FORT (BROOKLYN, NY)
                     718/630-1023
HAMPTON ROADS   757/788-4984
HARTSFIELD-JACKSON IAP
                     404/530-6770
HONOLULU IAP & HICKAM AMC TER-
MINAL   808/836-3351
HOUSTON BUSH AIRPORT
                     281/443-2451
HOUSTON HOBBY AIRPORT
                     713/644-1131
INDIAN HEAD, NAVAL SWC
                     301/744-6713
INDIANAPOLIS AIRPORT
                     317/241-6070
INDIANTOWN GAP, FORT
JACKSONVILLE   910/455-3411
JACKSONVILLE (ATLANTIC BEACH, FL)
                     904/246-3481
JACKSONVILLE AIRPORT
                     904/741-6655

JACKSONVILLE, NAS
                     904/778-2821
LEONARD WOOD, FORT
                     573/329-2039
LITTLE CREEK AMPHIBIOUS BASE
                     757/222-0472
LOGAN AIRPORT (BOSTON MA)
                     617/568-1978
LOS ANGELES IAP   310/645-3716
MCCHORD AFB   253/982-1100
MCGUIRE AFB AMC PASSENGER TER-
MINAL
MILWAUKEE WAR MEMORIAL
                     414/271-3133
NEWPORT NEWS SUPSHIP
                     757/223-1980
NEWPORT NEWS/WILLIAMSBURG
                     757/969-5604
NORFOLK IAP   757/233-0567
NORFOLK NS AMC TERMINAL
                     757/440-0939
ONTARIO IAP   909/390-4274
PALM SPRINGS AIRPORT
PENSACOLA AIRPORT & NAS
                     850/433-2475
PHILADELPHIA IAP   215/365-8889
PORT AUTHORITY BUS TERMINAL
                     212/695-5590/6160
RALEIGH-DURHAM IAP
                     919/840-0941
ROBINS AFB
RONALD REAGAN NATIONAL AIRPORT
                     703/419-3990
SAN ANTONIO DOWNTOWN
                     210/227-9373
SAN ANTONIO IAP   210/824-1081
SAN DIEGO AIRPORT
                     619/296-3192
SAN DIEGO DOWNTOWN
                     619/235-6503
SAN FRANCISCO IAP   650/761-
4611
SAN JOSE AIRPORT   408/288-7603
SAVANNAH/HILTON HEAD IAP
                     912/667-1124
SEA-TAC IAP   206/433-5438
ST. LOUIS' LAMBERT AIRPORT
                     314/429-7702
TRAVIS AFB PAX TERM
                     707/424-3316
WESTOVER ARB.   413/557-3290
WILLOW GROVE, NAS
WOODBRIDGE RUN FAMILY SUPPORT
SERVICES   703/494-5576

Tail Markings on Air Force Aircraft with the Home Unit; Location Mission Restrictions may prohibit Space-A Travel

State	Facility	Aircraft
AK	ELMENDORF AFB	C12J C12F C130H
AR	LITTLE ROCK ARB	C130E C130H
AL	BIRMINGHAM	KC135
AL	MAXWELL AFB	C130H
AZ	DAVIS-MONTHAN AFB	EC130E EC130 H
CA	BEALE ARB	KC135E
CA	CHANNEL ISLAND ANGS	C130E
CA	EDWARDS AFB	VARIOUS
CA	MARCH ARB	KC135R C141C
•CA	MOFFETT FEDERAL AIRPORT	MC130/P
CA	TRAVIS AFB	KC10A
CO	COLORADO SPRINGS	C150
CO	PETERSON AFB	C13E C13H
CO	PETERSON AFB	C21A
CO	PETERSON AFB	C130H
DE	DOVER AFB	C5A C5B
FL	EGLIN AFB	VARIOUS
FL	EGLIN AFB	MC130E HC130P
FL	PATRICK AFB	MC130P
FL	PATRICK AFB	HC130N C130E
GA	DOBBINS ARB	C130H
GA	ROBINS AFB	C130E C130H
GA	SAVANNAH	C130H

State	Facility	Aircraft
ID	MOUNTAIN HOME AFB	KC135
IL	PEORIA	C130E
IL	SCOTT AFB	C9A
IN	GRISSON ARB	KC135R
KS	MC CONNELL AFB	KC135R
MA	WESTOVER ARB	C5A
MD	ANDREWS AFB	C21 C22
MD	ANDREWS AFB	C141C
MD	BALTIMORE	C130E
MI	SELFRIDGE ANGB	C130E
MI	SELFRIDGE ANGB	KC135E
MN	MINN - ST. PAUL IAP/ARS	C130E
MN	MINNEAPOLIS-ST PAUL IAP ARS	C130E
MO	SAINT JOESPH	C130H
MS	KEESLER AFB	C12F C21A
MS	KEESLER AFB	WC130H C130E C130J
NC	SEYMOUR JOHNSON AFB	KC135R
NE	OFFUTT AFB	RC135S RC135U RC135V RC135W WC135 OC135B
NJ	MC GUIRE AFB	KC135E
NJ	MC GUIRE AFB	C141B KC10A
NY	NIAGARA FALLS IAP	C130H

State	Facility	Aircraft
OH	WRIGHT-PATTERSON AFB	C141B C141C
OH	YOUNGSTOWN-WARREN REG. AP ARS	C130H
OK	TINKER AFB	KC135R
OR	PORTLAND IAP	HC130P C130E
PA	HARRISBURG	EC130E
PA	PITTSBURGH IAP ARS	C130H
PA	WILLOW GROVE ARS	C130E
RI	QUONSET STATE AP	C130
SC	CHARLESTON AFB	C17A
TX	KELLY AFB	C5A
WA	MC CHORD AFB	C141B C17
WI	GEN. MITCHELL IAP ARS	C130H
WV	MARTINSBURG	C130E
ENGLAND	RAF MILDENHALL	KC135R
GERMANY	RAMSTEIN AB	T43 C9 C20 C21 C130E
JAPAN	KADENA AB	KC135R
JAPAN	YOKOTA AB	C130E C130H C9A C21A
JAPAN	KADENA AB	KC135R
JAPAN	YOKOTA AB	C130E C130H C9A C21A
KOREA	OSAN AB	C12J

• Possibly moved to new location

A/F Tail Marking

267

Principal Outside CONUS Flight Routes

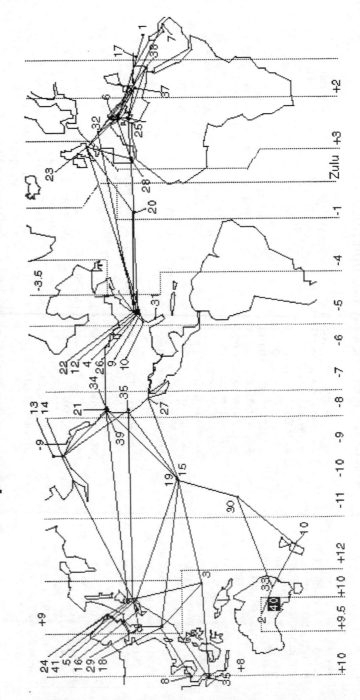

Standard time zones expressed in hours ± Zulu (GMT), applies only to installations shown.

International Terminal Map Reference

Map Location	Facility	State/Country	Quarters Available	Ground Transp. Available
1	Alice Springs A/P	AU	N	N
2	Andersen AFB	GU	D	Y
3	Andrews AFB	MD	D	Y
4	Atsugi	JA	Y	Y
5	Aviano AB	IT	D	Y
6	Bahrain A/P	BA	Y	Y
7	Bangkok A/P	TH	N	N
8	BWI A/P	MD	N	Y
9	Charleston AFB	SC	N	N
10	Christchurch A/P	NZ	D	Y
11	Dover AFB	DE	D	N
12	Eielson AFB	AK	Y	Y
13	Elmendorf AFB	AK	Y	Y
14	Hickam AFB	HI	Y	Y
15	Incirlik AB (Adana)	TU	Y	Y
16	Iwakuni, MCAS	JA	D	Y
17	Izmir A/P (Cigli)	TU	Y	Y
18	Kadena AB	OK	D	Y
19	Keflavic, NS	IC	D	Y
20	Kaneohe Bay, MCBH	HI	Y	Y
21	Lajes AB	AI	Y	Y
22	McChord AFB	WA	Y	Y
23	McGuire AFB	NJ	Y	Y
24	Mildenhall, RAF	UK	D	Y
25	Misawa AB	JA	Y	Y
26	Naples A/P	IT	Y	Y
27	Norfolk, NAS	VA	Y	Y
28	North Island, NAS	CA	Y	Y
29	Osan AB	RK	D	N
30	Pago Pago A/P	AS	N	Y
31	Ramstein AB	GE	D	N
32	Richmond, RAAF	AU	N	Y
33	Rota, NS	SP	D	N
34	Sea-Tac A/P	WA	N	Y
35	Sigonella, NAF	IT	Y	N
36	Singapore A/P	SG	N	Y
37	Souda Bay, NSA	GR	N	N
38	Tel Aviv A/P	IS	N	Y
39	Travis AFB	CA	D	N
40	Woomera A/P	AU	N	Y
41	Yokota AB	JA	D	Y

AVAILABILITY Symbols

Y Usually available
N Not available
D Difficult periods

2008 National Holiday List by Country & Date

Australia
Apr 25 2008 Anzac Day
May 5 2008 May Day NT
May 5 2008 Labour Day QLD
June 2 2008 Foundation Day WA
Jun 9 2008 Queen's Birthday All except WA
Aug 4 2008 Picnic Day NT
Aug 13 2008 Royal Queensland Show Day QLD Brisbane metro only
Sep 29 2008 Queen's Birthday WA
Oct 6 2008 Labour Day NSW/ACT/SA
Nov 3 2008 Recreation Day Parts of Northern TAS only
Nov 42008 Melbourne Cup Day VIC (Melbourne metropolitan only)
Dec 25 2008 Christmas Day All
Dec 26 2008 Boxing Day All except SA
Dec 26 2008 Proclamation Day SA

Bahrain
2 Oct Eid al-Fitr (End of Ramadan)
16 Dec National Day (two days)
9 Dec Eid al-Adha (Feast of the Sacrifice)
29 Dec Al-Hijrah (Islamic New Year)

Belgium
1 May Labour Day, Ascension Day
12 May Whit Monday
11 Jul Flemish Community Holiday
21 Jul Independence Day
15 Aug Assumption
27 Sep French Community Holiday
1 Nov All Saints' Day
11 Nov Armistice Day
15 Nov German Community Holiday
25 Dec Christmas Day

Germany
1 May Labour Day
1 May Ascension
12 May Whit Monday
22 May Corpus Christi
15 Aug Assumption
3 Oct Day of German Unity
31 Oct Day of Reformation
1 Nov All Saints' Day
19 Nov Repentance Day
25-26 Dec Christmas

Greece
25 Apr Orthodox Good Friday
28 Apr Orthodox Easter Monday
1 May Labour Day
16 Jun Day of the Holy Spirit
15 Aug Assumption
28 Oct Ochi Day
25 Dec Christmas Day
26 Dec Boxing Day

Indonesia
30 Jul Isra' and Miraj Limited closing
17 Aug Indonesian Independence Day Limited closing
30 Sep Eid al-Fitr (End of Muslim Ramadan) Everything closes
20 Dec Eid al-Adha (Muslim festival) Limited closing
25 Dec Christmas - Christian Limited closing

Israel
20-26 Apr Pesach (Passover)
8 May Yom Ha'Atzmaut (Israel Independence Day)
9 Jun Shavuot (Pentecost)
30 Sep-1 Oct Rosh Hashana (New Year)
9 Oct Yom Kippur (Day of Atonement)
14-20 Oct Sukkot (Tabernacles)
21 Oct Simchat Torah
22-29 Dec Chanukah (Festival of Lights)

Italy
25 Apr Liberation Day - Italy
25 Apr Anniversary of the Revolution - Portugal
1 May May Day / Labor Day
12 May Festival of the Tricolor
24 Jun Feast of St John the Baptist - Christian
15 Aug Assumption Day - Christian
1 Nov All Saints' Day - Christian
4 Nov Victory Day / National Unity Day - Italy
8 Dec Feast of the Immaculate Conception
25 Dec Christmas - Christian
26 Dec Day after Christmas, St Stephen's Day, Boxing Day

Japan
29 Apr Showa Day (Showa no hi) (now celebrated on May 4)
3 May Constitution Day (kenpo kinenbi)
4 May Greenery Day (midori no hi)
5 May Children's Day (kodomo no hi)
Third Monday of July Ocean Day (umi no hi)
Third Monday of September Respect for the Aged Day (keiro no hi)
Around September 23 Autum Equinox Day (shubun no hi)
Second Monday of October Health and Sports Day (taiiku no hi)
3 Nov Culture Day (bunka no hi)
23 Nov Labour Thanksgiving Day (kinro kansha no hi)
23 Dec Emperor's Birthday (tenno no tanjobi)
December 24-25 Christmas

2008 National Holiday List by Country & Date

Malaysia
1 May Labour Day
19 May Wesak Day (Birth of Buddha)
7 Jun King's Birthday
31 Aug National Day
1-2 Oct Hari Raya Puasa (End of Ramadan)
28 Oct Deepvali
8-9 Dec Hari Raya Haji (Feast of the Sacrifice)
25 Dec Christmas
29 Dec Awal Muharram (Islamic New Year)

New Zealand
Holiday Actual Date Date Observed
25 Apr ANZAC Day
2 June Queen's Birthday
27 Oct Labour Day
25 Dec Christmas Day
26 Dec Boxing Day

Puerto Rico
21 Apr Conmemoración del Natalicio de José de Diego (José de Diego Birthday)
11 May Día de las Madres (Mother's Day)
26 May Memorial Day
16 Jun Día de los Padres (Father's Day)
4 Jul Día de la Independencia de Estados Unidos (Independence Day)
21 Jul Conmemoración del Natalicio de Luis Muñoz Rivera (Luis Muñoz Rivera's Birthday)
25 Jul Conmemoración del Estado Libre Asociado (Commonwealth of Puerto Rico)
27 Jul Conmemoración del Natalicio de José Celso Barbosa (José Celso Barbosa Birthday)
1 Sep Día del Trabajo (Labor Day)
13 Oct Descubrimiento de América (Columbus Day)
11 Nov Día del Veterano (Veteran's Day)
19 Nov Día del Descubrimiento de Puerto Rico (Discovery of Puerto Rico Day)
27 Nov Día de Acción de Gracias (Thanksgiving Day)
25 Dec Navidad (Christmas Day)

Republic of Korea
1 May Labour Day (not an official public holiday but many companies and financial markets close)
5 May Children's Day.
12 May Buddha's Birthday
6 Jun Memorial Day.
15 Aug Liberation Day
13-15 Sep Harvest Moon (Chuseok)
3 Oct National Foundation Day
25 Dec Christmas Day

Scotland
4 Aug Summer Bank Holiday

Singapore
1 May Vesak Day
19 May 2008
9 Aug National Day
1 Oct Hari Raya Puasa
28 Oct Deepavali
8 Dec Hari Raya Haji
25 Dec Christmas Day

Thailand
6 April Chakri Day
7 April Substitution for Chakri Day
13 - 15 Apr (12+16+17 in some areas) Songkran Days
1 May Labour Day
5 May Coronation Day
9 May Ploughing Day
19 May Visakha Bucha Day
17 July Asarnha Bucha Day
18 July Buddhist Lent Day
12 August H.M. The Queen's Birthday
23 October Chulalongkorn Memorial Day
5 December H.M. The King's Birthday
10 December Constitution Day
31 December New Year's Eve

Turkey
23 Apr National Sovereignty and Children's Day
19 May Commemoration of Atatürk and Youth and Sports Day
30 Aug Victory Day
1-2 Oct Ramazan Bayrami (End of Ramadan)
28-29 Oct (28th is a half-day) Republic Day
8-9 Dec Kurban Bayrami (Feast of the Sacrifice)

Turkey
23 Apr National Sovereignty and Children's Day
19 May Commemoration of Atatürk and Youth and Sports Day
30 Aug Victory Day
20-21 Sep Ramazan Bayrami (End of Ramadan)
28-29 Oct (28th is a half-day) Republic Day
27-28 Nov Kurban Bayrami (Feast of the Sacrifice)

United Kingdom
5 May Early May Bank Holiday.
26 May Spring Bank Holiday
25 Aug Summer Bank Holiday (except Scotland)
25 Dec Christmas Day

2008 National Holiday List by Country & Date

26 Dec Boxing Day

United States
26 May Memorial Day (observed)
14 Jun Flag Day
4 Jul Independence Day
1 Sep Labor Day

13 Oct Columbus Day (United States)
11 Nov Veteran's Day
27 Nov Thanksgiving
25 Dec Christmas
Note:
Muslim festivals are timed according to
the phases of the moon and change each year. During the lunar month of Ramadan that precedes Ramazan Bayrami, Muslims fast during the day and normal business patterns may be interrupted. Some restaurants are closed during the day and there may be restrictions on smoking and drinking. Generally, centres of tourism are unaffected. Some disruption may continue into Ramazan Bayrami itself. Ramazan Bayrami and Kurban Bayrami may last anything from two to 10 days, depending on the region. Transport and hotels are very busy during these holidays, so book in advance

This list is a starting point. Before traveling it is wise to you make your own search for additional state, religious, & holidays. Spaceatravel.com does not guarantee the accuracy of the dates and suggests double checking with other sources.

Metric Conversions

Linear (U.S. to Metric)
1 inch - 2.54 centimeters
1 foot - 30.48 centermeters
1 yard - .914 meter
1 mile - 1.61 kilometers

Linear (Metric to U.S.)
1 millimeter - .03937 inch
1 centimeter - .3937 inch
1 meter - 3.2808 feet
1 kilometer - .621 mile

Cooking
Metric cooking is based on measuring utensils marked in millimeters and deciliters (1dl=10ml)

Measuring spoons:
1 tablespoon = 15 milliliters
1 teaspoon = 5 milliliters
1/2 teaspoon = 2.5 milliliters
1/4 teaspoon = 1.25 milliliters

Cooking Tempuratures
Boiling Point - F(212°) = C(100°)
Simmering Point - F(180°) = C(82°)
Slow Oven - F(300°) = C(149°)
Moderate Oven - F(350°) = C(177°)
Hot Oven - F(400°) = C(232°)
Very Hot Oven - F(450°) = C(250°)

To convert Centigrade into Farenheit, multiply Centigrade degrees by 9, then divide by 5 and add 32.

To convert Farenheit into Centigrade, subtract 32 from degrees Farenheit, multiply by 5 and divide by 9.

Temperatures

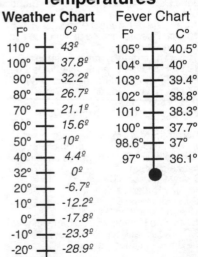

Weather Chart

F°	C°
110°	43°
100°	37.8°
90°	32.2°
80°	26.7°
70°	21.1°
60°	15.6°
50°	10°
40°	4.4°
32°	0°
20°	-6.7°
10°	-12.2°
0°	-17.8°
-10°	-23.3°
-20°	-28.9°

Fever Chart

F°	C°
105°	40.5°
104°	40°
103°	39.4°
102°	38.8°
101°	38.3°
100°	37.7°
98.6°	37°
97°	36.1°

Fisher Houses Directory

California

David Grant USAF Medical Center
100 Bodin Circle, Travis AFB, CA 94535
Phone: (707) 423-7551 Fax: (707) 423-7552
Manager: Charlene Hall
E-Mail Address: Charlene.Hall@60mdg.
travis.af.mil
Web Site: https://public.travis.amc.af.mil/
dgmc/fisherhouse

Naval Medical Center, San Diego
34800 Bob Wilson Drive
Building 46, San Diego, CA 92134-5000
Phone: (619) 532-9055 Fax: (619) 532-5216
Manager: David Esposito

Colorado

Denver VA Medical Center
1055 Clermont Street
Denver, CO 80220-3873
Phone: (888) 336-8262 Fax: (303) 393-4679
Manager: Jann Griffiths
E-Mail Address: Jann.Griffiths@med.
va.gov
Web Site: http://www.denverfisherhouse.
org

District of Columbia

Walter Reed Army Medical Center I, II & III
6825 Georgia Avenue, NW
Washington DC, 20307-5001
Phone: (301) 295-7374 Fax: (301) 295-8012
Manager: Vivian Conley
E-Mail Address: WRFisher2A@aol.com
Web Site: http://www.wramc.amedd.army.
mil/fisher/

Florida

Bay Pines VA Medical Center
10000 Bay Pines Boulevard
St. Petersburg, FL 33708
Phone: (727) 319-1350 Fax: (727) 319-1106
Toll Free Number: (888) 820-0230, extension 1350
Acting Manager: Patti DeFalco
E-Mail Address: BPFisherHouse@med.
va.gov
Web Site: http://www.falome.com/fisher.
html
Mailing Address:
PO Box 5005 (00FH)
Bay Pines, FL 33744

West Palm Beach VA Medical Center
7305 North Military Trail, Route 122
West Palm Beach, FL 33410-6400
Phone: (561) 882-7180 Fax: (561) 882-6565
Manager: Teresa del Rio
E-Mail Address: delrio.teresa_a@west-palm.va.gov

Georgia

Dwight David Eisenhower Army Medical Center
Fisher House Road, Building 280
Fort Gordon, GA 30905-5650
Phone: (706) 787-7100 Fax: (706) 787-5106
Manager: Andrew Hines
E-Mail Address: FHEAMC@aol.com
Web Site: http://www.ddeamc.amedd.army.
mil/Visitor/FISHER.HTM

Hawaii

Tripler Army Medical Center
315 Krukowski Road
Honolulu, HI 96819
Phone: (808) 433-1291 Fax: (808) 433-3619
Manager: Robin Renee Strader
E-Mail Address: FHTAMC@aol.com
CFC No. 9100 in the Hawaii-Pacific campaign.

Maryland

Malcolm Grow Medical Center
1076 West Perimeter Road
Andrews AFB, MD 20762
Phone: (301) 981-1243 Fax: (301) 981-7629
Manager: Janet Grampp
E-Mail Address: Janet.Grampp@andrews.
af.mil

National Naval Medical Center I & II
24 Stokes Road
Bethesda, MD 20814-5002
Phone: (301) 295-5334 Fax: (301) 295-5632
Manager: Albert Harrison
E-Mail Address: AlbertFish@mwrbethesda.
com

Minnesota

Minneapolis VA Medical Center
One Veterans Drive
Minneapolis, MN 55417
Phone: (612) 725-2106 Fax: (612) 970-5864
Acting Manager: Maggie Swenson

Mississippi

Keesler Medical Center
509 Fisher Street
Keesler AFB, MS 39534-2599
Phone: (228) 377-8264 Fax (228) 377-7691
Manager: Larry Vetter
E-Mail Address: FisherHouse@keesler.
af.mil
Web Page: www.keesler.af.mil/other_med_
svs.html

Fisher Houses Directory

New York

Stratton VA Medical Center
113 Holland Avenue
Albany, NY 12208
Phone: (518) 626-6919 Fax (518) 626-5452
Director: Jerry Jensen
E-Mail Address: FisherNY@aol.com
Web Page: www.va.gov/visns/visn02/alb/
fisherhouse.html

North Carolina

Womack Army Medical Center
12 Bassett Street
Fort Bragg, NC 28307-5000
Phone: (910) 432-1486 Fax: (910) 432-3825
Manager: Paula Gallero
E-Mail Address: FHWAMC@aol.com
CFC No. 9006 in the Southeastern North
Carolina (Fort Bragg)

Ohio

Cincinnati VA Medical Center
3200 Vine Street
Cincinnati, OH 45220
Phone: (513) 475-6571 Fax: (513) 487-6661
Manager: Karrie Hagan
E-Mail Address: Karrie.Hagan@med.
va.gov

Wright-Patterson Medical Center I & II
415 Schlatter Drive
Wright-Patterson AFB, OH 45433-1144
Phone: (937) 257-0855 Fax: (937) 656-2150
Manager: Julie Quinn
Assistant Manager: Pat Walters
E-Mail Address: Julie.Quinn@WPAFB.
AF.MIL

Texas

Brooke Army Medical Center I & II
Building 3623 George C. Beach Road
Fort Sam Houston, TX 78234-6200
Phone: (210) 225-4855, ext. 101 Fax: (210)
270-2560
Manager: Inge Godfrey
E-Mail Address: FHBAMC@aol.com

Darnall Army Community Hospital
36000 Darnall Loop
Fort Hood, TX 76544-4752
Phone: (254) 286-7927 Fax: (254) 286-7929
Manager: Issac Howard
E-Mail Address: FHHood@aol.com
Web Site: http://www.hood-meddac.army.
mil/default.asp?page=fisher

Wilford Hall Medical Center I, II, & III
1445 Foster Avenue
Lackland AFB, TX 78236
Phone: (210) 292-3000 Fax: (210) 292-3031
Manager: Vicky Locke

E-Mail Address: FHVolunteer@att.net
Web Site: http://www.fisherhouseinc.org

William Beaumont Army Medical Center
5005 North Piedras Street
El Paso, TX 79920-5001
Phone: (915) 569-1860 Fax: (915) 569-1862
Manager: Harry Hicks
E-Mail Address: FHWBAMC@aol.com

Virginia

Naval Medical Center, Portsmouth I (Apartments)
313 Green Street
Portsmouth, VA 23704
Phone: (757) 399-5461
Manager: Robin Shepherd
E-Mail Address: R.Shepherd@juno.com

Naval Medical Center, Portsmouth II (On-Base)
853 Williamson Drive, Building 287
Portsmouth, VA 23708
Phone: (757) 953-6889 Fax: (757) 953-7174
Manager: Loretta Loveless
E-Mail Address: FishrHouse@msn.com
Web Page: http://www-nmcp.med.navy.mil/
dpcs/fisherhouse

Washington

Madigan Army Medical Center
9999 Wilson Avenue
Fort Lewis, WA 98433
Phone: (253) 964-9283 Fax: (253) 968-3619
Manager: Jodi Land
E-Mail Address: FHMAMC@aol.com

Europe

Landstuhl Regional Medical Center
CMR 402
APO AE 09180
Phone: 49.6371.6183311
DSN: 486-6630
Manager: Kathy Gregory
Assistant Manager: Susan Johnson
EMail: Mary.Gregory@lnd.amedd.army.mil
German Address:
Fisher House
US Hospital Landstuhl
66849 Landstuhl/Kirchberg
Germany

Armed Forces Radio Frequencies in Europe & Western Asia

Location	AM Freq	FM Freq
Germany		
Amberg	1234	90.0
Ansbach	1485	
Bad Aibling		97.7
Bad Kissingen	1143	
Bamberg	1143	
Bitburg	1143	105.1
Bonn		107.6
Bremerhaven		107.9
Chiemsee		90.3
Frankfurt	873	98.7
Garmisch		90.3
Geilenkirchen		89.2
Giessen	1143	
Grafenwoehr	1107	101.4
Heidelberg	1143	104.6
Hohenfels	1485	89.4
Illesheim		104.9
Kaiserslautern	1107	100.2
Kalkar		106.1
Mannheim	1143	107.3
Moenchengladbach	1143	
Nuernberg		107.4
Pirmasens		103.0
Regensberg	1485	
Schweinfurt	1143	
Spangdahlem	1143	105.1
Stuttgart	1143	102.3
Vllseck	1107	107.6
Wuerzburg	1143	104.9
Belgium		
Brussels		101.7
Chievres (Z-FM)		107.9
Florennes AB		107.7
Kleine Broegel AB		106.2
SHAPE/Chievres		104.2
SHAPE (Z-FM)		106.5

Location	AM Freq	FM Freq
The Netherlands		
Brunssum		89.2
Schinen		89.2
Voekel AB		93.6
Italy		
Power Network		107.0
Z-FM		106.0
Bosnia		
Most Locations (Power Net)		91.1
Most Locations (Z-FM)		88.0 or 100.1
Hungary		
Taszar (Power Net)		102.1
Taszar (Z-FM)		93.1
Macedonia		
Most Locations (Power Net)		99.1
Most Locations (Z-FM)		88.0
Kosovo		
All Locations (P Net)		88.0,99.1or103.3
All Locations (Z-FM)		88.0, 99.1or103.3
Croatia		
Zagreb	n/a	99.1
Spain		
Rota		Cable 102.5
Turkey		
Incirlik	1590	(Cable) 107.1

Radio
Frequencies

Julian Date Calendar
(Leap Year) 2008, 2012

	1	2	3	4	5	6	7	8	9	10	11	12	13	14	15	16	17	18	19	20	21	22	23	24	25	26	27	28	29	30	31
Jan	1	2	3	4	5	6	7	8	9	10	11	12	13	14	15	16	17	18	19	20	21	22	23	24	25	26	27	28	29	30	31
Feb	32	33	34	35	36	37	38	39	40	41	42	43	44	45	46	47	48	49	50	51	52	53	54	55	56	57	58	59	60		
Mar	61	62	63	64	65	66	67	68	69	70	71	72	73	74	75	76	77	78	79	80	81	82	83	84	85	86	87	88	89	90	91
Apr	92	93	94	95	96	97	98	99	100	101	102	103	104	105	106	107	108	109	110	111	112	113	114	115	116	117	118	119	120	121	
May	122	123	124	125	126	127	128	129	130	131	132	133	134	135	136	137	138	139	140	141	142	143	144	145	146	147	148	149	150	151	152
Jun	153	154	155	156	157	158	159	160	161	162	163	164	165	166	167	168	169	170	171	172	173	174	175	176	177	178	179	180	181	182	
Jul	183	184	185	186	187	188	189	190	191	192	193	194	195	196	197	198	199	200	201	202	203	204	205	206	207	208	209	210	211	212	213
Aug	214	215	216	217	218	219	220	221	222	223	224	225	226	227	228	229	230	231	232	233	234	235	236	237	238	239	240	241	242	243	244
Sep	245	246	247	248	249	250	251	252	253	254	255	256	257	258	259	260	261	262	263	264	265	266	267	268	269	270	271	272	273	274	
Oct	275	276	277	278	279	280	281	282	283	284	285	286	287	288	289	290	291	292	293	294	295	296	297	298	299	300	301	302	303	304	305
Nov	306	307	308	309	310	311	312	313	314	315	316	317	318	319	320	321	322	323	324	325	326	327	328	329	330	331	332	333	334	335	
Dec	336	337	338	339	340	341	342	343	344	345	346	347	348	349	350	351	352	353	354	355	356	357	358	359	360	361	362	363	364	365	366

Julian Date Calendar
(Perpetual) 2009, 2010, 2011

	1	2	3	4	5	6	7	8	9	10	11	12	13	14	15	16	17	18	19	20	21	22	23	24	25	26	27	28	29	30	31
JAN	1	2	3	4	5	6	7	8	9	10	11	12	13	14	15	16	17	18	19	20	21	22	23	24	25	26	27	28	29	30	31
FEB	32	33	34	35	36	37	38	39	40	41	42	43	44	45	46	47	48	49	50	51	52	53	54	55	56	57	58	59			
MAR	60	61	62	63	64	65	66	67	68	69	70	71	72	73	74	75	76	77	78	79	80	81	82	83	84	85	86	87	88	89	90
APR	91	92	93	94	95	96	97	98	99	100	101	102	103	104	105	106	107	108	109	110	111	112	113	114	115	116	117	118	119	120	
MAY	121	122	123	124	125	126	127	128	129	130	131	132	133	134	135	136	137	138	139	140	141	142	143	144	145	146	147	148	149	150	151
JUN	152	153	154	155	156	157	158	159	160	161	162	163	164	165	166	167	168	169	170	171	172	173	174	175	176	177	178	179	180	181	
JUL	182	183	184	185	186	187	188	189	190	191	192	193	194	195	196	197	198	199	200	201	202	203	204	205	206	207	208	209	210	211	212
AUG	213	214	215	216	217	218	219	220	221	222	223	224	225	226	227	228	229	230	231	232	233	234	235	236	237	238	239	240	241	242	243
SEP	244	245	246	247	248	249	250	251	252	253	254	255	256	257	258	259	260	261	262	263	264	265	266	267	268	269	270	271	272	273	
OCT	274	275	276	277	278	279	280	281	282	283	284	285	286	287	288	289	290	291	292	293	294	295	296	297	298	299	300	301	302	303	304
NOV	305	306	307	308	309	310	311	312	313	314	315	316	317	318	319	320	321	322	323	324	325	326	327	328	329	330	331	332	333	334	
DEC	335	336	337	338	339	340	341	342	343	344	345	346	347	348	349	350	351	352	353	354	355	356	357	358	359	360	361	362	363	364	365

Find the sign-up month on the left, go to top and find day, drop to intersection of day and month and this is the sign-up date. Ask facility staff how long traveler sign-up will remain on their list. Record both dates.

Julian Date Tracking

Julian Dates are used to establish seat assignment seniority. Occasionally calendar dates are remembered and travelers start counting to figure days remaining on the a sign-up list or in estimating seat availability. Enter location, the period that terminal will honor a signup, and then use the Julian Date calendar to keep tract of when and where your signup remains active. **NOTE:** When passing through on a flight it is likely that your advance signup will be removed from the list.

Signup Location	Period Honored	Expiration Date
Sample Travis AFB, CA	60 days from 8126 date = 8186	Date 8186 = July 5, 2008

Vehicle Accident Information Form

√ If anyone is injured, call 911.
√ Call the police and make a report
√ Do not leave the scene of the accident
√ Take pictures of the accident scene and the vehicles before moving the vehicles. Be sure to photograph vehicle license numbers, state ID labels, interior of cars, **the other driver's face for ID purposes**, and if any signs of alcohol or drugs are visable in the other vehicle be sure to get these clearly in your pictures.
√ Write down the names and telephone numbers of any witnesses and all others involved in the accident.
√ Do **NOT** discuss the accident with others, including the other driver, at the scene.
√ At the scene, obtain the accident report number from the investigating police officer.

Weather & Road Condition ⎯⎯⎯⎯⎯⎯⎯⎯⎯⎯⎯

Date of Accident ⎯⎯⎯⎯⎯**Time**⎯⎯⎯⎯⎯**a.m. / p.m.**

The Other Driver & Vehicle Accident Information

Location of Accident⎯⎯⎯⎯⎯⎯⎯⎯⎯⎯
Other driver's name ⎯⎯⎯⎯⎯⎯⎯⎯⎯
Other driver's home address ⎯⎯⎯⎯⎯⎯⎯
Other driver's home telephone ⎯⎯⎯⎯⎯⎯
Other driver's Cell telephone⎯⎯⎯⎯⎯⎯⎯
Other driver's Driver's State⎯⎯⎯⎯⎯⎯⎯
Other driver's Driver's License No. ⎯⎯⎯⎯⎯
Other driver's Insurance Policy No. ⎯⎯⎯⎯⎯
Other driver's Insurance Company Name ⎯⎯⎯⎯
Other driver's Insurance Company telephone number ⎯⎯⎯
Other vehicle license number⎯⎯⎯⎯⎯⎯⎯
Year, make, color, and model of other vehicle⎯⎯⎯⎯

Witnesses: **Witnesses' Comments:**

Witness' Name ⎯⎯⎯⎯⎯ #1 ⎯⎯⎯⎯⎯⎯⎯
  Address ⎯⎯⎯⎯⎯⎯⎯   ⎯⎯⎯⎯⎯⎯⎯⎯
                        ⎯⎯⎯⎯⎯⎯⎯⎯
  Telephone ⎯⎯⎯⎯⎯⎯   ⎯⎯⎯⎯⎯⎯⎯⎯
Witness' Name ⎯⎯⎯⎯⎯ #2 ⎯⎯⎯⎯⎯⎯⎯
  Address ⎯⎯⎯⎯⎯⎯⎯   ⎯⎯⎯⎯⎯⎯⎯⎯
                        ⎯⎯⎯⎯⎯⎯⎯⎯
  Telephone ⎯⎯⎯⎯⎯⎯   ⎯⎯⎯⎯⎯⎯⎯⎯
Witness' Name ⎯⎯⎯⎯⎯ #3 ⎯⎯⎯⎯⎯⎯⎯
  Address ⎯⎯⎯⎯⎯⎯⎯   ⎯⎯⎯⎯⎯⎯⎯⎯
                        ⎯⎯⎯⎯⎯⎯⎯⎯
  Telephone ⎯⎯⎯⎯⎯⎯   ⎯⎯⎯⎯⎯⎯⎯⎯
Witness' Name ⎯⎯⎯⎯⎯ #4 ⎯⎯⎯⎯⎯⎯⎯
  Address ⎯⎯⎯⎯⎯⎯⎯   ⎯⎯⎯⎯⎯⎯⎯⎯
                        ⎯⎯⎯⎯⎯⎯⎯⎯
  Telephone ⎯⎯⎯⎯⎯⎯   ⎯⎯⎯⎯⎯⎯⎯⎯

Document Who, What, When, Why, Where, & How.

Accident Form

NOTES

Index

INDEX

Index

Index

Index

INDEX

Index

INDEX

Index

USE A TOP QUALITY BACKPACK

A sturdy backpack gets you to lodging offices while others wait.

A grip...

A backpack...

An Airport

bag...

All in one

Suggested Retail:
$170.00

From Publisher
$99 & $20 S&H

To order send e-mail to:

publisher@spaceatravel.com

Other luggage also available.

LUGGAGE